WESTMINSTER COMMENTARIES

EDITED BY WALTER LOCK D.D.

LADY MARGARET PROFESSOR OF DIVINITY IN THE UNIVERSITY OF OXFORD

AND D. C. SIMPSON, D.D.

ORIEL PROFESSOR OF THE INTERPRETATION OF HOLY SCRIPTURE, CANON OF ROCHESTER

THE BOOK OF NUMBERS

THE BOOK OF NUMBERS

WITH INTRODUCTION AND NOTES

BY

L. ELLIOTT BINNS, B.D., F.R.Hist.S.

LATE SCHOLAR OF EMMANUEL COLLEGE AND HULSEAN LECTURER, CAMBRIDGE;
EXAMINING CHAPLAIN TO THE BISHOP OF COVENTRY

METHUEN & CO. LTD.
36 ESSEX STREET W.C.
LONDON

First Published in 1927

PRINTED IN GREAT BRITAIN

PREFATORY NOTE

THE primary object of these Commentaries is to be exegetical, to interpret the meaning of each book of the Bible in the light of modern knowledge to English readers. The Editors will not deal, except subordinately, with questions of textual criticism or philology; but taking the English text in the Revised Version as their basis, they will aim at combining a hearty acceptance of critical principles with loyalty to the Catholic Faith.

The series will be less elementary than the Cambridge Bible for Schools, less critical than the International Critical Commentary, less didactic than the Expositor's Bible; and it is hoped that it may be of use both to theological students and to the clergy, as well as to the growing number of educated laymen and laywomen who wish to read the Bible intelligently and reverently.

Each commentary will therefore have

(i) An Introduction stating the bearing of modern criticism and research upon the historical character of the book, and drawing out the contribution which the book, as a whole, makes to the body of religious truth.

(ii) A careful paraphrase of the text with notes on the more difficult passages and, if need be, excursuses on any points of special importance either for doctrine, or ecclesiastical organization, or spiritual life.

But the books of the Bible are so varied in character that considerable latitude is needed, as to the proportion which the various parts should hold to each other. The General Editor will therefore only endeavour to secure a general uniformity in scope and character: but the exact method adopted in each case and the final responsibility for the statements made will rest with the individual contributors.

By permission of the Delegates of the Oxford University Press and of the Syndics of the Cambridge University Press the Text used in this Series of Commentaries is the Revised Version of the Holy Scriptures.

WALTER LOCK

PREFACE

IT is now more than twenty-three years since G. B. Gray's Commentary on Numbers in the *International Critical* Series made its appearance. During the interval which has elapsed no large work on the book has been published in English, but in Germany the Commentaries of Baentsch (1903) in *Hand-Kommentar zum A.T.* and Holzinger (1903) in *Kurzer Hand-Commentar zum A.T.* have been made available for the student. In addition to these works dealing with Numbers itself many works on the Old Testament, in whole or in part, throw additional light on Numbers: the background, too, of the book has been richly illuminated by the studies of specialists in Folk-lore and Comparative Religion. The archaeological advances of the present century give fresh insight into many smaller points, such as the meanings of personal names, and in not a few instances Sumerian roots seem to give us new information as to the origin of Semitic words. In the present series of commentaries philology must be kept in subordination to the more important task of exegesis, but I have in a number of places availed myself of the suggestions of specialists.

The interpretation of the Old Testament is a matter for specialists, but a real advantage is gained if those who specialize in the Old Testament have some knowledge of other fields of history, and even of the development of ideas and institutions amongst non-Semitic races. Much can be learned both from the similarities and from the contrasts which a comparison reveals. It has happened that during the preparation of this commentary I have been engaged, for other purposes, in the study of medieval history, and I cannot help feeling that the carrying on of the two lines of research at the same time has been a real advantage, especially in the study of the growth of laws and of literature.

In the great majority of commentaries on the Pentateuch the analysis of each separate section is prefixed to that section. Following the example of Dr McNeile, in his commentary on

Exodus, I have decided to group all such matter in the introduction, so as to lighten the notes on the text, and to remove to a place apart notes on technicalities which are often found wearisome by the ordinary reader. This arrangement, I need hardly say, does not imply any wish on my part to underestimate the value of a proper analysis of the books of the Pentateuch; on the contrary such an analysis is essential to a true understanding of their contents.

In conclusion I wish to acknowledge with gratitude the help which I have received from the general editor, Dr Lock, who has read through the book in both MS. and proof; and also from Dr S. A. Cook who has made several suggestions and criticisms.

L. E. B.

WEST HAM VICARAGE, E. 15
August 1926

CONTENTS

PRINCIPAL ABBREVIATIONS EMPLOYED

AHT. *Ancient Hebrew Tradition*, by Fr. Hommel.
AJTh. *The American Journal of Theology*.
ATLAO. *Das Alte Test. im Lichte des alten Orients*, by Alfred Jeremias.
A.V. The Authorised Version.
BBG. *Die Biblische und die Babylonische Gottesidee*, by J. Hehn.
BDB. *A Hebrew and English Lexicon of the Old Testament*, by F. Brown, S. R. Driver, and C. A. Briggs.
Bib. Sac. *Biblia Sacra*.
cf. Compare.
CH. *The Hexateuch &c.*, by J. E. Carpenter and G. Harford.
CIS. *Corpus Inscriptionum Semiticarum*.
CP. *Cuneiform Parallels to the Old Testament*, by R. W. Rogers.
D. The Deuteronomic Document of the Pentateuch.
E. The Elohistic Document of the Pentateuch.
EHH. *The Early History of the Hebrews*, by A. H. Sayce.
Ehrlich. *Randglossen zum Heb. Bibel*, vol. II. Lev.—Deut.
Enc. Bib. *Encyclopaedia Biblica*.
Enc. Brit. *Encyclopaedia Britannica*.
E.T. English Translation.
E.VV. English Versions of the Bible.
FLOT. *Folk Lore in the Old Testament*, by Sir James Frazer.
G.-K. or *Ges.-K*. *Gesenius' Hebrew Grammar, as edited and enlarged by E. Kautzsch*. Translated from the 28th German edition by A. E. Cowley.
H. The Holiness Document of the Pentateuch.
HCM. *The Higher Criticism and the Monuments*, by A. H. Sayce.
HDB. *A Dictionary of the Bible*, edited by J. Hastings.
HERE. *An Encyclopaedia of Religion and Ethics*, edited by J. Hastings.
HPN. *Hebrew Proper Names*, by G. B. Gray.
ICC. *The International Critical Commentary*, edited by S. R. Driver, A. Plummer, and C. A. Briggs.
IN. *Die Israeliten und ihre Nachbarstämme*, by E. Meyer and B. Luther.
J. The Jahvistic Document of the Pentateuch.
JBL. *The Journal of Biblical Literature*.
JE. The Combination of J and E.

JQR. *The Jewish Quarterly Review.*

JThS. *The Journal of Theological Studies.*

KAT. *Die Keilinschriften und das Alte Testament*, by E. Schrader.

LOT. *Introduction to the Literature of the Old Testament*, by S. R. Driver.

LXX. The Septuagint Version.

M.T. The Massoretic Text of the Hebrew O.T.

NOTH. *Notes on O.T. History*, by S. A. Cook.

NSI. *North Semitic Inscriptions*, by G. A. Cooke.

P, P^s, P^x. The Priestly Document of the Pentateuch and its various strata.

PEF(*QS*). *The Palestine Exploration Fund* (*Quarterly Statement*).

PSBA. *The Proceedings of the Society for Biblical Archaeology.*

Rev. bibl. *Revue biblique.*

R.V. The Revised Version.

Sam. The Samaritan Version.

SBOT. *The Sacred Books of the O.T.*, edited by Paul Haupt. The volume on Numbers is by J. A. Paterson.

Sum. The Sumerian language.

Syr. The Syriac Version.

TB. *Altorient. Texte mit Bilder zum A.T.*, edited by H. Gressmann, assisted by A. Ungnad and H. Ranke.

Vg., Vulg. The Vulgate Version.

ZAW. *Zeitschrift für die Alttestamentliche Wissenschaft.*

ZDMG. *Zeitschrift der Deutschen Morgenländischen Gesellschaft.*

ZDPV. *Zeitschrift des Deutschen Palästina-Vereins.*

INTRODUCTION

§ 1. The Book, and its characteristics.

Numbers forms the fourth book of the Pentateuch, as the five books of the Law, or of Moses, are named. Originally they were a single whole, but the division into five is very ancient, being found in LXX and Sam., and also later in Philo *de Abrah. init.* and Joseph. *c. Ap.* I. 39[1].

The name, which is perhaps not a very happy one[2], comes, by derivation through the Latin, from LXX title Ἀριθμοί (so in א and B). Originally the Greek title was transliterated into Latin—Tertullian, for example, cites it as *Arithmi* (*adv. Marc.* IV. 28)—as in the case of the other books of the Pentateuch; but for some unknown reason, in the case of Numbers only, the Greek was subsequently turned into the corresponding Latin, and *Numeri* is the Vulgate title of the Book.

The Hebrews called the book *Bemidhbar* (במדבר) or *Bammidhbar* from the fourth word *in the wilderness* (of Sinai). This custom of designating a book from its first word, or from some early phrase, is found also among the Babylonians.

The previous volumes of the Pentateuch carried on the narrative of the history of Israel from the creation, through the captivity in Egypt and the escape therefrom, down to the sojourn at Sinai. Numbers traces the march from Sinai, the wanderings in the wilderness (cf. the Heb. title of the book), and the arrival on the steppes of Moab opposite to Jericho. It includes amidst the narrative several groups of legislation.

Although Numbers, like the other books of the Pentateuch, has been compiled from a variety of sources (see pp. xv. ff.), yet, if its significance is properly to be apprehended, it is necessary to remember that for more than 2000 years it has been a single and complete volume. It is a living book, with its own history and

[1] See Kuenen *Onderzoek* I. 7, 331.

[2] Since the accounts of the numbering of the people occupy comparatively little space, the Hebrew title is much more apt, and gives the essential content of the book.

distinct characteristics; and during its long existence it has helped to meet the spiritual needs of real living men.

As a piece of literature it falls short of the highest class owing to its lack of unity and proportion. At the same time it cannot be denied that it contains narratives of the greatest merit, strung like pearls on a string[1], but the underlying idea has been obscured by too great a profusion of detail, and the various authors and editors—even down to the unknown scribe who gave the book its final form—were not at one in their aims.

Like every Hebrew scripture its main object is to exalt God and to exhibit Him in His majesty and holiness. The holiness and separateness of God involve also the holiness and separateness of His special representatives the Levites and priests, and even those of the people whom He has chosen. The people themselves form a vague mass, and by their murmuring and want of trust make all the clearer the patience and faithfulness of God. Here and there individuals are suddenly detached from the multitude for special notice, sometimes as shewing special zeal in the service of God, often enough for destruction. It is a remarkable feature of the book that there is no concealment of the weaknesses and shortcomings of professedly religious people. Moses himself, Miriam and Aaron, Balaam, the sons of Aaron, and even the miserable Korah and his crew, are examples of religious leaders who fall into sin, and have to suffer the consequences of their own folly.

From another point of view Numbers is a record of the invincible progress of the chosen people of God in the face of all opposition, whether of force or of guile, and of the folly of those who set themselves to thwart the divine purposes for Israel.

Less important characteristics which may be pointed out are—(*a*) the number of plagues recorded in the book, a thing likely in itself during the wilderness wandering with bad water and other encouragements of disease; (*b*) the large number of narratives explaining place names (xi. 1 ff., 4 ff., xii. 1 ff., xx. 1 ff. &c.); (*c*) the number of supplementary laws (see p. xlvii.); (*d*) a special interest in matters concerning women (xii., xxvii. 1–11, xxx., xxxvi.); and (*e*) the supremacy of Moses.

---

[1] Cf. Bishop Temple's criticism of Chopin: "one whose compositions are patchworks of beautiful pieces, but very often fail to be altogether beautiful precisely because they are incoherent and lack unity" (*Mens Creatrix* p. 114).

§ 2. The Sources and Literary Structure.

According to quite ancient tradition the books of the Pentateuch were written by Moses himself; it must, however, be remembered that there is in the Pentateuch itself no claim that, as a whole, it comes from his pen. On the contrary the statement in Num. xxxiii. 2 that the list of the encampments was made by Moses, suggests that other passages which are not so ascribed were not of his composition[1]. Furthermore, Moses is continually referred to in the third person, and although such a custom is by no means unknown, yet it is hard to imagine that a description like that in xii. 3 (*Now the man Moses was very meek, above all the men which were upon the face of the earth*: cf. Ex. xi. 3 also) could have come from the person himself[2]. In Dt. xxxiv. 5 ff. the death of Moses is described, and in spite of the fact that there are those who conceive it to be probable that the author recorded it by anticipation[3], the majority even of conservative critics regard the passage as a later addition, placed at the end of the Pentateuch in order to complete the life-story of its great hero.

The traditional authorship of the books must therefore be given up if any real understanding of the Pentateuch is to be possible. This does not mean, however, that none of the elements which go to compose it can be attributed to Moses, or that everything is to

---

[1] Even a conservative like Robertson rejects the traditional authorship and admits that "In point of fact...the books of the Pentateuch, like the historical books which follow them, are anonymous. The book of Genesis gives no hint of its authorship, neither does the book of Leviticus; and the few passages found in the other books which speak of Moses writing such and such things 'in a book,' will be discovered on examination to refer to certain specific things. Indeed the very fact of such expressions occurring within the books may even be taken as a presumption that it was not he who wrote the whole" (*The Early Rel. of Israel* p. 44; cf. p. 382).

[2] I cannot agree with Green when he states that "There is nothing in Ex. xvi. 35 which Moses could not have written; nor even in Num. xii. 3, when the circumstances are duly considered (cf. 1 Cor. xv. 10; 2 Cor. xi. 5, xii. 11)" (*The Higher Criticism of the Pentateuch* p. 51). The parallel with St Paul is much too distant to be of service by way of comparison.

[3] So Philo *Vit. Mos.* III. 39, and Joseph. *Ant.* IV. viii. 48. Even such a view is outdone by the naïveté of some of the Italian chroniclers. The *Annali di Ludovico Monaldesco* for example begins: "I Ludovico...was born at Orvieto...and died of old age (*morsi di vecchiezza*)": see Muratori *Rerum Ital. Script.* XII. col. 529. Perhaps even more striking is the ending of the *Chronicle of Milan* by Burigozzo: "As you will see in the Annals of my son, inasmuch as the death which has overtaken me prevents my writing more" (quoted by J. Addington Symonds *The Renaissance in Italy* I. pp. 188 ff.).

be brought down to a very late date. Some parts of the Pentateuch undoubtedly belong to early times, to the age of Moses himself, or even earlier. In fact the easiest way to explain the tradition of the Mosaic authorship of the Pentateuch is to suppose that laws actually given or collected by him formed the nucleus of the whole composition[1].

"A careful examination of the Pentateuch, especially if it be conducted in the original Hebrew, almost inevitably suggests that whoever gave the final form to the books and whenever this stage of their development was reached, many documents or oral traditions were combined in them; and further, that these traditions, whether oral or written, had their origins amongst people of different points of view and living in widely separated generations[2]." Applying this statement to Numbers we find that certain of the narratives contained in it have already appeared elsewhere, and that in some cases there are discrepancies both in detail and in outlook. For example the story of the quails (xi.) has been anticipated in Ex. xvi.; and the appointment of coadjutors for Moses, which also forms part of the same chapter (xi.), is repeated from Ex. xviii. 21 ff. The position assigned to both these narratives in Num. inspires much greater confidence than that in Ex. (see pp. 64 ff. below). So also the two stories of the striking of the Rock (Num. xx. 1 ff. and Ex. xvii. 1 ff.) seem to refer to the same incident: notice that the name Meribah appears in both narratives.

Narratives which contain inconsistencies are the accounts of the manna (xi. 7 ff.: cf. Ex. xvi. 14, 31), the taking of the census (i., already done at the time of Ex. xxxviii. 25 f.), the double narrative of the spies (xiii.), and the highly complicated story of Korah, Dathan and Abiram (xvi.). Also the two distinct locations of the death of Aaron (xxxiii. 38 and Dt. x. 6 *b*), the different accounts of the separation of Levi (iii., viii. and Dt. x. 8), the whole conception of the Tent of Meeting. Further in connexion with the laws many difficulties arise. In Robertson's words: "The laws are found, not collected together and systematised, but scat-

---

[1] Miss G. Lowthian Bell states that among the unlettered Arabs of the present day all poetry is ascribed to 'Antara, since his is the one well-known name in literature (*Syria: the Desert and the Sown* p. 59). So in times much more ancient the Hebrew would ascribe all legislation to Moses or all wisdom to Solomon.

[2] The above paragraph is quoted from my volume on *Exodus* in the *Cambridge R.V. for Schools* p. 2.

tered over several books. Not only is there a repetition in one collection of what may be found in another, but the same laws may be repeated with little or no alteration in the same collection[1]. And then there are discrepancies in the regulations found in different places on the same subject; and laws relating to subjects apparently the most diverse are brought into strange juxtaposition, as also are laws bearing upon what seem very different conditions of life and states of society[2]."

At the same time in our efforts to reconstruct the past and to devise theories to explain the growth of the ancient literature we need to act with caution. The inconsistencies which are so clear to us may have been clear also to the compilers (although the fact that many generations of scholars, blinded by tradition, failed to notice them makes it conceivable that this was not so), who may have had explanations of them which are no longer available. We must also be careful in our own reconstructions not to go beyond the evidence which we possess in our desire to round off some neat theory. Perhaps we do not allow sufficiently for the presence in the literature of quite colourless glosses, placed in the margin without any tendencious motive, and afterwards incorporated in the body of the narrative: in ancient times the only 'property' in a piece of literature was the possession of the manuscript, and the possessor felt quite as much at liberty to improve and alter it as would the owner of a house or garden in the present day. It is necessary, as J. R. Green long ago pointed out, to be sceptical of Heterodox reconstructions as well as of Orthodox traditions[3].

Numbers, then, like the rest of the Pentateuch, is no unity, if we use the word to mean that it comes from a single hand. This fact would be admitted by all schools of critics I imagine: but when attempts are made to arrange the various sources into groups, and to trace out the origins of these groups, then very wide differences of opinion reveal themselves. The majority of scholars in recent times accept the system associated with the names of Graf and Wellhausen, although no one of them, I suppose, holds it in exactly the same way. This system arranges the contents of the

---

[1] Cf. Num. xv. 1–16 with Lev. i.–xii.; Num. v. 5–10 with Lev. v. 5 ff., vi. 5 ff.; Num. xv. 22–28 with Lev. iv. 13 ff.

[2] Robertson *Early Rel. of Israel* pp. 381 f.

[3] See *Life and Letters of J. R. Green* pp. 153 f.

Pentateuch under four main sources, known as J, E, D, and P respectively. There is in addition another much smaller source known as H, that is the Law of Holiness. This source underlies Lev. xvii.–xxvi. and since in Numbers the only passages which come from it are x. 9f., (?) xv. 37–41, xxxiii. 50–53, 55f. it may be dismissed with the remark that in order of composition it seems to come between D and P[1].

Before turning to the examination of the Documentary Sources, their approximate date, and place of origin, it may be well to consider the various poetical compositions, a number of which occur in the book. The following is a list of them: x. 35f., xxi. 14f., 17f., 27–30, xxiii. 7–10, 18–24, xxiv. 3–9, 15–17, 18f., 20, 21f., 23f. and perhaps the Priestly benediction also (vi. 24–26). One of these poems is said to come from a collection called "the book of the Wars of the LORD" (xxi. 14); whilst xxi. 27–30 comes from the 'ballad-singers' (see on xxi. 27), evidently an oral source. These poems are for the most part very ancient.

In Germany several recent critics have advanced the theory that a large element of poetry underlies the present sources of the Pentateuch[2]. Sievers in his *Studien zur hebr. Metrik* has pushed this theory to extremes, and his arbitrary application of the principle has met with little favour among critics[3]. It is interesting to recall the similar theory of Niebuhr that the early history of Rome was preserved by the Pontifex Maximus in the form of songs, funeral odes, and annals, a theory which has recently been revived by the distinguished Italian historian Gaetano de Sanctis[4].

It was said above that the four main sources of the Pentateuch were J, E, D, and P. It must be remembered in this connexion that the majority of critics extend these sources into the book of Joshua which they group with the five books of Moses to form the

---

[1] Eissfeldt claims to have discovered a still earlier source, included in J, which he calls L (=Lay). This source represents the nomadic standpoint and is not limited to the Pentateuch but extends at least as far as Jud. ii. 2. He calls it the Lay document because its outlook is in contrast with that of P.

[2] Ehrlich *Randglossen zur hebr. Bibel* remarks on Gen. v. 22 "die Urquellen der Erzählungen des Pentateuchs alle Dichtungen waren." Procksch also considers that "mindestens viele Kapitel der Genesis ursprünglich metrisch zu lesen sind" (*Die Genesis übersetzt und erklärt* p. 8).

[3] See König *Hebr. Rhythmik* pp. 31 ff., Gressmann *Mose und seine Zeit* p. 345 &c. Eichrodt truly says of Sievers "die Anwendung des metrischen Prinzips zu willkürlich und einseitig sei" (*Die Quellen der Genesis* p. 2).

[4] See Gooch *Historians of the Nineteenth Century* pp. 19, 467.

Hexateuch. This re-grouping seems to me to be unnatural and to be inconsistent with the strong Jewish tradition which isolated the Torah or Pentateuch from the succeeding books. It is true that the style, language and ideas of J, E, D, and P can be traced in Joshua, but why stop short there? A critic like Sellin would carry J down to 1 K. ii., and Hölscher thinks that E goes right on to the fall of Jerusalem if not beyond[1]. The style of D and of P is found even later.

The extent of each document affects any theory which we may form as to its date, and also to some degree as to its origin. Hölscher, for example, brings the date of E down to the middle of the sixth century. Leaving aside extreme views the approximate dates may be taken to be J *c.* 850, E *c.* 750, and P *c.* 500–450.

As to the place of origin of J and E it is usual to assign J to Judah, E to Israel or Ephraim. Agreement on this point, however, is by no means complete, Smend, for example, derives both sources from Judah, and Eissfeldt is doubtful whether evidence exists sufficiently strong to differentiate between Israel and Judah as the homes of the documents.

The four main sources then come from different ages in the history of the Hebrew people; and indeed since each of the documents is the production, not so much of an individual writer as of a school, the separate documents have a long and extensive history of their own. The dates which may be assigned to the sources are therefore approximate only. On the one hand much that is early in time may have been included in a late source, on the other much that is late may have been added by way of gloss or correction to an early source. The latest of all the sources is that known as P or the Priestly, and since this source supplies more than three-quarters of the material in Num., and is moreover very readily distinguishable from the other sources, the simplest approach to the consideration of the documents is to start with it.

The main interest of the Priestly School is, to quote G. B. Gray, "to recapitulate the history of the origin and subsequent fortunes of the chosen people, and especially to describe the origin of their institutions." Although the date of the publication (to use a modern term) of P was post-exilic and late, much of the matter

---

[1] See *Gesch. der israel. u. jüd. Rel.* pp. 101 f.

in it is undoubtedly very ancient, and many primitive uses and customs are preserved in it[1]. Dealing as it does with ritual and legal procedure much of its contents was not designed originally for the public ear, but for those who were the guardians of the ritual and legal tradition, the priests. As H. M. Wiener well says: "The bulk of P was professedly only intended to reach the people mediately—through the teaching of the priests; Ezra's innovation was in direct conflict with the original intention of the legislation" (*Essays in Pent. Crit.* p. 219). The continual emphasis upon the teaching office of the priests suggests that there was in Israel a kind of Economy in Religious Teaching (cf. Ez. xliv. 23; Dt. xxiv. 8, xxxiii. 10 &c.).

There are in the Priestly source three distinct, though not very clearly defined, strata. Gray terms them P^g, the original source (referred to as P simply in my analysis pp. xxv ff.); P^s, certain supplementary matter; P^x, various legal regulations of doubtful date. The marks of P^s are as follows: (*a*) the use of a second altar, that of incense (Ex. xxx. 1–10: cf. xxv.–xxix. where it is unknown); (*b*) the unction of all the priests, not of the high-priest only (Ex. xl.: cf. xxix.); (*c*) the 'cords' of the tabernacle (Ex. xxxv. 18, xxxix. 40) not known in xxv.–xxix.; (*d*) the sweet incense of Ex. xxx. 7, 34 ff. which seems to have been missing originally from xxv.–xxix. Gray looks upon the retrospective dates in vii. 1, ix. 1, 5, 15 as being due to introductions of P^s.

In the analysis and notes which follow it is not intended to distinguish minutely between the various strata of P, but rather to treat the source as a whole; the distinction is not of primary importance in Numbers, except in passages like iii. 3, 26, 31 f., 37 &c., but the reader ought to know that such strata have been distinguished and to have some clue by which to recognise them.

The following is a selection of words and phrases occurring in Num. which are characteristic of P. (For a fuller list of such characteristics from the whole Pentateuch see *CH*.)

A dagger (†) after a series of references denotes that all passages in O.T. in which the word or expression occurs have been cited; an asterisk (*) that all such passages in the Hexateuch only have been cited.

[1] Gressmann claims that in some cases traditions in P are older than those in JE (*Mose* p. 241 &c.).

1. *Arboth (Plains of) Moab* xxii. 1, xxvi. 3, 63, xxxi. 12, xxxiii. 48–50, xxxv. 1, xxxvi. 13; Dt. xxxiv. 1, 8; Jos. xiii. 32 †.

2. *Beyond Jordan* (מעבר י״) xxii. 1, xxxii. 19 *bis*, 32, xxxiv. 15, xxxv. 14; Jos. xiii. 32, xiv. 3, xvii. 5, xviii. 7, xx. 8 *.

3. *Land of Canaan* xiii. 2, 17, xxvi. 19, xxxii. 30, 32, xxxiii. 40, 51, xxxiv. 2, 29, xxxv. 10, 14; 19 times in Gen., twice in Ex., 3 times in Lev., once in Dt., 7 times in Jos. In JE 14 times, nearly all in the Joseph story *.

4. *Wilderness of Zin* xiii. 21, xx. 1, xxvii. 14, xxxiii. 36, xxxiv. 3; Dt. xxxii. 51; Jos. xv. 1, 3 *.

5. *Aaron the priest* iii. 6, 32, iv. 16, xvi. 37, xviii. 28, xxv. 7, 11, xxvi. 1, 64, xxxiii. 38; Ex. 4 times; Lev. 3 times; Jos. xxi. 4, 13 *.

6. *According to the word of* (על פי) iii. 16, 39, 51, iv. 27, 37, 41, 45, 49, ix. 18, 20, 23, x. 13, xiii. 3, xxvii. 21, xxxiii. 2, 38, xxxvi. 5; Ex. xvii. 1, xxxviii. 21; Lev. xxiv. 12; Dt. xxxiv. 5; Jos. xix. 50, xxii. 9.

7. *All flesh* xvi. 22, xviii. 15, xxvii. 16; Gen. 10 times; Lev. xvii. 14.

8. *Among* (בתוך) of the Divine Presence in Israel &c. with pron. suffix. i. 47, v. 3, xiii. 32, xv. 14, 26, 29, xvi. 3, xviii. 20, xix. 10, xxv. 11, xxxii. 30, xxxv. 15, 34; Gen. xxiii. 6, 9; Ex. 6 times; Lev. 12 times; Jos. 5 times. Cf. Gen. xxxv. 2, xli. 8 (E) *.

9. *Assembly* (of Israel קהל) x. 7, xv. 15, xvi. 33, 47, xix. 20, xx. 6, 10, 12.

10. *Atonement, to make* (כפר). From Ex. xxix. 33–Num. xxxv. 33 70 times. Cf. use in other sources with non-technical meaning Gen. xxxii. 20 (J); Ex. xxxii. 30 (J); Dt. xxi. 8 (D), also in the Song of Moses (Dt. xxxii. 43) *.

11. *Between the two evenings* ix. 3, 5, 11, xxviii. 4, 8; Ex. xii. 6, xvi. 12, xxix. 39, 41, xxx. 8; Lev. xxiii. 5 †.

12. *Born in the land* (אזרח הארץ) ix. 14, xv. 13, 29; Ex. xii. 19, 48; Lev. 7 times; Jos. viii. 33 *.

13. *Charge* iii. 25, 31, 36, iv. 27, 31, xvii. 10, xviii. 8, xix. 9; Ex. xii. 6, xvi. 23, 32–34. Cf. i. 53, iii. 7, 28, 32, 38, viii. 26, ix. 19, 23, xviii. 3–5, xxxi. 30, 47.

14. *Congregation* (עדה) Ex. xii. 23–Jos. xxii. 30 125 times. Not in J, E, or D.

15. *Cut off from his people* ix. 13, xv. 30, xix. 13, 20; Gen. xvii. 14; Ex. 5 times; Lev. 9 times †.

16. *Drink offering* Num. 34 times; Ex. twice; Lev. 3 times. In J once (Gen. xxxv. 14) *.

17. *Face of, on the* (על פני) iii. 4 (xvi. 43, xx. 10 אל), xxi. 11, xxxiii. 7; Gen. 6 times; Lev. x. 3, xvi. 14; Dt. xxxii. 49, xxxiv. 1; Jos. 6 times.

18. *Families, after your* (with לְ) i. (13 times), ii. 34, iii.–iv. (15 times), xxvi. (16 times), xxxiii. 54; Gen. 5 times; Ex. 3 times; Jos. 28 times. Outside P xi. 10 *a* (J); 1 S. x. 21; 1 Chr. v. 7, vi. 62 (= Jos. xxi. 33, 40) †.

19. *Generations* (with לְ) ix. 10, x. 8, xv. 14, 21, 23, 38, xviii. 23, xxxv. 29; Gen. 4 times; Ex. 13 times; Lev. 13 times †.

20. *Heads of fathers* xvii. 3, xxxi. 26, xxxii. 28, xxxvi. 1; Ex. vi. 25; Jos. xiv. 1, xix. 51, xxi. 1 *.

21. *Head* (= take the sum נשא את־ראש) i. 2, 49, iv. 2, 22, xxvi. 2, xxxi. 26, 49; Ex. xxx. 12 †.

22. *Heave, to* xv. 19, 20, xvi. 37, xviii. 19, 24, 26, 28–30, 32, xxxi. 28, 52; Ex. twice; Lev. 7 times.

23. *Heave offering* (תרומה) Ex. xxv. 2–Num. xxxi. 52 40 times: cf. Dt. xii. 6, 11, 17 *.

24. *Oblation* (קרבן) Lev. i. 2–Num. xxxi. 50 78 times. Elsewhere Ez. xx. 28, xl. 43 †.

25. *Offer, to* (הקריב) Ex. xxviii. 1–Num. xxxi. 50 146 times.

26. *Plague* (נגף) viii. 19, xvi. 46; Ex. xii. 13, xxx. 12; Jos. xxii. 17; contrast Is. viii. 14 †.

27. *Possession* (אחזה) xxvii. 4, 7, xxxii. 5, 22, 29, 32, xxxv. 2, 8, 28; Gen. 9 times; Lev. 14 times; Dt. xxxii. 49; Jos. 4 times.

28. *Prince* (נשיא) more than 50 times in Num. Gen. 4 times; Ex. 3 times; Lev. iv. 22; Jos. 8 times.

29. *Serve, to, service* (צבא) iv. 3, 23, 30, 35, 39, 43, viii. 24, xxxi. 3, 4, 6, 7, 27, 42; Ex. xxxviii. 8; cf. Jos. xxii. 12, 33 *.

30. *Sweet savour* Ex. xxix. 18–Num. xxix. 13 38 times. Cf. Gen. viii. 21; Ez. vi. 13, xvi. 19, xx. 28, 41 †.

From the source known as D (i.e. Deuteronomic) one passage has been derived (xxi. 33–35), and that probably by deliberate borrowing from a parallel passage in the book of Deut. itself. There is therefore no need for any comment on this source[1].

The earliest of all the sources are J and E. Before they were combined with D, and subsequently with P, they appear to have been combined with one another. This amalgamation probably took place in the reign of Hezekiah for, as Sellin says, "just after the destruction of the Northern Kingdom in 722, when Judah could once more feel itself to be the spiritual leader of a united Israel and was making a special effort to concentrate all its powers, such a work would have a natural motive" (*Introd. to O.T.* p. 91). The redactor who carried out this task, although he seems to have treated the two sources with much respect, must have made many minor alterations for the sake of harmonising and connecting them.

In addition to special features which distinguish the separate documents J and E there are certain common characteristics which belong to JE, and mark it off from P. The most important of these characteristics are the following:

1. *Again* (Heb. idiomatic use of יסף). Gen. iv. 2–Num. xxii. 25 24 times. In D 11 times and in P (including xxxii. 15) 3 times*.

2. *Alone* (לבד with pron. suffix). In JE 19 times (including xi. 14, 17). In D 7 times and in P once *.

3. *Bring up, to* (Israel out of Egypt העלה) xiv. 13, xvi. 13, xx. 5, xxi. 5; 17 times elsewhere in JE. Dt. xx. 1 (D) and Lev. xi. 45 (P) *.

---

[1] The influence of D is probably also to be seen in xxxii. 7–13, 50–56.

4. *Cry, to* (צעק) xi. 2, xii. 13, xx. 16; Gen. iv. 10, xxvii. 34, xli. 55; Ex. 9 times; Jos. xxiv. 7. In D 3 times (Dt. xxii. 24, 27, xxvi. 7) *.

5. *Elders* (of Israel &c.) xi. 16 *bis*, 24, 30, xvi. 25, xxii. 4, 7 *bis*; Gen. l. 7 *bis*; Ex. 11 times; Jos. vii. 6, viii. 10, ix. 11. D 23 times, P 3 times *.

6. *Go, get thee, come* (לך, לכו). JE 57 times, D 3, P 1 *.

7. *Good and evil* (conjoined or opposed) xiii. 19, xxiv. 13; Gen. 9 times. Outside JE in Dt. i. 39 (D) *.

8. *Here* (בזה) xxii. 19, xxiii. 1 *bis*, 29 *bis*; Gen. xxxviii. 21, xlviii. 9; Ex. xxiv. 14 *.

9. *Look, to* (הביט) xii. 8, xxi. 9, xxiii. 21; Gen. xv. 5, xix. 17, 26; Ex. iii. 6, xxxiii. 8 *.

10. *Meet, to* (over against, against לקראת) xx. 18, 20, xxi. 23, xxii. 34, 36, xxiii. 3, xxiv. 1; Gen. 10 times; Ex. 7 times; Jos. 4 times. In D 6, in P 1 (xxxi. 13), also in Gen. xiv. 17 *.

11. *Let not...I pray* (אל נא) x. 31, xii. 11, 12, 13, xxii. 16; Gen. 8 times *.

12. *Now, and &c.* (ועתה). Gen. iii. 22–Jos. xxiv. 23 57 times. In D 10 times, also in Dt. xxxi. 19; in P 3 times including xxxi. 17.

13. *Stand, to* (יצב Hithp.) xi. 16, xxii. 22, xxiii. 3, 15; Ex. 6 times; Dt. xxxi. 14 *bis*; Jos. xxiv. 1. In D 4 times *.

14. *Well* (באר) xx. 17, xxi. 16, 18, 22; Gen. 20 times; Ex. ii. 15. Elsewhere in Gen. xiv. 10 *bis* *.

15. *Wroth, to be* (חרה אף) xi. 1, 10, 33, xii. 9, xxii. 22, 27, xxiv. 10, xxv. 3; Gen. 3 times; Ex. 5 times. In D 6 times, and in P (xxxii. 10, 13; Jos. vii. 1) *.

The two sources J and E must now be considered in themselves. The names come from the different names for the deity used in them before Ex. iii. 15, the Jahwistic source (J) using Jehovah (Jahweh) whilst E uses Elohim. Both regard events from the prophetic, as distinguished from the priestly, point of view, and both contain very early traditions of Israelite history. Probably J, which comes from Judah, is the earlier of the two sources, but this is by no means certain, and since the data for deciding the matter are differently regarded by different scholars the question is still to some extent an open one. In favour of the prior date of J the following arguments have been advanced: (*a*) the narrative as a whole gives the impression of greater freshness and originality; (*b*) the religious conceptions are more naïve, God is thought of as coming down to earth, and in general is conceived of in a much more anthropomorphic manner than in E; (*c*) J is less advanced in his ethical teaching; (*d*) J is less fond of miracles—cf. the story of the crossing of the Red Sea (Ex. xiv. 21 *b* and 16 *a*)[1]. Taken as

[1] The Northern Kingdom from which E most probably came seemed more fond of miracles than Judah; e.g. most of the miracles told of the prophets centre round Elijah and Elisha.

a whole J may be said to be practical and historical in outlook, he desires to bring back to his contemporaries the great things which Jehovah has done for the nation, and so to arouse their gratitude and to move them to real obedience.

Characteristics of J.

The following is a select list of words and expressions in Numbers which are generally held to be characteristic of J:

1. *Jahweh* is used for name of God.
2. *Angel of Jahweh* xxii. 22–27, 31, 34, and 16 times elsewhere in J, once in R^{JE} Ex. xxiii. 23 *.
3. *Before* (טֶרֶם) xi. 33; Gen. ii. 5 *bis*, xix. 4, xxiv. 15, 45; Ex. ix. 30, x. 7, xii. 34; Jos. ii. 8, iii. 1 *.
4. *Canaanite* for the natives of Palestine (cf. E 'Amorites'). xiv. 43, 45; Gen. x. 18, xii. 6, xxiv. 3, 37, l. 11.
5. *Flowing with milk and honey* xiii. 27, xiv. 8, xvi. 13; Ex. iii. 8, 17, xiii. 5, xxxiii. 3. Seven times in D, once in H (Lev. xx. 24), and outside the Hexateuch Jer. xi. 5, xxxii. 22; Ez. xx. 6, 15 †.
6. *Forasmuch as* (כִּי־עַל־כֵּן) x. 31, xiv. 43; Gen. xviii. 5, xix. 8, xxxiii. 10, xxxviii. 26 *.
7. *Ill, to deal* (הרע) xi. 11, xvi. 15; Gen. xix. 7, 9, xliii. 6, xliv. 5; Ex. v. 22. Three times in E (including xx. 15) and once each in D (Dt. xxvi. 6) and P (Lev. v. 4) *.
8. *Midst, in the* (or *among*, of Jahweh בְּקֶרֶב) xi. 20, xiv. 11, 14, 42; Ex. iii. 20, viii. 22, x. 1, xvii. 7, xxxiii. 3, xxxiv. 9; Jos. iii. 5, 10. Once in R^{JE} (Ex. xxxiii. 5) and 5 times in D *.
9. *Mighty, to be* (and *mighty* עצם) xiv. 12, xxii. 6; Gen. xviii. 18, xxvi. 16; Ex. i. 7, 9, 20. Seven times in D and once in P (xxxii. 1) *.
10. *Scatter, to* (פוץ) x. 35; Gen. x. 18, xi. 4, 8, xlix. 7; Ex. v. 12. Three times in D *.
11. *Sheol* xvi. 30, 33; Gen. xxxvii. 35, xlii. 38, xliv. 29, 31. Once also in Dt. xxxii. 22 *.
12. *Towns* or *villages* as *daughters* of a metropolis. xxi. 25, 32, xxxii. 42; in Jos. 6 times. Four times in R^{P} *.

A number of scholars find two distinct strata in J, and in fact almost two separate documents. This subject is too technical to be pursued here but fuller details may be found in Smend *Die Erzählung des Hexateuch*, Eichrodt *Die Quellen der Genesis*, and Eissfeldt *Hexateuchsynopse*: see above p. xviii, n. 1.

The Elohistic source (E) is marked by an interest in the supernatural, by a fondness for details, by a desire for edification, by a heightened sense of God's majesty (He no longer speaks on earth but from heaven or by means of dreams or an angel). That it is later than J is held by most scholars (see above) but is by no means certain. Winckler for example considers that E is the older on the ground that "it alone preserves recollections of the actual conditions of remote antiquity. For instance it still knows that the land must be won from the Amorites, while J usually speaks of Canaanites" (in Helmoth's *History of the World* III. p. 189). E also retains in its legends traces of a post-Israelite immigration of Edom, Moab, and Ammon; in J they are already settled.

Characteristics of E.

The following are some of the characteristic words and phrases which may be found in E:

1. *God* (*Elohim*). Although after Ex. iii. 15 the use of the name is no longer a distinctive feature of E, yet a preference for it seems still to mark certain passages: e.g. xxi. 5, xxii. 9, 12, 20, 22, 38, xxiii. 4, 27.

2. *Amorite* for the natives of Palestine instead of the Canaanite of J. xiii. 29, xxi. 13 *bis*, 21, 31; Gen. xv. 16, xlviii. 22; Jos. x. 5, 6, xxiv. 8, 12, 15, 18. In J 4 times (xxi. 25, 26, 32, xxxii. 39).

3. *On account of* (על אודות) xii. 1, xiii. 24; Gen. xxi. 11, 25; Ex. xviii. 8. Once in J and twice in R^D *.

4. *Pray, to* (התפלל) xi. 2, xxi. 7 *bis*; Gen. xx. 7, 17. Twice in D *.

5. *Prophet* and *to prophesy* (root נבא) xi. 25, 26, 27, 29, xii. 6; Gen. xx. 7; Ex. xv. 20. Ten times in D, once in P *.

6. *Speak with* (דבר עם) xi. 17, xxii. 19; Gen. xxxi. 24, 29; Ex. xix. 9, xx. 19 *bis*, 22, xxxiii. 9; Jos. xxiv. 27. Once in J and twice in D *.

7. *Suffer, to* (or *allow* נתן) xx. 21, xxi. 23, xxii. 13; Gen. xx. 6, xxxi. 7. Once in J, once in R^{JE}, and twice in D.

For a fuller discussion of the problems raised by the whole question of sources, and of those connected with each individual document, see *CH*, Driver *LOT*, Sellin *Introd. to O.T.* and for an excellent introductory treatment Simpson *Pentateuchal Criticism*[1].

§ 3. Analysis.

The following analysis of the contents of the book according to the several sources must in some respects be taken as approximate only. In view of the unanimity of scholars it is possible to allocate a section of the text to P or to JE with something approaching certainty; but to decide between J and E, P and P^s, respectively

[1] A summary of the present position of Pentateuchal criticism will be found in *The People and the Book* pp. 190 ff. and in Canon Harford's articles in *The Expositor* (July to Dec. 1925) now published under the title *Since Wellhausen*.

is often difficult; and this difficulty is increased with the further extension of the analysis. The work of previous scholars in the same field has been much used, especially *CH* and the commentaries of Gray, Holzinger, and Baentsch.

The meaning of the various symbols used, the peculiar characteristics of the sources which they represent, and also the approximate dates from which these come, have all been explained above (see pp. xv ff.).

Chapters i.–x. 10.

The whole of this part of the book comes from writers of the priestly school, as can be seen by the subject matter, the style and language, and the conception of the priesthood, the sacrifices, and the various other accompaniments of the system of worship which is represented as being practised by the Israelites in the wilderness. In this part, therefore, no attempt is made to go into any very great detail of analysis, or to justify the division of the contents; here and there notice is taken of usages peculiar to P, but the nature of the analysis does not demand that such notices should be exhaustive or numerous.

i.–iv. *The numbers and arrangements of the tribes.*

This opening section is typical of P, with its interest in statistics and love of genealogical lists. Some special terms may be pointed out, i. 2 *by their polls*, 4 *tribe* (מטה), 20 *and upwards* (ומעלה), 50 *tabernacle* (משכן), *testimony* (עדות), iii. 6 *set them*, 12 *and I, behold*, 13 *I am the* LORD, 46 *over and above*, iv. 2 *service* (צבא), 37 *according to...Moses*.

To the original groundwork of P many additions from Ps have been made, and the whole section has been worked over by a later redactor. The statement that Moses and Aaron took the census (i. 17 f.), together with 19 *a*, which should go with it, is the first of these additions[1]. The detailed statements of the numbers of the tribes also probably belong to Ps, as does the whole of ch. ii. Ch. iii., after 4, is not quite so easy to analyse[2], but on the whole it seems likely that the specification of the duties of the different

---

[1] Baentsch attributes 1–16 to Ps.

[2] The anointing of Aaron's sons marks 3, and probably the whole of 1–4, as Ps.

families of Levites is supplementary (23–26, 29–32, 35–38), as well as the entire passage dealing with the redemption of the first-born (44 f. possibly excepted). Ch. iv. is all P^s.

Analysis of i.–iv.

P	i. 1–16		19 *b*		5–22	
P^s		17–19 *a*		20–iii. 4		23–26
P	27 f.		33 f.		39	
P^s		29–32		35–38		40–iv. 49

v.–vi. *Various Laws and Regulations.*

One or two peculiarities of P deserve mention: v. 6 *soul* = *person*, 12 *commit a trespass*, 29 *this is the law of.* The opening passage (v. 1–4) may well have been P's original ending of the description of the camp, though *CH*, following Kuenen, attributes it to P^s. The next short passage 5–8, since it seems to be a supplement to Lev. vi. 1–7, belongs to P^s; whilst the various regulations contained in v. 11–vi. 21 may have come from some collection of legal decisions, earlier than P itself, the date of which is uncertain. The final passage 22–27 belongs also to an earlier age than P (in spite of Holzinger who regards it as P^s), but since P^x is reserved for legal matters, in the analysis it ranks as P.

Analysis of v.–vi.

P	v. 1–4			22–27
P^s		5–8		
P^x			9–vi. 21	

vii. *The oblations of the princes.*

The whole of this long chapter, with the probable exception of 10 and 89, belongs to P^s. The dating of the narrative appears to be inaccurate, since whilst taking i.–iv. for granted it relates what was supposed to have happened a month earlier. Further the anointing of an object (1) is a sign of P^s. The two *vv.* 10 and 89 seem, the one to be an insertion of an editor, the other to be a detached fragment, probably from P.

Analysis of vii.

P				89
P^s	1–9		11–88	
R^P		10		

viii.–x. 10. *Further laws and regulations.*

Practically the whole of chh. viii. and ix. comes from P^s. In viii. 1–4 Dillmann would limit the supplementary matter to *v.* 4 only. In the same way he regarded 5–26 as being mainly P, although containing expansions. In chh. iii. and iv. the Levites are represented as carrying on their duties without any consciousness that the special purification demanded by 5–22 was necessary; the latter passage would therefore seem to come from an even later supplement. The special Passover of ix. 1–14 comes from P^s, as does the account of the cloud in 15–22 which has a parallel in Ex. xvi. (partly J and partly P)[1]. x. 1–10 comes from P, into which an older passage 9f. has been incorporated. Certain expressions in these verses (e.g. בוא מלחמה, צר, בארצכם &c.) suggested to Dillmann a connexion with H.

Analysis of viii.–x. 10.

H						9 f.
P						x. 1–8
P^s	viii. 1–10		12–15 *a*		ix. 1–23	
R^p		11		15 *b*–26		

Chapters x. 11–xxii. 1.

These chapters form the second of the three parts into which the book of Numbers is divided[2]. Since J and E and P are all represented in this part greater care in the analysis is necessary, together with fuller notes and explanations.

x. 11–xii. *Incidents on the journey from Sinai to Paran.*

The earliest section (x. 11–28) belongs to P, the rest, except x. 34, to JE. The other sections are assigned to JE because their style and contents are not consistent with priestly authorship: cf. the use of נא, עזב, כי על כן, היטיב, ויחר אפו. In x. 12 P describes the Israelites as being in Paran, but in x. 33 they are only leaving Sinai, and in the same verse the ark goes before the people instead of in their midst as in iii. 31 (P). In the later sections the story of the manna and quails may be compared with P's account in Ex. xvi.

---

[1] LXX of ix. 15–23 makes several omissions.

[2] Gray ends this part at xxi. 9, Holzinger at xx. 13, Dillmann and McNeile at xxii. 1.

The priestly matter itself is not all from the same stratum, 11 f. belongs to P; whilst 13–28 because of its differences from ii. 17 will belong to P^s; x. 34 does not suit its present context[1], and its conception of the cloud is not that of P (cf. x. 11).

The rest of the matter has to be apportioned, as far as possible, between J and E. x. 29–36, except 33 and 34, may be assigned to J; note the use of Reuel rather than Jethro, and the phrase אל ארצי ואל מולדתי. 33, if we omit *of the covenant* which is a Deuteronomic insertion, seems to belong to E. 34 is P^s (see above). 35 f. is perhaps an ancient fragment embedded in J.

The account of the incident at Taberah (xi. 1–3) gives but little evidence in favour of either J or E, though the emphasis on intercession as powerful in arresting judgement (2) shews the influence of E. In xi. 4–35 two separate stories, the desire for flesh and the appointment of the seventy elders, have been amalgamated. This amalgamation, which must have involved a considerable amount of editing, and the absence of phrases characteristic of J or E as separate documents, makes the analysis peculiarly difficult. The fact that Joshua is prominent in 16 f., 24 *b*–30, is perhaps sufficient justification for assigning these *vv.* to E, to which source *CH* also assigns 14. It is true that 14 fits in badly after 13, being a sequel to 12, but it seems more likely to come from a redactor than from E[2]. Ch. xii may be more safely attributed to E since the references to the cloud (4), and to the tent (5), are in accordance with the conceptions contained in that document, rather than with those of J. Further the emphasis on dreams as a source of revelation is a characteristic of E.

Analysis of x. 11–xii.

J			29–33		35 f.		4–15		18–24 *a*		31–35		
E						xi. 1–3		16 f.		24 *b*–30		xii. 1–15	
P	x. 11 f.												
P^s		13–28		34									
R^{JE}													16

xiii., xiv. *The story of the spies and its sequel.*

The narrative includes fragments and sections from all the three main sources. The various strands, however, are so closely inter-

[1] In LXX it follows 36.

[2] Bacon includes it in J.

twined that the difficulty of unravelling them is very great. On any theory of the origin of these chh. certain incongruities, real or apparent, must be noticed. These may be divided into four, or perhaps five, groups: (*a*) the position of the Israelite camp; in 3 the wilderness of Paran is the starting point, and in 26 *a* the place to which they return: in 26 *b* the return is made to Kadesh, which is the starting point mentioned in xxxii. 8 and in Dt. i. 19 ff.; (*b*) the extent of the country surveyed: 2, 17 *a*, 21 state definitely that the whole of Canaan was visited; 22 ff. the country round Hebron only; (*c*) the report of the spies: in 32 the land is said to be evil, but in 27–31, 33 the land itself is good though difficult to invade and conquer[1]; (*d*) the composition of the minority: in xiii. 30 and xiv. 24 Caleb alone is mentioned, in xiv. 6 f., 38 Joshua is added; (*e*) a double account of the punishment; cf. xiv. 20–25 and 26–38.

These data are sufficient to shew the presence of matter from two distinct sources at least. Literary characteristics, apart from other evidence, enables us to identify one strand as coming from P: e.g. the use of תור (= *spy out*) xiii. 2, 16, 17 *a*, 21, 25, 32; xiv. 6, 7, 34, 38; מטה (= *tribe*) xiii. 2, 4–15; עדה (= *congregation*) xiii. 26, xiv. 1, 2, 5, 7, 10, 27, 35 f. The other strand had itself been made up of contributions from both J and E, and had been combined by the redactor, together with additions of his own, before being incorporated in P to form the present narrative.

The opening passage of xiii. up to 'Canaan' (17) comes from P, to which source also belongs 21 (the continuation of 17 *a*), 25–26 *a* (to 'Paran'), and 32, in whole or in part[2]. The first ten *vv.* of xiv. are very difficult, and there is much lack of agreement amongst critics as to the exact amount of JE which has got into them: 3 f. and 8 f. are not specially marked in style and the point of view suggested is that of the JE portion of the narrative, they should therefore probably be assigned to that source. The next section from P is 26–38, and here again a certain amount of material from JE seems to have been inserted: Bacon, for example, sees in 31–33 a continuation of 11–24; but, as Gray points out, 31 is not easily divided from 30, and 32 f. are connected with 29 by the use of

---

[1] I am not quite certain that there is any inconsistency here since "a land that eateth up &c." need not necessarily be an unfertile land: see note on text.

[2] Driver, Gray &c. regard 32 *b* as JE.

פגריכם. Probably 30–33 were incorporated from JE after being worked over by the redactor; Baentsch assigns them to P, but not to the main stratum. *CH* divide 39 (note the change of subject) between P and JE, but such a division is hardly necessary.

To analyse the material derived from JE is an impossible task, save that xiv. 11–24 seem to come from a later stratum, and perhaps xiii. 18 f. also. The attempt of Baentsch carries the analysis into minute detail, but it does not inspire complete confidence.

Analysis of xiii., xiv.

JE		17 *b*–20		22–24		26 *b*–31		33	
P	xiii. 1–17 *a*		21		25–26 *a*		32		
JE		3 f.	8 f.						39–45
P	xiv. 1 f.	5–7		10		26–29 (30–33) 34–38			
R^{JE}				11–24					
R					25				

xv. *Various regulations.*

The whole of this chapter comes from the priestly source, though some of its material seems to have been derived ultimately from H. The section dealing with the sabbath-breaker (32–36) is clearly supplementary, and perhaps very late. The final section (37–41) contains material older than P, and its style and ideas are so closely akin to the Holiness matter in Lev. xvii.–xxvi. that it may be assigned to that source, as is done by Baentsch amongst others.

Analysis of xv.

H			37–41
P	1–31		
P^s		32–36	

xvi., xvii. *The story of Korah, Dathan and Abiram.*

This story consists of two distinct narratives which have been combined together—the narrative of a revolt of laymen against the civil authority of Moses, this revolt was led by Dathan and Abiram; and the narrative of the revolt of Korah and his company against the claims of the Levites to a position of ecclesiastical superiority. The latter narrative has had further additions made to it, in order to emphasise the superiority of the priests to the ordinary Levites. The story of Dathan and Abiram comes from JE, the rest from P. Since the parts from JE are confined to xvi., we will consider that chapter first. As linguistic clues notice as characteristic of P the use of עדה (2 &c.), בתוך (3), הקריב (5) *and he spake...saying* (5 &c.), *the glory of the Lord* (19). In the same way the following words and phrases are characteristic of JE *land flowing with milk and honey* (13), חרה ל (15), *the elders* (25), כל אשר לכם (26 &c.), טף (27).

The priestly parts are themselves derived from P and from P^s; to the latter belong all the references to the separation of the Aaronic priests from their fellow Levites.

In xvi. 1 the descent of Korah from Levi probably comes from P^s, as in the story in P he was presumably a member of a lay tribe. 8–11 will also belong to P^s since in these *vv.* the rebels are represented as already in possession of the very rights which they had demanded in 3–5. The controversy against the Aaronic priesthood is continued in 16 f. The passage 36–40 can hardly belong to P itself as Ex. xxvii. 2 (P) represents the altar as overlaid with bronze from its first construction.

Analysis of xvi., xvii.

JE			1 *c*–2 *a*			12–15			25–34*			
P	xvi. 1 *a*			2 *b*–7				18–24		35		41–xvii. 13
P^s		1 *b*			8–11		16 f.				36–40	

* Apart from insertions.

xviii.–xix. *Further Laws and Regulations.*

The whole of this section belongs to the priestly school, but not all comes from the same stratum. xviii., in spite of much of it being a repetition of matter included in earlier passages, is best assigned to the main document: notice that only one altar is referred to (5, 17), and that the attitude towards possessions in 20 is in contrast with xxxv. 1–8 (P^s). It is possible, but not probable, that 25–32, since it is supplemental to 8–20, may be a later addition.

The two sections of xix. (1–13 and 14–22), whilst clearly of priestly origin, are yet not part of the original P; nor do they seem to come from the same hand, since the phraseology dealing with the same matter is quite distinctive. Some of these distinctions can only be seen by studying the original: e.g. the peculiar use of נפש for *corpse* in 11 and 13 (contrast 18 and 22), the different word for *ashes* אפר in 9 f. but עפר in 17; others are noticeable even in R.V.: e.g. compare the description of the dead body in 11 and 13 with the greater detail of 16 and 18, and the manner of cleansing in 12 (*himself*) with that in 19. *CH* regard 1–13 as belonging to P^s but 14–22 as part of the body of priestly *Torah* which was earlier than the code itself. The whole chapter, however, seems to contain very primitive ideas.

Analysis of xviii.–xix.

P	xviii.		
P^x		xix. 1–13	14–22

xx.–xxii. 1. *Events at the close of the wanderings.*

A variety of narratives is contained in this section, some of them containing matter of great antiquity. The first passage (xx. 1–13) has received very careful treatment by Cornill (*ZAW* xi. pp. 20–34). His conclusion is that much more of the story comes from P than was supposed by Dillmann. The opening statement is from this source, up to the word *month* (the word *year* having been deliberately omitted by the compiler), the rest of the *v.* is from J, except the statement in reference to Miriam which is from E. The first part of 3 comes from the compiler; *CH* attributes it to J, from whom no doubt the whole of 5, notice its similarity to 4 (P), has come. The rest of the passage is P, though various slight editorial changes have been made in it. Dillmann attributed 8–11 to E, mainly on account of the mention of the rod of Moses; whilst Bacon and *CH* assign 8 *b* to J, wishing to separate the *speaking* to the rock from its being *smitten*.

The next passage 14–21 by its very vividness shews its derivation from JE. As between the two documents the bulk of the story shews marks of E, although Wellhausen would assign it to J (*Composition* p. 110). Perhaps 19f. comes from J since it repeats 17. The passage dealing with the death of Aaron is clearly P, the mere fact that Mt. Hor is referred to being enough to place it, apart from linguistic evidence. Some scholars now refer 22 *a* to R (Dillmann), others to E (*CH*), on the grounds that P would have said *from the wilderness of Zin* (cf. 1) or *from Meribah Kadesh* (cf. xxvii. 14).

The short passage recording the origin of Hormah is non-priestly, and comes most probably from J; whilst the incident of the bronze serpent may safely be assigned to E: cf. use of אלהים (5) and

התפלל (7). The remainder of this section contains much interesting matter, including poetical passages which have the appearance of being old. The only trace of P is in 10, 11 *a* and xxii. 1, where notice ויסעו מן...ויחנו ב״. The rest of the material, if we except 33–35 (= Dt. i. 1–3), comes from JE; but on the division between the two sources there is no complete agreement between critics. Kittel, following Kuenen, assigns the whole of 17–30 to E; Wellhausen, on the other side, regarded 21–31 as all J. Perhaps the most satisfactory analysis is that of Bacon, with whom *CH* and Gray substantially agree, which makes 11 *b*–13, 21–24 *a*, 31 a complete and continuous narrative differing in several small points from the series (incomplete in itself) 16, 18 *b*–20, 24 *b*, 25, 32. The former belong to E since it has affinities with xx. 14–18, the latter probably to J.

Analysis of xx.–xxii. 1.

J						5			19 f.			xxi. 1–3					16–20		24 *b*–25		32	
E		1 *b*						14–18		21				4 *b*–9		11 *b*–15		21–24 *a*		26, 27–31		
D																						33–35
P	xx. 1 *a*		2		3 *b*–4		6–13				22–29				10, 11 *a*							xxii.
R^P				3 *a*									4 *a*									

Chapters xxii. 2–xxxvi. *Events in Moab.*

The great bulk of the contents of these chh. comes from the priestly school, part of it belonging to the later development of it. The only portions which can be assigned to JE are the story of Balaam (xxii. 2–xxiv. 25), part of the incident of Baal-peor (xxv. 1–5), and of the settlement of the East Jordan tribes (xxxii. 39–42).

xxii. 2–xxiv. *The Story of Balaam.*

This narrative consists of a number of poems linked together by prose passages, or perhaps of a prose narrative with poems inserted. The prose parts of xxii. can only be explained on the supposition that two distinct traditions have been combined, and that the compiler failed to notice certain inconsistencies in them. Some of these inconsistencies are in themselves very trifling (e.g. the duplication, unusual in prose, in 3; the difficulty of fitting in 4 after 2; the question of Balaam's home) and if each stood alone might be explained away: but the contradiction between 20 f. and 22 cannot be removed and is admitted by conservatives (see below p. 151). In xxiii. and xxiv. a certain number of inconsistencies and repetitions are also apparent; these suggest, not the combination of two sources into a single narrative, but that the two chh. themselves come from different authors. The opening of xxiv. seems to require, instead of xxiii., some lost narrative as its introduction: note the reference to the otherwise unknown 'enchantments.' The double appearance of xxiii. 22 f. = xxiv. 8 f., unless it is an interpolation in one passage, points to separate origins for xxiii. and xxiv.

Some critics regard the whole section as coming from E, whose peculiar usages are more prominent, with certain additions and insertions. The latest of them is Steuernagel in his *Einwanderung* pp. 72, 103 ff., but Kuenen held the same general position long before him. But a theory of interpolations and additions will not account for the inconsistencies, especially in xxii. 22–35, and it seems best to follow the majority of scholars in seeing the work of both J and E in the section.

Unfortunately distinguishing marks of style are almost entirely lacking, save that in xxii. 22–35 Jehovah is used consistently and not God; this suggests that the passage is J; a suggestion which is perhaps supported by the fact that the only other example of an animal speaking is also from J, the serpent in Gen. iii. In xxii. 2–21 references to God speaking in the night are suggestive of E. In E the messengers of Balak seem to be princes, in J less exalted people. In J Balaam is travelling with his own two servants, and this seems to infer a comparatively short journey; we may therefore assign *to Pethor which is by the river* in xxii. 5 to E who would thus regard Balaam as an Aramean (cf. xxiii. 7). xxiii. appears to resemble E (see 6, 7, 17) whilst xxiv. may well come from J (12 *messengers*).

Analysis of xxii. 2–xxiv.

J		3 *b*–7*		11		17 f.		22–34		36 *a*		37 *b*		39	
E	xxii. 2–3 *a*		8–10		12–16		19–21		35		36 *b*–37 *a*		38		40 f.
J								xxiv. 1–20							
E	xxiii. 1–21				24–26						25				
JE			22 f.				27–30				21–24				

* Omitting *to Pethor...river* (E).

xxv.–xxxi. *Various Laws and incidents.*

Except the first part of the first incident the whole of this section comes from the priestly document.

In the Baal-peor story (xxv.) the similarity of the offence has led to the combination of two separate stories. In 1–5 *Moabite* women seduce the Israelites into strange worship, a crime especially abhorrent to JE (cf. Ex. xxxiv. 14–16, xx. 3); in 6–18 a *Midianite* woman is taken to wife by an Israelite—an offence from the post-exilic standpoint (cf. Ezra x.). That 1–5 come from JE is suggested by marks of style: ויחר אף י״ (3), and חרון אף י״ (4). As 4 and 5 seem incompatible, elements derived from both J and E appear to be present, but to separate them is difficult. The rest of the chapter presupposes some lost opening, the final *vv.* (16–18) look like a connecting link with xxxi. and so must be later than P itself.

The second census (xxvi.), if it comes from P, has been annotated and expanded by a later editor—e.g. the writer of 8–11 knew xvi. in its present (JEP) form—but more probably the whole is late.

The ruling in the case of the daughters of Zelophehad is best assigned with *CH* to P^s, to which source the whole of the rest of the section belongs, excepting only xxvii. 12–23. Of this passage 12–14 is probably editorial, being an abbreviation of Dt. xxxii. 48–52, the remainder is from P.

Analysis of xxv.–xxxi.

JE	xxv. 1–5						
P		6–15				14–23	
P^s			16–18	xxvi. 1–xxvii. 11			xxviii.–xxxi.
R^p					12 f.		

xxxii.–xxxvi. *Miscellaneous topographical narratives.*

The first two passages of this section (xxxii. and xxxiii. 1–49) present us with a number of interesting problems; the rest are straightforward and belong obviously to some stratum of P.

xxxii. is a very difficult passage and critics in their attempts to analyse it offer a great variety of results. It seems likely that the passage, which contains quite old material, has been entirely re-cast; in other words that the editor has not, as in other places, been content merely to compile. This would account for the presence of clear traces of JE in the middle of obvious P passages, and for the mysterious D phrases (especially in 7–13). *CH* assign the whole of 1–38 to P in the main, Driver 1–17, 20–27, and 34–38 in the main to JE. My own analysis, which is purely tentative, takes account of the elaborate analysis of Baentsch; it is impossible, however, to feel confident that even this represents the true derivation of the fragments. The final passage (39–42) is a detached fragment written from the same standpoint as Judges i. Budde has made the interesting suggestion that it comes from J's account of the conquests of the Joseph tribes. Dillmann regarded 40 as coming from R^P and is followed by McNeile; in view, however, of Dt. iii. 15 it seems best to assign it to R^D.

The itinerary (xxxiii. 1–49) has some of the same peculiar problems as xxxii. It combines P and JE in a most baffling manner, and probably like the last section has been re-cast from matter belonging to the two sources, with further additions of unknown origin. Characteristic of P are the phrases ויסעו מן...ויחנו ב״, whilst all the stations mentioned in P, with the solitary exception of *the wilderness of Paran*, are included; most of those mentioned in JE are also included; and in addition sixteen stations not elsewhere alluded to. These last are *Dophkah* (12), *Alush* (13), the twelve stations from *Rithmah* (18) to *Hashmonah* (29), *Abronah* (34) and *Zalmonah* (41). Dillmann perhaps comes near to the real history of the section when he regards it as containing old matter incorporated by P, into which JE passages were inserted. The final form, however, seems to have been given to the passage by P^s. In a similar way P^s seems to have combined in 50–56 matter from D (or H) and P.

The statement of the boundaries of the West Jordan tribes is of course ideal, and might belong to any date (xxxiv. 1–15); as might also the list of princes who are appointed to see that the allotment is carried out (16–29).

The passage dealing with the Levitical cities (xxxv. 1–8) is later than xviii. (P), where it is stated that the priests and Levites are to be provided for since they are *not to possess any inheritance* (20, 24, 26).

The account of the cities of refuge and of the laws connected with them (xxxv. 9–34) contains a good deal of old material, and even shews traces of H. The present form, however, is late and the old material has been 'drastically re-written' (*CH*).

xxxvi. is entirely supplementary, though Baentsch regards 13 as possibly earlier.

Analysis of xxxii.–xxxvi.

JEP	xxxii. 1–17		20–27									
J					33 *a c*		39, 41 f.					
E						34–38						
D (?H)									50–53, 55 f.			
P		18 f.		28–32						54	xxxiv.	
Ps								xxxiii. 1–49				xxxv., xxxvi.
RD		(7–13?)			33 *b*		40					

§ 4. The Historical Value of Numbers.

Any conception of the Historical Value of Numbers, as of any other O.T. book, which we may adopt will depend almost entirely upon the critical position which we occupy. To the extreme conservative critic it is an account, accurate even in the minutest details, of the wanderings in the wilderness as described by the principal actor in the events, Moses himself. To the modern critic, however, such a conception of the book is not possible; not only does he feel constrained to deny the tradition that Moses was the author (see above p. xv), but further he divides the contents of the book among a number of separate sources (see pp. xvi ff.) whose value is of very different rank.

In other words Numbers must be regarded as having a twofold historical value: (*a*) a direct value, for the period with which the narratives profess to deal, and (*b*) an indirect value, as throwing light on the times when they were actually composed, and as exhibiting the ideals of the ecclesiastical organisation by which they were sustained. In regard to (*a*) the value is but slight. Certain broad facts must be accepted, the Exodus itself (although we are not bound to conclude that it affected the whole nation); the wanderings in the wilderness of which there is other early evidence (Hos. ix. 3, 10, xi. 1, xii. 9, xiii. 5); and the work done by some great leader and prophet such as Moses. Other less important facts no doubt lie behind the connexion of the Calebites with Hebron, and the struggle of Dathan and Abiram against Moses may point to some Reubenite attempt to obtain the supremacy in Israel in a time perhaps later than the Exodus. On the whole our knowledge of the real history of the Exodus period is very slight, and indeed until the period of the kings we can hardly dare to assert that we have much definite historical material to work upon. The lack of information is to some extent compensated for by extra-biblical sources such as the Tell el-Amarna Tablets; though in them the Israelites are not mentioned by name, probably they are, as Gressmann (*Mose* 393, 399) and other critics think, to be identified with the mysterious SA.GAZ or Ḥabiru[1].

We have to remember that in ancient times the writing of history was in an elementary stage, and restrictions and canons, which are now a commonplace, were then not dreamed of by the historian or chronicler. Speaking of Herodotus and his methods Sayce points out that "Now and again he refers to the older historians when he wishes to correct or contradict them; more frequently he silently incorporates their statements and words without mentioning them by name....Reviewers did not exist in his days, nor were marks of quotation or even footnotes yet invented" (*The Egypt of the Hebrews &c.* pp. 176f.). The critic is therefore often at a loss to know from what period or source any particular passage has been derived, and internal evidence, a somewhat uncertain criterion, is all that can give the clue.

Those who compiled the Pent. and collected the materials in the later times seem to have gone on the method of Baronius in his *Annales Ecclesiastici*. Whatever was edifying was included and the more miraculous the better. "The hagiographer had no idea of imposture, of palming off as true that which he knew was not true. The plenitude of his faith in the Church supported anything which was, or could be, told to the honour of the servants of Christ[2]."

The traditions which go to make up Hebrew history have come from many and varied sources. Much of the early tribal matter has been probably applied to the whole nation of which the various individual tribes formed but a part; age-long stories connected with sacred places were also, after proper adaptation, applied to heroes of Jewish story, for Canaan itself no doubt as well as the desert supplied much material. Later on the exile in Babylon was to make its contribution to the ever-growing story[3].

---

[1] Ḥabiru is a perfect equivalent to Hebrew. The SA.GAZ appeared in the N., the Ḥabiru in the centre and S. of Palestine, they were probably identical: see Jirku *Die Wanderungen der Heb.* p. 13; *Camb. Anct. Hist.* II. p. 733.

[2] Mark Pattison *Isaac Casaubon*[2] p. 327.

[3] Cf. an article by L. B. Paton in *AJTh.* VIII. (1908) pp. 658–82.

The oldest of our sources, J and E, come from a time in the early monarchy, possibly from before the division of the kingdoms (for the arguments in favour of this early date see Sellin *Int. to O.T.* pp. 56f., 67f.): but P is much later in date, and the information contained in it for the most part throws light on the post-exilic community. It is a very artificial production, the numbers of the people, the organisation of the tribes, the chronological statements, all bear this character upon their faces. The long lists of names, though many of them are ancient in form, may be only copied from older examples. At the same time these lists supply us with much information, since in them is contained a record not of family descent but often of tribal or other history. Just as the logographers who reduced the ancient legends of Greece to prose, tried to make a series of genealogies the framework of the whole, so the priestly school attached a high value to similar efforts[1]. As Hommel says "they preserve memories of past events under a genealogical garb" (*AHT* p. 235). In later times great care was exercised in preserving and recording genealogies (see Joseph. *c. Apion.* I. 7).

The fact that Hebrew history, in the early period at any rate, has not the substratum of fact which we expect to find in the history of a modern nation is disquieting to some minds. But the inspiration of the writers and editors was not given to fit them to be mere chroniclers and recorders. By their selections and by their re-arrangements of the matter they were able to impress upon the mind of the nation those lessons which it was God's object to convey to them. "History being to the nation what experience is to the individual, it is only through His providential ordering of history that God could express His dealings with a nation, and only through the prophetic interpretation of providence that His mind could be truly known[2]."

---

[1] See Holm *Hist. of Greece* I. pp. 34f. A further likeness between the lists of Greece and Israel is found in the fact that both included towns and peoples, in genealogical lists, as persons. This is such a commonplace of the O.T. that no example need be given; for the Greeks, however, reference may be made to the lists of the rulers of Argos which includes names like Aegialeus, Pelasgus, Epidamnus. The genealogical lists, like those of Israel, contain difficult and indeed contradictory statements (cf. Apollod. II. 1 with Pausanias II. 16).

[2] Skinner *Prophecy and Religion* p. 10. The comments of Holm upon ancient Greek legends apply almost exactly to ancient Hebrew literature: "poetry...seeks truth, but it is a special kind of truth,...an ethical meaning...(it has) no conception of the nature of real accuracy in facts" (*Hist. of Greece* I. pp. 32f.).

§ 5. The Religious Value of Numbers.

To the Jews history had above all else a didactic meaning, it was written in order to shew forth the wonders of God's dealings with His people: hence its supreme value for religion[1]. This value is quite independent of the exact truth of the narrative in which the teaching is conveyed, since as we saw above, a late account of an event may throw light on the ideas of the times in which it was put into writing. As a record of man's aspiration after God, and of the gradual response of God as man was able to receive His revelation, the importance of the book is undiminished by the work of critics, nay, since the true perspective is restored, its value is greatly enhanced.

Numbers, like any other book of the Old Testament, has a double significance. It is a vehicle for conveying to us the spiritual experiences of the Hebrew people, and from another point of view it is the record of the development amongst them of the knowledge of God. But since Numbers is no unity but comes from different ages of the history of Israel, and from writers whose ideas about God, and the demands which He makes upon men, were very diverse, its religious value in the first place is not that of the book as a whole but of the different sources from which it has been compiled[2]. The conceptions of the divine nature and of religion in the different strata are by no means identical[3].

Parts of Numbers have still a direct religious value for the present and for future ages; parts of it can only become available for us by means of allegorical interpretation. To the former belong the examples of noble and god-fearing men like Moses and Caleb, the warnings exhibited in the lives of the complaining Israelites, and the darker pictures of the fates of rebels, like Korah and his company (though here the offence, for which punishment fell upon them, is not one which seems heinous in our eyes, save as the sign of opposition to God and His servants). But many of the narratives

---

[1] Cf. Max Müller *Chips from a German Workshop* I. p. 21: "The real history of man is the history of religion: the wonderful ways by which the different families of the human race advanced towards a truer knowledge and a deeper love of God."

[2] The book as a whole has its own value: see above p. xiii.

[3] The two paragraphs above are taken with some few alterations from my volume on *Exodus* (*Camb. R.V. for Schools*) p. 8.

of the Old Testament, and even some of its laws, if they are to mediate to us real spiritual lessons, require a mystical, and not a literal, interpretation. The point of view of St Augustine must be adopted, when, in commenting upon this very book, he wrote "Eadem quippe sunt in vetere et novo; ibi obumbrata, hic revelata; ibi praefigurata, hic manifestata[1]."

In addition to some few characteristics of the book which distinguish it from other books of the Old Testament, not so much by their entire novelty as by the emphasis which they receive, there are many features which it has in common with the rest of the inspired writings. Since the book comes indeed from different sources and different ages it is in itself a kind of epitome, if the Wisdom literature be excluded, of the whole of the Old Testament. In other words, Numbers has no theology peculiar to itself but is a series of illustrations of Old Testament theology in general.

The great fundamental truth which underlies the whole national life of Israel is the central theme of Numbers, viz. the belief that Jehovah is a personal, living God, and that He stands in a peculiar relation to the people whom He has chosen[2]. The care which He exercises over them during the wanderings in the wilderness is but one mark of this. In the earliest times no doubt men regarded Him as in some ways a being like themselves, and thought of Him and described Him under anthropomorphic images, but even in E a higher stage has been reached (see above pp. xxiii f.); whilst in P the thought of His transcendence or holiness is ever in the writer's mind.

This God, Who was the protector and guide of Israel, demanded from His people obedience to His will as revealed in His laws (see below pp. xlvi ff.). So man began to learn that religion and morality were connected, and the purer and less magical became

---

[1] Quaest. 33 *in Num.* It may perhaps be worth noticing that Calvin, although he was much influenced by St Augustine, in this matter goes directly against him; of attempts to give a mystical significance to the Levitical Law he says "It is better to confess ignorance than to play with frivolous guesses." (Quoted by Farrar *Hist. of Interp.* p. 345.)

[2] It is not clear that true monotheism was taught even by the earlier prophets, it was certainly not accepted by the nation as a whole (see J. M. P. Smith *The Moral Life of the Hebrews* p. 234). So in Vedic religion the popular religion never accepted monotheism though a few monotheistic passages are found in the Rigveda: e.g. x. cxiv. 5: "Wise poets make the beautiful winged, though he is one, manifold by words," and I. clxiv. 46 "That which is one the wise call in divers manners."

his idea of God the higher became his ethical conceptions. The danger of the later priestly teaching, with its emphasis on the unapproachableness of Jehovah, was that it might make men think that He was also careless of mankind, that He would not see injustice and wrong. Any emphasis on the transcendence of God is apt to have this effect.

In these earlier stages of the moral life man had to learn the difference between right and wrong by means of positive commands, and by the bitter experience which followed a broken law. His conscience was not yet in a position to guide him without much outside direction, and so in the Law actions are commanded or forbidden, and little is said about the various motives which may prompt them[1].

For the lowest ideas about God we naturally turn to the oldest documents, but it must by no means be supposed that the later ones are free from superstitious and unworthy conceptions. If JE preserves traditions about the brazen serpent and its power to heal (xxi. 4–9), in P we find survivals of primitive customs like the appeal to the ordeal in the case of suspected unchastity (v. 11–31). In fact it would be true to say of the whole priestly school, and of its religious outlook, that it had a pathetic desire to magnify God's holy name, and yet a quite inadequate idea of what holiness really was and of the methods by which it was to be attained (cf. the two passages xv. 32–36 and 37–41).

So too all schools of thought held to the doctrine that prosperity was the reward of serving God and disaster the punishment of the offender. The shifts to which they had to resort in order to keep their hold on this doctrine are well known to every reader of the Old Testament. In the book of Numbers frequent outbreaks of plague are noticed, and always those who fall before them are held guilty of some offence against God[2]. For the writers of O.T. the

---

[1] In this respect our Blessed Lord went beyond, and fulfilled, the Law. Cf. Forbes Robinson's distinction: "The Jewish Law, adapted as it was to a less highly civilised society, dealt with actions: Christian ethics is concerned with the springs of actions, with motives and intentions" (*The Self-Limitation of the Word of God* p. 91).

[2] Cf. the different attitude of the Arabic writer Zuhair: "To-day I know and yesterday and the days that were, but for to-morrow mine eyes are sightless. For I have seen Doom let out in the dark like a blind camel; those it struck died and those it missed lived to grow old." (Quoted by Miss G. Lowthian Bell *Syria: the Desert and the Sown* p. 61.)

results of natural phenomena were regarded as the direct judgement of God. A later age, with wider knowledge of the causes underlying such phenomena, prefers to reserve its decision; moreover it cannot always see with so clear an insight into the "secret counsels of the inscrutable Godhead." In 1561 the steeple of Old St Paul's was struck by lightning, and a fire broke out which did much damage. "At a period of such fierce religious excitement, in the clash and collision of opinions and passions, both parties saw in this event a manifest sign from Heaven, a sign of the Divine wrath. Where could God, the avenger of sin, reveal Himself so awfully, so undesirably, so visibly, as in thus striking the great church of the metropolis, with that which all religions, which heathen poetry and Biblical imagery, had declared to be the chosen bolt of destruction from the right hand of the Almighty? Each party at once thrust itself into the secret counsels of the inscrutable Godhead, and read, without doubt or hesitation, the significance of this, as all agreed, supernatural event—the Protestants, as condemnatory of the old superstitious slavery to the usurping Bishop of Rome; the Papalists, of the rebellion against the Vicar of Christ, the sacrilegious profanation of the sanctuary[1]."

The presence of such primitive ideas in Numbers reminds us that the book, like the Old Testament itself, is but a stage (or better the record of a series of stages) in the divine revelation. We shall err equally if we attach too great an importance to its surviving superstitions, or too little. It had a part to play in the education of the human race by means of the experiences of the chosen people, and therefore it must not be despised, but since its completion or fulfilment in Christianity *primary* importance can no longer be attached to it[2].

Thus we have before us God's way of dealing with His children, illustrated in the life of Israel—to him that hath shall be given, those who apprehend divine truth, and use it, have as their reward a further revelation. The process is one of gradual development and evolution, not without failures and backslidings, of returning

---

[1] Dean Milman *Annals of St Paul's* p. 277.

[2] It is this fact which lends truth to the exaggerated utterance of Sir A. Quiller-Couch: "to connect in any child's mind the Book of Joshua with the Gospels, to make its Jehovah identical in that young mind with the Father of mercy to whom Jesus was the Son...is a blasphemous usage, and a curse" (*The Art of Reading* p. 50).

to primitive abuses. But if in its origins the religion of Israel was much the same as that of many another Semitic nation, in its developed form it was the complete disclosure of God's nature and purpose as far as man can bear it. Until the human race had been trained to worship its maker it was not in a position to receive the revelation of Him. As Ruskin puts it: "Nature keeps whatever she has done best, close sealed until it is regarded with reverence."

The ideal of the priestly religion, of which Numbers gives the most complete account, is that of a kind of Civitas Dei, a divine community living in the midst of an arid desert. The central fact of the whole scheme is that all the life and existence of the people is founded on the dwelling of Jehovah amongst them, their most important employment His worship. To serve this high and holy God a separate caste is required, who alone may approach Him, and round His Tabernacle, in ordered ranks, the tribes that bear His name take up their protecting stations. The mind of the priestly writer was an orderly and sagacious one, and his arrangements and conceptions are a striking anticipation of the heavenly hierarchies of the medieval Schoolmen.

The political ambitions of the Jewish race had come to nought, amid the disappointments of the exile and the return; the priestly school aroused in them a new ambition. "Originally a race, they had continually desired to become a nation, but never with real success; they ended in creating the idea of a Church[1]." In order that this ideal might become dominant in the nation they read it back into the very earliest stages of its existence[2].

In those parts of Numbers which come from JE several passages occur which throw an interesting light upon the idea of prophecy held by the early Israelites. In xii. 6 ff. two distinct methods of inspiration are contrasted, that of the ordinary prophet, by means of dreams and visions, and that of Moses by the direct revelation of God's will. Notice too the breadth of view which does not wish to limit the gift of prophecy to a single order of men (xi. 25 ff.) and does not deny it to one who was himself a member of another race (xx. 2 ff.).

---

[1] Headlam *The Doctrine of the Church and Reunion* p. 7.

[2] This involved the re-writing of the history of the nation. There was in Indian literature a similar development in order to throw off primitive crude ideas (see Bloomfield *The Relig. of the Veda* pp. 33 f., 215 f.), and even Pindar softened down some of the myths (Adam *Religious Teachers of Greece* p. 117).

§ 6. THE LEGISLATION IN NUMBERS.

The four later books of the Pentateuch, as they have come down to us, contain various groups of laws, all of which claim to go back to Moses as the spokesman of Jehovah. These various groups are attributed to four different periods of the history of Israel: (*a*) the eve of the departure from Egypt (Ex. xii.); (*b*) the sojourn at the Sacred Mount (Ex. xx.–Num. x. 10); (*c*) the wandering in the wilderness (Num. xv. ff.); (*d*) the time immediately before the crossing of the Jordan (Deut.). Some of these laws, such as the Book of the Covenant (xx. 22–xxiii. 33), and the second Decalogue (xxxiv. 11–26), both of which come from JE, belong to the earlier traditions of the race; but the vast mass of the legislation has been preserved in P and presumably is late in date.

To those who are used to modern legal codes such parts of the Old Testament as deal with the laws seem a strange miscellany, without any obvious arrangement or system to connect them. But in this they were not singular, other early attempts at the collection of legal matter are marked by the same features. The following description of the 'Capitularies' of Charles the Great might with few alterations be applied to parts of the Pentateuch. "They are a vast and miscellaneous accumulation of laws, regulations, judicial decisions, moral precepts, literary extracts, royal orders, articles of enquiry, civil and ecclesiastical circulars and special letters, down to inventories of farm stock, household furniture, and garden stuff and implements, in the king's residences....They cover the whole field of life. With scarcely an attempt at order, they show the confusion with which matters of every sort, political, religious, economical, were all thrown together in the attempt to regulate them. But they also show the strong instinct of early days as to the moral and spiritual laws, which underlie and animate the outward framework of civil society[1]."

So the collection of laws, which bears the name of Moses, comes from different ages, and contains much matter of different quality, and even represents different, and not very consistent, points of view. As a whole it cannot be dated for, as F. W. Maitland said of the register of the *Wryttes orygynall and judiciall*, "To ask for

[1] Dean Church *Beginning of the Middle Ages* p. 125.

its date would be like asking for the date of one of our great cathedrals[1]." Under what various circumstances it was codified and collected we do not know, analogy would make it probable that it was to meet some great crisis, or to register some great change. Amongst our Saxon forefathers "a publication of laws is the result of some political change or series of changes....The laws of Ethelbert of Kent were the result of the conversion; those of Wihtraed and Ini, of the changes which a century of Church organisation made necessary in that kingdom and in Wessex[2]." Greek history also furnishes us with a parallel to the priestly legislation, for just as the Laws of Lycurgus in Sparta consolidated the power of an aristocratic warrior class, so those of P established the position of the hierarchy in the nation of Israel.

If we could but trace out in its fullness the development of the Jewish legal system we should gain an unique insight into Jewish history[3]. That the system remained Mosaic in name is a tribute to the work of the first great leader of the Israelite race, and to the tenacity of Israelite memories, as well as to their power of adapting their laws to meet the changing needs of the times[4]. This power of adapting existing legislation to fresh circumstances, whilst preserving its original name and intention, can be well illustrated from Numbers, since it contains several legal provisions intended to supplement or modify the accepted codes. Such passages are (*a*) the Second Passover (ix. 6–14); (*b*) the Punishment for breaking the Sabbath (xv. 32–36); (*c*) the Tables of Sacrificial Dues (xxviii.–xxix.); (*d*) the question of the inheritance of daughters (xxvii. 1–11, xxxvi.). An attempt to arrange the laws in Numbers according to subject matter at once reveals two principal divisions, (A) laws concerned with the religious or ceremonial life of the nation, and (B) those intended to regulate the civil or

---

[1] *Memoir of F. W. Maitland* p. 72.

[2] Stubbs *Constitutional History of England* I. pp. 213f.

[3] Cf. Gibbon's dictum: "The laws of a nation form the most instructive part of its history" (*Decline and Fall of the Roman Empire* IV. p. 442).

[4] "We are not to suppose that...legislation has descended to us from the age of Moses without addition and change. Such a belief would be contrary to the history of other religious law-books, or indeed to historical probability. As the utterances of the Hebrew prophets were modified or enlarged according to the circumstances of the successive ages to which they are applied, so too the Mosaic legislation must have undergone revision and enlargement. Laws and regulations which suited the life in the desert needed adaptation to the changed conditions of life in Canaan... the Mosaic legislation was a matter of growth" (Sayce *EHH* p. 203).

social life of the community and of the individuals who composed it. It must be remembered that such a division would not have been made by the Hebrews themselves, for them the whole community was conceived of as being under the direct governance of Jehovah, all laws therefore were equally sacred. The distinction between religious and secular had not yet arisen. Hence perhaps the laws were intended in some cases to be an expression of the divine will, rather than regulations which could be carried out in their literal sense[1].

The following are the principal laws in Numbers arranged under appropriate headings and with references to parallel passages in the Pentateuch[2].

A. *Religious and Ceremonial Laws.*

These laws and regulations will be dealt with more fully in the next section. It may suffice to say here that, with one exception, the laws in Numbers belong to the priestly school of writers, in this respect they differ from those preserved in Exodus.

1. *Sacred Objects.*
   The Ark. See x. 33 *a*, *c*, 35 f. (JE): cf. Dt. x. 1–5, xxxi. 24–26; Ex. xxv. 10–22 (P).
2. *The Hierarchy.*
   Its origin. See iii. 5–10 (P).
   The Levites.
   - a. Age of Service. viii. 23–26 (P^s).
   - b. Consecration. viii. 5–22 (P).
   - c. Duties. iii. 5–9, xviii. 1–6 (P), i. 47–53, iii. 25 f., 29–32, 35–37, iv. 4 f., 15, 24–33 (P^s): cf. 1 Chr. xxiii. 1–5, 27–32, xxv. 1–8.
   - d. Property and means of support. xviii. 21, 23 f. (P), xxxi. 28–30, 47, xxxv. 1–8 (P^s): cf. Lev. xxv. 29–34 (P^s).
   - e. Subordination to the priests. iii. 5 f., 9, xviii. 1 f. (P), iv. 27 (P^s).

   The Priests.
   - a. Duties. xviii. 5, 7 *a* (P), iv. 11–15 *a*, 16 (P^s): cf. Lev. x. 8 *a*, 10 f., ii. 1 f. (P), Lev. vi. 6 f. (P^s).
   - b. Means of Support. v. 19 f., vi. 19 f. (P^x), xv. 20 f., xviii. 9–20, 25–32 (P), v. 5–8, xxxi. 25–29 (P^s): cf. Lev. vii. 11–14, 28–37, x. 14 f.; Ex. xxix. 27 f.; Lev. vi. 14–18 (P), Lev. vii. 8–10, x. 12 f. (P^s).

---

[1] The same was true of the Middle Ages. "All mediaeval law-making, civil and ecclesiastical alike," writes Professor Tout, "was but the promulgation of an ideal, rather than the issuing of precepts meant to be literally executed" (*The Empire and the Papacy* p. 334).

[2] Although I have by no means followed him very closely I wish to express my indebtedness to C. F. Kent *Israel's Laws and Legal Precedents*: his arrangement of all the necessary passages is a great boon to the student.

3. *The Sacred Dues.*

Firstborn Sons. iii. 11–13 (P), 46–51 (P^s): cf. Ex. xxxiv. 19 *a*, 20 *c*, xxii. 19 *b* (JE); Ex. xiii. 1 f. (P).
Firstborn of beasts. xviii. 15–18 (P): cf. Ex. xiii. 11–13 *a*, xxii. 30, xxxiv. 19 *b*–20 (JE); Dt. xiv. 23–27, xv. 19–22 (D).
Firstfruits. xv. 17–21 (P): cf. Ex. xxxiv. 26 *a* (JE); Dt. xviii. 4, xxvi. 1–11 (D); Lev. xix. 24, xxiii. 10 f. (H).
Tithes. xviii. 25–32 (P); Dt. xiv. 22–27, xxvi. 12–15 (D); Lev. xxvii. 30–33 (P^s).
Vows. vi. 13–21 (P^x), xxx. (P^s): cf. Dt. xxiii. 21–23, xii. 26 (D); Lev. xxvii. 1–29 (P^s).
Spoils of War. xxxi. 25–31 (P^s).

4. *The Sacred Calendar.*

The New Moon. xxviii. 11–15 (P^s).
The Sabbath. xv. 32–36, xxviii. 8 f. (P^s): cf. Ex. xxxi. 12–14; Lev. xix. 36 (H); Gen. ii. 2 f.; Ex. xxxv. 1–3 (P); Ex. xvi. 22–26, xxxi. 15–17; Lev. xxiii. 3 (P^s).
Passover and the Feast of Unleavened Bread. ix. 1–14, xxviii. 16–25 (P^s): cf. Lev. xxiii. 10–14 (H); Ex. xii. 1–13, 43, 45–50; Lev. xxiii. 4–8 (P); Ex. xii. 14–20 (P^s).
Feast of Weeks. xxviii. 26–31 (P^s): cf. Lev. xxiii. 15–21 (H).
Feast of Trumpets. xxix. 1–6 (P^s): cf. Lev. xxiii. 23–25 (P).
The Day of Atonement. xxix. 7–11 (P^s): cf. Lev. xvi. (P), xxiii. 26–32 (P^s).
Feast of Tabernacles. xxix. 12–38 (P^s): cf. Lev. xxiii. 39–44 (H), 33–36 (P).

5. *The Sacrifices.*

Cereal Offerings. xv. 1–16 (P): cf. Ex. xxxiv. 25 *a* (JE); Lev. ii. 1–16 (P).
Libations. xv. 3–10 (P): cf. Gen. xxviii. 18, xxxv. 14 (JE).
Guilt Offerings. [v. 5–8 (P)]: cf. Lev. xix. 20 (H), v. 14–19, vi. 1–7, xix. 21 f. (P).
Sin Offerings. xv. 22–31 (P): cf. Lev. v. 1–13 (P), iv. 1–35, vi. 24–29, viii. 14 f. (P^s).
Yearly Sin Offering. xvi. 29–34 *a* [1–28] (P).
The Red Heifer. xix. 1–13 [14–22] (P^x), [xxxi. 21–24] (P^s).
The Jealousy Offering. v. (P).
The Daily Sacrifice. [xxviii. 1–8 (P^s)]: cf. Ex. xxix. 38–42, xxx. 7 f. (P^s).

6. *Ceremonial Uncleanness.*

By the Dead. xix. 14–21 (P^x), 11–13, xxxi. 19 (P^z): cf. Dt. xxi. 1–5, 22 f. (D); Lev. xxii. 4 *b*, 6 *a* (H).
By contagion. xix. 22 (P^x): cf. Lev. v. 3 (P).
Spoils of War. xxxi. 20–24 (P^s).
The Nazirites. vi. 1–12 (P^x).

7. *The Law of Tassels.* xv. 37–41 (H): cf. Dt. vi. 8 f., xxii. 12 (D).

B. *Civil and Social Laws.*

1. *Political Organisation.*

The Census. i. 1–3, iii. 14 f. (P), iv. 1–3 (P^s).
The Division of the Land. xxvi. 52–56 (P^s): cf. Jos. xviii. 2–10 (D).

2. *Military Organisation.*

The Age of Service. xxvi. 2 *a*, 3 *a* (P^s).
Exemptions. i. 48 f., ii. 33 (P^s): cf. Dt. xx. 1 *a*, 5–7, xxiv. 5 (D).
Spoils and Captives. xxxi. 1 *a*, 2 f., 7–18, 21–23 (P^s): cf. Dt. vii. 1 f., 16, 22–26, xx. 10, 12–20, xxi. 10–14 (D).

3. *Judiciary.*

The number of witnesses. xxxv. 30 (P^s): cf. Dt. xvii. 6, xix. 15 (D).
The Cities of Refuge. xxxv. 9–15 (P^s): cf. Ex. xxi. 12–14 (JE); Dt. iv. 41–43, xix. 1–13 (D).

4. *Personal Relationships.*

Father and unmarried daughters. xxx. 3–5 (P^s).
Marriage with Aliens. xxv. 6–13 (P): cf. Ex. xxxiv. 12 *a*, 15 f.; Dt. vii. 1–4 (D).
The Husband's authority over the Wife. xxx. 6–8, 13–15 (P^s).
The Rights and Duties of Sojourners. ix. 14, xv. 14–16 (P), 29 f., xxxv. 15 (P^s): cf. Ex. xxii. 21 (JE); Dt. i. 16, xxiv. 14, 17 f., xxvii. 19 (D); Lev. xix. 33 f., xxiv. 22, xxv. 47 f., 53 (H).

5. *Property.*

The Inheritance of Daughters. xxvii. 1–11, xxxvi. 1–12 (P^s).

6. *Criminal Laws*[1].

Sacrilege. xviii. 22 (P), iii. 38 *b*, iv. 17–20 (P^s): cf. Lev. xix. 30 *b*, xxii. 3 *b* (H), vii. 20 f. (P^s).
Labour on the Sabbath. xv. 32–36 (P^s): cf. Ex. xxiii. 12, xxxiv. 21 (JE); Dt. v. 12–15 (D); Lev. xix. 3 *b*, xxvi. 2 *a* (H); Ex. xxxv. 2 f. (P), xxxi. 13 *b*–17 (P^s).
Deliberate defiance of the Law. xv. 30 f. (P): cf. Dt. xvii. 12 f. (D).
Adultery. v. (P): cf. Dt. v. 18, xxii. 22–24 (D); Lev. xviii. 20, xx. 10 (P).
Murder. xxxv. 14, 34 (P^s): cf. Ex. xxi. 12–14, 20 f. (JE); Dt. v. 17, xix. 11–13 (D); Lev. xxiv. 17, 21 *b* (H); Gen. ix. 5 f. (P).

§ 7. THE SACRIFICIAL SYSTEM[2].

The writers of the priestly school give us valuable information concerning the ecclesiastical organisation and system of the Jewish Church. This information, however, will only deceive us if we take it at its face value and as a description of the wilderness period. It belongs in reality to the post-exilic age.

---

[1] It must be remembered that "In ancient Israel, as in all early societies, criminal law was the business of the private individual, not of the state. Theft was punished by such reparation in property as would overcome the feeling of vengeance which would otherwise have led to bloodshed. The punishment of a murderer was primarily the business of the avenger of blood, and the most the law could hope to do was to step in and regulate the feud." H. M. Wiener *Pentateuchal Studies* p. 176; see further the same writer's *Studies in Biblical Law* chap. iv.

[2] In the following section the Sacrificial System as a whole is but slightly dealt with: its object is to collect the contributions made to the system by Numbers. For a full study of the Jewish Sacrificial System see G. B. Gray *Sacrifice in O.T.*

In order to be complete a sacrificial system must provide for four things, (*a*) the place at which the sacrifices may be offered; (*b*) the times of the various sacred seasons; (*c*) the form of the several offerings; and (*d*) the persons who may offer the sacrifice. In regard to each of these four requirements the Pentateuch makes ample provision.

(*a*) *The place of sacrifice.*

This subject is fully dealt with in Ex. xxv.–xxxi., and xxxv.–xl., and the reader is recommended to study these chh. with the notes in McNeile's excellent commentary in the present series, paying especial attention to the Essay on *The Tabernacle: its structure, historicity and religious significance* (pp. lxxii.–xcii.). Numbers provides little that is new on the subject, beyond the regulations for the care of the sacred objects and for their removal on the march through the wilderness; information which has but little value since it presupposes artificial conditions.

(*b*) *The sacred seasons.*

The custom of holding a number of sacred feasts during the course of each year is not, of course, peculiar to the Israelites, or even to the Semites. Amongst the Germanic races, for example, there were three great annual festivals; one in the autumn for peace and plenty, one at Yuletide for growth, and one in the early summer for victory[1].

The observing of these great festivals was also a mark of the Jewish calendar, though the times differ, and there is no provision made for any stated festival in order to obtain success in arms. The three occasions upon which all males were to appear before Jehovah (Ex. xxiii. 17) were the Passover and Unleavened Cakes, the Feast of Weeks, and the Feast of Tabernacles or Booths. These feasts go back to the earliest documents of the Pentateuch. In JE the regulations are very simple (see Ex. xii. 21–27, xiii. 3–10, xxiii. 14–18, xxxiv. 18–23); in D they become more elaborate (Dt. xvi. 1–17); and in P minute rules and regulations are laid down. It should be remembered that these festivals were really pilgrimages; for the Heb. חַג *ḥag* (usually translated *feast*), like the

[1] See *Camb. Med. Hist.* II. p. 489.

corresponding Arabic *Haj*, implies a journey to a sanctuary: see further Driver *Deut.* (*ICC*) pp. 188 f.

To these three great annual Pilgrimages other lesser public festivals were added. In Num. xxviii.–xxx. 1 we have a list of these, and of the appropriate sacrifices to be offered on them. A similar, though less complete, list of appointed feasts is to be found in Lev. xxiii. and in Ez. xlv. 18–xlvi. 15.

The list in Lev. xxiii. is interesting because it contains matter from both H and P, as well as editorial additions. The following feasts are set out in it:

	Lev.	*Num.*
(*a*) Sabbath	1–3 (Ps)	xxviii. 9 f.
(*b*) Passover and Unleavened Cakes	4–8 (P)	
	9–14 (H and Ps)	16–25
(*c*) Weeks	15–22 (H mainly)	26–31
(*d*) New Year	23–25 (P)	xxix. 1–6
(*e*) Day of Atonement	26–32 (P)	7–11
(*f*) Booths	23–36 (P)	12–38
	39–43 (H)	

The fuller list in Num. has in addition the daily sacrifice (xxviii. 3–8) and the New Moon (11–15). The former of these provisions orders that certain offerings are to be made, one in the morning, and the other in the evening. This law Wellhausen regards as "the fundamental element of the worship, for even the sacrifices of Sabbaths and feast-days consist only of its numerical increase" (*Proleg.* p. 80). The cessation of the daily or continual offering (see on xxviii. 3) was a great disaster (Dan. viii. 11 ff. &c.), being apparently equivalent to the downfall of the whole sacrificial system. Some kind of daily sacrifice seems to have been offered before the exile though its exact nature is not quite clear. Wellhausen (*op. cit.* p. 79) points out that in 2 K. xvi. 15 a burnt offering and a meal offering were made, the one in the evening and the other in the morning, in the time of Ahaz; but Ezekiel (xlvi. 13–15) mentions only the burnt offering made in the morning.

In connexion with the sacred seasons it should be noted that Num. provides a Supplementary Passover (ix. 1–14) for those prevented by absence from keeping the first.

(c) *The form of the several offerings.*

The various set feasts had each of them its own appointed offering or offerings. In Num. xxviii.–xxx. 1 we have, as we have seen, an elaborate list of the sacred feasts, and also a schedule of dues similar to those found in connexion with Carthaginian temples.

	Burnt Offering			
Season	He-lambs of the 1st year	Young bullocks	Rams	*Sin Offering* He-goats
Every morning	1	—	—	—
Every evening	1	—	—	—
Sabbath Day	7	—	—	—
New Moon	7	2	1	1
Feast of Unleavened Cakes (daily from 15th to 21st of 1st month)	7	2	1	1
Feast of Weeks	7	2	1	1
Seventh Month: 1st day	7	1	1	1
10th „	7	1	1	1
Feast of Tabernacles: 15th day	14	13	2	1
16th „	14	12	2	1
17th „	14	11	2	1
18th „	14	10	2	1
19th „	14	9	2	1
20th „	14	8	2	1
21st „	14	7	2	1
22nd „	7	1	1	1

It should be noted that the law requires that on special occasions the ordinary offerings should still be made in addition to those specially prescribed.

With the animal sacrifices went offerings of meal, oil and wine, the quantities of which were duly appointed (xv. 1–16).

The requirements under Ezekiel's ideal scheme differ considerably from those here set forth. The following table is based upon Ez. xlv. 21–xlvi. 15:

Season	Lambs	Rams	Bullocks	Goats
Every morning	1	—	—	—
Every evening	0	—	—	—
Sabbath Day	6	1	—	—
New Moon	6	1	0	0
Feast of Unleavened Bread. Daily for 7 days	0	7	7	1
Feast of Weeks	0	0	0	0
Seventh Month: 1st day	0	0	0	0
10th „	0	0	0	0
Feast of Tabernacles (15th–21st of 7th month)	0	7	7	0
22nd day	0	0	0	0

Further differences will also be found in the quantities of meal, oil, and wine, appointed to accompany the offerings.

In addition to the regular public offerings a number of offerings which apply to special cases are regulated in Num., these are the meal offering of jealousy (v. 15), and the offering of the Nazirite (vi. 10 ff.).

(*d*) *The offerers of Sacrifice.*

In Lev. i.–vii. we have a manual of sacrifice giving instructions to the worshipper and to the priest upon that important ritual art. In the Israelite public worship prayer and exhortation were almost entirely ignored, the priest's office was to offer sacrifice and to attend to those who came to inquire of God[1].

A recent writer, however, makes the suggestion that these two parts of the priestly function were originally separated in early Israelite religion. He sees in Moses, for example, a priest-King like to the Assyrian *patesi* or the Sabaean *mukarrib* or the Arabic *kâhin*. As such Moses delivered judgements and had charge of the sacred oracle. Over against him stood the Levitical priest who was concerned with the cultus of the God and the care of His sanctuary[2].

In the parts of the Pentateuch which come before Numbers the appointment of Priests and their consecration have been provided for (Ex. xxix. &c.), and even the special vestments which they are to wear (Ex. xxviii., xxix.). But little or nothing has been said of the Levites. It is true that the tribe of Levi has been mentioned from time to time, possibly in Ex. iv. 14, xxxii. 26–28 (both JE), as sacred. In Ex. xxxviii. 21 and Lev. xxv. 32 f. (P^s) only have we an unmistakable reference to its ecclesiastical character.

To the development of the hierarchy, Num. contributes little, beyond recording the obscure struggle which lies behind the story of Korah, and insisting that the priests alone have the right to offer incense (xvi.–xvii.); it also deals with the question of priestly revenues (see below).

---

[1] Cf. Gwatkin *Knowledge of God* II. p. 145: "Preaching and ghostly counsel were not his work, but cutting up beasts and answering legal questions." Private prayer was common in early times and is frequently mentioned in 1 and 2 Sam.: e.g. 1 S. i. 3, 10, viii. 6, 2 S. vii. 27, xii. 16. For the development of public prayer see Oesterley *The Jewish Background of the Christian Liturgy* ch. iii.

[2] See Nielsen *Altarab. Mondreligion* pp. 137 ff.

As regards the Levites, however, we have a good deal of information. The whole tribe is excluded from the census and its duties marked out (i. 47 ff.); and in iii. 5–13 the appointment of the Levites as a caste of priestly servants is definitely made and their duties more fully defined, viz. the care and transport of the sanctuary and all its furniture (iv. 1–32). In viii. 5–22 we have an account of their purification, and presentation, on behalf of Israel (11) and in the place of the firstborn (6–18). The Levites are to stand between the priests and the congregation, they are to assist the former, but they are not to handle any of the sacred objects directly (xviii. 3). It should be noticed that the writer looks upon the Levites mainly as a body of ecclesiastical porters; there is nothing for example, which suggests the Levitical choirs of later times[1].

A matter with which Num. deals at some length is the revenue of the ecclesiastics. Before the exile we have little information on the subject; no doubt the priests partook of the sacrifices and received gifts from those who came to the sanctuaries, sometimes evidently seizing more than custom allowed them (1 S. ii. 12 ff.). From the last days of the Jewish monarchy onwards the priests seem to have advanced more extravagant claims to power and to have become possessed of steadily increasing revenues. This advance can be seen by comparing the different provisions for the priests in D, Ezekiel, and P; and a still further advance can be traced in the Mishnah.

The important ch. in Num. is xviii. where the following sources of revenue are permitted:

(1) All meal, sin and guilt offerings (xviii. 9 f., cf. Ecclus. vii. 31). This provision is also made in Ez. xliv. 29, but was unknown before, with the possible exception of 2 K. xii. 16 where there is a reference to some kind of fine (?) for guilt and sin offerings which was the priests' property.

(2) Part of the peace offering (11: cf. Lev. vii. 32 ff.). This was allowed by Dt. xviii. 3, but on a less liberal scale.

(3) The firstfruits (12 f.). In pre-exilic days the priests prob-

---

[1] For a history of the development of the Priesthood, real and imaginary, the reader is referred to McNeile *Exodus* pp. lxvi. ff.; Burney *Judges* pp. 44 ff.; Steuernagel *Einwanderung &c.* pp. 99 ff.; Hölscher *Gesch. der israel. u. jüd. Rel.* pp. 64 ff.; and above all to Gray *Sacrifice* pp. 179 ff.

ably derived a small revenue from this source since firstfruits were to be brought to the sanctuary: see Ex. xxiii. 19, xxxiv. 26 (JE).

(4) All devoted things (14). These are allowed by Ez. xliv. 29 but are not mentioned before.

(5) The firstborn (15 ff.). The offspring of human beings are to be redeemed at five shekels, and unclean animals are also to be redeemed; the firstborn of clean animals are to be sacrificed and the priests are to take their appointed share. This provision is not found in Ezekiel, and the laws in Dt. xv. 19–23, xii. 17 f., xiv. 23 (dealing only with the firstborn of clean cattle) are incompatible and evidently earlier: see Driver *Deut.* p. 187, and Gray pp. 229 f.

(6) The Levites are to have the tithes (21–24).

(7) A tithe of the Levites' tithe is to go to the priests (25–32).

Additional revenue came to the priests from the skins of burnt offerings (Lev. vii. 8), from the shewbread (Lev. xxiv. 5–9: cf. 1 S. xxi. 3 ff.). They also took possession of unredeemed fields (Lev. xxvii. 21) and of fines in certain cases where no one else claimed them (Num. v. 8: cf. Lev. v. 16, xxii. 14). They had also certain special dues from the Nazirites (Num. vi. 19 f.).

These elaborate and extensive provisions were based on the principle that the Levites were to have no property as had the other tribes; this is distinctly laid down in xviii. 20, 24, "Thou shalt have no inheritance in their land, neither shalt thou have any portion among them....Among the children of Israel they (i.e. the Levites) shall have no inheritance." Later on, however, the Levites did obtain for themselves possessions and an inheritance (xxxv.), but since the provisions of xviii. were not repealed presumably they still retained their original endowments.

§ 8. The position of Moses.

It has been pointed out by Lord Morley[1] that the early history of many nations is marked by the emergence of "half-divine legislators" who figure mysteriously against the dark background of primitive times. Such were Lycurgus and Solon, and greatest of all, the lawgiver of the Hebrew people. Around each of these

---

[1] *Burke* p. 240.

figures much has gathered that is of doubtful historic value; but, as Gwatkin has said with characteristic emphasis, "A man is not proved to be legendary if a good deal of legend has grown up round him[1]."

Our knowledge of Moses, it need hardly be pointed out, comes from other sources beside the present book; but since Numbers contains much important material it will be worth while considering the conception, or to speak more accurately the different conceptions found in the various sources[2], of the prophet therein set forth.

In Exodus we have the story of his early life, in Numbers we have the picture of his developed character as it was revealed under the stress and strain of continued difficulties. The greatest and most oppressive of these difficulties came from the insubordination and ingratitude of the people to whom he was a God-given leader. Moses would have appreciated to the full, from his own experience (cf. especially xiv. 41 ff., xvi. 14), the advice given by the Duke of Alva to Don John of Austria: "Recollect that the first foes with whom one has to contend are one's own troops, with their clamours for an engagement at this moment, and their murmurs about results at another[3]."

The importance of Moses for the history of Israel can scarcely be exaggerated; in every department of the nation's life, religious, social and political, and even military, he stands alone[4]. It is one of the characteristics of Numbers that emphasis should be laid on this supremacy: see xii. 1–15, xvi. 12 f., 28 ff. (all JE)[5]; although in those portions of it which come from P Aaron is introduced much more freely, and in one case at least (iii. 1) his name is put before that of Moses. The position of Moses was, however, so firmly fixed that even in P he remains supreme; and the priestly conception of the true relation of the secular and ecclesiastical

---

[1] *The Knowledge of God* II. pp. 17 f. It is remarkable that the historicity of Moses is now almost unquestioned: see the various studies by Baentsch, Beer, Gressmann, Sellin, and Volz.

[2] Cf. Lofthouse in *The People and the Book* pp. 225 f.

[3] Quoted by Motley *The Rise of the Dutch Republic* pt. III. ch. 1.

[4] Philo saw in Moses one who was at the same time a king, a lawgiver, a priest and a prophet: *De vit. Mos.* III. 23 (Mang. II. 163).

[5] Cf. use of אדני in Num. xi. 28, xxxii. 25, 27, xxxvi. 2; also Ex. xxxii. 22; Jos. v. 14.

leaders had to be exhibited in the dependence of Joshua upon Eleazar (xxvii. 21).

(*a*) The work which Moses accomplished as a military and political leader must have been exceedingly great. The account of the wilderness period, as it now stands, has been idealised by later writers; but, when allowance has been made for their labours, enough remains to witness to the stupendous achievement of welding together a heterogeneous mob of desert tribes, and leading them to the conquest of Palestine. Although the carrying out of the actual entry was left to other leaders, it was the preparatory work of Moses which made it possible; and, if Sayce is right, the conquest of the East Jordan territories was, from a military point of view, a greater triumph than that of Joshua[1]. His fame as a leader is not dependent on the accounts in the Pentateuch alone, it is an unvarying tradition in the prophets: see Hos. xii. 13, Mic. vi. 4, and much later Is. lxiii. 11. It was this aspect of the work of Moses which appealed to earlier generations: to them Moses was primarily a man of action, not a writer of books. It is interesting in this connexion to remember Bishop Stubbs' summary of the rise of the German peoples: "A great family of tribes whose institutions are all in common, and their bonds of political cohesion so untrustworthy, are singularly capable of entering into new combinations; singularly liable to be united and dissolved in short-lived confederations, and to reappear under new names, so long as they are without a great leader. Yet in that very community of institutions and languages, in the firmness of the common basis, and the strength of the lower organisation, if a leader can be found to impress on them the need of unity, and to consolidate the higher machinery of political action into a national constitution, instead of small aggregations and tumultuary associations, they possess a basis and a spring of life, from and by which they may rise into a great homogeneous people, symmetrically organised and united, progressive and thoroughly patriotic[2]."

(*b*) But if the deeds of Moses appealed to the earlier generations, to their children his writings were the most important part of his work and the Law of Moses became the national code. The first

---

[1] *Early Hist. of Hebs.* p. 271.
[2] *The Constitutional History of England* I. p. 39.

appearance of any definite reference to a code of Moses is Mal. iv. 4, "Remember ye the law of Moses my servant, which I commanded unto him in Horeb for all Israel, even statutes and judgements"; here possibly nothing more than Dt. is intended by the law of Moses[1].

(*c*) In addition to his achievement as a leader and lawgiver Moses was also a great religious genius, the first of the prophets. He it was in reality who laid the foundation of Hebrew religion and introduced a new conception of God, a conception which moulded the whole future of the nation[2]. As a prophet he had an intercourse with Jehovah such as none other might claim, not even the priestly Aaron (xii. 1–15). This power was used consistently in an ungrudging spirit (cf. xi. 29) for the glory of Jehovah and the benefit of His people. Like Jeremiah after him, Moses was preeminently an intercessor: see xii. 11 ff., xiv. 11–24 (both JE); and cf. Jer. xv. 1; Job xlii. 7 f.

To form any clear estimate of the character of Moses is an almost impossible task. Each several source looked upon him as the ideal leader of the nation and formed its own conception, into which was incorporated all that seemed desirable in such a personage. As the points of view of JE, of D, and of P, were manifestly different the picture which is presented to us is a composite one; and although P had, as it were, the last word, yet so firmly were the earlier stories and traditions concerning Moses fixed in the minds of the men of Israel that they were strong enough to defy even the editing of P. With D's conception of Moses we are not now concerned since that source hardly appears in Numbers; that of JE shews a leader of courage and devotion, with great ideals and an enthusiasm which is only thrown into brighter relief by an occasional lapse into despondency or impatience. The predominant characteristic of the man is that 'meekness' without which even the greatest leaders have made shipwreck of their plans; high principles and noble aims are not sufficient in themselves, they must in order to produce the highest type of character be combined with stern self-control and endless patience. Simon de Montfort the younger, a man of deep religious convictions, is

---

[1] See further § 6, *The Legislation in Numbers*.
[2] Cf. Stade *Gesch. des Volkes Isr.* I. p. 130.

a noteworthy example of failure through this fundamental deficiency. Creighton says of him "He could combine men for action in a great crisis; but the same fiery earnestness of purpose which then made him capable of kindling their enthusiasm, was a hindrance to him in less stormy times. Himself engrossed in a great purpose, he was intolerant of the weaknesses of others. He had not the art of getting his own way without the appearance of self-assertion. He demanded the same obedience in small things as in great[1]." Even St Paul had to learn this lesson by sad experience: cf. Gal. i. 5f. and Phil. i. 18. In the case of Moses, this 'meekness' came with the realisation of the splendour of his vocation as God's servant. Face to face with his Creator he was content to submit:

> "Yet take thy way, for sure thy way is best,
> Stretch or contract me thy poore debtor.
> This is but tuning of my breast,
> To make the music better."

Yet even this giant of meekness fell at last in the part where he was strongest; and for some combination of unbelief and disobedience he was excluded from the land of promise. The exact nature of the offence is uncertain; no doubt it was clear in JE, but in the later documents it has been so modified as to be almost unintelligible[2].

In the end God took him and buried him and "even the site of his tomb was forgotten. His only memorial was the people whose future greatness he rendered possible, and of whose religious and social life he determined the direction for centuries to come[3]."

§ 9. The Text of Numbers.

The textual criticism of O.T. has never received the same amount of attention as that of N.T. That this should be so is quite natural in view of the difference in the amount of material available. The standard Hebrew text is that of the Massoretes[4], and the earliest MS. of the whole O.T. known to us is dated as late as 1010 A.D.

---

[1] *Simon de Montfort* p. 184.

[2] D gives as the cause—Jehovah's anger with him that *the people* were disobedient as early as the second year of the Exodus (Dt. i. 37, iii. 24, iv. 21).

[3] Wade *O.T. Hist.* p. 133.

[4] The Massoretes were so called from being the authors, anonymous for the most part, of the *Massorah*. This consisted of a number of traditional rules and formulae dealing with the text of O.T., and also with its interpretation.

Although the text is standardised there are a number of slight variations in the different codices; these have been collected by Kennicott[1] and De Rossi[2], but much work probably still remains to be done. It is quite evident that in not a few places the original text has been completely lost. As H. M. Wiener, a conservative critic, says: "There are passages that violate the ordinary rules of grammar, passages from which no sense can be extracted, passages that can indeed be translated and will give some sense from which however no satisfactory meaning can be elicited[3]." Additional evidence for the Pentateuch comes from the Samaritan Version and the Septuagint. The former of these versions has probably no great critical value, the consonants alone are printed and the text has been "disfigured by errors of transcription and by arbitrary treatment[4]." It is written in the so-called Samaritan characters which are really the old Hebrew, and in so far as it has escaped alteration it represents the text as it existed *c.* 330 B.C. The Septuagint (LXX) of Numbers (which itself, of course, has to be subjected to textual criticism) was probably composed in Alexandria early in the third century B.C.; different MSS. of this version, most of which contain the text of N.T. and are known by the same symbols, are occasionally quoted where interesting readings occur in them; in addition the recension of Lucian (†311 A.D.) is also to be noted.

A comparison of these various materials does not reveal any great variety of readings, and even in corrupt passages, like the poems, little assistance can be obtained from the versions. The Hebrew text itself seems fixed save for a few minor differences in reading.

The following is a sketch of the probable development of the text. Behind our present Hebrew, LXX, and Sam. texts lay an archetype which most resembled our present M.T.—to this archetype various additions were made, in the case of the Hebrew only slight ones, in the case of the versions much more considerable.

(*a*) As regards amplifications in the Hebrew it is difficult, as Gray points out, "to draw a sharp line between the latest editors

---

[1] *Vetus test. hebr. cum var. lect.* (Oxford 1776–80).
[2] *Var. lect. veteris Test.* (Parma 1784–8).
[3] *Pent. Studies* p. 6.
[4] Buhl *Canon and Text of O.T.* p. 89.

...whose remarks might be regarded as part of the original work in its final form, and the early scribes who transmitted the text of the completed work." These amplifications are only slight and unimportant, such as the gloss in xiii. 33 (missing from LXX), and possibly additions in ix. 20–23. The unique phrase "holy water" in v. 17, which W. R. Smith took to be "an isolated survival of an obsolete expression[1]," seems to be a Hebrew modification of an original "living water" (so in LXX). Gray thinks that in its use of "LORD" and "God" the Hebrew does not always preserve so early a text as Sam. or LXX[2].

(*b*) The additions in LXX are more numerous, and in quite a number of passages it has a text not only longer than the Hebrew but also than the Sam. This longer text does not seem to have any special significance, and often consists merely of expansions of formulae.

(*c*) The Sam. text is characterised by a number of additions from Dt. i–iii. which have been incorporated into Numbers in order to supplement the narrative. The following is a list of these additions:

Dt.			
Dt. i.	6–8	after Num.	x. 10
	20–23 *a*	"	xii. 16
	27–33	"	xiii. 33
	42	"	xiv. 40
	44 *a*, *b*	"	45 *a*
iii.	24–25 *a*, 26 *b*–28, ii. 2–6	"	xx. 13
ii.	9	"	xxi. 11
	17–19	"	12
	24 f.	"	20
	28, 29 *a*	"	22
	31	"	23 *a*
iii.	21 f.	"	xxvii. 13

As was pointed out above in (*b*) Sam. has occasionally a shorter text than LXX; but in only a few passages is it shorter than Heb., though sometimes it is probably nearer the archetype.

---

[1] *Rel. Sem.*[2] p. 181.

[2] See *Numbers* (*ICC*) pp. 310 ff. where statistics are given for the Balaam narratives.

§ 10. The Contents of Numbers.

PART I. THE SOJOURN AT SINAI. I.–X. 10.

(*a*) *The numbers and arrangements of the tribes.* (i.–iv.)

The taking of the census i.
The order of encampment ii.
The special position of the Levites iii.
The numbers and the duties of the Levites iv.

(*b*) *Various laws and regulations.* (v.–vi.)

The exclusion of the unclean v. 1–4.
Some priestly dues 5–10.
The ordeal of jealousy 11–31.
The law of the Nazirite vi. 1–21.
The Aaronic Blessing 22–27.

(*c*) *The oblations of the princes.* (vii.)

(*d*) *Further laws and regulations.* (viii.–x. 10.)

The golden lampstand viii. 1–4.
The service of the Levites 5–26.
The supplementary Passover ix. 1–14.
The cloud over the Tabernacle 15–23.
The silver trumpets x. 1–10.

PART II. THE WANDERINGS IN THE WILDERNESS. X. 11–XXII. 1.

(*a*) *Incidents on the journey from Sinai to Paran.* (x. 11–xii. 16.)

The departure from Sinai x. 11–36.
The incidents of the journey xi.
The vindication of Moses xii.

(*b*) *The story of the spies and its sequel.* (xiii.–xiv.)

The mission and the report of the spies xiii.
The despair and punishment of the congregation xiv. 1–38.
The defeat at Hormah 39–45.

(*c*) *Various Regulations.* (xv.)

Sacrificial directions 1–21.
Unconscious trespasses 22–31.
The punishment of the Sabbath-breaker 32–36.
The wearing of fringes 37–41.

(*d*) *The story of Korah, Dathan and Abiram.* (xvi.–xvii.)

The rebellion and its punishment xvi.
The rod that budded xvii.

(*e*) *Further laws and regulations.* (xviii.–xix.)

The duties and revenues of the priests and Levites xviii.
Rules for purification from defilement by the dead xix.

(*f*) *Events at the close of the wanderings.* (xx.–xxii. 1.)

Events at Kadesh xx. 1–21.
The journey to Moab 22–xxii. 1.

PART III. EVENTS IN MOAB. xxii. 2–xxxvi.

(*a*) *The story of Balaam.* (xxii. 2–xxiv. 25.)

His summons and journey to Balak xxii. 2–41.
Balaam's first utterance xxiii. 1–13.
Balaam's second utterance 14–26.
Balaam's last utterances 27–xxiv. 25.

(*b*) *Various laws and incidents.* (xxv.–xxxi.)

Baal-peor xxv.
The second census xxvi.
The inheritance of daughters xxvii. 1–11.
Moses and his successor 12–23.
Regulations concerning public offerings xxviii., xxix.
The vows of women xxx.
The holy war against Midian xxxi.

(*c*) *Miscellaneous topographical narratives.* (xxxii.–xxxvi.

The East Jordan territories xxxii.
The journeyings from Egypt to Moab xxxiii.
The West Jordan territories xxxiv.
The Levitical cities xxxv.
The daughters of Zelophehad xxxvi.

List of New Testament References.

Num. vi. 3 = Lk. i. 15
,, vi. 5 = Acts xxi. 26
,, xi. 34 = 1 Cor. x. 6
,, xii. 7 = Heb. iii. 2, 5f., x. 21
,, xiv. 3f. = Acts vii. 39
,, xiv. 16 = 1 Cor. x. 5
,, xiv. 29 = Heb. iii. 17
,, xiv. 33 = Acts vii. 36
,, xvi. 5 = 2 Tim. ii. 19
,, xvi. 38 (xvii. 3) = Heb. xii. 3
,, xxiv. 6 = Heb. viii. 2
,, xxv. 1f. = Apoc. ii. 20
,, xxvii. 14 = Acts vii. 51
,, xxvii. 17 = Mt. ix. 36, Mk. vi. 34
,, xxx. 2 = Mt. v. 33
,, xxxi. 16 = Apoc. ii. 14

THE BOOK OF NUMBERS.

PART I.

THE SOJOURN AT SINAI.

CHAPTERS I.—X. 10.

The whole of this the first part of the Book is an account of the events which occurred, and the regulations which were made, in the period immediately before the departure of the people from Sinai. A comparison of i. 1 with x. 11 shews that this period consisted of nineteen days. The following divisions of the matter will help to make the contents of the Part a little clearer.

(*a*) The numbers and arrangements of the tribes. i.–iv.
(*b*) Various laws and regulations. v. and vi.
(*c*) The oblations of the princes. vii.
(*d*) Further laws and regulations. viii.–x. 10.

Chapters I.—IV.

The Numbers and Arrangements of the Tribes.

The arrangements recorded in these early chh. have been described, a little crudely perhaps, as "a mathematical demonstration of the theocracy in the wilderness." The conception of God's character which underlies them is one which would emphasise His love of order and His hatred of confusion, divine attributes which are sometimes forgotten or ignored.

The order in which the events and commands are narrated is not without difficulty; it would have been much simpler, for example, if the command to omit the Levites from the census had been recorded before it was tacitly anticipated by the actual numeration of the tribes (cf. i. 49). Objection may also be brought against the many repetitions, a very familiar characteristic of the document known as P: for example, if the whole of i. 17–43 and of iv. 1–33 were to be eliminated little would be lost from the account, except the insistence on the Levites not touching the articles entrusted to them until they had been covered over by the priests, and the order to number Levites between thirty and fifty years of age. The contents may be summarised as follows:

The taking of the census. i.
The order of encampment. ii.
The special position of the Levites. iii.
The numbers and the duties of the Levites. iv.

CHAPTER I.

The taking of the Census.

The idea of a census was not altogether new, since the poll-tax mentioned in Ex. xxx. 30 ff., xxxviii. 25 ff., was a direct preparation for such an enterprise. No doubt the principal reason for the census in the mind of the writer was the necessity for having some record of the numbers of the people, to serve as a basis for taxation and for military service; a motive similar to that which inspired the order for a census in 2 Sam. xxiv. there attributed to God's anger against Israel[1]. No definite command is given as to the exact method of recording the numbers, probably it was done according to the divisions suggested by Jethro, in tens and fifties, hundreds and thousands (see Ex. xviii. 21). The round numbers in which the results are stated make it probable that some such method was adopted. At the same time it must not be forgotten that, according to Maine, "The unit of an ancient Society was the Family[2]....The Aggregation of Families forms the Gens or House. The Aggregation of Houses makes the Tribe. The Aggregation of Tribes constitutes the Commonwealth." (*Ancient Law* pp. 126 ff.)[3]

(*a*) *The appointment of agents.* 1–19.
(*b*) *The numbers of the several secular tribes.* 20–46.
(*c*) *The Levites not numbered.* 47–54.

I. 1 And the LORD spake unto Moses in the wilderness of *P*

I. 1–19. Moses, by the commandment of God, announces the names of the twelve men who are to assist in making a census of the tribes.

1. *And.* The book by its beginning shews that it is not complete in itself, but is connected with previous matter: cf. Ex. i. 1; Lev. i. 1.

the LORD. When so printed *the LORD* represents the divine personal name JHVH for which the Jews, because it was ineffable, substituted Adonai (*Lord*) in reading. The modern word Jehovah is a combination of the vowels of the latter word with the consonants of the original, which was probably pronounced Jahweh.

spake unto Moses...saying. Sanday does not consider that such a statement compels us to suppose that an actual voice was audible to the bodily ear. "There is," he says, "a great tendency in an age and in a state of civilisation like that to which the prophets belonged to

---

[1] This is not the only passage in which a census is thought to be dangerous, a similar idea underlies the payment of the ransom in Ex. xxx. 12 (see Driver *ad loc.*). The superstitious aversion to numbering people or cattle is still found amongst savage tribes in the present day: see Frazer *FLOT* II. pp. 555 ff.

[2] Amongst the ancient Germans a young man was a member of the Family only until he became fit to use arms: cf. Tacitus *Germ.* XIII.

[3] The organisation of the Tartars was still more detailed. Six or more blood-related tents (Mongol—*yúrta*) formed a camp (Turk. *aul*; Mongol, *khoton*, *khotun*; Roumanian, *catun*); several camps made a clan (Turk. *tire*; Mongol. *aïmak*); several clans formed a tribe (*uruk*); and finally, several tribes made a folk (Turk. *il*, Mongol. *ūluss*). See further *Camb. Med. Hist.* I. pp. 333 ff.

Sinai, in the tent of meeting, on the first day of the second month, in the second year after they were come out of the land of Egypt, saying, 2 Take ye the sum of all the congregation of the children of Israel, by their families, by their fathers' houses, *P*

express the higher and more abstract processes of the human mind in terms of the lower and more concrete." *Inspiration* p. 146[1].

wilderness of Sinai. The exact locality is uncertain since the evidence for the traditional site is not very early, it cannot indeed be traced beyond the third century A.D., and has recently been challenged mainly on the ground of its inconsistence with O.T. references. (See McNeile's discussion in *Exodus* pp. xcviii ff.; also Weill *Le séjour des Israélites au désert*, and P. Haupt *Midian u. Sinai* in *ZDMG* (1909) pp. 506 ff.)

the tent of meeting (Heb. אֹהֶל מוֹעֵד). Zimmern, and Haupt (*JBL* XIX. pp. 58 and 70) suggest that the phrase originally described the tent where a propitious or appointed time for an undertaking was declared. Later it came to mean the place which the LORD had appointed for meeting Moses (cf. Ex. xxv. 22)[2]. The relation of this *tent* to the tabernacle is complicated, since in three distinct respects it seems to be distinguished from it by both E and P. The tent of E is apparently a portable shrine, such as was common amongst Semitic peoples from very early times; it was erected outside the camp; and it had but a single guardian, Moses' servant Joshua, who was a non-Levite. But the tabernacle of P (sometimes also called *the tent of meeting*, though distinguished in Ex. xxxix. 32 &c.) is an elaborate structure requiring complicated arrangements for its transport; it is placed in the midst of the camp; and carefully guarded by the Levites.

the first day. Ehrlich suggests that the first day was chosen as being a holiday: cf. also Dt. i. 3; Ezek. xxvi. 1, xxix. 17, &c.

the second month. The designating of the months by numbers, rather than by names, is a sign of late date (so Wellh. *Proleg.* p. 109). The use of numbers in 1 K. xii. 32 f. is probably no exception, as there are reasons for regarding this passage as late (see Skinner *ad loc.* in the Century Bible).

2. *Take ye the sum.* Lit. *lift* or *take the head*, a phrase common in P, and especially in this book (*v.* 49; iv. 2, 22; xxvi. 2; xxxii. 26, 49).

the congregation (Heb. עֲדַת־), the favourite word of P to represent the whole people of Israel. In LXX it is usually rendered as here by συναγωγή, never by ἐκκλησία: see further on xx. 4.

families...fathers' houses. These terms might be rendered by 'clan' and 'family' respectively; the former includes the latter as one of its divisions.

---

[1] Cf. St Basil *Hom. in Ps. xxviii*: "What is meant by the voice of the Lord? Are we to understand thereby a disturbance caused in the air by the vocal organs? Is it not rather a lively image, a clear and sensible vision imprinted on the mind of those to whom God wishes to communicate His thought?"

[2] Gressmann *Mose* p. 246 compares הַר־מוֹעֵד (Is. xiv. 13), and בֵּית מוֹעֵד (Job xxx. 23).

according to the number of the names, every male, by their *P* polls; 3 from twenty years old and upward, all that are able to go forth to war in Israel, thou and Aaron shall number them by their hosts. 4 And with you there shall be a man of every tribe; every one head of his fathers' house. 5 And these are the names of the men that shall stand with you: of Reuben; Elizur the son of Shedeur. 6 Of Simeon; Shelumiel the son of Zurishaddai. 7 Of Judah; Nahshon the son of Amminadab. 8 Of Issachar;

names. i.e. persons: cf. Acts i. 15.

their polls (Heb. גלגלתם cf. Golgotha). Used four times in this ch., in iii. 45; and in Ex. xvi. 16, xxxviii. 26. The word often has the literal meaning of a skull as in Ju. ix. 53 &c.

3. *twenty years old and upward.* The age at which an Israelite became liable to pay the temple shekel (Ex. xxx. 14), and to partake of the passover (Jub. xlix. 17): the rabbis however said at fourteen.

and Aaron. Aaron was to assist in the census, although it did not extend to the Levites; many critics accordingly think the name is an insertion here. The derivation of the name *Aaron* is not known; some scholars would derive it from *ha'aron* (= the ark); Neubauer suggests that it may be a Minaean form of *aron*: see Sayce *Early Hist. of the Hebs.* p. 34.

by their hosts. The expression is late: cf. Borchert *Der Gottesname Jahwe Z^e^baoth* in *Theo. Stud. u. Krit.* 1896, pp. 626 f.

5–15. These *vv.* contain a list of twenty-four Israelite chiefs, and are in close agreement with similar lists in ii. 3 ff., vii. 12 ff., and x. 14 ff. Hommel in his volume *Ancient Hebrew Tradition* defends the antiquity of this and other lists; his conclusions have not however met with much agreement (see G. B. Gray *The Character of the Proper Names in the Priestly Code: a reply to Prof. Hommel* in the *Expositor* for Sept. 1897 pp. 173 ff.). For the whole subject of Hebrew Proper Names see G. B. Gray's volume under that title, and Nestle *Isr. Eigennamen.* Of the names in the following list, nine are compounds of El, three of Shaddai, three of Zur, six are of the form Abi, Ahi, Ammi, which postulate some relationship to the deity. Holzinger compares the names on account of their religious character, a common feature of Hebrew nomenclature, with those of the English Puritans.

5. *Elizur* i.e. *God* (or *my God*) *is a rock.* For *ẓur* (צוּר) as a title of God see Wiegand *Der Gottesname* צוּר in *ZAW* (1890) pp. 85 ff., also Hommel *op. cit.* p. 32.

Shedeur i.e. *Shaddai is a flame.*

6. *Shelumiel.* This and the name following appear in the ancestry of Judith (viii. 1) though Salasadai (= *Zurishaddai*) is there said to be the son of Israel.

7. *Nahshon the son of Amminadab.* These two names appear in Ex. xx. 23, Ruth iv. 20. *Amminadab* was also father of Elisheba, the wife of

Nethanel the son of Zuar. 9 Of Zebulun; Eliab the son of Helon. *P*
10 Of the children of Joseph: of Ephraim; Elishama the son of Ammihud: of Manasseh; Gamaliel the son of Pedahzur. 11 Of Benjamin; Abidan the son of Gideoni. 12 Of Dan; Ahiezer the son of Ammishaddai. 13 Of Asher; Pagiel the son of Ochran. 14 Of Gad; Eliasaph the son of [1]Deuel. 15 Of Naphtali; Ahira the son of Enan. 16 These are they that were called of the congregation, the princes of the tribes of their fathers; they were the heads of the [2]thousands of Israel. 17 And Moses and *Ps* Aaron took these men which are expressed by name: 18 and they assembled all the congregation together on the first day of

[1] In ch. ii. 14, *Reuel.* [2] Or, *families*

Aaron, so that *Nahshon* would be his brother-in-law. The latter was an ancestor of David (Ruth iv. 20), and also of our Lord (Matt. i. 4). *Nahshon* probably means *serpent* (*nahash* itself a proper name), and *Amminadab* means *the* (*divine*) *kinsman is munificent.*

8. *Nethanel.* Common in O.T., but once only in N.T., *Nathaniel* in Jn. i. 45. The name *Na-tan-ilâni* appears in the cuneiform texts of the Bab. Exped. of Univ. of Pennsylvania IX. 67, 15.

10. *Elishama.* The grandfather of Joshua (1 Chron. vii. 26 ff.). See also 2 Sam. v. 16 and Jer. xxxvi. 12 for others of this name, the meaning of which is *God hath heard.*

Ammihud. See also xxxiv. 20, 28; 2 Sam. xiii. 37; 1 Chron. ix. 4.

Gamaliel. A common name in N.T. times, see Acts v. 24; *Pirke Aboth* I. 16, II. 2. The meaning is *God is* (*my*) *reward.*

Pedahzur. The rock hath redeemed. Here and ii. 20. Cf. *Pedahel* (xxxiv. 28), *Pedaiah* (Neh. iii. 25) and the similar names in Assyr. *Pudu-ilu*, *Pudi-ilu*, and in Phoenician בעלפדא; and for the second half of the name ברצר in the Zenjirli inscription (*NSI* No. 62, *l.* 1).

12. *Ammishaddai.* As it stands the meaning of this name is puzzling (cf. Gray). Ehrlich suggests pointing עִמִּי שַׁדַּי (cf. עִמָּנוּאֵל: Is. vii. 17, viii. 8) which gives a suitable meaning, *Shaddai is with me.*

14. *Deuel.* The correction of R.V. margin *Reuel* (so LXX) is to be adopted: cf. ii. 14.

15. *Ahira.* Kerber *Heb. Eigennamen* pp. 75 ff. sees in *-ra* (Heb. רע) the Egyptian deity.

16. *princes.* The spies are also called by this title (cf. xiii. 2).

thousands. A military rather than a civil division (xxxi. 5; 2 Sam. xviii. 1; though cf. Ex. xviii. 21 ff.); capable however of more general use (x. 36), here, for example, it evidently means a tribal division: see further Nowack *Arch.* I. pp. 301, 307, and for the use of the corresponding Arab. term Nöldeke *ZDMG* (1886) pp. 175 f.

17. *expressed.* Lit. *pierced, pricked off*: cf. 1 Chron. xii. 31; Ezra viii. 20.

the second month, and they declared their pedigrees after their families, by their fathers' houses, according to the number of the names, from twenty years old and upward, by their polls. 19 As the LORD commanded Moses, | so he numbered them in the wilderness of Sinai. P^s P

20 And the children of Reuben, Israel's firstborn, their generations, by their families, by their fathers' houses, according to the number of the names, by their polls, every male from twenty years old and upward, all that were able to go forth to war; 21 those that were numbered of them, of the tribe of Reuben, were forty and six thousand and five hundred. P^s

22 Of the children of Simeon, their generations, by their families, by their fathers' houses, those that were numbered thereof, according to the number of the names, by their polls, every male from twenty years old and upward, all that were able to go forth to war; 23 those that were numbered of them, of the tribe of Simeon, were fifty and nine thousand and three hundred.

24 Of the children of Gad, their generations, by their families, by their fathers' houses, according to the number of the names, from twenty years old and upward, all that were able to go forth to war; 25 those that were numbered of them, of the tribe of Gad, were forty and five thousand six hundred and fifty.

26 Of the children of Judah, their generations, by their families, by their fathers' houses, according to the number of the names, from twenty years old and upward, all that were able to go forth to war; 27 those that were numbered of them, of the tribe of Judah, were threescore and fourteen thousand and six hundred.

28 Of the children of Issachar, their generations, by their families, by their fathers' houses, according to the number of the names, from twenty years old and upward, all that were able to go forth to war; 29 those that were numbered of them, of the tribe of Issachar, were fifty and four thousand and four hundred.

18. *declared their pedigrees*. As was done in former times by landowners in England at the various visitations of Crown representatives.

20–46. These *vv.* give the numbers of the separate tribes, the formula in each case being exactly the same.

P^s

30 Of the children of Zebulun, their generations, by their families, by their fathers' houses, according to the number of the names, from twenty years old and upward, all that were able to go forth to war; 31 those that were numbered of them, of the tribe of Zebulun, were fifty and seven thousand and four hundred.

32 Of the children of Joseph, *namely*, of the children of Ephraim, their generations, by their families, by their fathers' houses, according to the number of the names, from twenty years old and upward, all that were able to go forth to war; 33 those that were numbered of them, of the tribe of Ephraim, were forty thousand and five hundred.

34 Of the children of Manasseh, their generations, by their families, by their fathers' houses, according to the number of the names, from twenty years old and upward, all that were able to go forth to war; 35 those that were numbered of them, of the tribe of Manasseh, were thirty and two thousand and two hundred.

36 Of the children of Benjamin, their generations, by their families, by their fathers' houses, according to the number of the names, from twenty years old and upward, all that were able to go forth to war; 37 those that were numbered of them, of the tribe of Benjamin, were thirty and five thousand and four hundred.

38 Of the children of Dan, their generations, by their families, by their fathers' houses, according to the number of the names, from twenty years old and upward, all that were able to go forth to war; 39 those that were numbered of them, of the tribe of Dan, were threescore and two thousand and seven hundred.

40 Of the children of Asher, their generations, by their families, by their fathers' houses, according to the number of the names, from twenty years old and upward, all that were able to go forth to war; 41 those that were numbered of them, of the tribe of Asher, were forty and one thousand and five hundred.

42 Of the children of Naphtali, their generations, by their families, by their fathers' houses, according to the number of the names, from twenty years old and upward, all that were able to go forth to war; 43 those that were numbered of them,

of the tribe of Naphtali, were fifty and three thousand and four hundred. *P*[s]

44 These are they that were numbered, which Moses and Aaron numbered, and the princes of Israel, being twelve men: they were each one for his fathers' house. 45 So all they that were numbered of the children of Israel by their fathers' houses, from twenty years old and upward, all that were able to go forth to war in Israel; 46 even all they that were numbered were six hundred thousand and three thousand and five hundred and fifty.

47 But the Levites after the tribe of their fathers were not numbered among them. 48 For the LORD spake unto Moses, saying, 49 Only the tribe of Levi thou shalt not number, neither shalt thou take the sum of them among the children of Israel: 50 but appoint thou the Levites over the tabernacle of the testimony, and over all the furniture thereof, and over all that belongeth to it: they shall bear the tabernacle, and all the furniture thereof; and they shall minister unto it, and shall encamp round

47–54. The Levites are not numbered; but are appointed to certain offices in connexion with the care of the tabernacle.

47. *the Levites...were not numbered.* This statement anticipates the following section. Wellhausen attaches this *v.* to *vv.* 17–46 and considers that the whole has been displaced (*Comp.* pp. 178 f.).

48. *For the LORD.* This rendering does not represent the Heb. which reads *And the LORD*, but is an attempt to avoid the consequences of the statement in *v.* 47 that the omission had already taken place. In the Heb. division of the text *v.* 47 is attached to *vv.* 44–46 (see previous note), and the section beginning *v.* 48 is evidently in the wrong context.

49. *Levi thou shalt not number.* In 1 Chron. xxi. 6 Benjamin, as well as Levi, is omitted from David's census by Joab; possibly, as Wellhausen thinks, because the Holy City was within its borders, but more probably because of "the fact that the tabernacle of Yahweh, which the Chronicler considered the centre of worship in David's time, was set up at Gibeon within the borders of Benjamin": see Curtis *Chronicles* (*ICC*) p. 248.

50. *the tabernacle of the testimony.* The ark is called *the testimony* as containing the tables of the law; this usage is found in P only, as indeed is the whole phrase.

they shall minister. The Heb. verb (שׁרת) is used generally of some form of sacred service, especially of the service of the Priests and Levites (in Num. of the Levites alone). It is sometimes applied to various forms of secular service, usually those of special importance or responsibility:

about the tabernacle. 51 And when the tabernacle setteth forward, the Levites shall take it down: and when the tabernacle is to be pitched, the Levites shall set it up: and the stranger that cometh nigh shall be put to death. 52 And the children of Israel shall pitch their tents, every man by his own camp, and every man by his own standard, according to their hosts. 53 But the Levites shall pitch round about the tabernacle of the testimony, that there be no wrath upon the congregation of the children of Israel: and the Levites shall keep the charge of the tabernacle of the testimony. 54 Thus did the children of Israel; according to all that the LORD commanded Moses, so did they. *P*[s]

e.g. Ex. xxiv. 13, xxxiii. 11 (of Joshua as the servant of Moses); 1 K. x. 5 (of Solomon's servants); 1 K. xix. 21 (of Elisha).

51. *stranger*. The *stranger* in this connexion is any person, whether a native-born Israelite or a sojourner, who had no right to approach the tabernacle,—in other words a non-Levite. The same usage is found in xvi. 40 (= xvii. 5 Heb.) in connexion with the offence of Korah, and is common in H and P.

52. *standard*. Gray is not inclined to accept this rendering as he thinks the context is better suited by some parallel to *company*[1]: and his objection receives support from LXX, Syr., and Targum. The use of words from the same root supports the rendering of R.V., see especially Cant. vi. 4, 10 "terrible as a bannered host." The banners or standards of the ancients were for the most part symbolic figures carried on the end of a pole. Jewish tradition says that a lion was the standard for Judah (cf. Enoch xlix. 9; Rev. v. 5); a human head for Reuben; an ox for Ephraim (cf. Deut. xxxiii. 17); an eagle for Dan. See further on ii. 2.

53. *no wrath*. By reason of the breach of the 'taboo' forbidding laymen to touch the sanctuary: cf. xvi. 46; 1 Sam. vi. 10.

CHAPTER II.

The order of encampment.

This ch. contains an account of the arrangements for camping in the wilderness; each group of tribes is settled in its appointed place on the four sides of the camp, whilst the tribe of Levi is in the midst around the sanctuary. The camp thus forms a perfect square[2] (cf. Ezek. xl. 47; Rev. xxi. 16), with the leading tribe of each group of three in the centre of the respective sides.

---

[1] דגל = *company* in the Elephantine Papyri. Gibbon mentions a tribe of Huns who were divided up into hordes or banners: III. p. 83.

[2] Egyptian camps in the time of Ramses II were of this formation (see the illustration in Gressmann *T.B.* II. No. 50) whereas Assyrian camps were circular or elliptical (see *op. cit.* No. 52).

Niebuhr has compared this ideal camp to that of an army of toy soldiers with the officers on horseback in front and everything in its exact place (*Ebr. Zeitalter* p. 243: quoted by Baentsch). Others have seen in it perhaps more happily a parallel to the catalogue of ships in the second Book of the *Iliad* (see De Wette *Beiträge* p. 339).

The idea which is expressed by the camp so arranged is "that of the sanctifying presence of God in Israel's midst" (cf. v. 3; Lev. xv. 31), in other words its significance is not military or utilitarian, but religious.

II. 1 And the LORD spake unto Moses and unto Aaron, saying, *P*[s] 2 The children of Israel shall pitch every man by his own standard, with the ensigns of their fathers' houses: over against the tent of meeting shall they pitch round about. 3 And those that pitch on the east side toward the sunrising shall be they of the standard of the camp of Judah, according to their hosts: and the prince of the children of Judah shall be Nahshon the son of Amminadab. 4 And his host, and those that were numbered of them, were threescore and fourteen thousand and six hundred. 5 And those that pitch next unto him shall be the tribe of Issachar: and the prince of the children of Issachar shall be

II. 1. *Moses and...Aaron.* Since Moses is alone mentioned in *v.* 34 Aaron may well be an addition here. The address to the two is common in P: cf. Ex. vii. 8, ix. 8, xii. 1, 43 &c.

2. *standard...ensigns.* The two symbols refer to larger and smaller groups of people; the *standard* to the 'camp' of three tribes (cf. *vv.* 3, 10, 18, and 25), the *ensign* to the clan or family (see Holzinger, and Nowack *Arch.* p. 362), just as in the Roman army the legion had its *aquila*, the cohort its *signum*. The Heb. word (דֶּגֶל), which is translated *standard*, is one of very wide use, and can be applied to any sign or mark; e.g. a prophetic sign (Ex. iii. 12), or a miracle (Josh. xxiv. 17), or a memorial (Josh. iv. 6), or even to the heavenly bodies (Gen. i. 14: cf. Jer. x. 2). In the present passage the meaning of *pole* or *ensign* (cf. i. 52 with note) seems to be demanded, as in Ps. lxxiv. 4 "they set up their signs for signs" (the various E.VV., including the Prayer Book, obscure the fact that the same word is used in both cases in the original). In modern times an Arab chief will indicate the spot for a camp by driving his spear into the ground (see Doughty *Arabia Deserta* I. p. 221). LXX τάγμα reads רגל for דגל.

3. *the east side toward the sunrising.* This expression is tautological; the doubling of the quarters of the compass, however, is common in P (cf. Ex. xxvi. 18 "for the south side southwards"; and see Baentsch's note *ad loc.*).

Judah. As P always regards Judah as the pre-eminent tribe, the position of honour, that on the east, must be given to him; just as in the inner camp it belongs to the priests.

Nethanel the son of Zuar: 6 and his host, and those that were numbered thereof, were fifty and four thousand and four hundred: 7 *and* the tribe of Zebulun: and the prince of the children of Zebulun shall be Eliab the son of Helon: 8 and his host, and those that were numbered thereof, were fifty and seven thousand and four hundred. 9 All that were numbered of the camp of Judah were an hundred thousand and fourscore thousand and six thousand and four hundred, according to their hosts. They shall set forth first.

P[s]

10 On the south side shall be the standard of the camp of Reuben according to their hosts: and the prince of the children of Reuben shall be Elizur the son of Shedeur. 11 And his host, and those that were numbered thereof, were forty and six thousand and five hundred. 12 And those that pitch next unto him shall be the tribe of Simeon: and the prince of the children of Simeon shall be Shelumiel the son of Zurishaddai: 13 and his host, and those that were numbered of them, were fifty and nine thousand and three hundred: 14 and the tribe of Gad: and the prince of the children of Gad shall be Eliasaph the son of [1]Reuel: 15 and his host, and those that were numbered of them, were forty and five thousand and six hundred and fifty. 16 All that were numbered of the camp of Reuben were an hundred thousand and fifty and one thousand and four hundred and fifty, according to their hosts. And they shall set forth second.

17 Then the tent of meeting shall set forward, with the camp of the Levites in the midst of the camps: as they encamp, so shall they set forward, every man in his place, by their standards.

[1] In ch. i. 14, *Deuel.*

10. *the south side.* Lit. *on the right hand*: the quarters of the compass being named from the point of view of one facing east. The Heb. word here used (תֵּימָנָה) is found chiefly in P, Ezek., and in the poetical books. In Ex. xxvi. 18 &c. the south side of the tabernacle is literally 'towards the Negeb' (see on Num. xiii. 17), an expression which could only have come from one writing in Palestine or one who wrote from that standpoint.

17. *with.* Does not appear in the original which reads *the tent of meeting, the camp of the Levites, shall &c.*

in the midst of the camps. This order of marching does not agree with that of x. 17–21.

in his place. Lit. *upon his hand*: cf. xiii. 29; Deut. xxiii. 12; Jer. vi. 3.

18 On the west side shall be the standard of the camp of Ephraim according to their hosts: and the prince of the children of Ephraim shall be Elishama the son of Ammihud. 19 And his host, and those that were numbered of them, were forty thousand and five hundred. 20 And next unto him shall be the tribe of Manasseh: and the prince of the children of Manasseh shall be Gamaliel the son of Pedahzur: 21 and his host, and those that were numbered of them, were thirty and two thousand and two hundred: 22 and the tribe of Benjamin: and the prince of the children of Benjamin shall be Abidan the son of Gideoni: 23 and his host, and those that were numbered of them, were thirty and five thousand and four hundred. 24 All that were numbered of the camp of Ephraim were an hundred thousand and eight thousand and an hundred, according to their hosts. And they shall set forth third. P[s]

25 On the north side shall be the standard of the camp of Dan according to their hosts: and the prince of the children of Dan shall be Ahiezer the son of Ammishaddai. 26 And his host, and those that were numbered of them, were threescore and two thousand and seven hundred. 27 And those that pitch next unto him shall be the tribe of Asher: and the prince of the children of Asher shall be Pagiel the son of Ochran: 28 and his host, and those that were numbered of them, were forty and one thousand and five hundred: 29 and the tribe of Naphtali: and the prince of the children of Naphtali shall be Ahira the son of Enan: 30 and his host, and those that were numbered of them, were fifty and three thousand and four hundred. 31 All that were numbered of the camp of Dan were an hundred thousand and fifty and seven thousand and six hundred. They shall set forth hindmost by their standards.

18. *Ephraim.* The camp of Ephraim is really the gathering of the descendants of Rachel.

25. *the camp of Dan.* The descendants of the concubines, with the exception of Gad, are grouped together here. With the importance here assigned to Dan contrast the later disfavour into which the tribe fell (see my note on Jer. viii. 16).

31. *standards.* The plural is strange, as each camp had only one standard; the same phrase is used in *v.* 17 of the Levites, as to the number of whose standards we are not informed, but not of the three other camps.

32 These are they that were numbered of the children of Israel by their fathers' houses: all that were numbered of the camps according to their hosts were six hundred thousand and three thousand and five hundred and fifty. 33 But the Levites were not numbered among the children of Israel; as the LORD commanded Moses. 34 Thus did the children of Israel; according to all that the LORD commanded Moses, so they pitched by their standards, and so they set forward, every one by their families, according to their fathers' houses. P^s

CHAPTER III.

The special position of the Levites.

The various regulations collected in this ch. are concerned with the position and status of the ecclesiastical portion of the Hebrew nation, both in its external and internal relationships, and also with the numbers and duties of those who composed it.

(*a*) *The sons of Aaron.* 1–4.
(*b*) *The appointment of the Levites as servants to the priests.* 5–13.
(*c*) *The census of the Levites.* 14–39.
(*d*) *The substitution of the Levites for the firstborn.* 40–51.

III. 1 Now these are the generations of Aaron and Moses in the day that the LORD spake with Moses in mount Sinai. 2 And these are the names of the sons of Aaron; Nadab the firstborn, and Abihu, Eleazar, and Ithamar. 3 These are the names of the

III. 1–4. These *vv.* form an introduction to the account of the institution of the Levites: they contain little beyond what has already been given in Ex. vi. 23; Lev. x. 1 f.

1. *These are the generations.* A common phrase in Genesis (see v. 1, vi. 9 &c.), where it forms a framework for the whole narrative, marking the beginning of each new epoch: cf. Driver *Genesis* p. ii. The rendering *generations*, though it gives the literal meaning of the original, does not always harmonise with what follows: e.g. Gen. ii. 4, xxxvii. 2.

Aaron and Moses. As no mention is made of any descendants of *Moses*, the inclusion of his name seems unnecessary. An interpolator, however, would hardly have ventured to break the usual order by which *Moses* comes before *Aaron*. The latter, as the elder brother (Ex. vii. 7), would very naturally come first in a genealogical list.

in mount Sinai. Perhaps a reference to Ex. xxiv. 1 where Nadab and Abihu are mentioned, though not it should be observed as sons of Aaron: see Gressmann *Mose* p. 258.

sons of Aaron, the priests which were anointed, whom he consecrated to minister in the priest's office. 4 And Nadab and Abihu died before the LORD, when they offered strange fire before the LORD, in the wilderness of Sinai, and they had no children: and Eleazar and Ithamar ministered in the priest's office in the presence of Aaron their father. *P*[s]

5 And the LORD spake unto Moses, saying, 6 Bring the tribe of Levi near, and set them before Aaron the priest, that they may minister unto him. 7 And they shall keep his charge, and *P*

3. *anointed.* In Ex. xxix. 7 the high-priest only is anointed, the anointing of the sons also is regarded by many critics as a mark of a later stratum of P: see McNeile *Exodus* p. 188. According to 1 K. xix. 16 Elisha was to be anointed as the successor of Elijah. The significance of the rite was originally perhaps the desire to impart to the person anointed the virtues of the sacred animal from which the unguent was derived: see Wade in *Peake's Comm.*

consecrated: lit. *filled the hand.* This phrase which is found as early as Jud. xvii. 5, 12, is of uncertain origin. It must in some way be connected with the similar Assyr. phrase *umalli ḳâta* by which the appointment to any position of authority is signified: see Nowack *Arch.* II. p. 121; Muss-Arnolt *Dict.* I. p. 542. There exists amongst scholars a considerable difference of opinion as to the object placed in the priest's hand at the time of his consecration: Sellin suggests arrows, such as were used in primitive ages for purposes of divination (*Beiträge* II. pp. 118 f.), Baudissin a portion of the sacrifice (*HDB* IV. p. 71: cf. also van Hoonacker *Le Sacerdoce lévitique &c.* pp. 134 f.).

4. *Nadab and Abihu.* See also Ex. vi. 23, xxiv. 1; Lev. x. 1 ff. The latter passage gives a fuller account of the incident here referred to.

strange fire. In this and similar contexts *strange* means unlawful, just as the stranger is the unauthorised person in i. 51. It is hard to know what is meant by strange or common fire, for in the sanctuary all fire would be holy. Dr Kennett suggests to me that the *fire* in the tabernacle was produced by some unusual means in later times (cf. 2 Macc. i. 19 ff. where the *fire* hidden by the pre-exilic priests is really naphtha). The two men may thus have been thought of as introducing ordinary fire into the sacred place.

no children. Hence all the different lines of the priesthood trace their descent from Eleazar or Ithamar.

in the presence of &c. This need not be taken literally but is rather equivalent to *during the lifetime of*: so in Gen. xi. 28.

5–13. The Levites are placed under Aaron's orders, thus fulfilling their dedication to God's service as substitutes for the firstborn of the whole people.

6. *before Aaron.* Aaron here represents the whole priestly caste, in *v.* 9 the more usual phrase *Aaron and his sons* is used.

the charge of the whole congregation before the tent of meeting, *P*
to do the service of the tabernacle. 8 And they shall keep all
the furniture of the tent of meeting, and the charge of the
children of Israel, to do the service of the tabernacle. 9 And
thou shalt give the Levites unto Aaron and to his sons: they are
[1]wholly given unto him [2]on the behalf of the children of
Israel. 10 And thou shalt [3]appoint Aaron and his sons, and
they shall keep their priesthood: and the stranger that cometh
nigh shall be put to death.

11 And the LORD spake unto Moses, saying, 12 And I, behold,
I have taken the Levites from among the children of Israel
instead of all the firstborn that openeth the womb among the
children of Israel; and the Levites shall be mine: 13 for all the
firstborn are mine; on the day that I smote all the firstborn in

[1] Heb. *given, given.* [2] Or, *from* [3] Or, *number*

9. *given unto him.* Cf. viii. 16 ff. where the Levites are first given to Jehovah, and then by Him to the priests.

10. *the stranger.* See on i. 51, though in the present context the Levite is included. It was in the light of prohibitions such as this that later opinion so severely condemned the action of Jeroboam (1 K. xii. 31) who allowed non-Levites to perform priestly functions.

12. *taken.* Cf. Am. vii. 15 (of the prophet); 2 S. vii. 8 (of David); Ex. vi. 12 (of all Israel).

instead of...the firstborn. Jehovah's right to the *firstborn* is very ancient being found already in JE (Ex. xxii. 28, xxxiv. 19 f.), though according to J it was not exercised until the entry into Canaan (Ex. xiii. 11 ff.). It has been suggested that the substitution of the Levites was a compensation for the loss of the services of the eldest sons as natural priests, for as such they were apparently regarded by some ancient peoples. This theory finds favour with Baudissin *Priesterthum* pp. 55 ff., and Smend *A. T. Religionsgesch.*[2] p. 282: cf. also Targum Jonathan on Ex. xxiv. 5, and *Z'baḥim* xiv. 4. Wellhausen however is strongly opposed to the theory, and points out that there is not in the O.T. "a single trace of the priesthood of the first-born" (*Hist. of Isr.* p. 121). In early times the father seems to have acted as priest to the family (Ex. xiii. 8 ff.: cf. Jud. xvii. 10). Baentsch finds difficulty in the fact that the *firstborn* are elsewhere said to be redeemed by a money payment (xviii. 15 f.; cf. also Ex. xiii. 13, xxxiv. 20). It is possible to reconcile the two conceptions by supposing that the taking of the Levites is a substitution for all the firstborn then existing, and that the redemption by payment was intended to refer to those born subsequently.

the land of Egypt I hallowed unto me all the firstborn in Israel, *P* both man and beast: mine they shall be; I am the LORD.

14 And the LORD spake unto Moses in the wilderness of Sinai, saying, 15 Number the children of Levi by their fathers' houses, by their families: every male from a month old and upward shalt thou number them. 16 And Moses numbered them according to the word of the LORD, as he was commanded. 17 And these were the sons of Levi by their names; Gershon, and Kohath, and Merari. 18 And these are the names of the sons of Gershon by their families; Libni and Shimei. 19 And the sons of Kohath by their families; Amram, and Izhar, Hebron, and Uzziel. 20 And the sons of Merari by their families; Mahli and Mushi. These are the families of the Levites according to their fathers' houses.

13. *hallowed unto me.* They belonged to Jehovah because He slew them not with the Egyptians, they are in other words 'devoted' or 'taboo' (cf. Baudissin *Studien* II. p. 63, and Frazer *The Dying God* pp. 174 ff.).

I am the LORD. A formula which is especially characteristic of H: see Chapman *Introd.* p. 112.

14–39. The census of the Levites is taken by God's command and a list of names is given. Similar lists of Levite names are found in xxvi. 57 ff. and in Ex. vi. 16 ff., 1 Chron. vi. 16 ff., xxiii. 7 ff.; in each case with unimportant variations.

15. *from a month old &c.* As all the firstborn were not to be redeemed until they reached that age, so the Levites who were to be substituted for them were only numbered from above that age.

17. *Gershon.* This name Wellhausen would connect with Gershom the eldest son of Moses (*Hist. of Isr.* pp. 142 f.).

18. *Libni and Shimei.* So in Ex. vi. 17 and 1 Chron. vi. 17: in 1 Chron. xxiii. 7 (cf. xxvi. 21) *Ladan and Shimei.*

19. *Amram.* The father of Moses and Aaron (Ex. vi. 18, 20), who thus belonged to the family of Kohath.

Hebron. Curteis thinks that the appearance of this name "shows that a portion of the ecclesiastical tribe of Levi came from priests who had ministered at the sanctuary at Hebron" (see his note on 1 Chron. vi. 2 in *ICC*).

20. *Mahli.* Cf. the feminine form Mahlah (xxvi. 33 &c.), and also the first husband of Ruth, Mahlon (Ruth i. 2 &c.).

Mushi. Perhaps connected with Moses: so Wellhausen *Hist. of Isr.* p. 143.

the Levites. Lit. *the Levi.* The use of the article with a tribal name is unusual in Hebrew: see Driver on Deut. iii. 13.

21 Of Gershon was the family of the Libnites, and the family *P* of the Shimeites: these are the families of the Gershonites. 22 Those that were numbered of them, according to the number of all the males, from a month old and upward, even those that were numbered of them were seven thousand and five hundred. 23 The families of the Gershonites shall pitch behind the taber- *P*[s] nacle westward. 24 And the prince of the fathers' house of the Gershonites shall be Eliasaph the son of Lael. 25 And the charge of the sons of Gershon in the tent of meeting shall be the tabernacle, and the Tent, the covering thereof, and the screen for the door of the tent of meeting, 26 and the hangings of the court, and the screen for the door of the court, which is by the tabernacle, and by the altar round about, and the cords of it for all the service thereof.

21–26. The numbers, station, and charge of the family of Gershon. The families of the Levites formed an inner circle round the tabernacle, Gershon being on the west in front of the camp of Ephraim, Kohath on the South in front of Reuben, Merari on the North in front of Dan, and the Priests on the east in front of Judah. In this section, and in the two following, there is a change from narrative to command: *vv.* 21 f., 27 f., 33 f. and 39 being narrative, and the other *vv.* commands.

21. *the Shimeites.* This family alone is mentioned in Zech. xii. 13 of the house of Levi, possibly in a representative capacity.

23. *behind...westward.* That is facing east. *Westward* is lit. *seawards*, and the term was originally coined by people dwelling in Palestine with the Mediterranean Sea to the west: cf. the phrase in Ezek. xli. 12 "toward the west" which is literally "the way of the sea."

24. *Lael.* "Belonging to El." Gray points out the great interest of this word from a philological point of view, since it is formed from a preposition and the divine name; the only other example of this in Hebrew being Lemuel in Prov. xxxi. 1 (see *HPN* pp. 206 f.)[1].

25. *the tabernacle.* The curtains only are here meant (cf. iv. 25; Ex. xxvi. 1–6), since the structure itself is in the care of the Merarites (*v.* 36).

the Tent. A description of the tent and its fittings will be found in Ex. xxvi. 7 ff.

26. *the cords.* According to *v.* 37 these were part of the charge of the family of Merari. In the original account of the arrangements for the construction of the tabernacle (Ex. xxvii. 19) they are not mentioned, but are added in the later description of the actual construction (Ex. xxxv. 18).

---

[1] Other examples could be drawn from cognate languages: e.g. Palmyrene לשמש (*NSI* No. 117 *l.* 3); Phoenician Λεάσταρτος (Joseph. *c. Apion* I. 18) &c.

P 27 And of Kohath was the family of the Amramites, and the family of the Izharites, and the family of the Hebronites, and the family of the Uzzielites: these are the families of the Kohathites. 28 According to the number of all the males, from a month old and upward, there were eight thousand and six hundred, keeping the charge of the sanctuary. P^s 29 The families of the sons of Kohath shall pitch on the side of the tabernacle southward. 30 And the prince of the fathers' house of the families of the Kohathites shall be Elizaphan the son of Uzziel. 31 And their charge shall be the ark, and the table, and the candlestick, and the altars, and the vessels of the sanctuary wherewith they minister, and the screen, and all the service thereof. 32 And Eleazar the son of Aaron the priest shall be prince of the princes of the Levites, *and have* the oversight of them that keep the charge of the sanctuary.

P 33 Of Merari was the family of the Mahlites, and the family of the Mushites: these are the families of Merari. 34 And those that were numbered of them, according to the number of all the males, from a month old and upward, were six thousand and two hundred. P^s 35 And the prince of the fathers' house of the families of Merari was Zuriel the son of Abihail: they shall pitch

28. *six hundred.* The omission of a Hebrew letter has caused this reading, instead of the correct number three hundred (שש for שלש). As LXX and M.T. agree, the error is of ancient date.

30. *Elizaphan.* Cf. 1 Chron. xv. 8; 2 Chron. xxix. 13. The meaning is *God has sheltered*: see further *HPN* pp. 205, 303, and cf. Baal-zephon xxxiii. 7.

31. *the ark.* See Ex. xxv. 10–22.

the table. See Ex. xxv. 23–30.

the candlestick. See on viii. 1 ff. and Ex. xxv. 31–40.

the altars. Originally there was one altar only (see Ex. xxvii. 1); another altar, that of incense, is mentioned (Ex. xxx. 1–10) after all the furniture of the tabernacle has been described. The second altar is regarded by many critics as belonging to a later stratum of P. In the present passage Syr. and Targ. Onkelos have the singular.

the screen. Syr. *the veil of the screen* (cf. iv. 5, xviii. 7). See the description in Ex. xxvi. 31–33.

32. *Eleazar.* As the eldest surviving son of Aaron he is the chief prince of the Levites, being also a member of the family of Kohath: he is mentioned at the end of the passage dealing with them. Dillmann considers the *v.* to be an interpolation.

35. *Abihail.* The same name as the father of Esther (Esth. ii. 15),

on the side of the tabernacle northward. 36 And [1]the appointed P^s charge of the sons of Merari shall be the boards of the tabernacle, and the bars thereof, and the pillars thereof, and the sockets thereof, and all the instruments thereof, and all the service thereof; 37 and the pillars of the court round about, and their sockets, and their pins, and their cords. 38 And those that pitch before the tabernacle eastward, before the tent of meeting toward the sunrising, shall be Moses, and Aaron and his sons, keeping the charge of the sanctuary [2]for the charge of the children of Israel; and the stranger that cometh nigh shall be put to death. 39 All that were numbered of the Levites, which *P* Moses and Aaron numbered at the commandment of the LORD, by their families, all the males from a month old and upward, were twenty and two thousand.

40 And the LORD said unto Moses, Number all the firstborn P^s males of the children of Israel from a month old and upward,

[1] Heb. *the office of the charge.* [2] Or, *even*

also of a Gadite (1 Chron. v. 14). In 1 Chron. ii. 29; 2 Chron. xi. 18 the name is that of a woman.

36. *the boards.* See Ex. xxvi. 15–18.

the bars. See Ex. xxvi. 26–28.

the pillars. See Ex. xxvi. 32, 37.

the sockets. See Ex. xxvi. 19–21.

37. *pillars of the court.* See Ex. xxvii. 10 ff.

their cords. See on *v.* 26.

38. *Moses.* As the command is addressed to Moses it is strange that he is mentioned in the third person.

39. *twenty and two thousand.* The details of this total, as given in the previous *vv.*, make up 22,300; the explanation will be found in the note on *v.* 28. According to the Talmud the excess represents the firstborn of the Levites themselves. Jerome records a tradition that the *twenty-two* here is a mystic sign of the number of books in the Hebrew Bible: *Praefat. in libr. Samuel et Malachim* quoted by Ryle *Canon of O.T.* p. 299.

40–51. The substitution of the Levites for the firstborn. The number of the firstborn is hard to reconcile with the total population. According to i. 46 the male Israelites over twenty years of age exceeded 600,000, which would mean that the whole people numbered some 2,000,000: if we allow an equal number of firstborn daughters, the total of firstborn would be about 45,000; this would give to each family between forty and fifty children. Dr Orr tries to reduce this figure by suggesting that only the firstborn still at home were reckoned (cf. Ex. xii. 30 one dead in each house); he also suggests that dead firstborn ought to be allowed for—though unless these had been sacrificed their death rate should

and take the number of their names. 41 And thou shalt take the Levites for me (I am the LORD) instead of all the firstborn among the children of Israel; and the cattle of the Levites instead of all the firstlings among the cattle of the children of Israel. 42 And Moses numbered, as the LORD commanded him, all the firstborn among the children of Israel. 43 And all the firstborn males according to the number of names, from a month old and upward, of those that were numbered of them, were twenty and two thousand two hundred and threescore and thirteen. *P*[s]

44 And the LORD spake unto Moses, saying, 45 Take the Levites instead of all the firstborn among the children of Israel, and the cattle of the Levites instead of their cattle: and the Levites shall be mine; I am the LORD. 46 And for [1]the redemption of the two hundred and threescore and thirteen of the firstborn of the children of Israel, which are over and above *the number of* the Levites, 47 thou shalt take five shekels apiece by the poll; after the shekel of the sanctuary shalt thou take them (the shekel is twenty gerahs): 48 and thou shalt give the money wherewith the odd number of them is redeemed unto Aaron and to his sons. 49 And Moses took the redemption-money from them that were over and above them that were redeemed by the Levites: 50 from the firstborn of the children of Israel took he the money; a thousand three hundred and threescore and five *shekels*, after the shekel of the sanctuary: 51 and Moses gave [2]the redemption-money unto Aaron and to his sons, according to the word of the LORD, as the LORD commanded Moses.

[1] Or, *those that are to be redeemed, the &c.*
[2] Or, *the money of them that were redeemed*

not differ materially from that of the rest of the people—and also the existence of polygamy and concubinage (*Problem of O.T.* pp. 367 f.).

41. *all the firstlings.* There is evidently some error here, as according to xviii. 17 cattle fit for sacrifice are not to be redeemed. It has been suggested that this provision is a later substitute for that in xviii. 17, which may have proved difficult to carry out in practice: cf. Baudissin *Priesterthum* pp. 42 f.

47. *shekel of the sanctuary.* The phrase suggests settled times. The value of this coin was about 2*s.* 5*d.*, and the whole price of redemption would be about 12*s.* in English money: see *HDB* III. pp. 422.

gerah. Ass. *girû.* Found only in connexion with the shekel; its English value would be about 3*d.*

CHAPTER IV.

The numbers and the duties of the Levites.

The status and duties of the Levitical families having been dealt with in general terms, the writer now gives, in more minute detail, the various duties of the different branches. This account of their duties is given in the setting of the command to take the sum of their separate families. It should be noticed that the sons of Kohath have, in this ch., displaced the sons of Gershon as the first in the list: cf. iii. 25 f.

(*a*) *The service of the sons of Kohath.* 1–20.
(*b*) *The service of the sons of Gershon.* 21–28.
(*c*) *The service of the sons of Merari.* 29–33.
(*d*) *The numbers of the Levites.* 34–49.

IV. 1 And the LORD spake unto Moses and unto Aaron, saying, 2 Take the sum of the sons of Kohath from among the sons of Levi, by their families, by their fathers' houses, 3 from thirty years old and upward even until fifty years old, all that enter upon the [1]service, to do the work in the tent of meeting. 4 This is the [2]service of the sons of Kohath in the tent of *P*[s]

[1] Heb. *warfare*, or, *host* (and so in vv. 35, 39, 43). [2] Or, *work*

IV. 1–20. Moses is commanded to take the numbers of the sons of Kohath between the ages of thirty and fifty: he is also informed of the nature of the duties assigned to them.

3. *from thirty years old &c.* The period of Levitical service is differently represented elsewhere: in viii. 23–26 from twenty-five until fifty, though even then the Levite is to remain as a kind of supernumerary. Later writers place the beginning of the time of service at twenty (1 Chron. xxiii. 24, 27; 2 Chron. xxxi. 17; Ezra iii. 8; 1 Esdras v. 58), and make no mention of the age of release. Keil sees in the regulations of the present passage a temporary measure. LXX assimilates this passage to viii. 23 ff. by reading twenty-five in both places.

service. Mg. *warfare* or *host* (Heb. צָבָא). The use of the noun to represent the service of the sanctuary is found in this ch. and viii. 24 f. only, though possibly the phrase in Dan. viii. 13 "both the sanctuary and the host" is another instance. The root in both Heb. and cognate languages referred originally to warlike endeavours[1], but in later times it had so far lost its distinctive meaning as to be applied to the work of the women who served at the door of the tent of meeting (Ex.

[1] Ball points out that the symbol for Assyr. *çâbu* (=Heb. צבא) was in Sumerian ERIM, ERIN, ZAB, meaning *bowman, warrior* (*Job* p. 170).

meeting, *about* the most holy things: 5 when the camp setteth *P* forward, Aaron shall go in, and his sons, and they shall take down the veil of the screen, and cover the ark of the testimony with it: 6 and shall put thereon a covering of sealskin, and shall

xxxviii. 8; 1 Sam. ii. 22)[1]. In our own day, and indeed since the time of St Paul, the conception of the service of God as a warfare is perfectly familiar. A famous preacher of the last generation went so far as to say "that work for God, of whatever kind it be, which Christian people are bound to do, and which is mainly service for men for God's sake, will never be rightly done until we understand that it is *warfare* as well as work." Alex. Maclaren *Expositions of Holy Scripture* II. p. 297.

4. *the most holy things*. In the Heb. the phrase is the same as that used for the holy of holies in Ex. xxvi. 33.

5–14. In these *vv.* is described the work of the priests in wrapping up the furniture and vessels of the tabernacle before their removal by the Kohathites. The objects, which do not include the laver, are divided up into six groups: (*a*) the ark (*vv.* 5 f.); (*b*) the table of the shewbread, with its utensils and the loaves themselves (*vv.* 7 f.); (*c*) the candlestick and its utensils (*vv.* 9 f.); (*d*) the golden altar (*v.* 11); (*e*) a group of miscellaneous utensils (*v.* 12); (*f*) the altar of burnt offering (*vv.* 13 f.). All these objects were covered with a *blue* cloth, except the altar of burnt offering which had one of *purple*, and over everything went a waterproof covering made of *sealskin*. In the case of the table and its utensils a *scarlet* cloth was used in addition to the blue one; and in the case of the ark the *blue* cloth came outside the waterproof sheet (underneath it being the veil of the screen), no doubt to distinguish it from the other objects that were transported with it. All these objects were to be carried by hand, by means of poles or staves; the lampstand and the miscellaneous objects, however, were suspended from a *frame*. The other families of Levites were provided with wagons for their heavier burdens.

5. *the veil of the screen*. So in Ex. xxxv. 12, xxxix. 34 &c.[2]

6. *sealskin* (Heb. תַּחַשׁ). This word is found in late writers only (Ezek. and P) and its meaning is a matter for conjecture. It is generally thought to refer to the skin of some animal (cf. Arab. *tuḥas* = dolphin), though the versions translated it as a colour (LXX ὑακίνθινον). Bondi *Aegyptiaca* pp. 1 ff. suggests that the word is derived from the Egyptian *tḥs* = leather. This would agree with Ezek. xvi. 10, where sandals are

[1] In a similar way *militia* could be used, not merely of military service, but of any employment; it is interesting to notice that the medieval lawyer Irnerius referred to the clergy as those who *divinam militiam gerunt*: see Carlyle *Medieval Polit. Theory &c.* II. p. 81.

[2] The word rendered *veil* (פָּרֹכֶת) comes from Ass. *parakku* = *shrine*; this word is generally connected with *parâku* = *to shut off*. Landersdorfer questions this derivation considering that it is a Sum. word BARAG: see *Sum. Sprachgut im A.T.* p. 54, also Theis *Sum. in A.T.* p. 33 (but cf. Leander *Sum. Lehnwörter* p. 31).

spread over it a cloth all of blue, and shall put in the staves thereof. 7 And upon the table of shewbread they shall spread a cloth of blue, and put thereon the dishes, and the spoons, and the bowls, and the cups to pour out withal: and the continual bread shall be thereon: 8 and they shall spread upon them a cloth of scarlet, and cover the same with a covering of sealskin, and shall put in the staves thereof. 9 And they shall take a cloth of blue, and cover the candlestick of the light, and its lamps, and its tongs, and its snuffdishes, and all the oil vessels thereof, wherewith they minister unto it: 10 and they shall put it and all the vessels thereof within a covering of sealskin, and shall put it upon [1]the frame. 11 And upon the golden altar they shall spread a cloth of blue, and cover it with a covering of sealskin, and shall put in the staves thereof: 12 and they shall take all the vessels of ministry, wherewith they minister in the sanctuary, and put them in a cloth of blue, and cover them with a covering of sealskin, and shall put them on the frame. 13 And they shall take away the ashes from the altar, and spread

P^s

[1] Or, *a bar*

said to be made of this material. Many scholars think the dugong or sea-cow is meant. For an excellent discussion of the various views see *Enc. Bib.* Badgers' Skins.

blue. Better *violet* or *purple-blue* (LXX ὑακίνθινον as for above). A dye made from a shell-fish, perhaps the *Helix Ianthina* (see *HDB* I. p. 457).

staves. According to Ex. xxv. 15 the staves were not to be removed.

7. *the table of shewbread.* Better *of the presence*: see further McNeile's note on Ex. xxv. 30.

the continual bread (Heb. לֶחֶם הַתָּמִיד). The phrase is not found elsewhere.

8. *cloth of scarlet.* Why the Table had an extra covering cannot now be explained. *Scarlet* (Heb. תּוֹלַעַת שָׁנִי: i.e. *scarlet-worm*) is obtained from the cochineal insect (*Coccus ilicis*) which is called in Arab. *ḳirmiz,* whence we get our word crimson.

9. *candlestick of the light.* Here and Ex. xxxv. 14 only in this full form: see further on viii. 1 ff.

10. *the frame* (Heb. הַמּוֹט). The word occurs here, xiii. 23, and Nah. i. 13 only. In the latter passage it is rendered *yoke* in agreement with the usual meaning of מוֹט; LXX ἀναφορέων is also used to represent the Hebrew word translated staves. Some flat surface, such as a tray, seems to be required by the context here.

11. *the golden altar.* The altar of incense: see on iii. 31.

13. *the altar.* See Ex. xxvii. 1 ff

a purple cloth thereon: 14 and they shall put upon it all the vessels thereof, wherewith they minister about it, the firepans, the fleshhooks, and the shovels, and the basons, all the vessels of the altar; and they shall spread upon it a covering of sealskin, and put in the staves thereof. 15 And when Aaron and his sons have made an end of covering the sanctuary, and all the furniture of the sanctuary, as the camp is to set forward; after that, the sons of Kohath shall come to bear it: but they shall not touch the [1]sanctuary, lest they die. These things are the burden of the sons of Kohath in the tent of meeting. 16 And the charge of Eleazar the son of Aaron the priest shall be the oil for the light, and the sweet incense, and the continual meal offering, *P*[s]

[1] Or, *holy things*

a purple cloth. The altar of burnt offering may have had a cloth of a different colour, because it stood in the court outside the actual sanctuary. *Purple* (Heb. אַרְגָּמָן which LXX here renders ὁλοπόρφυρον) was a dye obtained from a shell-fish; both *Murex brandaris* and *Murex trunculus* are found in Phoenicia (cf. Virgil *Aen.* IV. 262: Tyrioque ardebat murice laena).

14. At the beginning of this *v.* LXX and Sam. add provision for the transport of the laver and its base: cf. Ex. xxx. 17.

basons. These were used for tossing the blood against the altar. The same word occurs in Am. vi. 6 for *wine-bowls*, perhaps to represent the 'intemperate greed' of the drinkers: see Edghill *ad loc.*

15. *after that.* The holy things are not to be touched by the Levites until they are covered up.

bear it. Different accounts are contained in O.T. of the manner in which the ark was transported. Here and in 2 Sam. xv. 24 ff. it is by the hands of the Levites, in Josh. iii. 13 &c. by the priests, and in 2 Sam. vi. 3 (cf. 1 Sam. vi. 8 ff.) David places it in a cart. As the two latter occasions were of a special nature it is not necessary to see any inconsistency in this change.

they shall not...die. The R.V. rendering does not quite represent the original, where the negative is not adversative, but circumstantial (see Driver *Heb. Tenses* § 159). Gray renders *without, however, touching the holy things, and so suffering death.*

the sanctuary. Better with mg. *holy things.*

16. *oil.* See Ex. xxvii. 20.

sweet incense. See Ex. xxv. 6, xxx. 34 ff. (where Driver renders *incense of fragrant powders*)[1].

continual meal offering. Phrase here only in Pent. (cf. Neh. x. 33).

---

[1] The word rendered *fragrant powders* (סַמִּים) occurs in the plural only, and is peculiar to P and Chron. Its meaning is dubious though it is sometimes connected

and the anointing oil, the charge of all the tabernacle, and of all that therein is, the sanctuary, and the furniture thereof. *P*[s]

17 And the LORD spake unto Moses and unto Aaron, saying, 18 Cut ye not off the tribe of the families of the Kohathites from among the Levites: 19 but thus do unto them, that they may live, and not die, when they approach unto the most holy things: Aaron and his sons shall go in, and appoint them every one to his service and to his burden: 20 but they shall not go in to see the [1]sanctuary even for a moment, lest they die.

21 And the LORD spake unto Moses, saying, 22 Take the sum of the sons of Gershon also, by their fathers' houses, by their families; 23 from thirty years old and upward until fifty years old shalt thou number them; all that enter in to [2]wait upon the service, to do the work in the tent of meeting. 24 This is the service of the families of the Gershonites, in serving and in bearing burdens: 25 they shall bear the curtains of the tabernacle, and the tent of meeting, its covering, and the covering

[1] Or, *holy things* [2] Heb. *war the warfare.*

It may represent the daily offering for the priests (Lev. vi. 22), or less probably the offering which accompanied the continual burnt offering (Ex. xxix. 38 ff.).

anointing oil. See Ex. xxx. 22 ff.

18. *the tribe* (Heb. שֵׁבֶט). The use of this word for anything less than a tribe of Israel is probably unique, for the apparent exceptions (Jud. xx. 12, and 1 Sam. ix. 21 where the *tribes* of Benjamin are referred to) are almost certainly due to textual corruption: in each case the singular should be read, unless indeed an archaic form of the construct case is used (cf. *Ges.-K.* § 90 l).

20. *shall not...see.* Cf. 1 S. vi. 19.

the sanctuary. See on *v.* 15.

for a moment. Lit. *as a swallowing* (Heb. כְּבַלַּע[1]) i.e. of one's spittle. The full phrase, which is also found in Arabic, occurs in Job vii. 19 where Bishop Gibson gives as an equivalent "in the twinkling of an eye."

21–28. The task of the Gershonites was simpler, and perhaps less honourable, than that of the Kohathites; they were responsible for the transport of the various coverings and curtains of the tent and its court. According to vii. 7 they had the use of wagons for this purpose.

23. *service.* See on *v.* 3.

---

with Ar. شَمّ *smell.* Landersdorfer, however, suggests a derivation from the Sumerian ŠEM, ŠIM *spicery* (*Sum. Sprachgut im A.T.* p. 50).

[1] Apparently an accusative of time with כְּ: see *BDB* p. 453 (1 *a*).

of sealskin that is above upon it, and the screen for the door of the tent of meeting; 26 and the hangings of the court, and the screen for the door of the gate of the court, which is by the tabernacle and by the altar round about, and their cords, and all the instruments of their service, and whatsoever shall be done with them, therein shall they serve. 27 At the commandment of Aaron and his sons shall be all the service of the sons of the Gershonites, in all their burden, and in all their service: and ye shall appoint unto them in charge all their burden. 28 This is the service of the families of the sons of the Gershonites in the tent of meeting: and their charge shall be under the hand of Ithamar the son of Aaron the priest. P

29 As for the sons of Merari, thou shalt number them by their families, by their fathers' houses; 30 from thirty years old and upward even unto fifty years old shalt thou number them, every one that entereth upon the service, to do the work of the tent of meeting. 31 And this is the charge of their burden, according to all their service in the tent of meeting; the boards of the tabernacle, and the bars thereof, and the pillars thereof, and the sockets thereof; 32 and the pillars of the court round about, and their sockets, and their pins, and their cords, with all their instruments, and with all their service: and by name ye shall [1]appoint the instruments of the charge of their burden. 33 This is the service of the families of the sons of Merari, according to all their service, in the tent of meeting, under the hand of Ithamar the son of Aaron the priest.

[1] Or, *number*

27. *ye shall appoint.* LXX has the singular, referring to Moses alone.

in charge. LXX ἐξ ὀνομάτων agreeing with *v.* 32. Probably this reading should be adopted here as the difference in the Heb. is not very great.

28. *Ithamar.* Though himself a Kohathite, being son of Aaron (see on iii. 19), Ithamar has charge of both the Gershonites and Merarites. The name occurs amongst the Sabaeans, Ithamar paying tribute to Sargon after the battle of Raphia: see Sayce *Egypt of the Hebs. &c.* p. 114.

29–33. The duty of the Merarites is to attend to the transport of the actual structure or framework of the tabernacle itself. Like the Kohathites they have wagons provided for them: see vii. 8.

34–49. The Levites are numbered according to their separate families, and in fulfilment of the divine command to Moses.

34 And Moses and Aaron and the princes of the congregation P^s numbered the sons of the Kohathites by their families, and by their fathers' houses, 35 from thirty years old and upward even unto fifty years old, every one that entered upon the service, for work in the tent of meeting: 36 and those that were numbered of them by their families were two thousand seven hundred and fifty. 37 These are they that were numbered of the families of the Kohathites, all that did serve in the tent of meeting, whom Moses and Aaron numbered according to the commandment of the LORD by the hand of Moses.

38 And those that were numbered of the sons of Gershon, by their families, and by their fathers' houses, 39 from thirty years old and upward even unto fifty years old, every one that entered upon the service, for work in the tent of meeting, 40 even those that were numbered of them, by their families, by their fathers' houses, were two thousand and six hundred and thirty. 41 These are they that were numbered of the families of the sons of Gershon, all that did serve in the tent of meeting, whom Moses and Aaron numbered according to the commandment of the LORD.

42 And those that were numbered of the families of the sons of Merari, by their families, by their fathers' houses, 43 from thirty years old and upward even unto fifty years old, every one that entered upon the service, for work in the tent of meeting, 44 even those that were numbered of them by their families, were three thousand and two hundred. 45 These are they that were numbered of the families of the sons of Merari, whom Moses and Aaron numbered according to the commandment of the LORD by the hand of Moses.

46 All those that were numbered of the Levites, whom Moses and Aaron and the princes of Israel numbered, by their families, and by their fathers' houses, 47 from thirty years old and upward even unto fifty years old, every one that entered in to do

34. *princes of the congregation.* Cf. xvi. 2, xxxi. 13; Ex. xvi. 22; Jos. ix. 15. LXX οἱ ἄρχοντες Ἰσραήλ is generally considered to be a later usage: cf. Driver *LOT* pp. 133 f. (Nos. 32 and 38).

37. *by the hand of Moses.* A phrase typical of P.

47. *thirty years old.* Cf. the age of our Lord when He began His ministry (Lk. iii. 23).

the work of service, and the work of bearing burdens in the tent P^s of meeting, 48 even those that were numbered of them, were eight thousand and five hundred and fourscore. 49 According to the commandment of the LORD they were numbered by the hand of Moses, every one according to his service, and [1]according to his burden: thus were they numbered of him, as the LORD commanded Moses.

[1] Or, *according to his burden and his duty, as &c.*

49. This *v.* is so corrupt that it cannot be translated as it stands. R.V. probably represents what was originally intended by the writer.

CHAPTERS V.—VI.

VARIOUS LAWS AND REGULATIONS.

The various provisions in these and the following chh. seem to have no obvious order or arrangement. Those which have been collected into the present section begin in each case with the formula "And the LORD spake unto Moses, saying," which is generally held to be characteristic of P.

(*a*) *The exclusion of the unclean.* v. 1–4.
(*b*) *Some priestly dues.* 5–10.
(*c*) *The ordeal of jealousy.* 11–31.
(*d*) *The law of the Nazirite.* vi. 1–21.
(*e*) *The Aaronic blessing.* 22–27.

V. 1 And the LORD spake unto Moses, saying, 2 Command P the children of Israel, that they put out of the camp every leper,

V. 1–4. All unclean persons, whatever the origin or nature of their condition, are to be excluded from the camp as being a source of defilement to the sanctity which it derived from the presence of Jehovah in its midst. "The notion of pure and impure is exclusively religious: it is neither moral nor utilitarian" Loisy *Rel. of Isr.* p. 70.

2. *put out.* In other places leprosy alone involves exclusion, and Dillmann would account for the greater severity of the present regulations by supposing that they apply to a military camp. That special regulations were imposed on Hebrews during military service cannot be denied: see Dt. xx. 1 ff., xxiii. 9 ff. and cf. Schwally *Semitische Kriegsalterthümer* pp. 59 ff., but the inclusion of women (*v.* 3) seems to rule out such a reference here.

every leper. For the various forms of leprosy see Lev. xiii. The reason for the exclusion of the leper was probably religious rather than sanitary; just as the Persians excluded lepers as being under punishment for some specially grievous crime (see Herodotus I. § 138). In O.T. leprosy is

and every one that hath an issue, and whosoever is unclean by the dead: 3 both male and female shall ye put out, without the camp shall ye put them; that they defile not their camp, in the midst whereof I dwell. 4 And the children of Israel did so, and put them out without the camp: as the LORD spake unto Moses, so did the children of Israel. *P*

5 And the LORD spake unto Moses, saying, 6 Speak unto the children of Israel, When a man or woman shall commit any sin that men commit, to do a trespass against the LORD, and that soul be guilty; 7 then they shall confess their sin which they *Ps*

often a mark of the divine displeasure: cf. xii. 12 (Miriam); 2 K. v. 27 (Gehazi), xv. 5 f. (Uzziah)[1]; there is no evidence, however, for the idea, found elsewhere, that leprosy is a penalty for a breach of 'taboo': see Frazer *Spirits of the Corn &c.* II. pp. 26 f.

issue. See Lev. xv.

unclean by the dead. See on xix. 11 ff. *Dead* is lit. *spirit, ghost* (*nephesh*) as in vi. 6, 11, ix. 6 ff. &c. See on this H. W. Robinson's Essay on "Heb. Psychology" in *The People and the Book* pp. 353 ff.

3. *female.* The seclusion of women in the East at the time of their periods was kept up until the Middle Ages: cf. Maimonides *Moreh Nebuchim* III. 47. See further Frazer *Balder the Beautiful* I. pp. 22 ff., *Taboo* pp. 145 ff.

in the midst whereof &c. Cf. xxxv. 34 where the same phrase is used of the promised land, and as a warning against polluting it by bloodshed.

5–10. Regulations are laid down providing that in cases where no relative exists to claim compensation for certain injuries, the amount shall go to the priests. The original law, to which this is supplementary, will be found in Lev. vi. 1 ff.

6. *man or woman.* Cf. the different Heb. of *v.* 3. The same distinction is found in the story of the flood, though the E.VV. do not disclose it: e.g. Gen. vii. 2 compared with vi. 19, vii. 3 &c.

man...men. The words here are also different in the original, corresponding to *vir* and *homo*, or *Mann* and *Mensch*.

to do a trespass: lit. *to treacherously do an act of treachery.* It might seem that this section dealt with sins against God Himself, but *v.* 7 *b* makes it plain that the compensation is to be paid to the representatives of the injured party: to sin against a fellow man is to act treacherously against the LORD: cf. Lev. vi. 2.

7. *shall confess.* Here and in Lev. v. 5 (sin offering), xvi. 21 (day of atonement), some kind of public confession is required: cf. Jos. vii. 19; Ezra x. 11; Dan. ix. 4.

---

[1] So too as late as Pope Alexander III (†1181) who refers to the leprosy of Baldwin of Jerusalem as a scourge "under the righteous judgement of God": see Roger of Hoveden *Annals* II. p. 4 (Bohn's edition).

have done: and he shall make restitution for his guilt in full, and add unto it the fifth part thereof, and give it unto him in respect of whom he hath been guilty. 8 But if the man have no kinsman to whom restitution may be made for the guilt, the restitution for guilt which is made unto the LORD shall be the priest's; besides the ram of the atonement, whereby atonement shall be made for him. 9 And every heave offering of all the holy things of the children of Israel, which they present unto the priest, shall be his. 10 And every man's hallowed things shall be his: whatsoever any man giveth the priest, it shall be his.

Ps

Px

11 And the LORD spake unto Moses, saying, 12 Speak unto

make restitution for his guilt: lit. *return his guilt*. This phrase is a good example of the Heb. idiom, by which the abstract is used for the concrete, *guilt* here means *the profits of the guilty deed*.

fifth part. So in Lev. vi. 5, xxii. 14: cf. also Lev. xxvii. 11 ff., 27, 31 and see Cook *Laws of Moses &c*. p. 67.

8. The priest as Jehovah's representative stands in the place of the man who dies without kin (cf. Lev. xxiii. 20), just as the state does in English law.

kinsman. Heb. גֹּאֵל: *gō'ēl*. In the passage in Lev. vi. 1–7 no mention is made of the kinsman, though doubtless as the representative of the injured party his rights were taken for granted: see further on xxxv. 12.

besides the ram of the atonement. Lev. vi. 6 requires this as the appropriate guilt offering. The greater part of this offering went to the priest, and the offender might easily have supposed that the restitution made to him would have rendered the sacrifice unnecessary.

9. *every heave offering* (Heb. תְּרוּמָה). "An examination of the passages in which תְּרוּמָה, and the cognate verb הֵרִים, occur, shews that it denotes properly what is *lifted off* a larger mass, or separated from it, for sacred purposes....(It) is only used exceptionally in connexion with sacrifices." Driver *Deut*. (*ICC*) p. 142. A whole tractate of the Mishna *Terumoth* is devoted to the subject: see also *Aboda Zara* II. 7.

shall be his. That is the individual priest's.

10. In this *v*. there is a description of the two sources from which the priestly revenue was derived, (*a*) dues to Jehovah, (*b*) actual gifts to the priests. In each part of the *v*. *his* should be taken to refer to the individual priest.

11–31. If a husband suspects his wife of adultery, but has no proofs of her offence, he can compel her to submit to "the ordeal of jealousy[1]." Bringing an offering for his wife, the husband presents her before the priest, who "sets her before the LORD." The woman then swears that

[1] See Additional Note pp. 35, 36.

the children of Israel, and say unto them, If any man's wife go P^x
aside, and commit a trespass against him, 13 and a man lie with her carnally, and it be hid from the eyes of her husband,

she is innocent, and having done so, drinks "the water of bitterness," which contains in it dust from the tabernacle floor; if she be really innocent nothing further happens, but if she have committed perjury a punishment, probably miscarriage, befalls her.

The punishment inflicted on the woman depended entirely on the working of the ordeal itself, and was in reality much more merciful than that inflicted, for example, on witches in later ages. No time limit is mentioned for the curse to take effect, and it may be supposed that it would begin its operations immediately. It should be noted that for cases of proved adultery the punishment was death for both parties in early times (Lev. xx. 10; Dt. xxii. 22 f.); in N.T. times the woman, at least, was liable to be stoned (Jn. viii. 5), though since the Jews did not possess the power of inflicting a death sentence (Jn. xviii. 31), the penalty could hardly have been inflicted. Later still by a further modification the adulteress lost her property rights under the marriage settlement, and in addition, was scourged (see *Jew. Enc.* I. p. 217 *a*). Until recent times the death sentence was still inflicted in Palestine, either by the aggrieved husband or by the next of kin (*PEFQS* (1897) pp. 127 ff.)[1].

The Israelite Law worked very unfairly against the woman in regard to sexual offences; since she was regarded merely as the property of the husband he had rights against her, but she had none against him; a man, for example, could not commit adultery against his wife, but only against another man. When compared with the Arabs, the Israelites are markedly lacking in chivalrous feelings, and the matter of fact way in which stories are told of the readiness with which even Abraham was ready to sacrifice his wife, in order to preserve his own safety, reveals the low estimate of women which existed amongst the chosen people: see Gen. xii. 10 ff., xix. 8, xx., xxvi., and cf. Jud. xix. 24 with Moore's note.

The narrative as it stands bears traces of confusion, as the Heb. can mean nothing less than that the woman had to take two draughts of the bitter water, if not three (*vv.* 24 and 26). In addition Gray considers that she had twice to swear (*vv.* 19 and 21) and was twice brought before Jehovah (*vv.* 16 and 18).

12. *go aside.* The word occurs elsewhere only in Prov. iv. 15, vii. 25. The corresponding root in Ethiopic is used with the meaning 'be seduced.'

---

[1] See further Cook *Laws of Moses &c.* pp. 105 ff., and for the usages of non-Semitic peoples Diod. Sic. I. 78; Aelian. *Var. Hist.* XIII. 24; Tacitus *Germ.* XIX. Plutarch *Quaestt. Gr. init.* VII. 171 (I owe these references to Jeremy Taylor's *Rule and exercise of Holy Living* II. iii. 10).

and be kept close, and she be defiled, and there be no witness P against her, neither she be taken in the act; 14 and the spirit of jealousy come upon him, and he be jealous of his wife, and she be defiled: or if the spirit of jealousy come upon him, and he be jealous of his wife, and she be not defiled: 15 then shall the man bring his wife unto the priest, and shall bring her oblation for her, the tenth part of an ephah of barley meal; he shall pour no oil upon it, nor put frankincense thereon; for it is a meal offering of jealousy, a meal offering of memorial, bringing iniquity to remembrance. 16 And the priest shall bring her near, and set her before the LORD: 17 and the priest shall take holy water in an earthen vessel; and of the dust that is on the

13. *be kept close.* The subject of the verb (which is feminine) is the woman: *she be undetected.*

in the act. Cf. Jn. viii. 4; Code of Ḥammurabi § 130.

14. The husband's rights were very comprehensive (see above and cf. Ecclus. ix. 1, where there is a warning against needless jealousy); but in later times he had to bring some kind of evidence before the ordeal could be imposed (*Sōṭah* I. 1 f.; cf. Philo *De Spec. Leg.* x.).

15. *tenth part of an ephah.* About seven pints.

barley meal. A less valuable form of cereal than 'fine meal,' the usual offering.

no oil...frankincense. As in the case of a poor man's sin offering (Lev. v. 11). Here the omission is made because the occasion was not a happy one.

to remembrance. The object of the offering is to draw Jehovah's attention to the supposed crime, so that He may give a right decision; in x. 9 the trumpets are blown in order that God may not forget His people.

16. *before the LORD.* In P this means to bring to the tabernacle, and possibly to the altar. In the earlier legislation it refers to the local sanctuary.

17. *holy water.* Though this expression is familiar in Christian worship, it occurs nowhere else in the Bible. Perhaps the water was taken from the laver (so *Sōṭah* II. 2), where pure water was kept for the priests to use in their ablutions, for as it had been placed in a holy vessel it would itself be holy (Ex. xxx. 28 f.). LXX paraphrases ὕδωρ καθαρὸν ζῶν, or possibly represents the original Heb.[1], from which the present text has arisen by a corruption: cf. Robertson Smith *Rel. Sem.*[2] p. 181.

an earthen vessel. As in Lev. xiv. 5, 50. After the ceremony the vessel being 'holy' would be destroyed: cf. Lev. vi. 28.

the dust. Special sanctity would attach to the dust of the tabernacle,

---

[1] קדשים being read for חיים.

floor of the tabernacle the priest shall take, and put it into the *P*x water: 18 and the priest shall set the woman before the LORD, and let the hair of the woman's head go loose, and put the meal offering of memorial in her hands, which is the meal offering of jealousy: and the priest shall have in his hand the water of bitterness that causeth the curse: 19 and the priest shall cause her to swear, and shall say unto the woman, If no man have lien with thee, and if thou hast not gone aside to uncleanness, [1]being under thy husband, be thou free from this water of bitterness that causeth the curse: 20 but if thou hast gone aside, [1]being under thy husband, and if thou be defiled, and some man have lien with thee besides thine husband: 21 then the priest shall cause the woman to swear with the oath of [2]cursing, and the priest shall say unto the woman, The LORD make thee a [2]curse and an oath among thy people, when the LORD doth make thy thigh to fall away, and thy belly to swell;

[1] Or, with another *instead of thy husband* See Ezek. xxiii. 5, Rom. vii. 2.
[2] Or, *adjuration*

and so the test would be made more severe. Lane says that cakes are made from the dust of Muhammed's tomb, and used as charms against disease: see *Modern Egyptians* (Minerva edition) p. 235.

18. *hair...go loose.* As a sign of shame and of mourning. The priests were forbidden to let their hair go loose (Lev. x. 6, xxi. 10): see further Nowack *Arch.* II. p. 114.

water of bitterness. That is water which causes bitterness or pain: cf. Jer. ii. 19, iv. 18. In actual practice bitter potions have been used in similar ordeals in modern times[1].

19. *under thy husband*: mg. *instead of thy husband.* Either translation is possible, but the text seems the better rendering in view of the use of the same preposition in Ez. xxiii. 5—"when she was mine"—is lit. *under me*: cf. also Rom. vii. 2 ὕπανδρος.

21. *a curse and an oath.* May thy fate be so terrible as to be used in cursings; cf. Jer. xxix. 22, where the full form of the curse is given. For the opposite expression see Gen. xii. 2 f.

thy thigh...thy belly. Gray quotes the opinion of H. W. Robinson that the water "may have been regarded as affecting the offspring of a guilty intercourse, so that, though the woman grows great with child ("the swelling belly"), the birth is abortive." *Thigh* is in any case almost certainly a euphemism.

---

[1] The ideogram ḪUL denoted both *limnu* (evil) and *marru* (bitter). By *bitter* water the Semite understood any water unfit for drinking. See Morgenstern in *Mitteilungen der Vorderas. Gesell.* 1905, 3 p. 32.

22 and this water that causeth the curse shall go into thy bowels, *P^x*
and make thy belly to swell, and thy thigh to fall away: and the woman shall say, Amen, Amen. 23 And the priest shall write these curses in a book, and he shall blot them out into the water of bitterness: 24 and he shall make the woman drink the water of bitterness that causeth the curse: and the water that causeth the curse shall enter into her *and become* bitter. 25 And the priest shall take the meal offering of jealousy out of the woman's hand, and shall wave the meal offering before the LORD, and bring it unto the altar: 26 and the priest shall take an handful of the meal offering, as the memorial thereof, and burn it upon the altar, and afterward shall make the woman drink the water. 27 And when he hath made her drink the water, then it shall come to pass, if she be defiled, and have

23. *a book* (Heb. סֵפֶר). The derivation, and original meaning, of the word are not certainly known. Professor Margoliouth claims that it comes from an Arabic word meaning 'stone,' and sees this conception in the words of Job xix. 23 "inscribed in a book" or better "engraved" (*Lines of Defence of the Bib. Rev.* p. 156). Such a rendering would well suit this present passage, if the words were written on a stone, and then washed off. Lane describes a similar method of charming away illness amongst the modern Egyptians. Verses from the Koran are written on the inner surface of an earthenware cup or bowl, water is then poured into it, and when the words have been washed off the patient drinks the water (*op. cit.* p. 233)[1]. Others think that the book may have been of skin, such as is described by Herodotus (v. 58); the roll of Jer. xxxvi. 23 would hardly have been of such tough material: cf. Buhl *Canon* pp. 195 f.

25. *shall wave.* Like so much of the ritual of this ceremony this act is abnormal.

26. *memorial* (Heb. אַזְכָּרָה). A technical term used here and in Lev. only (ii. 2, 9, 16, v. 12, vi. 15, xxiv. 7): the handful is a memorial or representation of the whole offering.

27. *made her drink.* This is the second, or perhaps the third, taking of the draught. To readers of the E.V. it might seem that there is no need to suppose that this is so (cf. Finn *Unity of Pentateuch* p. 386), but as the 'tenses' of the original Heb. are what is known as 'consecutive,' no other interpretation of the text as it stands is possible.

---

[1] "The ancient Egyptian had a profound belief in the magical virtue of the written word, and one of his favourite ways of possessing himself of knowledge was to wash off in beer the writing of any roll whose contents he wished to make infallibly his own, subsequently drinking the beer." Baikie *Egyptian Papyri &c.* pp. 19 f.

committed a trespass against her husband, that the water that *P^x* causeth the curse shall enter into her *and become* bitter, and her belly shall swell, and her thigh shall fall away: and the woman shall be a curse among her people. 28 And if the woman be not defiled, but be clean; then she shall be free, and shall conceive seed. 29 This is the law of jealousy, when a wife, [1]being under her husband, goeth aside, and is defiled; 30 or when the spirit of jealousy cometh upon a man, and he be jealous over his wife; then shall he set the woman before the LORD, and the priest shall execute upon her all this law. 31 And the man shall be free from iniquity, and that woman shall bear her iniquity.

[1] Or, *goeth aside* with another *instead of her husband*

28. *free.* That is free from guilt, declared innocent: cf. Jer. ii. 35; Ps. xix. 13.

29. *jealousy.* Cf. Prov. vi. 34; *Test. Twelve Patriarchs* (T. Reub. VI. 5).

ADDITIONAL NOTE ON V. 11–31.

Trial by Ordeal.

The ordeal was not much resorted to in Israel; with the probable exception of Ex. xxii. 8 f. this is the only example of it in the Law; but at times of great crisis the servants of Jehovah challenged their opponents to some such test. Of this latter type of occasional ordeal—if one may so call it—there is a good example in xvi. 16 ff. (the censers), another instance is to be found in 1 K. xviii. (Elijah on Mt. Carmel). In later times adultery became so common, according to Maimonides (on *Sōṭah*), that the Sanhedrin abolished the ordeal. J. Lightfoot has an interesting note on Jn. viii. 1–11 in which he states that the author of this advice was Johanan ben Zacchai, a contemporary of our Lord's, and possibly one of those who brought the adulterous woman to Him. In the Code of Ḥammurabi the ordeal is used "only in two cases, and on each occasion it is by water. The river-god (*ilu Nāru*) has to decide whether a man upon whom a spell has been cast has suffered unjustly (§ 2), and whether a wife who has fallen under the suspicion of unchastity is innocent (§ 132)": S. A. Cook *The Laws of Moses &c.* p. 64. Further illustrations of similar customs amongst races akin to the Israelites will be found in Robertson Smith *Rel. Sem.*[2] pp. 179 ff.

During the Middle Ages trial by ordeals of various kinds was very common, and formed part of the legal system[1]. The Church, however, always seems to have regarded such means of discovering guilt with a certain suspicion. Pope Stephen V issued a decree in 816 in which he stated that "The holy canons do not approve of confession by the ordeal...and what is not sanctioned by the holy Fathers, no modern superstitious invention must presume to do." Later still Agobard of Lyons (d. 840) protested against both the duel, and the ordeal, but the only effect was to draw unfavourable attention to himself.

[1] Cf. Stubbs *Constitutional Hist.* I. 654 (for England), and for the various Teutonic tribes Milman *Latin Christianity* II. pp. 60 ff.

Even so great a man as his later contemporary Hincmar of Rheims (d. 882), could uphold its use, and in mystic fashion compare the water to that of the flood, which was the means of salvation to the righteous, but of overwhelming disaster to the wicked. A decree of the Lateran Council of 1215 formally condemned and abolished the practice. St Thomas Aquinas (d. 1274) seems not to recognise the present passage as an ordeal, for he states that: "The ordeal ...is intended for the detection of secret sin by means of something done by man: still there is further expected a miraculous effect to be wrought by God. Hence this kind of judicial inquiry is rendered unlawful, both because it is directed to the judging of secret things that are reserved to the divine judgement; and also because such a judicial procedure is not sanctioned by divine authority," *Summa Theologica* II. II. Q. XCV. viii. 3 (see Jos. Rickaby *Aquinas Ethicus* II. pp. 172 f.). In spite however of these strong opinions the ordeal long survived, and in the notorious case of Savonarola great ecclesiastics invoked its aid.

Amongst the Greeks and Romans the custom prevailed widely, especially in connexion with the punishment of perjury by the gods. For the former see Frazer's edition of Pausanias *Description of Greece* IV. 175 f. and 253 ff. and cf. Sophocles *Antigone* 264 ff.

> ἦμεν δ' ἕτοιμοι καὶ μύδρους αἴρειν χεροῖν,
> καὶ πῦρ διέρπειν, καὶ θεοὺς ὁρκωμοτεῖν,
> τὸ μήτε δρᾶσαι, μήτε τῳ ξυνειδέναι
> τὸ πρᾶγμα βουλεύσαντι μήτ' εἰργασμένῳ.

Amongst the Romans evidence of a similar practice, and a similar belief, is not hard to find: e.g. Polybius VI. 56; cf. Virgil *Aeneid* XI. 787 f.

> "Et medium freti pietate per ignem
> Cultores multa premimus vestigia pruna."

Juvenal, however, tells us that by his time the apprehension of divine punishment was but a slight deterrent to the false swearer. Pliny mentions a river which had the power of detecting and punishing perjury *Hist. Nat.* XXXI. 2.

For later times, and for the prevalence of the custom amongst uncivilised peoples of our own day, see Frazer *FLOT* III. pp. 304–414 and for the whole subject the article "Ordeal" in *Enc. Brit.* by Sir E. B. Tylor.

VI. 1 And the LORD spake unto Moses, saying, 2 Speak unto *P^x*

VI. 1–21. The law for men or women who take upon them the Nazirite vow. They are to give up all products of the vine, to let the hair grow, and to avoid contact with the dead. In case this latter defilement is incurred, a special rite of purifying must be undergone. At the end of the period for which the vow is made, an oblation is to be offered, and various ritual acts to be performed, before the normal life may be resumed.

The subject of the Nazirite in Israel is a very puzzling one, as apparently the term Nazirite was used at different times with various connotations. The institution seems to have existed from very early days (see Jud. xiii.–xvi.; Am. ii. 11 f.), and survived into the days of our Lord (1 Macc. iii. 49 f.; Joseph. *Ant.* XIX. vi. 1, and cf. the description of St James by Hegesippus in Eusebius *Hist. Eccles.* II. xxiii. 4), and even later[1].

---

[1] For the later Nazirites see the tractate *Nazir* and Gray *Sacrifice* pp. 38 f.

the children of Israel, and say unto them, When either man or *P^x^*
woman shall make a special vow, the vow of [1]a Nazirite, to
[2]separate himself unto the LORD: 3 he shall separate himself
from wine and strong drink; he shall drink no vinegar of wine,
or vinegar of strong drink, neither shall he drink any liquor of
grapes, nor eat fresh grapes or dried. 4 All the days of his

[1] That is, *one separated* or *consecrated*. [2] Or, *consecrate*

The case of Samson presents peculiar features when compared with the regulations here set out. In the first place, his dedication was no temporary measure enforced by a vow, but a life-long service, undertaken in response to a divine command which preceded his own birth. The most important regulation concerning him was that by which no razor came upon him (Jud. xvi. 17); whether he himself had to avoid the use of intoxicants does not appear, though his mother was to abstain from such before his birth (Jud. xiii. 4); in regard to the third of the prohibitions here laid down Samson seems to have been quite unconcerned (Jud. xiv. 8).

2. *man or woman*. The mother of Samson seems to have been an example of a woman Nazirite (Jud. xiii. 4, 7): the case of Bernice is sometimes cited (Joseph. *Bell. Jud.* II. xv. 1) as another instance.

Nazirite. The word means someone separated or devoted, and the full phrase Nazirite of God (Jud. xiii. 5), seems to be suggested by this shorter form.

3 f. The first prohibition laid upon the Nazirite is from drinking intoxicating liquors[1]. A similar prohibition was laid upon the priests, but only before ministering in the tent of meeting (Lev. x. 8 f.); the mother of Samson (Jud. xiii. 4) and John the Baptist (Lk. i. 15) were also to observe a like abstinence. In Jer. xxxv. there is a description of a whole 'family,' who, in obedience to an ancestral command, practised the same self-denial; in their case, and probably in that of the Nazirite, the avoidance of wine and allied products was not a temperance measure, but a protest against the use of fruits which were the gift of the Baalim (see the writer's note on Jer. xxxv. and cf. Frazer *Taboo* p. 13). The use of intoxicants is forbidden to Moslems: Koran II. 116, IV. 46 &c.

3. *strong drink*. This term includes wine or any other intoxicant.

vinegar. Sour beer or wine is still used to manufacture inferior kinds of vinegar.

liquor of grapes. It is hard to know what is meant by this drink or how it differed from wine: see Pattison *SBOT*.

dried. Possibly there is a reference here to the raisin-cakes mentioned in 2 S. vi. 19; Hos. iii. 1 (as part of the Canaanite cult).

---

[1] The antiquity of the use of intoxicating liquors is seen in the similarity of the word used to describe them: Assyr. *inu*, Heb. יין, cf. *ϝοῖνος*, vinum &c. Ball would also add the Chinese *yün* and Sumerian MUN.

[1]separation shall he eat nothing that is made of the grape-vine, from the kernels even to the husk. 5 All the days of his vow of separation there shall no razor come upon his head: until the days be fulfilled, in the which he separateth himself unto the LORD, he shall be holy, he shall let the locks of the hair of his P^x

[1] Or, *consecration* Or, *Naziriteship*

4. *kernels...husk.* The meaning of these two words is not known with any certainty, though the context shews that some part of the vine must be meant. *Kernels* (חַרְצַנִּים: *ḥarẓannim*) is connected with a root meaning sharp, and the reference seems to be to the bitter, acrid flavour of some product of the vine. *Husk*, or better *skin* (זָג: *zāg*), comes from a root meaning transparent and is connected with the Arabic word for glass: see *BDB*[1].

5. The second regulation, that no razor was to come upon the Nazirite, was originally the most important (see above), and a feature common to the different types of Nazirite recorded in O.T. The vow which was undertaken by St Paul at Cenchreae (Acts xviii. 18), evidently involved the reverse of the Nazirite prohibition, unless either of Rackham's explanations be adopted: (*a*) that he cut short his hair at the beginning of the period, or (*b*) that he was shorn at the end of the period, and kept the hair to present it at Jerusalem.

no razor. Cf. Lev. xxi. 5; Jud. xiii. 5, xvi. 17; 1 S. i. 11. The Roman, and Sabine, priests were not allowed to use razors made of iron (Frazer *Taboo* p. 262); the prohibition here is more comprehensive. For further examples and explanations see Robertson Smith *Rel. Sem.*[2] pp. 324 ff.

the days be fulfilled. Cf. Acts xxi. 26.

locks of the hair. The long locks of the Nazirite were such a familiar sight that 'an undressed vine' (Lev. xxv. 5, 11) is in the original a 'Nazirite' vine. St Paul's statement in 1 Cor. xi. 14 that long hair was a dishonour to a man was not intended to apply to those who incurred this shame for a religious purpose.

6 f. The third prohibition insists on the avoidance of the neighbourhood of the dead. The Greeks felt that even the gods would be defiled by any contact with death; this idea applied above all to Apollo and Artemis, the divinities who were especially associated with light and purity. Cf. Apollo's excuse for withdrawing from the house of Admetus on the approach of Death:

> ἐγὼ δέ, μὴ μίασμά μ' ἐν δόμοις κίχῃ,
> λείπω μελάθρων τῶνδε φιλτάτην στέγην.
>
> Euripides *Alcestis* 22 f.

and the desertion of Hippolytus by Artemis:

> ἐμοὶ γὰρ οὐ θέμις φθιτοὺς ὁρᾶν
> οὐδ' ὄμμα χραίνειν θανασίμοισιν ἐκπνοαῖς.
>
> Euripides *Hippolytus* 1437 f.

---

[1] Neither word is found elsewhere in M.T., though Klostermann suggests חַרְצַנִּים for the obscure חרייונים of 2 K. vi. 25.

head grow long. 6 All the days that he separateth himself unto the LORD he shall not come near to a dead body. 7 He shall not make himself unclean for his father, or for his mother, for his brother, or for his sister, when they die: because his separation unto God is upon his head. 8 All the days of his separation he is holy unto the LORD. 9 And if any man die very suddenly beside him, and he defile the head of his separation; then he shall shave his head in the day of his cleansing, on the seventh day shall he shave it. 10 And on the eighth day he shall bring two turtledoves, or two young pigeons, to the priest, to the door of the tent of meeting: 11 and the priest shall offer one for a sin offering, and the other for a burnt offering, and make atonement for him, for that he sinned by reason of the dead, and shall hallow his head that same day. 12 And he shall separate unto the LORD the days of his separation, and shall bring a he-lamb of the first year for a guilt offering: but the former days shall be void, because his separation was defiled. P^x

The Christian believes in One who has power even over Death (1 Cor. xv. 26; Rev. i. 18).

6. *a dead body*: lit. *the soul of one dead*. The idea of defilement by the ghost of the dead man may be suggested: see on xix. 11 ff.

7. *for his father &c*. The same rule applies to the high priest (Lev. xxi. 11), but not to his assistants (Lev. xxi. 1 ff.).

separation...upon his head. The outward sign is taken as the symbol of the separation for which it stood. In 1 Cor. xi. 10 the veiled hair of the woman is *the sign* of her subordination (cf. Goudge *ad loc*.).

9–12. The Nazirite who offends, even by accident, against the foregoing regulation must purify himself for seven days, and then undertake his vow afresh. It is to be noticed that in the eyes of the Hebrews unintentional, or 'hidden' sin (Ps. xix. 12) or defilement, was just as serious as that which was deliberate (cf. however xv. 30).

9. *head of his separation*. See on *v*. 7 above.

shave. The hair thus taken from the man's head could not be offered to Jehovah, since it was defiled, and so had to be buried, cf. Robertson Smith *Rel. Sem*.² pp. 369 ff. for similar methods of disposing of 'dangerous' objects, and see *Temûrah* VII. 4.

10. *turtledoves...pigeons*. So in Lev. v. 7, xii. 8, xiv. 22 (all as substitutes for a more expensive offering), xv. 14, 29 (man or woman with an issue). The ordinary Israelite who was defiled by the dead made no offering (cf. xix. 9).

12. *guilt offering*. The reason for this offering is obscure. Two lines of explanation have been suggested, (*a*) that it was a compensation for the delayed offering of the hair (Stade *Gesch. des Volk. Isr*. II. p. 257),

13 And this is the law of the Nazirite, when the days of his separation are fulfilled: he shall be brought unto the door of the tent of meeting: 14 and he shall offer his oblation unto the LORD, one he-lamb of the first year without blemish for a burnt offering, and one ewe-lamb of the first year without blemish for a sin offering, and one ram without blemish for peace offerings, 15 and a basket of unleavened bread, cakes of fine flour mingled with oil, and unleavened wafers anointed with oil, and their meal offering, and their drink offerings. 16 And the priest shall present them before the LORD, and shall offer his sin offering, and his burnt offering: 17 and he shall offer the ram for a sacrifice of peace offerings unto the LORD, with the basket of unleavened bread: the priest shall offer also the meal offering thereof, and the drink offering thereof. 18 And the Nazirite shall shave the head of his separation at the door of the tent of meeting, and shall take the hair of the head of his separation, and put it on the fire which is under the sacrifice of peace offerings. 19 And the priest shall take the sodden shoulder of the ram, and one unleavened cake out of the basket, and one *P^x*

and (*b*) because the accident was really a punishment for some secret sin (cf. Jn. ix. 2).

13–21. At the end of the period of the vow, the Nazirite makes his offerings, and then having shaved off his hair places it on the fire beneath the sacrifice; the ceremony is concluded by various other ritual acts. In the Arabian vow of *Ihram*, which is like the Nazirite vow in many respects, the offering is the main purpose of the vow, the latter being merely an incidental restraint: see Wellhausen *Arab. Heidenthum* p. 116.

13. *shall be brought.* Cf. v. 13 where the wife suspected of adultery might be unwilling to come. The Nazirite presumably would be anxious to accomplish his vow, and compulsion would not be required. Rashi would turn the phrase into a reflexive, but his suggestion is not supported by other examples of the usage. It should be noticed, however, that no one is named whose duty it is to *bring* the Nazirite.

14. The mention of the burnt offering before the sin offering is strange since the latter would first be offered up.

18. *door of the tent.* In *v.* 9 no place is specified.

take the hair. Gray sees in the destruction of the hair a survival of the custom of hair offerings: cf. Robertson Smith *Rel. Sem.*[2] pp. 331 ff.; Frazer *Magic Art* I. pp. 28 ff. In any case, since the hair was devoted to Jehovah, its destruction is necessary lest it should in any way be defiled.

unleavened wafer, and shall put them upon the hands of the Nazirite, after he hath shaven *the head of* his separation: 20 and the priest shall wave them for a wave offering before the LORD; this is holy for the priest, together with the wave breast and heave [1]thigh: and after that the Nazirite may drink wine. 21 This is the law of the Nazirite who voweth, *and of* his oblation unto the LORD for his separation, beside that which he is able to get: according to his vow which he voweth, so he must do after the law of his separation. P^x

22 And the LORD spake unto Moses, saying, 23 Speak unto Aaron and unto his sons, saying, On this wise ye shall bless the children of Israel; ye shall say unto them, *P*

24 The LORD bless thee, and keep thee:

[1] Or, *shoulder*

19. *the sodden shoulder*. No command has been made in regard to the boiling of the shoulder, it is taken for granted. This casual reference is important in view of Wellhausen's statement "that the flesh of the sacrifice in the Priestly Code is no longer boiled" *Hist. of Isr.* p. 68: cf. Wiener *Essays &c.* pp. 211 f.

upon the hands: lit. *palms*. Cf. Ex. xxix. 24; Lev. viii. 27.

22–27. Moses is commanded to convey to Aaron and his sons the form of blessing which they are to pronounce over the people. This fragment is quite obviously out of its context, and the suggestion that it originally came after Lev. ix. 22 has much to recommend it on grounds of fitness, though there is no actual evidence in support of it. The threefold form of the Blessing (cf. Gen. xlviii. 15 f.) naturally suggested, in earlier times, the persons of the Blessed Trinity (see Pusey on Micah ii. 4), and indeed "the three portions of the blessing—Preservation, Enlightenment, Peace—bear a relation, by no means fanciful, to the work of the Father, the Son, and the Holy Spirit" Watson *Expos. Bible* p. 68. The same threefold form is found amongst the Babylonians—but with one important difference, three gods are invoked instead of one. The following is taken from Hehn *Siebenzahl und Sabbat bei den Babylon. und im A.T.* p. 65, being part of a hymn to Shamash:

"May *Ea* be gracious unto thee,
Damkina, the queen of the ocean, make her face to shine upon thee,
Marduk the great overseer of the Igigi, lift up thine head."

In the Prayer of the Raising of the Hand to Ishtar part of the ritual was the threefold recitation of the incantation: see Rogers *CP* p. 161.

23. *On this wise.* Hooker cites this passage and the giving of the Lord's prayer as justification for use the of set forms: *Eccles. Polity* Bk. v. xxvi. 2.

24. *The LORD.* That is *Jehovah*, the divine personal name (see on i. 1). After the Jews had ceased to use this name it was still retained, so

25 The LORD make his face to shine upon thee, and be gracious unto thee: P

26 The LORD lift up his countenance upon thee, and give thee peace.

27 So shall they put my name upon the children of Israel; and I will bless them.

tradition says, in pronouncing this blessing in the Temple services, but not in the synagogue. (See Schürer *Gesch. des jüd. Volkes im Zeitalter J.C.*[4] II. p. 355.)

bless...keep. The positive and negative sides of God's love; the bestowal of good things, and the prevention of evil.

25. Hort has beautifully paraphrased this *v.* as "the smile and the merciful help of the Lord of heaven and earth": quoted by Goudge on 1 Cor. i. 3.

his face to shine. That is *take delight*: cf. Sumerian KA-ZAL (lit. *face-shine*) rendered *tašîltu, pleasure*, in Assyr. A common expression in the Psalms: e.g. xxxi. 16, lxvii. 1, lxxx. 3, 7, 19.

be gracious. Cf. Gen. xliii. 29 and Pss. passim. The expression is said never to appear in P.

26. *lift up his countenance.* Cf. Ps. iv. 6; Jub. x. 3, xxii. 28. A favourite expression, used of the Babylonian deities, to represent the bestowal of love or favour upon a particular individual or place: see Delitzsch *Babel and Bible* pp. 33, 94 ff.

peace. The characteristic blessing of O.T., to which St Paul added that characteristic of the New 'grace': cf. Armitage Robinson *Ephesians* pp. 141, 221 ff.

27. *put my name.* Cf. Dt. xxviii. 10 for the favourable consequences of this. The ancients believed that names appropriately used had much potency: see Böhmer *Das biblische...im Namen*; Giesebrecht *Die alttest. Schätzung des Gottesnamens* especially pp. 94 ff.; Heitmüller *Im Namen Jesu* pp. 162 ff., 167 ff. Amongst the Phoenicians the 'name' of Baal was actually made a deity: cf. the inscription of Eshmun-'azar *l.* 18 (in *NSI* pp. 30 f.).

CHAPTER VII.

THE OBLATIONS OF THE PRINCES.

This ch., perhaps the longest in the whole Bible, owes its size to the monotonous repetition of a long formula "consisting of 118 English words" (*CH* II. p. 194) with hardly any variation; it exhibits the peculiar style of P carried to its logical conclusion. The object of the ch. is presumably to arouse in the writer's contemporaries the spirit of emulation, and, in the importance which it assigns to the secular rulers as the support of the ecclesiastical establishment, it follows the example of Ezekiel (xlv. 17, xlvi. 2 &c.). According to Ex. xxxv. 21 the whole congregation had previously made voluntary offerings in which the rulers had taken a big part.

The offerings of the Princes (i.e. the heads of the twelve non-Levite tribes) consisted of six wagons and twelve oxen; one third of these was given to the Gershonites, and the rest to the Merarites for the work of transporting the tabernacle (cf. iv. 21 f.). In addition the princes offered a 'dedication gift' on the day of the consecration of the altar, the details of which will be found repeated after each name.

VII. 1 And it came to pass on the day that Moses had made *P*[s] an end of setting up the tabernacle, and had anointed it and sanctified it, and all the furniture thereof, and the altar and all the vessels thereof, and had anointed them and sanctified them; 2 that the princes of Israel, the heads of their fathers' houses, offered; these were the princes of the tribes, these are they that were over them that were numbered: 3 and they brought their oblation before the LORD, six covered wagons, and twelve oxen; a wagon for every two of the princes, and for each one an ox: and they presented them before the tabernacle. 4 And the LORD

VII. 1. *on the day.* According to Ex. xl. 17 this was the first day of the second year of the wanderings. There would however seem to be some mistake in the dating, as the contents of the ch. presuppose the legislation of I.—IV., which chh. are dated a month later. The mistake must be due to the compiler.

anointed it. Cf. Ex. xl. 9 f.; Lev. viii. 10 f. Objects as well as persons were consecrated by this method.

2. *the princes of Israel.* This phrase, which is an equivalent to the more usual *princes of the congregation* (see on iv. 34), is found only in Num. in the Pent. (here *v.* 84, i. 44, iv. 46): elsewhere it is used by Ezekiel (xxi. 25, xxii. 6, xlv. 9) as a general term for the rulers of Israel.

offered. The object of this verb is missing.

these were &c. These words form a parenthesis following the breaking off of the sentence. It is strange to find such a breach of good style in a calm and leisurely writer like P, though it is quite easy to account for the similar phenomenon which recurs in the writings of St Paul.

3. *covered wagons*[1]. (LXX ἁμάξας λαμπηνικάς.) The Heb. word for covered (צב) is found elsewhere only in Is. lxvi. 20 where it is rendered *litters* by R.V., its meaning is quite uncertain. The reading of Symm. ὑπουργίας is interesting and suggests that צבא *service* (see on iv. 3) stood in text before him.

before the tabernacle. This phrase corresponds to *before the* LORD in the earlier part of the *v.*

---

[1] The Heb. word for עֲגָלָה *wagon* is generally thought (*see BDB*) to be so named from the *rolling* (√עגל) of the wheels: but this would not distinguish it from the chariot (רכב). A derivation from עֶגְלָה *heifer* seems much more probable: cf. 1 S. vi. 7 f. &c. and see Ehrlich *op. cit.* p. 133.

spake unto Moses, saying, 5 Take it of them, that they may be to do the service of the tent of meeting; and thou shalt give them unto the Levites, to every man according to his service. 6 And Moses took the wagons and the oxen, and gave them unto the Levites. 7 Two wagons and four oxen he gave unto the sons of Gershon, according to their service: 8 and four wagons and eight oxen he gave unto the sons of Merari, according unto their service, under the hand of Ithamar the son of Aaron the priest. 9 But unto the sons of Kohath he gave none: because the service of the sanctuary belonged unto them; they bare it upon their shoulders. 10 And the princes offered [1]for the dedication of the altar in the day that it was anointed, even the princes offered their oblation before the altar. 11 And the LORD said unto Moses, They shall offer their oblation, each prince on his day, for the dedication of the altar. P^s R^P P^s

12 And he that offered his oblation the first day was Nahshon the son of Amminadab, of the tribe of Judah: 13 and his oblation was one silver charger, the weight thereof was an hundred and thirty *shekels*, one silver bowl of seventy shekels, after the shekel of the sanctuary; both of them full of fine flour mingled with oil for a meal offering; 14 one golden spoon of ten *shekels*, full of incense; 15 one young bullock, one ram, one he-lamb of the first year, for a burnt offering; 16 one male of the goats for a sin offering; 17 and for the sacrifice of peace offerings, two oxen, five rams, five he-goats, five he-lambs of the first year: this was the oblation of Nahshon the son of Amminadab.

[1] Or, *the dedication-gift*

7 ff. The Gershonites, who had to remove only the curtains and hangings of the tent, did not require so much space as the Merarites, who had to transport the structure itself (iv. 21–33). The Kohathites carried the ark on their shoulders (iv. 15).

9. *the sanctuary.* Better *the holy things*, see on iv. 15. These were carried on poles, and not placed in wagons: cf. however 2 S. vi. 3.

10. *for the dedication.* The same word is used in the title to Ps. xxx.

13. *silver charger.* Cf. Ex. xxv. 29, xxxvii. 16. The weight would be equal to about 60 oz. Troy weight.

silver bowl. Cf. Ex. xxvii. 3. The weight is about 33 oz.

shekel of the sanctuary. See on iii. 47.

14. *spoon.* Heb. כַּף means *the palm of the hand*; some kind of hollow vessel is meant, LXX renders *θυίσκην*.

18 On the second day Nethanel the son of Zuar, prince of Issachar, did offer: 19 he offered for his oblation one silver charger, the weight thereof was an hundred and thirty *shekels*, one silver bowl of seventy shekels, after the shekel of the sanctuary; both of them full of fine flour mingled with oil for a meal offering; 20 one golden spoon of ten *shekels*, full of incense; 21 one young bullock, one ram, one he-lamb of the first year, for a burnt offering; 22 one male of the goats for a sin offering; 23 and for the sacrifice of peace offerings, two oxen, five rams, five he-goats, five he-lambs of the first year: this was the oblation of Nethanel the son of Zuar.

P[s]

24 On the third day Eliab the son of Helon, prince of the children of Zebulun: 25 his oblation was one silver charger, the weight thereof was an hundred and thirty *shekels*, one silver bowl of seventy shekels, after the shekel of the sanctuary; both of them full of fine flour mingled with oil for a meal offering; 26 one golden spoon of ten *shekels*, full of incense; 27 one young bullock, one ram, one he-lamb of the first year, for a burnt offering; 28 one male of the goats for a sin offering; 29 and for the sacrifice of peace offerings, two oxen, five rams, five he-goats, five he-lambs of the first year: this was the oblation of Eliab the son of Helon.

30 On the fourth day Elizur the son of Shedeur, prince of the children of Reuben: 31 his oblation was one silver charger, the weight thereof was an hundred and thirty *shekels*, one silver bowl of seventy shekels, after the shekel of the sanctuary; both of them full of fine flour mingled with oil for a meal offering; 32 one golden spoon of ten *shekels*, full of incense; 33 one young bullock, one ram, one he-lamb of the first year, for a burnt offering; 34 one male of the goats for a sin offering; 35 and for the sacrifice of peace offerings, two oxen, five rams, five he-goats, five he-lambs of the first year: this was the oblation of Elizur the son of Shedeur.

36 On the fifth day Shelumiel the son of Zurishaddai, prince of the children of Simeon: 37 his oblation was one silver charger, the weight thereof was an hundred and thirty *shekels*, one silver bowl of seventy shekels, after the shekel of the sanctuary; both of them full of fine flour mingled with oil for a meal offering; 38 one golden spoon of ten *shekels*, full of incense; 39 one young

bullock, one ram, one he-lamb of the first year, for a burnt offering; 40 one male of the goats for a sin offering; 41 and for the sacrifice of peace offerings, two oxen, five rams, five he-goats, five he-lambs of the first year: this was the oblation of Shelumiel the son of Zurishaddai. *P*[s]

42 On the sixth day Eliasaph the son of Deuel, prince of the children of Gad: 43 his oblation was one silver charger, the weight thereof was an hundred and thirty *shekels*, one silver bowl of seventy shekels, after the shekel of the sanctuary; both of them full of fine flour mingled with oil for a meal offering; 44 one golden spoon of ten *shekels*, full of incense; 45 one young bullock, one ram, one he-lamb of the first year, for a burnt offering; 46 one male of the goats for a sin offering; 47 and for the sacrifice of peace offerings, two oxen, five rams, five he-goats, five he-lambs of the first year: this was the oblation of Eliasaph the son of Deuel.

48 On the seventh day Elishama the son of Ammihud, prince of the children of Ephraim: 49 his oblation was one silver charger, the weight thereof was an hundred and thirty *shekels*, one silver bowl of seventy shekels, after the shekel of the sanctuary; both of them full of fine flour mingled with oil for a meal offering; 50 one golden spoon of ten *shekels*, full of incense; 51 one young bullock, one ram, one he-lamb of the first year, for a burnt offering; 52 one male of the goats for a sin offering; 53 and for the sacrifice of peace offerings, two oxen, five rams, five he-goats, five he-lambs of the first year: this was the oblation of Elishama the son of Ammihud.

54 On the eighth day Gamaliel the son of Pedahzur, prince of the children of Manasseh: 55 his oblation was one silver charger, the weight thereof was an hundred and thirty *shekels*, one silver bowl of seventy shekels, after the shekel of the sanctuary; both of them full of fine flour mingled with oil for a meal offering; 56 one golden spoon of ten *shekels*, full of incense; 57 one young bullock, one ram, one he-lamb of the first year, for a burnt offering; 58 one male of the goats for a sin offering; 59 and for the sacrifice of peace offerings, two oxen, five rams, five he-goats, five he-lambs of the first year: this was the oblation of Gamaliel the son of Pedahzur.

60 On the ninth day Abidan the son of Gideoni, prince of the

children of Benjamin: 61 his oblation was one silver charger, *P*[s] the weight thereof was an hundred and thirty *shekels*, one silver bowl of seventy shekels, after the shekel of the sanctuary; both of them full of fine flour mingled with oil for a meal offering; 62 one golden spoon of ten *shekels*, full of incense; 63 one young bullock, one ram, one he-lamb of the first year, for a burnt offering; 64 one male of the goats for a sin offering; 65 and for the sacrifice of peace offerings, two oxen, five rams, five he-goats, five he-lambs of the first year: this was the oblation of Abidan the son of Gideoni.

66 On the tenth day Ahiezer the son of Ammishaddai, prince of the children of Dan: 67 his oblation was one silver charger, the weight thereof was an hundred and thirty *shekels*, one silver bowl of seventy shekels, after the shekel of the sanctuary; both of them full of fine flour mingled with oil for a meal offering; 68 one golden spoon of ten *shekels*, full of incense; 69 one young bullock, one ram, one he-lamb of the first year, for a burnt offering; 70 one male of the goats for a sin offering; 71 and for the sacrifice of peace offerings, two oxen, five rams, five he-goats, five he-lambs of the first year: this was the oblation of Ahiezer the son of Ammishaddai.

72 On the eleventh day Pagiel the son of Ochran, prince of the children of Asher: 73 his oblation was one silver charger, the weight thereof was an hundred and thirty *shekels*, one silver bowl of seventy shekels, after the shekel of the sanctuary; both of them full of fine flour mingled with oil for a meal offering; 74 one golden spoon of ten *shekels*, full of incense; 75 one young bullock, one ram, one he-lamb of the first year, for a burnt offering; 76 one male of the goats for a sin offering; 77 and for the sacrifice of peace offerings, two oxen, five rams, five he-goats, five he-lambs of the first year: this was the oblation of Pagiel the son of Ochran.

78 On the twelfth day Ahira the son of Enan, prince of the children of Naphtali: 79 his oblation was one silver charger, the weight thereof was an hundred and thirty *shekels*, one silver bowl of seventy shekels, after the shekel of the sanctuary; both of them full of fine flour mingled with oil for a meal offering; 80 one golden spoon of ten *shekels*, full of incense; 81 one young bullock, one ram, one he-lamb of the first year, for a burnt

offering; 82 one male of the goats for a sin offering; 83 and for the sacrifice of peace offerings, two oxen, five rams, five he-goats, five he-lambs of the first year: this was the oblation of Ahira the son of Enan. *Ps*

84 This was the [1]dedication of the altar, in the day when it was anointed, [2]by the princes of Israel: twelve silver chargers, twelve silver bowls, twelve golden spoons: 85 each silver charger *weighing* an hundred and thirty *shekels*, and each bowl seventy: all the silver of the vessels two thousand and four hundred *shekels*, after the shekel of the sanctuary; 86 the twelve golden spoons, full of incense, *weighing* ten *shekels* apiece, after the shekel of the sanctuary: all the gold of the spoons an hundred and twenty *shekels*: 87 all the oxen for the burnt offering twelve bullocks, the rams twelve, the he-lambs of the first year twelve, and their meal offering: and the males of the goats for a sin offering twelve: 88 and all the oxen for the sacrifice of peace offerings twenty and four bullocks, the rams sixty, the he-goats sixty, the he-lambs of the first year sixty. This was the [1]dedication of the altar, after that it was anointed. 89 And when Moses went into the tent of meeting to speak with him, then he heard the Voice speaking unto him from above the mercy-seat that was upon the ark of the testimony, from between the two cherubim: and he spake unto him. *P*

[1] Or, *dedication-gift* [2] Or, *at the hands of*

89. This *v.* has no connexion with what precedes or what follows. The fragment is an instance of some specific fulfilment of the promise contained in Ex. xxv. 22.

when. That is *on a certain occasion* not *whenever*, the 'tenses' are not frequentative.

with him. There is no previous mention of Jehovah.

he spake unto him. The contents of the speech have been lost or displaced.

Chapters VIII.—X. 10.

Further Laws and Regulations.

The miscellaneous regulations and provisions here collected seem to have no binding link between them; nor, with the possible exception of (*d*) and (*e*), can we discover any reason to account for their position in regard either to one another or the matter which has preceded them.

(*a*) *The golden lampstand.* viii. 1–4.
(*b*) *The service of the Levites.* 5–26.
(*c*) *The supplementary Passover.* ix. 1–14.
(*d*) *The cloud over the Tabernacle.* 15–23.
(*e*) *The silver trumpets.* x. 1–10.

VIII. 1 And the LORD spake unto Moses, saying, 2 Speak *P*s unto Aaron, and say unto him, When thou [1]lightest the lamps, the seven lamps shall give light in front of the candlestick. 3 And Aaron did so; he [2]lighted the lamps thereof *so as to give light* in front of the candlestick, as the LORD commanded Moses. 4 And this was the work of the candlestick, [3]beaten work of gold; unto the base thereof, *and* unto the flowers thereof, it was beaten work: according unto the pattern which the LORD had shewed Moses, so he made the candlestick.

5 And the LORD spake unto Moses, saying, 6 Take the Levites

[1] Or, *settest up* [2] Or, *set up* [3] Or, *turned*

VIII. 1–4. Moses instructs Aaron concerning the lighting, or better the setting up, of the lamps. According to Ex. xxx. 7; Lev. xxiv. 1–4, the lamps burned during the night only; in later times some of the lamps were kept burning continuously (*Tamid* III. 9, VI. 1; Joseph. *Ant.* III. viii. 3). In the days of Samuel the lamps would seem to have gone out at night, and to have burned during the day (1 S. iii. 3). The temple of Solomon was lighted by separate candlesticks, five on each side (1 K. vii. 49). The subject of "Light in the Temple" inspired one of Keble's most beautiful poems: see *Lyra Apostolica* LX.

2. *Aaron.* So in Ex. xxx. 8 and Lev. xxiv. 3 where, as here, he is solely responsible: in Ex. xxvii. 21 and 2 Chr. xiii. 11, however, the office is shared with his sons. The charge is left undefined in Ex. xxv. 37 (M.T.), LXX and Syr. read Moses.

lightest. Better with mg. *settest up.*

seven lamps. So in Zech. iv. 2; Rev. iv. 5 &c. According to Josephus (*Ant.* III. vi. 7, vii. 7, *B.J.* V. v. 5) these symbolised the sun, moon, and planets: cf. Gunkel *Schöpfung und Chaos* p. 130.

candlestick. Better *lampstand.* The lamps were fixed upon it.

4. *beaten work*: mg. *turned.* Probably some kind of hammered work is meant, what is technically known as *repoussé* work.

the pattern. Cf. Ex. xxv. 9, 40.

5–26. This section deals with the service of the Levites; in *vv.* 5–22 with their purification and presentation, in *vv.* 23–26 with the period during which they are to minister. In regard to the former passage we have, as Kuenen pointed out, an attempt to supply a formal account of the institution of the Levites which shall correspond to the institution

from among the children of Israel, and cleanse them. 7 And P^s thus shalt thou do unto them, to cleanse them: sprinkle the water of expiation upon them, and let them cause a razor to pass over all their flesh, and let them wash their clothes, and cleanse themselves. 8 Then let them take a young bullock, and its meal offering, fine flour mingled with oil, and another young bullock shalt thou take for a sin offering. 9 And thou shalt present the Levites before the tent of meeting: and thou shalt assemble the whole congregation of the children of Israel: 10 and thou shalt present the Levites before the LORD: and the children of Israel shall lay their hands upon the Levites: 11 and R^s Aaron shall [1]offer the Levites before the LORD for a wave

[1] Heb. *wave*, and in vv. 13, 15, 21.

of the priests as recorded in Lev. viii. Most of the matter contained in this account is parallel with iii. 5–13, *vv.* 6 *b*–13 being the only new matter. The rules for the Levites were less stringent than those for the priests; they were merely to be sprinkled (*v.* 7) and not washed (Lev. viii. 6); and their ordinary garments to be cleansed (*v.* 7; cf. Ex. xix. 10, 14) not new ones provided (Lev. viii. 13). For the Levites, the negative process of cleansing was all that their office required; for the priests, there must be the positive sanctification (Ex. xxix. 1; Lev. viii. 12): see further Weinel *ZAW* (1898) pp. 35 f., 62 f.

There are in the section a number of repetitions; the command to cleanse is twice given (*vv.* 6 and 15), and the order for their 'waving' three times, to be performed once by Aaron (*v.* 11) and twice by Moses (*vv.* 13 and 15).

7. Moses as the agent of God cleanses the Levites, they then continue the process for themselves.

water of expiation. Here only. Sin is conceived of as something almost physical. Similar language survives in the Baptismal Service, though there it is spiritually interpreted.

cause a razor. So of the head of the Nazirite (vi. 9), and of the leper who is to be cleansed (Lev. xiv. 8). The Egyptian priests shaved their bodies every other day as a measure of purification: see Herod. II. 37.

wash their clothes. So of the congregation (Ex. xix. 14), and of the leper (Lev. xiv. 8 f.): see further Robertson Smith *Rel. Sem.*[2] pp. 452 f.

10. *lay their hands*. By their representatives presumably, perhaps the twelve princes. If the idea of substitution were present, the hands of the firstborn ought to have been placed on the heads of the Levites: cf. *v.* 12.

11. *offer*. Heb. *wave*, as in *vv.* 13, 15, 21. This action must have been performed in a symbolic manner, or else the word had lost its original force. There is possibly some connexion with the 'wave-breast' which

offering, [1]on the behalf of the children of Israel, that they may *R*[P] be to do the service of the LORD. 12 And the Levites shall lay *P*[s] their hands upon the heads of the bullocks: and offer thou the one for a sin offering, and the other for a burnt offering, unto the LORD, to make atonement for the Levites. 13 And thou shalt set the Levites before Aaron, and before his sons, and offer them for a wave offering unto the LORD. 14 Thus shalt thou separate the Levites from among the children of Israel: and the Levites shall be mine. 15 And after that shall the Levites go in to do the service of the tent of meeting: | and thou shalt *R*[P] cleanse them, and offer them for a wave offering. 16 For they are [2]wholly given unto me from among the children of Israel; instead of all that openeth the womb, even the firstborn of all the children of Israel, have I taken them unto me. 17 For all the firstborn among the children of Israel are mine, both man and beast: on the day that I smote all the firstborn in the land of Egypt I sanctified them for myself. 18 And I have taken the Levites instead of all the firstborn among the children of Israel. 19 And I have given the Levites as [3]a gift to Aaron and to his sons from among the children of Israel, to do the service of the children of Israel in the tent of meeting, and to make atonement for the children of Israel: that there be no plague among the children of Israel, [4]when the children of Israel come nigh unto the sanctuary. 20 Thus did Moses, and Aaron, and all the congregation of the children of Israel, unto the Levites: according unto all that the LORD commanded Moses touching the

[1] Or, *from* [2] See ch. iii. 9. [3] Heb. *Nethunim*, given.
[4] Or, *through the children of Israel coming nigh*

was offered to God at His altar, and then returned to Aaron and the priests, as God's representatives (Lev. vii. 30 f.).

16. See on iii. 9.

17. Cf. iii. 13.

19. *as a gift*. Heb. נְתֻנִים: cf. mg. *Nethunim*, that is *given*. In Ezra and Nehemiah the lowest grade of ecclesiastics are the Nethinim: see Batten on Ezra ii. 43 ff. in *ICC*.

to make atonement. The Levites come between God and the people, for the protection of the latter.

no plague. In i. 53, the Levites are to pitch round about the tent, to prevent the approach of any unauthorised person: here they are the servants of a duly consecrated order of ministers.

Levites, so did the children of Israel unto them. 21 And the Levites purified themselves from sin, and they washed their clothes; and Aaron offered them for a wave offering before the LORD; and Aaron made atonement for them to cleanse them. 22 And after that went the Levites in to do their service in the tent of meeting before Aaron, and before his sons: as the LORD had commanded Moses concerning the Levites, so did they unto them. R^P

23 And the LORD spake unto Moses, saying, 24 This is that which belongeth unto the Levites: from twenty and five years old and upward they shall go in [1]to wait upon the service in the work of the tent of meeting: 25 and from the age of fifty years they shall [2]cease waiting upon the work, and shall serve no more; 26 but shall minister with their brethren in the tent of meeting, to keep the charge, and shall do no service. Thus shalt thou do unto the Levites touching their charges.

IX. 1 And the LORD spake unto Moses in the wilderness of Sinai, in the first month of the second year after they were come P^s

[1] Heb. *to war the warfare in the work.*
[2] Heb. *return from the warfare of the work.*

21. *purified themselves*: lit. *unsinned themselves.* In view of the almost physical idea of sin which was current amongst the Hebrews, the nearest English equivalent is perhaps 'disinfect.'

22. *before.* Suggests *under the direction of*: cf. 1 Chr. xxiv. 6.

23–26. Levites were to serve between the ages of twenty-five and fifty (for the different traditions as to the age of service see on iv. 3), when they were to retire from compulsory work, though they were still permitted to give voluntary help.

24. *to wait upon the service.* LXX B paraphrases ἐνεργεῖν: cf. Armitage Robinson *Ephesians* pp. 242 f.

25. *fifty years.* This provision for the compulsory retirement of ecclesiastics at a certain age is an anticipation of modern demands in the same direction.

IX. 1–14. The people keep the passover on the appointed day. On complaint being made to Moses that certain men have been unable to partake in it, owing to defilement, or absence, he is ordered by Jehovah to institute a second or supplementary passover. This second passover is interesting as exhibiting a spirit of accommodation in the law, such as is often supposed to be lacking in it.

Jeroboam also ordained a feast, "like unto the feast that is in Judah" (1 K. xii. 32 f.), to be held on the fifteenth day of the eighth month; this was not a supplementary but a rival festival.

1. *in the first month.* The incident here related, like that in ch. vii,

out of the land of Egypt, saying, 2 Moreover let the children of Israel keep the passover in its appointed season. 3 In the fourteenth day of this month, [1]at even, ye shall keep it in its appointed season: according to all the statutes of it, and according to all the ordinances thereof, shall ye keep it. 4 And Moses spake unto the children of Israel, that they should keep the passover. 5 And they kept the passover in the first *month*, on the fourteenth day of the month, [1]at even, in the wilderness of Sinai: according to all that the LORD commanded Moses, so did the children of Israel. 6 And there were certain men, who were unclean by the dead body of a man, so that they could not keep the passover on that day: and they came before Moses and before Aaron on that day: 7 and those men said unto him, We are unclean by the dead body of a man: wherefore are we kept back, that we may not offer the oblation of the LORD in its appointed season among the children of Israel? 8 And Moses said unto them, Stay ye; that I may hear what the LORD will command concerning you. *P*[s]

[1] Heb. *between the two evenings.*

is earlier in time than the regulations which come before it, the census having been made in the second month (i. 1). The exact day is not mentioned, presumably it is earlier than the tenth day, since according to Ex. xii. 3 the lamb, though it was not slain until the fourteenth, had to be selected on that day.

2. *Moreover let &c.* Heb. reads *And let*: some utterance has evidently fallen out, and the translators inserted *Moreover* in order to fill up the gap. LXX supplies 'speak,' εἰπὸν καὶ κ.τ.λ.

3. *at even.* Heb. *between the two evenings.* The exact meaning of this phrase is uncertain. According to one tradition, it meant the time between the sunset and actual darkness; according to another, the time between the sun's declension and its setting. In later times the Pharisees supported the latter view, the Sadducees the former.

4. For the unusual construction in this *v.* see Ehrlich *op. cit.* p. 137.

5. *they kept the passover.* The first occasion since the original institution in Egypt.

6. *certain men.* It has been suggested that these were Mishael and Elizaphan who buried Nadab and Abihu within a week of this passover (Lev. x. 4 f.).

unclean by the dead. See on vi. 6.

could not keep. Cf. Lev. vii. 20.

before Aaron. Probably an insertion: cf. *him* in next *v.*

8. *that I may hear.* Other cases which were referred to divine direction are mentioned in xv. 34, xxvii. 5; Lev. xxiv. 12.

9 And the LORD spake unto Moses, saying, 10 Speak unto *Ps* the children of Israel, saying, If any man of you or of your generations shall be unclean by reason of a dead body, or be in a journey afar off, yet he shall keep the passover unto the LORD: 11 in the second month on the fourteenth day [1]at even they shall keep it; they shall eat it with unleavened bread and bitter herbs: 12 they shall leave none of it unto the morning, nor break a bone thereof: according to all the statute of the passover they shall keep it. 13 But the man that is clean, and is not in a journey, and forbeareth to keep the passover, that soul shall be cut off from his people: because he offered not the oblation of the LORD in its appointed season, that man shall bear his sin. 14 And if a stranger shall sojourn among you, and will keep the passover unto the LORD; according to the statute of the passover, and according to the ordinance thereof, so shall he do:

[1] Heb. *between the two evenings.*

10. *in a journey afar off.* Holzinger sees in this phrase the influence of post-exilic times, when the Jews had become traders, and were in the habit of making long journeys in connexion with their affairs. Wiener, on the other hand, sees in it a provision for a time when the whole nation will be settled in its own land, and none of them absent except on temporary journeys: *Essays &c.* p. 222. The original reference to Jehovah did not include anything beyond the case of persons defiled by the dead. This deferred passover might however be held for other reasons: see 2 Chr. xxx. 2, 15.

11. *with unleavened bread &c. with* is here represented by עַל in Heb.: so Ex. xii. 8.

12. *nor break a bone.* So in the original regulations (Ex. xii. 46). Cf. Ps. xxxiv. 20; Jn. xix. 36.

13. *cut off.* It is not certain whether this sentence was intended to be executed by divine or human means, whether death or merely excommunication would be the penalty. Outlawry was the punishment for certain crimes under the Code of Ḥammurabi (see S. A. Cook *The Laws of Moses &c.* pp. 51, 101, and 174). In ancient Arabia a murderer was either exiled (cf. Cain: Gen. iv. 12), or solemnly put to death. For modern Arab customs of outlawry see Jaussen *Coutumes des Arabes* pp. 226 ff., and Von Alois Musil *Arabia Petraea* III. pp. 60 and 335.

bear his sin. That is the consequences of the sin.

14. *a stranger.* Better *a sojourner* (גֵּר: *Gêr*), one living under the temporary protection of the tribe. A real *stranger* (תּוֹשָׁב: see on xxxv. 15) was not allowed to eat of the passover (Ex. xii. 45).

ye shall have one statute, both for the stranger, and for him that is born in the land. Ps

15 And on the day that the tabernacle was reared up the cloud covered the tabernacle, even the tent of the testimony: and at even it was upon the tabernacle as it were the appearance of fire, until morning. 16 So it was alway: the cloud covered it, and the appearance of fire by night. 17 And whenever the cloud was taken up from over the Tent, then after that the children of Israel journeyed: and in the place where the cloud abode,

one statute. The placing of the sojourner and the native on the same level is, according to Driver, a sign of the later legislation: "In P the *Gêr* is placed practically on the same footing as the native Israelite: he enjoys the same rights, and is bound by the same laws, whether civil, moral and religious, or ceremonial...the only specified distinctions being that the *Gêr*, if he would keep the passover, must be circumcised, and that an Israelite in servitude with him may be redeemed before the jubile, a privilege not granted in the case of the master's being an Israelite" (*Deut.* p. 165).

him that is born in the land: lit. *one arising* (i.e. from the soil), *an aborigine.* The word is seldom found outside H and P. In Ps. xxxvii. 35 it is used of a tree.

15–23. On the completion of the tabernacle the cloud descended upon it to be a guide to the Israelites, and also a symbol of the divine protection, both by day and by night. This cloud is mentioned in three of the main documents which make up the Pent., though with different features. In J the emphasis is upon the pillar of fire and cloud going before the people (xiv. 14; Ex. xiii. 21); in E there is no mention of the appearance of fire, nor does the cloud go in front of the people (xi. 25, xii. 5, 10); in P it stands over or upon the tabernacle, and appears as fire at night (*vv.* 15 ff., Ex. xxiv. 15 ff., xl. 34 ff.).

Delitzsch compares the promise to Esar-haddon: "I, Ishtar of Arbela, will make to ascend on thy right hand smoke, and on thy left hand fire" (*Babel and Bible* p. 174). Other writers quote the passage from Quintus Curtius describing the fiery cresset hung on a pole above the tent of Alexander the Great, "the flame of it was seen by night, and the smoke by day" (v. ii. 7). See further Frazer *Magic Art* II. p. 264, *FLOT* I. p. 16.

15. *the tent of the testimony.* This phrase occurs only here and in xvii. 7, 8, xviii. 2 in the Pent. The more usual expression is *the tent of meeting*: see on i. 1.

as it were...fire. Cf. Acts ii. 3. In Gen. xv. 17 God is represented under the forms of a smoking furnace and a flaming torch.

until morning. When daylight came the glow of the fire would no longer be discerned; the image may be taken from the cloud over a volcano which would exhibit the same phenomena.

there the children of Israel encamped. 18 At the commandment of the LORD the children of Israel journeyed, and at the commandment of the LORD they encamped: as long as the cloud abode upon the tabernacle they remained encamped. 19 And when the cloud tarried upon the tabernacle many days, then the children of Israel kept the charge of the LORD, and journeyed not. 20 And sometimes the cloud was a few days upon the tabernacle; then according to the commandment of the LORD they remained encamped, and according to the commandment of the LORD they journeyed. 21 And sometimes the cloud was from evening until morning; and when the cloud was taken up in the morning, they journeyed: or *if it continued* by day and by night, when the cloud was taken up, they journeyed. 22 Whether it were two days, or a month, or a year, that the cloud tarried upon the tabernacle, abiding thereon, the children of Israel remained encamped, and journeyed not: but when it was taken up, they journeyed. 23 At the commandment of the LORD they encamped, and at the commandment of the LORD they journeyed: they kept the charge of the LORD, at the commandment of the LORD by the hand of Moses. P^s

X. 1 And the LORD spake unto Moses, saying, 2 Make thee P

18. *At the commandment*: lit. *at the mouth*. This might seem to involve an oral command, in addition to the lifting of the cloud: probably, however, the word had lost its original force.

The picture of Israel's dependence on the divine guidance is a very beautiful one. At the same time we must not forget that, as Alexander Maclaren has well said, "The children of Israel in the wilderness, surrounded by miracle, had nothing which we do not possess....Their guidance came by this supernatural pillar; ours comes by the reality of which that pillar was nothing but a picture." *Expositions of Holy Scripture* (*Exodus &c.* p. 305).

20. *a few days*. Heb. ימים מספר is unusual; the final ם is due to dittography and should be omitted.

22. *a year*: lit. *days*. יָמִים so LXX ἡμέρας. An indefinite period is here meant evidently of a longer duration than a month. Gray rejects the rendering of R.V. which he terms 'unjustifiable.' But יָמִים clearly has the meaning of *a year* (R.V. *a full year*) in 1 S. xxvii. 7, so too in 1 S. i. 3; Jud. xvii. 10, and other passages.

X. 1–10. Moses is commanded to make two silver trumpets. These instruments were to be used for five different purposes, three of which were connected with the wanderings, the remaining two with the time after the settlement in Canaan: (1) the calling together of the whole congregation, *v.* 3; (2) or of the princes alone (*v.* 4); (3) for giving the

two trumpets of silver; of [1]beaten work shalt thou make them: *P*
and thou shalt use them for the calling of the congregation, and for the journeying of the camps. 3 And when they shall blow with them, all the congregation shall gather themselves unto thee at the door of the tent of meeting. 4 And if they blow but with one, then the princes, the heads of the thousands of Israel, shall gather themselves unto thee. 5 And when ye blow an alarm, the camps that lie on the east side shall take their journey.

[1] Or, *turned*

signal for marching (*vv.* 5 f.). In Canaan they were to be blown for a memorial before God, to remind Him of His people, whether (4) in war (*v.* 9), or (5) in the day of gladness and sacrifice (*v.* 10).

Since the march of the people was to be determined by the movement of the cloud (ix. 17) and to be announced by the sounding of the trumpet (*v.* 2) there is a possible connexion between this section and that which preceded it.

2. *trumpets.* There are in Heb. three words which are alike translated *trumpet* (*a*) שׁוֹפָר *shōphār*, (*b*) יוֹבֵל *jōbhēl*, and (*c*) חֲצֹצְרָה *ḥăẓōẓĕrāh.* The two former words are derived from roots which have some connexion with ram, for (*a*) cf. the Assyr. *shappar*(*u*) wild goat, and for (*b*) see the use in Jos. vi. 5 &c. It is probable that (*b*) remained always an actual 'horn,' whilst (*a*) retained its curved, hornlike shape even when made in metal. The word used in the present passage (*c*) is rendered by *BDB clarion*, and is described as "a long straight, slender metal tube, with flaring end." For a description of these various *trumpets* see Benziger *Heb. Arch.* pp. 276 f.; also Driver's illustrated note on Amos ii. 2 in *Camb. Bible.* Besides differing in appearance the instruments were used for different purposes; (*a*) was almost confined (except in late passages) to secular affairs, such as warfare; (*b*) was sounded at Sinai (Ex. xix. 13), and at Jericho (Jos. vi. 5), and survived to give its name to the fiftieth year, which was ushered in by its sounds (see on xxxvi. 4); (*c*) is a late word (mostly used in P, Chron. &c.), and except in two passages, Hos. v. 8 and 2 K. xi. 14 (= 2 Chr. xxiii. 13), is confined to religious purposes.

beaten work. See on viii. 4.

3. *they shall blow.* The sound of the trumpets for calling together the people, and the princes, was apparently different from that which gave the signal for journeying, though scholars are by no means agreed as to the exact nature of the distinction.

them. Both trumpets were to be used for summoning all the congregation, one only to summon the leaders.

all the congregation. Cf. Joel ii. 15 f. Certain assemblies of the Roman people were called together by the blast of a trumpet, and in much later times ordinances or proclamations of the council were made known by the sound of the trumpet in the Swiss towns (see Jussie *Levain du Calvinisme* p. 21).

5. *blow an alarm.* The word is used of a *war-cry* (Am. i. 14; Jer. xx.

6 And when ye blow an alarm the second time, the camps that *P* lie on the south side shall take their journey: they shall blow an alarm for their journeys. 7 But when the assembly is to be gathered together, ye shall blow, but ye shall not sound an alarm. 8 And the sons of Aaron, the priests, shall blow with the trumpets; and they shall be to you for a statute for ever throughout your generations. 9 And when ye go to war in your land *H* against the adversary that oppresseth you, then ye shall sound an alarm with the trumpets; and ye shall be remembered before the LORD your God, and ye shall be saved from your enemies. 10 Also in the day of your gladness, and in your set feasts, and in the beginnings of your months, ye shall blow with the trumpets over your burnt offerings, and over the sacrifices of your peace offerings; and they shall be to you for a memorial before your God: I am the LORD your God.

16 &c.), or a blast for a march as here (xxxi. 6; 2 Chr. xiii. 12), or for any religious shout (1 S. iv. 5 f. &c.).

7. *blow, but...not sound an alarm.* In Hos. v. 8 the two terms are used in parallelism. Procopius tells us that Belisarius distinguished the *charge* by sounding a metal trumpet (*ex aere crassiori*), the *retreat* by sounding on a leather one (*ex corio lignoque tenuissimo*). This distinction was made, he is careful to tell us, by his own advice: *De Bello Goth.* Bk. II. ch. 23.

8. *a statute for ever.* A phrase characteristic of P.

9. *in your land.* That is Canaan, the promised inheritance.

ye shall be remembered. Cf. Ps. xliv. 24 ff., and see on v. 15.

ye shall be saved. 2 Chr. xiii. 12 ff. is an illustration of the fulfilment of this promise.

10. In connexion with religious festivals there is to be a blowing of the trumpets[1]. A similar observance marked the spring festival of Cybele and Attis held at Rome; see Frazer *Adonis* I. pp. 267 f.

day of your gladness. Any special time of rejoicing, such as the completion of Solomon's temple (2 Chr. v. 12), or its cleansing under Hezekiah (2 Chr. xxix. 26).

set feasts. The regularly recurring feasts such as those specified in chh. xxviii.–xxix.; Lev. xxiii. The rendering of A.V. *solemn assemblies* may be compared with the Latin *sollemnis* which had originally the meaning of recurring or appointed.

memorial before your God. So the stones of memorial on the high priest's shoulders (Ex. xxviii. 12), and on the breastplate (Ex. xxviii. 29), were intended to bring the people to God's notice.

---

[1] In the Pent. no music, in the wider sense of the word, is ordered in connexion with the ritual.

PART II.

THE WANDERINGS IN THE WILDERNESS.

CHAPTERS X. 11—XXII. 1.

The present division of the book of Numbers has been described as a record of man's murmurings and sins, in contrast with the previous division, which contained the divine commands and provisions for the way. The period covered is probably intended to be the full forty years of the wanderings (xiv. 33), although the year of the final arrival at Kadesh has been omitted (see on xx. 1). This period is an almost complete blank except at its beginning and at its close, though perhaps some of the undated incidents may also belong to it[1]. The following are the main divisions:

(*a*) Incidents on the journey from Sinai to Paran. x. 11–xii. 16.
(*b*) The story of the spies and its sequel. xiii.–xiv.
(*c*) Various laws and regulations. xv.
(*d*) The story of Korah, Dathan and Abiram. xvi.–xvii.
(*e*) The ecclesiastical dues. xviii.
(*f*) Cleansing from defilement by the dead. xix.
(*g*) Incidents on the way to Moab. xx.–xxii. 1.

CHAPTERS X. 11—XII. 16.

INCIDENTS ON THE JOURNEY FROM SINAI TO PARAN.

A double account of the departure from Sinai is given (x. 11–28 and 29–33), and then various incidents on the journey to Paran are narrated. The subject of prophesying forms the main interest of chh. xi. and xii. and may be the link connecting them.

The departure from Sinai. x. 11–36.
The incidents of the journey. xi.
The vindication of Moses. xii.

CHAPTER X. 11–36.

The departure from Sinai.

Following the instructions of the cloud, the Israelites journey by their hosts to the wilderness of Paran. Hobab is invited to go with them in order to act as guide, although the ark is said to go before them to find a camping place.

---

[1] Several interesting attempts to reconstruct, in whole or in part, the wilderness period have been made in recent times; e.g. Van Hoonacker *Le Sacerdoce lévitique* p. 146; H. Wiener *Essays in Pent. Crit.* pp. 123ff. Such efforts, however, are not convincing as the data which we possess are insufficient for the task.

The address to Jehovah on the starting out and coming to a standstill of the ark.

(*a*) *The date of the setting forth.* 11–13.
(*b*) *The order of the march.* 14–28, 34.
(*c*) *Another account of the departure.* 29–33.
(*d*) *The prayers said over the ark.* 35 f..

11 And it came to pass in the second year, in the second month, on the twentieth day of the month, that the cloud was taken up from over the tabernacle of the testimony. 12 And the children of Israel set forward according to their journeys out of the wilderness of Sinai; and the cloud abode in the wilderness of Paran. 13 And they first took their journey according to the commandment of the LORD by the hand of Moses. 14 And in the first *place* the standard of the camp of the children of Judah set forward according to their hosts: and over his host was Nahshon the son of Amminadab. 15 And over the host of the tribe of the children of Issachar was Nethanel the son of Zuar. 16 And over the host of the tribe of the children of Zebulun was Eliab the son of Ḥelon. 17 And the tabernacle

P

*P*s

11. According to Ex. xix. 1 the children of Israel reached Sinai on the third month after leaving Egypt (the exact day has fallen out), some ten or eleven months must therefore have been spent before the sacred mount.

the cloud was taken up. This would be the first occasion on which the cloud gave directions for journeying: cf. ix. 17–22.

the tabernacle of the testimony. See on i. 50.

12. *the wilderness of Paran*[1]. The exact locality indicated by this term is not certainly known, most scholars however identify it with the desert *et-Tīh*; it seems however to have had a wider usage, and to have included the wilderness of Zin and Kadesh (cf. xiii. 26 with note). Later writers seem to have been led astray by the similarity of the names, and to have confused *Paran* with the *Wady Feiran* north of *Jebel Serbal* in the Sinai Peninsula (see Ptolemy V. XVII. 1; Eusebius *Onom.* 298; cf. also Greene *Hebrew Migration* p. 319; Meyer *IN* pp. 60 f.).

13. *first.* This has perhaps been repeated from the *v.* following. Dillmann thinks, probably correctly, that it draws attention to the first occasion upon which the guidance of the cloud was manifested.

14–16. Cf. ii. 3–9.

14. *Judah.* In Jud. i. 2, xx. 18, Judah is represented as leading the entry into Canaan.

---

[1] P. Haupt has recently suggested that the name means *glowing land* 'Glutland' *ZDMG* (1910), p. 714).

was taken down; and the sons of Gershon and the sons of Merari, who bare the tabernacle, set forward. 18 And the standard of the camp of Reuben set forward according to their hosts: and over his host was Elizur the son of Shedeur. 19 And over the host of the tribe of the children of Simeon was Shelumiel the son of Zurishaddai. 20 And over the host of the tribe of the children of Gad was Eliasaph the son of Deuel. 21 And the Kohathites set forward, bearing the sanctuary: and *the other* did set up the tabernacle against they came. 22 And the standard of the camp of the children of Ephraim set forward according to their hosts: and over his host was Elishama the son of Ammihud. 23 And over the host of the tribe of the children of Manasseh was Gamaliel the son of Pedahzur. 24 And over the host of the tribe of the children of Benjamin was Abidan the son of Gideoni. 25 And the standard of the camp of the children of Dan, which was the rearward of all the camps, set forward according to their hosts: and over his host was Ahiezer the son of Ammishaddai. 26 And over the host of the tribe of the children of Asher was Pagiel the son of Ochran. 27 And over the host of the tribe of the children of Naphtali was Ahira the son of Enan. 28 Thus were the journeyings of the children of Israel according to their hosts; and they set forward. *P*[s]

17. *Gershon...Merari.* According to ii. 17 the three families of the Levites in 'one camp' followed the 'camp of Reuben.' The present arrangement seems more suitable, as it allows an interval to elapse in which the tabernacle could be erected at each halting place, in readiness to receive the sacred objects borne by the Kohathites (cf. v. 21).

18–20. Cf. ii. 10–16.

20. *Deuel.* Read *Reuel* (cf. i. 14).

21. *the Kohathites.* See note on *v.* 17 above.

the sanctuary. Not the tabernacle, for this was carried by the Gershonites and Merarites. The holy things are meant: cf. iv. 15 mg. The ark would be included amongst these according to iii. 31 (P), though *v.* 33 places it in the front of the march.

22–28. Cf. ii. 18–31.

29–34. The following section is really parallel to *vv.* 1–28 (which contains P's account of the start from Sinai) and comes from JE, which is here resumed after being unused from Ex. xxxiv. 28. Some conservative critics think that Moses shewed lack of faith in desiring Hobab's assistance, when he had the 'cloud and pillar' for guide; they would see in *v.* 33 *b* an implied rebuke: it is simpler to suppose that the narratives came originally from different sources, one of which was ignorant

29 And Moses said unto Hobab, the son of Reuel the Midianite, Moses' father in law, We are journeying unto the place of which the LORD said, I will give it you: come thou with us, and we will do thee good: for the LORD hath spoken good concerning *J*

of the tradition of the ark as a guide. LXX and Targ. avoid the difficulty by rendering the tense of *v.* 31 as past instead of future.

The final reply of Hobab has not been preserved. Kittel considers that he accepted, but that the editor has omitted his consent, because it would have been at variance with Ex. xxviii. 27 (*Gesch. des Volkes Israels* I. p. 471 note 3). If חֹבָב הַקֵּינִי be read in Jud. i. 16 (with Moore and others) for בְּנֵי קֵינִי (i.e. *Hobab the Kenite* instead of *the children of the Kenite* which is not good Hebrew) there is evidence in support of his having gone at this juncture, though it is by no means conclusive (cf. Sayce *EHH* pp. 213 f.). Consistency can be given to the account by supposing that Hobab refused to accompany the people, but provided the ark as a substitute: cf. Gressmann *Mose und seine Zeit* p. 236.

29. *Hobab.* The meaning of this name has exercised the ingenuity of scholars, and various interpretations have been put forward. By Wellhausen it is connected with the Arabian deity *Ḥubâb serpent, Reste Arab. Heid.*[2] p. 146, whilst Cheyne sees in it merely another form of Jehonadab. Schwally thinks that the name was originally *Hobab-jah* or *Hobab-el* (*Semit. Kriegsalter.* I. p. 1); in support of this last theory may be mentioned the name Χωβαβιηλ, which is found in a Greek fragment of Enoch[1]. According to the present text of the Pent. *Hobab* has not previously been mentioned, his abrupt introduction here suggests that something has fallen out, or been omitted.

the son of Reuel. Gray thinks that Hobab was a member of the clan *Reuel*, and that his name has fallen out before *Reuel* in Ex. ii. 18. LXX renders the name Ῥαγουήλ: this name is given to one of the archangels in Enoch xx. 2–8[2].

the Midianite. In Jud. iv. 11 he is called the Kenite.

father in law. In Jud. iv. 11, also probably in i. 16, Hobab is referred to as the father-in-law of Moses, in E he is called Jethro (Ex. iii. 1, xviii. 1).

the place. Cf. Ex. xxxiii. 1; Jud. xi. 19.

for the LORD. There is special emphasis on the promise having been made by *Jehovah*, as if that would attract Hobab: cf. Ex. xviii. 11. If Jehovah had been the God of Jethro before His revealing Himself to Moses, this emphasis can readily be explained.

---

[1] Clay *Empire of the Amorites* p. 88 connects Hobab with Ḥumbaba in the Gilgamish Epic (m drops out very easily in Semitic languages), and also with Κομβαβος mentioned by Lucian *De Dea Syria* as the guardian of Queen Stratonike in the legend of the construction of the sanctuary at Hierapolis.

[2] Artapanus says that Raguel was ἄρχων of the country (quoted by Alex. Polyhistor, B.C. 140).

Israel. 30 And he said unto him, I will not go; but I will depart *J* to mine own land, and to my kindred. 31 And he said, Leave us not, I pray thee; forasmuch as thou knowest how we are to encamp in the wilderness, and thou shalt be to us instead of eyes. 32 And it shall be, if thou go with us, yea, it shall be, that what good soever the LORD shall do unto us, the same will we do unto thee.

33 And they set forward from the mount of the LORD three days' journey; and the ark of the covenant of the LORD went before them three days' journey, to seek out a resting place for them. 34 And the cloud of the LORD was over them by day, *P*s when they set forward from the camp.

30. *I will depart.* According to Ex. xviii. 27 (E) Jethro (= Hobab) has already departed.

land...kindred. Midian probably lay on the far side of the Gulf of Akaba and east of the Arabah (xxii. 4, xxv. 5 ff.; Gen. xxv. 6, xxxvi. 35; Jud. vi.–viii.). The march of the Israelites was due north-west, and if the traditional site of Sinai is retained, would coincide for the earlier stages with that of the route to Midian. From these data scholars have arrived at different conclusions, some would infer that the traditional site of Sinai is incorrect (Sayce *EHH* pp. 186 ff., 213); others that the interview here narrated took place when the point of dividing had been reached; others again that Hobab's clan—as distinguished from the other Midianites—were living in the Sinai peninsula.

31. *eyes.* LXX renders πρεσβύτης, Vulg. *doctor.* To those who know the desert all kinds of landmarks are recognisable such as would be quite unnoticed by a stranger. The Midianites knew the desert from their regular trips with merchandise (Gen. xxxvii. 28).

33. *the mount of the LORD.* Here only of the mount of the lawgiving. The phrase is used elsewhere of Zion (Is. ii. 3, xxx. 29; Mic. iv. 2; Ps. xxiv. 3). A similar phrase Mount of God is used of Horeb; this expression would seem to come from the Northern kingdom as it is found only in E (Ex. iii. 1, iv. 27, xviii. 5, xxiv. 13) and in 1 K. xix. 8.

went before them. According to the reading of the text the ark was always three days in front of the rest of the host, a position useless to those who came after and dangerous to the advance party. Gray and Baentsch think that the ark like the cloud moved of its own accord; Klostermann, Holzinger, and Kennedy, think that it was placed on a cart and drawn by oxen (cf. 1 S. vi. 7 ff.; 2 S. vi. 3). The statement in this *v.* cannot easily be reconciled with P's conception of the march as set forth in *vv.* 13–28.

34. This *v.* comes from P and is attached here but loosely.

the cloud...was over them. Not as a guide, but as a protection, perhaps from the heat. When Pope Zacharias went to interview the Lombard

35 And it came to pass, when the ark set forward, that Moses *J* said, Rise up, O LORD, and let thine enemies be scattered; and let them that hate thee flee before thee. 36 And when it rested, he said, Return, O LORD, unto the ten thousands of the thousands of Israel.

king Liutprand a cloud, by the special intercession of St Peter, hovered above his company to guard them from the sun's rays (see Milman *Hist. of Latin Christianity* III. p. 5).

35 f. This small section, like Gen. i. 1, was regarded, according to an ancient Jewish tradition, as being in itself a separate book of the law, these two making up the number of books to the sacred seven. It is the smallest section (*Parashah*) in the law, and contains only 85 Hebrew words: see *Yadayim* III. 5. The connexion with the wilderness period seems only slight. The rising up and going out of Jehovah against His enemies is the situation demanded, not the regular progress of the journeyings. Gressmann points out that the Philistines took their gods with them to battle (2 S. v. 21), as did the Carthaginians (Polybius 7–9. 2).

35. *when the ark.* Here also the ark is thought of as moving of itself.

O LORD. The ark is the throne of Jehovah according to Gressmann *Mose* p. 353 (cf. Dibelius *Die Lade Jahves* pp. 8 ff.), and He is addressed before the ark is moved; or perhaps the ark itself as the visible manifestation of His presence is addressed by His name.

let thine enemies &c. Quoted in Ps. lxviii. 1.

36. *Return.* This address is not suited to the conditions of the wanderings as described in *v.* 33; some settled sanctuary seems to be inferred. Baentsch refers the saying to the pre-Davidic period of Israel's sojourn in Canaan.

the thousands. See note on i. 16.

CHAPTER XI.

The incidents of the journey.

The incidents collected in this ch. come from JE; attempts to discriminate between the two sources and to carry the analysis a stage further are not really convincing. Two separate narratives, one concerning the murmurings because of the manna, and the other the appointment of the elders, seem to have been combined; Gray has endeavoured to separate them. Van Hoonacker would locate all the incidents (except *vv.* 6 *b*–9, 33 f.) at Taberah which he equates with Alush (xxxiii. 13) and places before the visit to Sinai. Gressmann (*Mose* pp. 161 ff.) connects *vv.* 11 f., 14–17, 24 *b*–30 with Jethro's visit to Moses described in Ex. xviii. (cf. Meyer *IN* p. 66). The contents of the section may be analysed as follows:

(*a*) *The murmurings at Taberah.* 1–3.
(*b*) *The murmurings because of the manna.* 4–10.
(*c*) *The complaint of Moses.* 11–15.
(*d*) *The divine response.* 16–24 *a*.
(*e*) *The appointment of the seventy elders.* 24 *b*–30.
(*f*) *The coming of the quails.* 31–35.

XI. 1 And the people were as murmurers, [1]*speaking* evil in the ears of the LORD: and when the LORD heard it, his anger was kindled; and the fire of the LORD burnt among them, and devoured in the uttermost part of the camp. 2 And the people cried unto Moses; and Moses prayed unto the LORD, and the fire abated. 3 And the name of that place was called [2]Taberah: because the fire of the LORD burnt among them. *E*

4 And the mixed multitude that was among them fell a *J*

[1] Or, which was *evil* [2] That is, *Burning.*

XI. 1–3. The reason for the murmuring at Taberah is not given, but the ordinary hardships of a desert march would doubtless provide many occasions for such outbursts. In P there is no mention of Taberah as a stopping-place, Kibroth-hattaavah being given as the first halt after leaving Sinai (xxxiii. 16), D mentions both places (Dt. ix. 22), putting Taberah first. Keil and Dillmann regard the two names as meaning one and the same place.

1. *as murmurers.* For the use of *as* see *G-K*[28] § 118 *x*.

speaking *evil.* Evil here (רע) means misfortune and should be connected with the previous words and 'speaking' omitted. Gray renders "as those complaining of misfortune."

the fire of the LORD. Probably an outburst of fire caused by lightning: cf. xvi. 35; Ex. xix. 18; 1 K. xviii. 38 &c. Loisy speaks of "a murderous explosion of that divine electricity which was diffused everywhere" (*Rel. of Isr.* p. 55).

2. *Moses prayed.* Cf. xxi. 7; Gen. xx. 17.

3. *Taberah.* Here and Dt. ix. 22 only. The site is unknown and perhaps the story is later than the name. Amongst the ancients places struck by lightning were regarded as unsafe or 'taboo' and often were enclosed by a wall.

4–10. Dissatisfied with the manna, and remembering the varied diet of Egypt, the children of Israel, probably incited by the rabble who had accompanied them, demand flesh to eat. A similar incident is recorded in Ex. xvi. (P) though there both quails and manna are given at one and the same time, whilst here (JE) some interval sufficiently long to cause the people to grow weary of the manna must have elapsed. P in its present form places the incident in the wilderness of Sin[1], JE apparently at Kibroth-hattaavah (*v.* 34) though no mention is made of any departure from Taberah (*v.* 3).

4. *the mixed multitude.* In Ex. xii. 38 (J) the presence of a *mixed multitude* at the departure from Egypt is noted though the word is different (ערב). McNeile suggests 'riff-raff' as a rendering of אספסף

[1] As Ex. xvi. 33 f. presupposes the erection of the Tent of Meeting it must originally have come later in the narrative (see Baentsch *ad loc.*, and cf. S. A. Cook in *JQR* (1906) pp. 742 ff.).

lusting: and the children of Israel also wept again, and said, *J*
Who shall give us flesh to eat? 5 We remember the fish, which
we did eat in Egypt for nought; the cucumbers, and the melons,
and the leeks, and the onions, and the garlick: 6 but now our

which is used here. Other passages in the Hexateuch recognise the presence of strangers in the host (Dt. xxix. 11; Jos. viii. 35). Allegorically interpreted *the mixed multitude* represents that element of decay and corruption which finds its place in even the purest of spiritual movements: cf. Mt. xiii. 24 ff., 47 ff.

fell a lusting. So Ps. lxxviii. 29, xvi. 14; 1 Cor. x. 6.

wept. The Israelites are frequently represented as so doing: cf. xiv. 1; Dt. i. 45, xxxiv. 8; Jud. ii. 4, xx. 23, 26, xxi. 2. It must be remembered that ancient peoples shewed their emotions much more freely than modern Britons: in Homer and Virgil the heroes often give way to their feelings in this way (in the *Aeneid lacrimae* alone occurs 43 times), and even Caesar could say of his soldiers *neque interdum lacrimas tenere poterant* (*De Bell. Gall.* I. 39); cf. also Cicero *In Cat.* IV. 3.

again. There is no previous mention of weeping. LXX renders καθίσαντες reading וַיֵּשְׁבוּ for וַיָּשֻׁבוּ.

Who shall give us flesh. The Heb. idiom would better be represented by *would that we had flesh.* The shortage of flesh is hard to understand since according to J the people were rich in cattle (Ex. xii. 32, 38, xvii. 3, xix. 13, xxxiv. 3; Num. xiv. 33, xxxii. 1), and quite obviously the sacrificial system of P requires a large number. A possible explanation is that the offering of beasts in sacrifices had used up the people's supplies, but no hint of this is anywhere given.

5. *We remember.* The same longing for the luxuries of Egypt is shewn in Ex. xvi. 3. Memory in looking back not seldom delights in what was pleasant, forgetting what was harsh and burdensome.

the fish. Fish were very common in Egypt: cf. Ex. vii. 21; Is. xix. 8; Herod. II. 92.

cucumbers. Cf. Is. i. 8. A favourite food in hot climates. The vegetable here referred to is probably a variety of melon *Cucumis chate*: see Löw *Aram. Pflanzennamen* 278, 330, 408.

melons. Here only in O.T. but frequent in later Heb. Löw (*op. cit.* 297) identifies them with *Cucumis citrullus.*

leeks. Heb. *grass.* In Aram. the cognate word occasionally has the meaning *leeks.* Pliny speaks of these vegetables in connexion with Egypt, *Hist. Nat.* XIX. 33. The botanical name is *Allium porrum*: see Löw *op. cit.* 169.

onions. Herodotus tells us that *onions* and leeks were common food amongst labourers (II. 125). Sayce questions the accuracy of the statement but regards it as a testimony to their popularity (*Egypt of Hebs. &c.* p. 258).

garlick. Löw identifies the cognate Aramaic word with *Allium sativum*

soul is dried away; there is nothing at all: we have nought save *J* this manna to look to. 7 And the manna was like coriander seed, and the [1] appearance thereof as the appearance of bdellium. 8 The people went about, and gathered it, and ground it in mills, or beat it in mortars, and seethed it in pots, and made cakes of it: and the taste of it was as the taste of [2] fresh oil. 9 And when the dew fell upon the camp in the night, the manna

[1] Heb. *eye*. [2] Or, *cakes baked with oil*

(*op. cit.* 336)[1]. In the Zenjirli Inscription (*NSI* No. 61) Panammu thanks Hadad for a land of wheat and of *garlick*.

7. *the manna*. The story of the *manna* probably has some natural foundation, and from the description given here and in Ex. xvi., the true source is not difficult to find. Certain trees (e.g. *Tamarix gallica*) have exudations which arise during the night and fall to the earth, and when the sun's heat touches them melt away. To those ignorant of the manner of its production the *manna* would seem to have fallen from heaven. See further the articles in *HDB* and *Enc. Bib.*, also the additional information in McNeile's note on Ex. xvi. 15.

coriander seed. So Ex. xvi. 31 and not elsewhere. The so-called seed (really fruit) of the coriander is about the size of a peppercorn (*Enc. Bib.*).

the appearance. Heb. *the eye*. This idiom is not infrequent: cf. Lev. xiii. 55 (of leprosy); Ez. x. 9 (of the wheels); Zech. v. 6 &c. The rendering of A.V. *colour* has no support.

bdellium. Here and Gen. ii. 12 only. LXX evidently thought that the stone was meant and renders κρυστάλλου. The reference is of course to the transparent gum which is common in the East (see Pliny *Hist. Nat.* XII. 9). Peiser claims to have found a cognate word in the Babylonian contract-tablets (*ZAW* XVII. 347 f.).

8. *mills...mortars*. As amongst the Romans the use of *mortars* was earlier than that of *mills*: see *Enc. Bib.* 3091 ff., 3201 ff., and Driver on Dt. xxiv. 6.

taste. According to Wisd. xvi. 20 the manna had "the virtue of every pleasant savour, and agreeing to every taste," i.e. it tasted to each man like his favourite food. St Augustine refers to the tradition in *Retractationes* II. 20 but knows of no other reference to it but this passage from Wisdom. The tradition would seem to ignore *v.* 6 above.

fresh oil. Heb. לְשַׁד (*lĕshad*) here and Ps. xxxii. 4 only. In the latter passage it has the meaning *fat*. Baentsch compares Arab. *lasada* = dainty.

9. *when the dew fell*. The writer does not suggest any supernatural origin for the manna: cf. Ex. xvi. 5 ff.; Dt. viii. 3.

---

[1] The detailed notice of vegetables is quite in accordance with modern Semitic usage. Miss Lowthian Bell has observed that the Arabs though they do not trouble to distinguish between the different varieties of flowers have separate names for the smallest vegetable (*Syria, the Desert and the Sown* p. 18).

fell [1]upon it. 10 And Moses heard the people weeping throughout their families, every man at the door of his tent: and the anger of the LORD was kindled greatly; and Moses was displeased. 11 And Moses said unto the LORD, Wherefore hast thou evil entreated thy servant? and wherefore have I not found favour in thy sight, that thou layest the burden of all this people upon me? 12 Have I conceived all this people? have I brought them forth, that thou shouldest say unto me, Carry them in thy bosom, as a nursing-father carrieth the sucking child, unto the land which thou swarest unto their fathers? 13 Whence should I have flesh to give unto all this people? for they weep unto me, saying, Give us flesh, that we may eat. 14 I am not able to bear all this people alone, because it is too heavy for me. 15 And if thou deal thus with me, kill me, J

[1] Or, *with*

10. *Moses heard &c.* The narrative apparently goes back to *v.* 6, but some obscurity clings to the *v.*, possibly *the anger of the LORD &c.* should be omitted, otherwise *and Moses was displeased* is an anti-climax.

11–15. Overborne by the continual complaining of the people the patience of Moses comes to an end and he turns to God in expostulation. We might not unnaturally have expected a rebuke of the Israelites, but as Baentsch points out the situation is quite in accordance with psychological knowledge. Bacon *Triple Trad.* pp. 139 ff., 168 would place the passage after Ex. xxx. 1–3 when Jehovah refused to accompany the people into the wilderness: this suggestion meets with Gray's approval.

11. *evil entreated.* So Dt. i. 9, 12; 1 K. iii. 8 f.

thy servant. A periphrasis characteristic of J: cf. Gen. xviii. 3, 5.

found favour. Cf. Ex. xxx. 12, xxxiv. 9 &c. Another phrase common in J.

12. *Have I conceived.* The *I* is emphatic. Moses reminds the LORD that He is the begetter of Israel (cf. Dt. xxxii. 18) who is therefore Jehovah's son (cf. Hos. xi. 1). In Ex. xxxii. 7 Jehovah speaks of Israel as 'thy people' putting the responsibility upon Moses.

in thy bosom &c. Cf. the phrases used of the divine protection and care in Dt. i. 31; Is. xl. 11, xlvi. 3; Hos. xi. 3.

nursing-father. Cf. Is. xlix. 23.

13. *Whence should I &c.* Cf. the question of the disciples in Mk. viii. 4; Mt. xv. 33; (cf. John vi. 5).

14. *I am not able...alone.* Quoted with a small omission in Dt. i. 9 but in a slightly different setting: a good illustration of D's manner of treating earlier sources: see Driver *Deut.* pp. 9 f.

15. *kill me...out of hand.* Cf. Ex. xxxii. 32 and the despair of Elijah (1 K. xix. 4). Holzinger compares Jer. xv. 15 ff., xx. 7 ff.

I pray thee, out of hand, if I have found favour in thy sight; *J*
and let me not see my wretchedness.

16 And the LORD said unto Moses, Gather unto me seventy *E*
men of the elders of Israel, whom thou knowest to be the elders of the people, and officers over them; and bring them unto the tent of meeting, that they may stand there with thee. 17 And I will come down and talk with thee there: and I will take of the spirit which is upon thee, and will put it upon them; and they shall bear the burden of the people with thee, that thou bear it not thyself alone. 18 And say thou unto the people, *J*
Sanctify yourselves against to-morrow, and ye shall eat flesh: for ye have wept in the ears of the LORD, saying, Who shall

see my wretchedness. Better *gaze upon* cf. Gen. xxi. 16, xliv. 34 where the same use is found: see *G-K*[28] § 119 *k*.

16–24 *a*. In reply to the expostulations of Moses Jehovah promises to give him the help of seventy elders to share his burdens: a message is also sent to the people that flesh in plenty shall be provided for them. The connexion of the two parts of Jehovah's reply is not very close and probably the conjunction is artificial.

16. *seventy men.* The number of the nations mentioned in Gen. x., of our Lord's messengers (Lk. x. 1–16) and also in all probability of the Sanhedrin and of various other Jewish councils (see Joseph. *Bell. Jud.* II. xx. 5, IV. v. 4). In Enoch lxxxix. 59 seventy shepherds are mentioned.

the elders. Amongst primitive peoples age was often the main qualification for any office of government, such was the case among the Greeks and Romans; and also amongst our Saxon forefathers, the word alderman being really elder (cf. Stubbs *Constitutional Hist.* I. p. 178). For further details concerning the elders in Israel see Driver's note on Dt. xix. 12, also Nowack *Arch.* I. pp. 300 ff.; Benzinger *Arch.* §§ 41 ff.

officers. The same word is used in Ex. v. where it refers to the Israelite foremen working under Egyptian overseers.

17. *come down.* Cf. Gen. xi. 5, xviii. 21; Ex. iii. 8.

take of the spirit. That the elders received of the spirit which was upon Moses, and not a gift direct from God, shews their subordination: Moses alone had direct relations with Jehovah: cf. Ex. xxxiii. 7 ff. So men recognised that the spirit of Elijah was upon Elisha (2 K. ii. 15). Hooker makes use of this passage in discussing the grace received in Ordination (*Eccles. Pol.* Bk. v. lxxvii. 8).

thou bear it not...alone. Moses cried to God for divine aid and God replied by giving him the help of human agents.

18. *Sanctify yourselves.* As for a sacrifice: cf. Gen. xxxv. 2; Ex. xix. 10 f. In Jer. xii. 3 the word means prepare for slaughter, and Rashi would take it in the same sense here.

give us flesh to eat? for it was well with us in Egypt: therefore the LORD will give you flesh, and ye shall eat. 19 Ye shall not eat one day, nor two days, nor five days, neither ten days, nor twenty days; 20 but a whole month, until it come out at your nostrils, and it be loathsome unto you: because that ye have rejected the LORD which is among you, and have wept before him, saying, Why came we forth out of Egypt? 21 And Moses said, The people, among whom I am, are six hundred thousand footmen; and thou hast said, I will give them flesh, that they may eat a whole month. 22 Shall flocks and herds be slain for them, to suffice them? or shall all the fish of the sea be gathered together for them, to suffice them? *J*

23 And the LORD said unto Moses, Is the LORD's hand waxed short? now shalt thou see whether my word shall come to pass unto thee or not. 24 And Moses went out, and told the people the words of the LORD: | and he gathered seventy men of the elders of the people, and set them round about the Tent. 25 And the LORD came down in the cloud, and spake unto him, and *E*

20. *a whole month.* Lit. *a month of days,* the same phrase occurs in Gen. xxix. 14 and a similar one in Dt. xxi. 13; 2 K. xv. 13.

until it come out. Vigorous if unpleasant language is used.

out of Egypt. See on xiv. 4.

23. *hand waxed short.* Cf. Is. l. 2, lix. 1[1].

my word. "A divine word was thought to possess a certain real and independent existence; once uttered it pursued its own course" (Gray). Cf. Is. lv. 11.

24 *b*–30. Jehovah fulfils His promise to Moses and takes of his spirit and places it upon the seventy elders who thereupon prophesy: cf. the effect of the gift of the Spirit at Pentecost (Acts ii. 4). Two others, Eldad and Medad, who had remained in the camp, also prophesied to the indignation of Moses' servant Joshua. Two points seem to stand out in this narrative; the importance attached by primitive people to the prophetic frenzy, and the teaching that God's grace is not confined to certain offices and rites; this last point is of great importance in view of the narrow and rigid ideas of the priesthood held by later Judaism.

24 *b*. *gathered.* Nothing is said, either here or in *v.* 16, of the method of selection beyond the fact that those chosen were to be known by Moses as elders of the people.

25. *in the cloud.* See on ix. 15–23.

---

[1] Some interesting remarks, accompanied by illustrations, on the 'hand of God' are to be found in Nielsen *Die altarab. Mondreligion* p. 155.

took of the spirit that was upon him, and put it upon the seventy *E* elders: and it came to pass, that, when the spirit rested upon them, they prophesied, but they did so no more. 26 But there remained two men in the camp, the name of the one was Eldad, and the name of the other Medad: and the spirit rested upon them; and they were of them that were written, but had not gone out unto the Tent: and they prophesied in the camp.

put it upon. Presumably by the outstretched hand: cf. xxvii. 18 with note.

rested. So in 2 K. ii. 15; Is. xi. 2.

they did so no more. The rendering of A.V. *did not cease* is misleading. The prophetic frenzy came upon them and after they had recovered from it they prophesied no more for "their proper function was to be that of government not prophesying" (Speaker's Commentary). The same phrase is used in Dt. v. 22.

26. *Eldad...Medad.* Nothing is known of these two men though there is a reference to a Book of Eldad and Modat (sic) in *The Shepherd of Hermas* Vis. II. iii. 4, and it occurs amongst the list of Apocryphal books of N.T. in the *Athanasian Synopsis* and in the *Stichometry of Nicephorus.* Some think that the quotation from 'the prophetic word' in 2 Clem. XI. 2 ff. (referred to as 'Scripture' in 1 Clem. XXIII. 3 f.) is also from the same lost book. Holzinger suggests that the original forms were Elidad (cf. xxxiv. 21) and Elmodad; the latter form receives support from LXX and Sam. which both have Modad, and Hommel compares the name Mūdadi found in Babylonian contract tablets (*Altisr. Ueberlief.* 75, 112). Wellhausen (*Reste Arab. Heident.*[2] pp. 14 ff.) mentions an Arabic deity Wadd which may underlie the two names (which if Holzinger's suggestion is adopted will come from the same root). This deity is worshipped by the Sabeans, and the name Modad has been found amongst them (*ZDMG* XXXVII. pp. 13, 18). For the assonance Gray compares Jabel and Jubal (Gen. iv. 20 f.), Gog and Magog (Ez. xxxviii. 2 &c.), Hārūt and Mārūt (Koran II. 96), an additional instance may be adduced in Hadūdmadūd who is expected to appear at the end of the world by the Yezidis: see Lowthian Bell *Syria &c.* p. 293.

and they were of them that were written. It is interesting to notice that there was a written register: cf. xxxiii. 2; Jud. viii. 14; and the present writer's note on Jer. xxxvi. 1–8. The words however are probably a gloss inserted by an ecclesiastically minded scribe (*Enc. Bib.* 1256).

but had not gone out &c. Perhaps they were unclean (cf. 1 S. xx. 26) —though in this case the gift of the spirit seems strange—or unwilling. Ruskin thinks they were occupied with special labours: "don't try to be a prophet; go on quietly with your hard camp-work, and the spirit will come to you in the camp, as it did to Eldad and Medad, if you are appointed to have it" (*Modern Painters* Pt. v. ch. II. § 4). Certain MSS. of LXX—Holmes and Parsons 16, 52, 73, 77 and 131 (first hand)—omit the words.

27 And there ran a young man, and told Moses, and said, Eldad *E* and Medad do prophesy in the camp. 28 And Joshua the son of Nun, the minister of Moses, [1]one of his chosen men, answered and said, My lord Moses, forbid them. 29 And Moses said unto him, Art thou jealous for my sake? would God that all the LORD'S people were prophets, that the LORD would put his spirit upon them! 30 And Moses gat him into the camp, he and the

[1] Or, *from his youth*

28. *Joshua...the minister of Moses.* He stood towards Moses in much the same relationship as Samuel to Eli, Elisha to Elijah. For the problems concerning Joshua the minister of Moses and Joshua the conqueror see Additional Note below.

one of his chosen men. Heb. מִבְּחֻרָיו: the rendering of the mg. *from his youth* is to be preferred.

forbid them. The disciple is more concerned for the honour of his master than the master himself[1]: cf. Mk. ix. 38 f.; Lk. ix. 49. When Erasmus printed his text of N.T. in 1515, and published it immediately, he anticipated the publication of the great Complutensian edition which had been in print the year before but whose publication was delayed. Cardinal Ximenes who was responsible for the edition, on hearing Stunica, one of the scholars working under him, belittle Erasmus' achievement, rebuked him saying: "Would that all might thus prophesy; if you can do better work, produce it; but don't condemn the industry of another."

29. In *vv.* 11 ff. Moses is exhibited to us in a bad light, this *v.* shews his true nobility of character: for a similar expression of it cf. Dt. i. 9 ff.

would God &c. Cf. Bishop Andrewes: "I wish with all my heart (as did Moses) that all God's people were prophets: but till they be so, I wish they may not prophesie; no more would Moses neither" (Sermon XI *Of the Holy Ghost*: quoted by Goudge on 1 Cor. xiv. 31).

put his spirit. The same wish underlies the great prophecy in Joel ii. 28 ff. (M.T. III. 1 ff.).

ADDITIONAL NOTE ON XI. 28.

Joshua.

In O.T. Joshua appears in three characters: as one of the spies (Num. xiii. 8 a passage from P in which he is called Hoshea[2]); as the servant of Moses (Num. xi. 28); and finally as a great soldier and the leader of Israel in the

---

[1] According to the Talmud Joshua himself aspired to some kind of superiority over the elders: "Moses said to Joshua, You will act with the elders: God said to Joshua, One leader and not two leaders at the same time." *Sanhedrin* 8 *a*.

[2] It has been pointed out by Ehrlich *Randglossen* pp. 156 ff. that הושע is the oldest form of the name, being used up to 2 K. xvii. 1; in Hag. and Zech. the form יהושע is used, and latest of all, in Ezra and Neh. ישוע appears.

conquest of Palestine. Have we here the amalgamation of a series of different traditions?

Joshua seems never to have aroused any great enthusiasm amongst the Jews, if the neglect of him in later literature is any criterion, being completely overshadowed by Moses; P, it should be remembered, places him in a position of inferiority to the head of the ecclesiastical organisation. It is also very doubtful whether he found any place in the earliest traditions of Ex. and Num.[1]

In the story of the spies in its original form, Caleb was the only survivor (Num. xiv. 24); the necessities of the case seem to have led to Joshua also being included, since he was to lead Israel into Palestine. As a leader he seems to have been connected with the House of Joseph only, or at most with the combination of tribes which settled in Central Palestine. Budde would read Joshua for Jehovah in Jud. i. 22 and so find a definite statement to this effect; but the emendation is barely convincing in view of Jehovah in *v.* 19.

Certain critics regard Joshua as earlier than Moses, considering that the invasion from the East of Jordan corresponded with the activity of the Ḫabiru or SA.GAZ. Moses on their view arose much later, and, forming a confederation in the Negeb, invaded Palestine from the South thus making the beginnings of Judah[2].

Joshua may have arisen owing to a natural desire to provide Moses with attendants and to name the chief of them, and then to regard him as his leader's successor (see *Enc. Bib.* 2600); his name was certainly a very suitable one for the conqueror of Palestine.

Against these arguments, however, must be placed the strong Israelite tradition in favour of the historical existence of the Ephraimite leader: cf. Wiener *Essays in Pent. Crit.* p. 142.

elders of Israel. 31 And there went forth a wind from the LORD, *J* and brought quails from the sea, and let them fall [1]by the camp, about a day's journey on this side, and a day's journey on the

[1] Or, *over*

31–35. The coming of the quails and the plague which followed. The name of the place is given as Kibroth-hattaavah. The narrative of *vv.* 18–24 *a* is here resumed.

31. *a wind.* As in the flood-story according to P (Gen. viii. 1), and in J's account of the bringing up and dispersal of the locusts in Egypt (Ex. x. 13, 19).

quails. These birds still fly northward over the Mediterranean each spring and return again early in the autumn. The description of them in this passage is in full accord with what is known of their habits at the present time and evidently comes from a source well acquainted with them.

from the sea. That is from the Gulf of Akaba.

let them fall. Quails are soon exhausted in their flight and fall to the ground.

---

[1] Cf. S. A. Cook *NOTH* p. 126.

[2] See an article by T. J. Meek "A Proposed Reconstruction of Early Heb. Hist." in *AJTh* XXIV. pp. 209 ff.

other side, round about the camp, and about two cubits above the face of the earth. 32 And the people rose up all that day, and all the night, and all the next day, and gathered the quails: he that gathered least gathered ten homers: and they spread them all abroad for themselves round about the camp. 33 While the flesh was yet between their teeth, ere it was chewed, the anger of the LORD was kindled against the people, and the LORD smote the people with a very great plague. 34 And the name of that place was called [1]Kibroth-hattaavah: because there they buried the people that lusted. 35 From Kibroth-hattaavah the people journeyed unto Hazeroth; and they abode at Hazeroth. J

[1] That is, *The graves of lust.*

two cubits. That is about three feet.

32. *ten homers.* A homer was about ten bushels.

spread them. In order to cure them, a practice known to the ancient Egyptians: cf. Herod. II. 77.

33. *ere it was chewed.* Heb. יִכָּרֵת: lit. *it was cut off.* The rendering is a guess from the context, Gray rejects it in favour of LXX, Vulg. &c. *ran short.*

the LORD smote. The various plagues which befell the people in the wilderness were all the result of rebellion (cf. xvi. 49, xxv. 9); the LORD had promised freedom from disease in return for obedience (Ex. xv. 26).

34 f. Topographical notes connecting the incident with Kibroth-hattaavah and recording the next stage on the journey.

34. *Kibroth-hattaavah.* LXX Μνήματα τῆς ἐπιθυμίας. Palmer would identify the site with *Erweis el Ebeirig* where he found remains of a large camp with graves outside. The Arabs have a legend that these remains are the relics of a caravan of pilgrims which was afterwards lost in the wilderness (*Desert of the Exodus* pp. 257 ff.). The identification is not however generally accepted. *Erweis el Ebeirig* is a day's march from *'Ain-Hudherah* which Palmer would identify with Hazeroth.

35. *Hazeroth.* *'Ain-Hudherah* (better *'Ain el-Ḥadra*) according to Palmer (*op. cit.* pp. 260 ff., 313 ff.) and Burckhardt *Syrien* p. 808. Dillmann and others including Gray question the identification.

CHAPTER XII.

The vindication of Moses.

Moses is attacked by members of his own family, the LORD sanctions the uniqueness of his position and punishes Miriam. E. Meyer, who regards the legend that Moses had a sister Miriam as late, and possibly arising through a grave of Miriam being found at Kadesh, finds in this story an allegorical account of a controversy for precedence between different ranks of the priesthood (*IN* pp. 92 ff.).

Women take a very high place in Hebrew story especially as prophetesses, though there is no real trace of their having been priestesses as in other ancient religious systems. That women acted as ministers at Hebrew sanctuaries, probably in some inferior, and often degrading, capacity, we know from Ex. xxxviii. 8 and 1 S. ii. 22 where the Heb. for *served* (צבא) is a technical term (see on iv. 3).

(*a*) *The attack on Moses.* 1–3.
(*b*) *The divine vindication and punishment.* 4–10.
(*c*) *Moses intercedes for Miriam.* 11–16.

XII. 1 And Miriam and Aaron spake against Moses because of the Cushite woman whom he had married: for he had married a Cushite woman. 2 And they said, Hath the LORD indeed *E*

XII. 1–3. Miriam (and Aaron) murmur against Moses questioning the lawfulness of his privileged position. The reason for their complaint alleged in *v.* 1 seems pointless unless the narrator intended to represent the whole affair as a product of female jealousy.

1. *Miriam and Aaron. Miriam*[1] is referred to in Ex. xv. 20 as the sister of Aaron, Moses being unmentioned. Muhammed placed her among his four perfect women, together with the Blessed Virgin, the prophet's own wife Khadija, and his favourite daughter, Fatima.

spake. The verb in the original is in the fem. sing. which suggests that Aaron is an afterthought; the fact that Miriam alone is punished points in the same direction.

against Moses. Though Aaron is stated to be older than Moses in Ex. vii. 7 Baentsch infers from Ex. ii. 1 f. that Moses was the firstborn of Amram and Jochebed.

Cushite woman. LXX, Syr., Vulg. render *Ethiopian* but see below. In Ex. ii. 21 Moses marries Zipporah the daughter of the priest of Midian, and in Ex. xviii. 5 f. after Moses had left her with her father she is brought to him by Jethro. The question arises as to the identity of the Cushite woman and Zipporah. Two objections against it must be considered, the difference between Cush and Midian, and the unlikelihood of Miriam suddenly blaming her brother for a marriage which had taken place so many years before. It is possible to dispose of the first objection, for though Cush generally refers to Ethiopia (Josephus has built up on this identification a story of Moses and the daughter of the king of Ethiopia *Ant.* II. x.), yet it also refers to a district east of Babylon (see Driver on Gen. x. 8), and in addition to a North Arabian people who appear in the inscriptions as the Kusi (see *Enc. Bib.* 'Cush'). This last identification has been accepted by Bacon *Triple Trad.* pp. 9 f. and other scholars and is quite a possible way of meeting the above

---

[1] Margoliouth thinks that *Miriam*=*love* or *desire*: *Schweich Lectures* p. 15. He bases his opinion on the use of רם in Liḥyani inscriptions.

spoken only [1]with Moses? hath he not spoken also [1]with us? *E*
And the LORD heard it. 3 Now the man Moses was very meek, above all the men which were upon the face of the earth. 4 And the LORD spake suddenly unto Moses, and unto Aaron, and unto Miriam, Come out ye three unto the tent of meeting. And they three came out. 5 And the LORD came down in a pillar of cloud, and stood at the door of the Tent, and called Aaron and Miriam: and they both came forth. 6 And he said, Hear now my words: if there be a prophet among you, I the

[1] Or, *by*

objection. In regard to the second difficulty Wiener (*Essays in Pent. Crit.* p. 99) thinks that Ex. xviii. 5 f. should come before this passage, in which case Zipporah will have but recently joined the Israelites and have thus given Miriam occasion for her outbreak of jealousy.

2. *spoken only with Moses.* Cf. Dt. xxxiv. 10 ff. The matter in dispute here seems not the leadership of Moses, but his uniqueness, as Gray points out. The use of the preposition in the Heb. is a little strange, בְּ being used instead of the more usual אֶל: the same usage occurs, however, in Hos. i. 2, Hab. ii. 1; also several times in Zech. (see Pusey on i. 9).

with us. Miriam is called a prophetess in Ex. xv. 20, and in Mic. vi. 4 both Miriam and Aaron are coupled with Moses as being "sent before" the people.

the LORD heard. Cf. xi. 1; 2 K. xix. 4 (= Is. xxxvii. 4); Ez. xxxv. 12 f.: all of words spoken against God or His servants.

3. *the man Moses.* Cf. Ex. xi. 3. It seems hardly likely that Moses would thus refer to himself. See Introd. p. xv.

meek. The word often has the meaning *poor, afflicted* (Heb. ענו), but the idea of 'meekness' is also present: see *BDB*. Moses anticipated the virtue commended and exhibited by our Blessed Lord. "Christianity as in the case of other 'passive' virtues not only confers a higher place upon the virtue than it had ever gained in the scale of pagan ethics, cf. Arist. *Ethic. Nic.* IV. 5, but also reveals the character of an ideal meekness and gentleness" (Knowling *Epistle of St James* p. 90).

4–10. The LORD intervenes in the dispute and vindicates Moses. The divine anger falls upon Miriam and she becomes leprous.

4. *suddenly.* That is *immediately*, the word however is missing from LXX though added by the second and third hands of B.

Come out...unto the tent of meeting. The tent is thought of as being outside the camp: see further on i. 1.

5. *pillar of cloud.* See on ix. 15 ff.

6. *Hear now.* Cf. Lamech's song (Gen. iv. 23). This passage (*vv.* 6–8) was also poetical in structure.

a prophet among you. Heb. *your prophet be Jehovah.* The change of a word gives the meaning of R.V. and is generally accepted though

LORD will make myself known unto him in a vision, I will speak *E* with him in a dream. 7 My servant Moses is not so; he is faithful in all mine house: 8 with him will I speak mouth to mouth, even manifestly, and not in dark speeches; and the form of the LORD shall he behold: wherefore then were ye not afraid to speak against my servant, against Moses? 9 And the anger of the LORD was kindled against them; and he departed. 10 And the cloud removed from over the Tent; and, behold, Miriam was leprous, as *white as* snow: and Aaron looked upon Miriam,

entirely conjectural. The word for prophet (נביא) is thought by *BDB* to have come into use after Elijah's time: cf. 1 S. ix. 9.

vision...dream. This method of revelation is characteristic of E and forms one of the few means of distinguishing it from J: see Gen. xx. 3, 6, xxviii. 12, xxxi. 11, 24, &c. In later times dreams were not regarded favourably by some of the prophets: see Jer. xxiii. 25 with the present writer's note.

7. *My servant Moses.* So described in Dt. xxxiv. 5 (JE); Ex. xiv. 31 (? editorial), and repeatedly in Joshua, especially in passages from D; similarly used of many other of God's agents: e.g. Gen. xxvi. 24; Job i. 8; cf. the servant of Jesus Christ (Ro. i. 4; 2 Pet. i. 1; Jude 1)[1].

mine house. Not here the temple or even the tabernacle but the whole people of God (see Pusey on Hos. viii. 1 and cf. Gen. xli. 40; Jer. xii. 7; *Assump. Moses* XI. 16; Heb. iii. 2).

8. *mouth to mouth.* This actual expression is found here only though the similar *face to face* occurs in Ex. xxxiii. 11; Dt. xxxiv. 10 (both probably E).

dark speeches (LXX δι' αἰνιγμάτων: cf. 1 Cor. xiii. 12). The Heb. חִידָה is sometimes rendered *riddle* and is often used in parallelism to מָשָׁל *proverb* (e.g. Ez. xvii. 2; Prov. i. 6; Hab. ii. 6) a dark, enigmatic saying.

form of the LORD (LXX τὴν δόξαν). Driver in his note on Dt. iv. 12 defines this as an "intangible, yet quasi-sensual manifestation of the Godhead."

10. *Miriam was leprous.* For leprosy as a punishment for offences against God see on v. 2; also Benzinger *Arch.* pp. 481 f. According to the Talmud there were seven sins which incurred this punishment: denunciation, bloodshed, false oaths, immorality, haughtiness, robbery, and grudging (*'Arakhin* 16 *a*).

white as *snow.* To the ordinary reader this description seems to add to the horror of the disease, strictly speaking it suggests a milder form of leprosy.

---

[1] Sellin *Mose* pp. 81 ff. thinks that Moses was the original of the servant of the LORD in the later chh. of Isaiah.

and, behold, she was leprous. 11 And Aaron said unto Moses, *E* Oh my lord, lay not, I pray thee, sin upon us, for that we have done foolishly, and for that we have sinned. 12 Let her not, I pray, be as one dead, of whom the flesh is half consumed when he cometh out of his mother's womb. 13 And Moses cried unto the LORD, saying, Heal her, O God, I beseech thee. 14 And the LORD said unto Moses, If her father had but spit in her face, should she not be ashamed seven days? let her be shut up without the camp seven days, and after that she shall be brought in again. 15 And Miriam was shut up without the camp seven days: and the people journeyed not till Miriam was brought in again. 16 And afterward the people journeyed from Hazeroth, *R*^{JE} and pitched in the wilderness of Paran.

11–16. Aaron appeals to Moses to use his power with God in order that the leprosy of Miriam may be cured. In response to the intercession of Moses she is forgiven and the disease removed.

11. *Aaron said.* In the *Books of Adam and Eve* xx. 2 f. Eve appeals to Adam to intercede with God for her; cf. also Job xlii. 8.

sin. Rather the consequences of sin.

us. Aaron deserved the same punishment as Miriam and perhaps in an older form of the story actually incurred leprosy.

12. *as one dead.* In actual fact the leper was treated as a dead person or as one mourning for the dead (i.e. himself).

13. *O God.* Heb. אֵל־נָא, an unusual expression: cf. Holz. and *G-K*[28] § 105 *b*. Dillmann suggests pointing אַל (cf. Gen. xix. 18) *Nay now.* Ehrlich rejects this suggestion as it robs the prayer of any mention of God: he would read אלהינו.

14. *spit in her face.* Spitting seems to be not only an act of contempt, but also to carry a curse with it. See Holz. *ad loc.* and cf. the supposed magic effects amongst the Babylonians[1] and amongst the Arabs (Wellhausen *Arab. Heiden.*[2] pp. 161, 174). Spittle, however, not only had power to bring harm but also good: see the prayer to Marduk 'holder of the spittle of life' in *Babel and Bible* p. 174, and cf. Mk. vii. 33, viii. 23.

15. *without the camp.* Rank was no protection for the leper, all alike were excluded from amongst the people of Israel (cf. 2 K. xv. 5; 2 Chr. xxvi. 21), though the Syrians seem not to have been so strict (2 K. v. 1).

16. *Paran.* Many critics regard this as an editorial link with x. 12.

---

[1] The Sumerian UǴ-RIA *witchcraft* is connected with RIR (cf. רִיר 1 S. xxi. 14) *spittle.*

CHAPTERS XIII. AND XIV.

THE STORY OF THE SPIES AND ITS SEQUEL.

Before making any attempt to invade Canaan the Hebrews send spies to report on the land itself and also upon those who dwell in it. The extent to which the promised land was surveyed is not quite clear (cf. xiii. 2, 17 *a*, 21 with 22 ff.), but on the return of the expedition cowardice and want of faith cause the people to break out into murmuring. As a result they are condemned to wander in the wilderness: in spite of this an unofficial and futile attempt to force their way through is made at Hormah. The obvious intention of the story is to explain the long delay in making the entry into Canaan.

Burney sees behind the narrative of J traces of an old Calibbite tradition, according to which an invasion from the south took place carried out by the clan of Caleb and its kindred (*Schweich Lectures* p. 30: cf Paton *JBL* (1913) pp. 1–53 and S. A. Cook *NOTH* pp. 38 f., 81 f.). For an analysis of the narrative and an attempt to deal with its obvious difficulties see Introd. pp. xxix f. The following are the main sections of the division.

The mission and report of the spies. xiii.
The despair and punishment of the congregation. xiv. 1–38.
The defeat at Hormah. xiv. 39–45.

CHAPTER XIII.

The mission and report of the spies.

A number of men, one chosen from each of the twelve tribes according to P, are dispatched into the promised land. They are charged to make a survey of the country, paying special attention to its productiveness, its possibilities for settlement, the cities in it, and the character of its inhabitants. The expedition returns after an absence of forty days during which it had explored the region round about Hebron in the south (P extends the survey so as to reach the boundaries of the future kingdom), and brings back evidences of the fruitfulness of the country, but also of the strength of those who dwell in it and of their cities[1]: except Caleb the members of the expedition are against any invasion of such a 'man-eating' land.

(*a*) *The choice of the spies.* 1–17 *a*.
(*b*) *The charge to the spies.* 17 *b*–20.
(*c*) *The journey into Canaan.* 21–26.
(*d*) *The report of the spies.* 27–33.

XIII. 1–17 *a*. The account of the choice of the spies here given comes from P (see Introd. p. xxx) who gives a list of twelve names taken severally from the twelve tribes. As the present narrative stands JE gives no number of spies, and mentions one name only, that of Caleb: it is however probable that the account of the sending of the spies in

---

[1] A similar account of Palestine, describing its agriculture and the strength of its cities (some with walls 50 ft. high), is given by a Pharaoh of the 6th Dynasty (*c.* 2700). See Clay *Amurru* p. 30.

XIII. 1 And the LORD spake unto Moses, saying, 2 Send *P* thou men, that they may spy out the land of Canaan, which I give unto the children of Israel: of every tribe of their fathers shall ye send a man, every one a prince among them. 3 And Moses sent them from the wilderness of Paran according to the commandment of the LORD: all of them men who were heads of the children of Israel. 4 And these were their names: of the tribe of Reuben, Shammua the son of Zaccur. 5 Of the tribe of

Dt. i. 22 f. is based on JE, the early part of whose narrative is lost (see Driver *ad loc.*), and in that account the number twelve does appear.

1. *the* LORD *spake*. According to Dt. i. 22 the people asked Moses to send spies, a sign of their want of faith in Jehovah's leadership; this presumably represents the point of view of JE (see above). Holzinger points out that it is characteristic of P to make the command come from God. Ehrlich suggests that because the enterprise was a failure D left out the divine command and referred it to the people: this suggestion would have had greater probability if it had been the later document (P) which had made the omission.

2. *the land of Canaan*. This designation of the promised land is typical of P. The expression is rare after Joshua; it occurs in Jud. xxi. 12, once in the prophets (Ez. xvi. 29), and once in the other writings (Ps. cv. 11 = 1 Chr. xvi. 18).

a prince. See on i. 16. The names are different from those in the list of i. 16 (where see note). In Jos. vi. 23 the spies are merely young men, but the expedition which they had to undertake was of military importance only; this expedition had a much wider scope, hence the employment of people of consequence whose judgement would carry weight.

3. *the wilderness of Paran*. See on x. 12.

4. *And these were their names*. This formula is characteristic of P: it gives (with the omission of the pronoun) the Heb. name to the book commonly called Exodus. The list which follows contains twenty-four names, of which eleven do not occur elsewhere, and of the persons whom they represent Caleb and Hoshea alone are known. Characteristics of this list are the small number of compound names and especially of names compounded with the divine name (see however notes on *vv.* 7, 9), and the abnormally large number which end in *-i*. Ehrlich has also pointed out that in four cases (*vv.* 5, 7, 14, 15) the name of the prince begins with the same letter as that of his tribe. Hommel defends the genuineness of the list *AHT* pp. 299 ff.

4. *Shammua*. The other occurrences of this name except 2 S. v. 14 are late: Neh. xi. 17, xii. 18.

Zaccur. Another name common in late writers: Neh. iii. 2, x. 12, xiii. 13 &c. It has been suggested (see *Enc. Bib.* 5372) that the name may ultimately be connected with the Zakkara or Zakkala (*r* and *l* being interchangeable in Egyptian) who appear in the inscriptions of

Simeon, Shaphat the son of Hori. 6 Of the tribe of Judah, Caleb *P* the son of Jephunneh. 7 Of the tribe of Issachar, Igal the son of Joseph. 8 Of the tribe of Ephraim, Hoshea the son of Nun. 9 Of the tribe of Benjamin, Palti the son of Raphu. 10 Of the tribe of Zebulun, Gaddiel the son of Sodi. 11 Of the tribe of Joseph, *namely*, of the tribe of Manasseh, Gaddi the son of Susi. 12 Of the tribe of Dan, Ammiel the son of Gemalli. 13 Of the

Ramses III as amongst the invaders of Syria; they subsequently settled to the north of the Philistines in Dor, as we are informed by Wen-Amon (B.C. 1110 *c.*): see Macalister *Hist. of the Philistines* p. 30. The same writer also mentions a prince of Byblos Zakar-Baal the first part of whose name, or title (see Reinach *Rev. archéol.* IV. XV. p. 45), is the same as *Zaccur*.

5. *Shaphat.* The name of the father of Elisha (1 K. xix. 16).

Hori. The name of a Horite or Edomite clan (Gen. xxxvi. 22).

6. *Caleb.* According to xxxii. 12 Caleb was a Kenizzite, and therefore ultimately an Edomite if Gen. xxxvi. 11 is to be trusted. The meaning of the word is *dog* and it may have a totemistic origin: see Robertson Smith *Rel. Sem.*² pp. 137 ff.[1]. Radau thinks that the real names of the kings of Shirpurla (= Lagash) commonly rendered Ur-Nina and Ur-Bau should be Kalbi-Nina and Kalbi-Bau (*Early Bab. Hist.* p. 144).

Jephunneh. In 1 Chr. ii. 18 Caleb is the son of Hezron. A member of the tribe of Asher is named Jephunneh in 1 Chr. vii. 38.

7. *Igal.* The meaning of the name is *He (God) redeems.* This name occurs in 2 S. xxiii. 36 as one of David's heroes.

8. *Hoshea.* See on *v.* 16. So named in Dt. xxxii. 44 where however the versions LXX, Sam., Vg., read Joshua.

9. *Palti.* The name of the husband of Michal (1 S. xxv. 44) called in 2 S. iii. 15 Paltiel, which is probably the correct form. In this case as in that of Igal (*v.* 7) part of the name has been omitted.

Raphu. Here only. Hommel compares the South Arabian *Ili-rapa'a*, *AHT* pp. 83, 301.

10. *Gaddiel.* The fuller form of the name Gad (cf. Dan and Daniel), or Gaddi (*v.* 11). Names compounded with Gad, who was an Aramaean deity, are common amongst the Phoenicians: see *NSI* Nos. 27 *l.* 3, 59 C *l.* 2; whilst *Ga-di-ilu* is a Bab. name: see Johns *Deeds* No. 443, 1.

Sodi. Here only.

11. *Gaddi.* See on Gaddiel above and cf. Γαδδι[ς] 1 Macc. ii. 2.

Susi. Here only.

12. *Ammiel.* The name of the father of Machir (2 S. ix. 4), also of Bathsheba (1 Chr. iii. 5: cf. 2 S. xi. 3). Names compounded with *Ammi* are not uncommon = kinsman or uncle.

Gemalli. Here only.

---

[1] Dante's friend and protector Can Grande della Scala, to whom he dedicated the *Paradiso*, derived his name from *cane*=*dog*.

tribe of Asher, Sethur the son of Michael. 14 Of the tribe of Naphtali, Nahbi the son of Vophsi. 15 Of the tribe of Gad, Geuel the son of Machi. 16 These are the names of the men which Moses sent to spy out the land. And Moses called Hoshea the son of Nun Joshua. 17 And Moses sent them to spy out the land of Canaan, | and said unto them, Get you up this way [1]by the South, and go up into the mountains: 18 and see the land, what it is; and the people that dwelleth therein, whether they be strong or weak, whether they be few or many; 19 and what *P* *JE*

[1] Or, *into*

13. *Sethur.* Here only.

Michael. A name of common occurrence in post-exilic times: see further *Enc. Bib.*

14. *Nahbi...Vophsi.* Both names occur here only.

15. *Geuel...Machi.* Here only.

16. *Joshua.* According to P (Ex. vi. 2 f.) the name Jehovah (Jahweh) was not known when Joshua was born, he could not therefore have had a name given to him of which Jo- (Jeho-) was a part. According to the Talmud (Tal. Bab. *Sanh.* 107 *a*) the name was changed by the use of the *yod* (*i* or *j*) which was taken by Jehovah from Sarai when her name was changed to Sarah[1]. Early Christian thought saw in the change a forecast of our Lord: see Ep. Barnabas XII. 8.

17 *b*–20. Moses sends out the spies with a definite commission covering two aspects of the land (*a*) its military power, this with a view to the conquest, and (*b*) its economic resources, this with a view to the settlement there. It is hardly likely that even a number of Bedawin tribes such as were the followers of Moses could have been so entirely ignorant of the conditions of Canaan as the charge to the spies would suggest.

17. *this way.* Better *then*: cf. *G-K*[28] § 136.

by the South. Better *into the Negeb.* The *South* is a geographical term for the country south of Judah, it is not a point of the compass, as A.V. seemed to think, their translation *southward* makes nonsense as the spies were to travel due north. For a description of the Negeb, the name of which comes from a root meaning 'dry' or 'parched,' see Palmer *Desert of the Exodus* pp. 292 ff., 359 ff. and G. A. Smith *Hist. Geog.* pp. 278 ff. The use of the term as a point of the compass represents the standpoint of one dwelling in Canaan to whom the Negeb was the Southland.

the mountains. So Dt. i. 24. Palmer suggests that a detour was made into the hill-country of Judah in order not to arouse the suspicions of the dwellers in the Negeb (*op. cit.* p. 511).

---

[1] St Jerome evidently thought that the change in the case of Joshua was made by God: Osee in lingua nostra Salvatorem sonat, quod nomen habuit etiam Josue filius Nun, antequam ei a Deo vocabulum mutaretur (*In Osee* cap. I. v. 1).

the land is that they dwell in, whether it be good or bad; and *JE* what cities they be that they dwell in, whether in camps, or in strong holds; 20 and what the land is, whether it be fat or lean, whether there be wood therein, or not. And be ye of good courage, and bring of the fruit of the land. Now the time was the time of the firstripe grapes. 21 So they went up, and spied *P* out the land from the wilderness of Zin unto Rehob, to the entering in of Hamath. 22 And they went up [1]by the South, *JE*

[1] Or, *into*

19. *the land.* Cf. *v.* 20. Ehrlich thinks that *land* is here used in the sense of climate.

camps...strong holds. Cf. the statement made by Thucydides (I. 10) that Sparta was inhabited as a city κατὰ κώμας. The word for *strong hold* was not primarily applied to the city itself but to its defences, as the use of the full phrase in xxxii. 17, 36 and Jer. iv. 5 makes clear: see further Nowack *Arch.* I. p. 368.

20. *fat.* Cf. Neh. ix. 25, 35.

be ye of good courage. Gray translates *exert yourselves,* and compares Gen. xlviii. 2 where the same Heb. word is rendered 'strengthened himself.'

firstripe grapes. That would probably be the middle or end of July or the beginning of August, though the time would differ according to the position of the place visited and the forwardness or otherwise of the season: see Benzinger *Arch.* p. 212.

21–26. The description of the journey of the spies comes from both P (*vv.* 21, 25, 26 *a*) and JE (*vv.* 22–24, 26 *b*): see Introd. p. xxx. Steuernagel thinks that the spying of Hebron originally formed the introduction to the story of its capture in Jud. i. 10: see *Die Einwanderung der isr. Stämme* p. 74. Gressmann also supports this theory *Auswahl* p. 112, *Mose* pp. 294 f.

21. *the wilderness of Zin.* Not to be confused with the wilderness of Sin (Ex. xvi. 1). According to P *the wilderness of Zin* lay to the north of that of Paran (xx. 1); a difficulty here arises because P apparently regards Kadesh itself as being in the same wilderness (xx. 1 *a*, xxvii. 14, xxxiii. 36; Dt. xxxii. 51), yet *v.* 26 *b* gives Kadesh as the place to which the spies returned. As in the case of the wilderness of Paran there is some looseness in the use of the term.

Rehob. Mentioned in 2 S. x. 8, and in the fuller form Beth-Rehob in Jud. xviii. 28; 2 S. x. 6. It lay at the head of the Jordan valley near to Dan and Mount Hermon: see Buhl *Geog.* pp. 65, 237. Two other places of the same name are mentioned, both in Asher, one in Jos. xix. 28, 30; Jud. i. 31, the other in 1 Chr. vi. 75. The name is found in Egyptian lists: see W. Max Müller *Asien u. Europa* p. 153.

the entering in of Hamath. A very common expression for the ideal northern boundary of Israel (xxxiv. 8; Jos. xiii. 5; Am. vi. 14 &c.).

and came unto Hebron; and Ahiman, Sheshai, and Talmai, the *JE*

Hamath itself is the modern *Ḥamā* situated on the Orontes some 150 miles north of Dan; it was probably in existence before the time of the Exodus, being known to the Egyptians as *Ḥa-mā-ti* (cf. W. Max Müller *op. cit.* pp. 174, 256). The exact situation of *the entering in* is a matter of dispute. The majority of scholars identify it with the cleft between Lebanon and Hermon (see Buhl *Geog.* pp. 66, 110), van Kasteren *Rev. Bib.* 1895 pp. 23 ff. definitely locating it in the *Merj 'Ayūn* at the southern end of *el-Buḳā'*, an identification which is accepted by Holzinger. Moore *Judges* (*ICC*) p. 80 thinks that it "is probably the plain Ḥoms, some 30 miles south of Ḥamā, at the intersection of four passes, and of main roads from the coast, the Syrian desert, and north and south through Coele Syria." Furrer *ZDPV* VIII. pp. 27 ff. places *the entering in* at *er-Restān*, the ancient Arethusa. Burney has pointed out the difficulty of van Kasteren's identification in view of Jos. xiii. 5 and Jud. iii. 3 (see *Judges* pp. xcix f., 63) and his arguments seem to be decisive for the northern end of *el-Buḳā'* in these passages: the term may, however, have been loosely applied to the whole pass, sometimes with emphasis on its southern mouth, sometimes on the northern.

22. *Hebron.* This city lies nearly twenty miles south of Jerusalem. According to Jud. i. 10 its original name was Kirjath-Arba, a statement which is confirmed by the appearance of *Rubuti* in the Tell el-Amarna Tablets. The meaning of Kirjath-Arba is the Tetrapolis, the town of four, and various suggestions have been made as to the substantive which should follow 'four' in this connexion[1]; that which meets with most favour being 'confederates' (Ḥabiru) from which the later name Hebron may have been derived (cf. Hommel *AHT* p. 232). Another suggestion would supply 'gods' (cf. Arbela = Arba-il), and sees in the four deities Abraham and the three men who there appeared to him (Gen. xxiii. 2), the latter were none other than Ahiman, Sheshai, and Talmai.

Ahiman. A Levite of this name is mentioned in 1 Chr. ix. 17 but the passage is probably corrupt (see Curtis *ICC ad loc.*). The name on the analogy of Ahijah means *Mān* (some deity) *is my brother.* Burney suggests (*Judges* p. 10) that *Mān* may be the *Meni* of Is. lxv. 11 or the *Manōthū* which appears in Nabataean inscriptions.

Sheshai. Sayce would connect this word with the Bedawin tribes mentioned in the Egyptian inscriptions under the name of Shashu (*HCM* p. 189). On the other hand Burney (*op. cit.* p. 10) would connect with Shisha (1 K. iv. 3) or Shavsha (1 Chr. xviii. 16) which he thinks were undoubtedly forms of Shamsha[2]: cf. the late Bab. form *šaššu* for *šamšu* = sun.

Talmai. The name occurs elsewhere in O.T. as that of a king of

---

[1] 'Four' may however be itself a title for the deity: cf. Burney *Judges* p. 43.

[2] Cheyne cites in support of this (*Enc. Bib.* 4433) Aram. *Ki-šavaš* which is used as the equivalent of Ass. *Ki-šamaš* in a bilingual inscription of B.C. 504 (*CIS* II. 65).

children of Anak, were there. (Now Hebron was built seven years before Zoan in Egypt.) 23 And they came unto the valley of Eshcol, and cut down from thence a branch with one cluster *JE*

Geshur (2 S. iii. 3, xiii. 37). Sayce mentions the similar name *Talmī* borne by two kings of Liḥyân in inscriptions found at el-'Olâ near Teima (*HCM* p. 189, citing D. H. Müller *Epigraphische Denkmäler aus Arabien* p. 5). A form Talmu or Talimu occurs in Nabataean inscriptions (*CIS* II. 321, 344, 348).

the children of Anak. This form appears also in *v.* 28 and Jos. xv. 14: other forms are *sons of Anak v.* 33; Dt. ix. 26, and with slight variations in Jos. xv. 14 *a*; Jud. i. 20: in Dt. i. 28, ix. 2 *a* the sons of the Anakim: in addition the term Anakim alone is used in Dt. ii. 10 f., 21; Jos. xi. 21 f., xiv. 12, 15. *Anak* is not a personal name, its Heb. meaning is *neck* and the phrase *sons of neck*, by a common idiom, means long-necked or tall men. The sons named above represent probably not individuals but tribes of Amorite or North Arabian people settled round Hebron. Many traditions survived in Canaan of gigantic peoples most of whom were the original dwellers in the land; perhaps *the sons of Anak* in spite of their names were also pre-Canaanite: cf. Macalister's interesting remarks on these giant aborigines who, after being destroyed in Israel, survived in Gaza, Gath, and Ashdod (Jos. xi. 22) and perhaps amalgamated with the Philistines, giving them their gigantic champions (*Schweich Lectures* pp. 60 f., 68). For other theories see Schwally *ZAW* XVIII. pp. 139 ff.

Zoan. Mentioned also in Is. xix. 11, 13; Ez. xxx. 14; Ps. lxxviii. 12, 43. The city was of very great antiquity and the reference here may be to its rebuilding in the time of the nineteenth dynasty (see Sayce *HCM* p. 190). Ed. Meyer (*IN* p. 447, *Gesch. des Altertums*[2] I. pp. 293 ff.) refers it to the founding of the temple of Seth at Zoan in B.C. 1670: cf. Gressmann *ZAW* xxx. p. 31. Zoan is situated in the east of the Delta; it was known to the Greeks as Tanis: see Flinders Petrie *Tanis* (*Egypt. Explor. Fund Memoirs* 1885 and 1888).

23. *the valley of Eshcol*. The position of this valley is not certainly known, Buhl *Geog.* p. 89 suggests the *Wady Bît Iskâhil* to the north-west of Hebron. But there is no necessary connexion between Eshcol and Hebron (cf. xxxii. 9; Dt. i. 24), and there are signs of vine cultivation far to the south of it. Palmer thinks that the clusters would be gathered on the homeward journey, and as far south as possible, on account of the perishable nature of figs and of the difficulty of carrying the grapes through hostile territory (*Desert of the Exodus* p. 352); he himself suggests the *Wady Hanein*, a little to the north of Kadesh (*op. cit.* p. 512).

one cluster. The context suggests that it was exceedingly heavy. When Alboin wished to persuade the Lombards to invade Italy he shewed them specimens of the wonderful fruits which grew there: see Paulus Diaconus *De Gest. Langobard.* Bk. II. ch. v (in Muratori *Rerum Ital. Script.* I. 427).

of grapes, and they bare it upon a staff between two; *they* JE
brought also of the pomegranates, and of the figs. 24 That place
was called the valley of [1]Eshcol, because of the cluster which
the children of Israel cut down from thence. 25 And they re- P
turned from spying out the land at the end of forty days.
26 And they went and came to Moses, and to Aaron, and to all
the congregation of the children of Israel, unto the wilderness
of Paran, | to Kadesh; and brought back word unto them, and JE
unto all the congregation, and shewed them the fruit of the land.
27 And they told him, and said, We came unto the land whither
thou sentest us, and surely it floweth with milk and honey; and

[1] That is, *a cluster*.

staff. Better *frame*: see on iv. 10.

pomegranates...figs. These fruits are still found in abundance: see Robinson *Biblical Researches in Pal.* I. p. 316.

24. The story may have arisen in consequence of the name.

25. *forty days*. This seems to fit in with JE: cf. *v.* 20 the time of the firstripe grape. Westcott has pointed out that "The space of forty days is always in scripture a period of solemn waiting followed by issues of momentous interest" (*Revelation of the Risen Lord* p. 175). The present story certainly justifies this generalisation.

26. *Kadesh*. The usual identification is with the modern *'Ain Ḳadîs* some 75 miles south-west of Hebron: see Clay Trumbull *Kadesh Barnea* pp. 238–275, also Guthe *ZDPV* VIII. pp. 182 ff., 196; von Alois Musil *Arabia Petraea* II. i. pp. 176 ff. (the doubt thrown on the identification on p. 236 is not very convincing). As the text stands *Kadesh* is said to be in the wilderness of Paran: it is possible that as the wilderness of Paran and that of Zin were close to one another (*vv.* 3 and 21) it might be regarded as belonging to either. Cheyne regards Paran as sometimes including Zin (*Enc. Bib.* 3583). The site, to judge from its name Kadesh, was already a sanctuary.

27–33. The spies bring back a good report of the fertility of the land (*v.* 32 *a* belongs to P), but they are dismayed by the strength of its fortifications and the huge size of the inhabitants.

27. *with milk and honey*[1]. A very common phrase in J where it occurs eight times, and in D where it is almost as frequent. It is strange that *milk and honey* rather than 'corn and wine' should be taken as marks of a fertile country. In Is. vii. 15 the eating of *milk and honey* is a sign that the land is spoiled and uncultivated according to most critics:

---

[1] דְּבַשׁ *honey* may be derived from Sum. root GAB = DAB *rounded* or *humped*; since honey is found massed together in combs. דְּבוֹרָה *bee* may mean the clustering insect: see C. J. Ball in *Hilprecht Anniv. Vol.* p. 35. It is certainly remarkable that דב should be included in the words for both *bee* and *honey*.

this is the fruit of it. 28 Howbeit the people that dwell in the *JE* land are strong, and the cities are fenced, *and* very great: and moreover we saw the children of Anak there. 29 Amalek dwelleth in the land of the South: and the Hittite, and the Jebusite, and the Amorite, dwell in the mountains: and the

contrast Gray *ad loc.* in *ICC*. The origin of the conjunction of the two products may have been mythological: cf. the Greek association of *milk and honey* with the cult of Dionysus, and see Schwally *ZAW* XXII. pp. 321 ff. Canaan however can never have been exceedingly fertile as a whole[1]. See further Guidi in *Rev. bibl.* 1903 pp. 241 ff.

28. *fenced.* Cf. Dt. i. 28; Jos. xiv. 12. The walls of Lachish were more than twenty-eight feet thick (cf. Sayce *HCM* p. 288). The tribes of the desert have always dreaded the city: cf. G. A. Smith *Isaiah* ii. pp. 190 f.[2]

Anak. See on *v.* 22.

29. *Amalek.* The Amalekites were nomad tribes frequenting the deserts in the south of Palestine; their attack on the Israelites described in Ex. xvii. 8 ff. was long remembered and resented. See further the notes on xxiv. 20.

the Hittite. See Additional Note pp. 89 f.

the Jebusite. A small tribe living round Jerusalem, probably of Semitic race: they were afterwards conquered by David (2 S. v. 6 ff.). Nothing is known of them beyond the scanty particulars contained in O.T.

the Amorite...the Canaanite. The *Amorites* are connected with the hill-country in Dt. i. 19 f., 44: Sayce says of them that they "belonged to the white race, and, like other members of the white race, were tall in stature and impatient of the damp heat of the plains" (*Early Israel* p. 71). In some passages, however, generally attributed to E and D, the term is used of the inhabitants of Canaan as a whole, without regard to the race to which they belong (cf. Sayce *op. cit.* p. 73): J uses 'Canaanite' with this meaning. Flinders Petrie thinks that the *Amorites* represent the 'pre-Israelite Semites' as distinguished from the 'neolithic troglodytes,' the aboriginal people of Canaan for whom the term *Canaanite*

---

[1] Frederick II who visited Palestine during the Crusades was very scornful of it. "When he saw the Holy Land (which God had so oft-times commended as a land flowing with milk and honey and most excellent above all lands) it pleased him not, and he said that if the God of the Jews had seen *his* lands of Terra di Lavoro, Calabria, Sicily, and Apulia, then He would not so have commended the land which He promised to the Jews": quoted by G. G. Coulton *From St Francis to Dante* p. 242.

[2] When the Goths and other tribes conquered Italy they destroyed the walls of the cities and ordered that they should not be rebuilt, for being accustomed to live in the open deserts of the North, they held walled cities in abhorrence: see Testa *The War of Fred. I against the Communes &c.* p. 11. For earlier times see Tacitus *Hist.* IV. 64.

Canaanite dwelleth by the sea, and along by the side of Jordan. *JE* 30 And Caleb stilled the people before Moses, and said, Let us go up at once, and possess it; for we are well able to overcome it. 31 But the men that went up with him said, We be not able to go up against the people; for they are stronger than we. 32 And *P* they brought up an evil report of the land which they had spied out unto the children of Israel, saying, The land, through which we have gone to spy it out, is a land that eateth up the inhabitants thereof; and all the people that we saw in it are men

should be reserved: see *Eastern Exploration* p. 24[1]. There is an interesting study of the use of the two names *Amorite* and *Canaanite* by Dhorme entitled *Les pays bibliques au temps d'el-Amarna* in *Rev. bibl.* 1908 pp. 501 ff. He shews that in the Tell el-Amarna tablets *A-mur-ru* is the country round Beyrout in North Syria, *Ki-na-aḥ-ni*, the land south of Lebanon. According to E and D the Canaanites were the dwellers in the lowlands of west and south-west Palestine (Dt. i. 7, xi. 30; Jos. v. 1 &c.: contrast Num. xiv. 45). See further Driver *Deut.* p. 11, Burney *Judges* pp. lviii ff., 41.

the side of Jordan: lit. *hand*. The same use occurs in Ex. ii. 5; Dt. ii. 37; Jer. xlvi. 6; Dan. x. 4 &c.

30 f. The attempt of Caleb to still the people seems out of place here since no murmuring has yet been mentioned. The *vv.* would fit in more suitably after xiv. 7.

Caleb. There is here no mention of Joshua: cf. xiv. 6.

32. *evil report*. Not necessarily a false report: cf. Gen. xxxvii. 2.

eateth up the inhabitants. The usual interpretation of the phrase is that the land is so unfertile that it provides insufficient nourishment for its people (so Gray, McNeile &c.): cf. Ez. xxxvi. 13 f.; Lev. xxvi. 38[2]. The difficulty of this interpretation is the reference in *v.* 27 to 'milk and honey' for the compiler could hardly have failed to notice the contradiction: see Finn *Unity of Pent.* p. 87. The spies may have represented the inhabitants as cannibals. Wellhausen saw in the report the impression of the post-exilic community: cf. Hag. i. 6, ii. 19; Neh. v.

all the people. Terror makes the spies exaggerate: cf. *v.* 28.

The American archaeologist, A. T. Clay, has an interesting theory concerning the Amorites. He holds that they were once a great empire, and that the Semitic Babylonians had their origin in Amurru. The culture of the West Semites or Amorites was carried to Mesopotamia where it amalgamated with that of the Sumerians. Although Clay's theory has not been proved it seems worthy of serious attention for we can no longer regard the Amorites as a mere Palestinian tribe just as we can no longer regard the Hittites as such. For the evidence in support of the theory see Clay *The Empire of the Amorites,* and *Amurru: the Home of the Northern Semites*: cf. also Ungnad *Die ältesten Völkerwanderungen Vorderasiens.*

[2] When Croesus was preparing to invade Persia a certain Lydian tried to turn him from his purpose by pointing out that the Persians were a poor people and their land very barren: see Herodotus I. 71.

of great stature. 33 And there we saw the [1]Nephilim, the sons of Anak, which come of the Nephilim: and we were in our own sight as grasshoppers, and so we were in their sight. *JE*

[1] Or, *giants*

men of great stature. According to Am. ii. 9 the Amorites were tall as 'cedars.'

33. *the Nephilim.* The word seems to be from Heb. root meaning *to fall* (נפל). The Fathers accordingly identified the Nephilim with the fallen angels. Schwally endeavouring to interpret the name from this root suggests that they are the fallen (i.e. the dead): see *Das Leben nach dem Tode* p. 63 note 1, and *ZAW* (1898) pp. 143 ff. The word occurs in Gen. vi. 4 of the offspring of angels and human mothers.

grasshoppers. Cf. Is. xl. 22 where the comparison is between Jehovah and the dwellers upon earth.

Additional Note on XIII. 29.

The Hittites.

The Hittites form for the history of the ancient East the unknown quantity which is supplied by the Etruscans in that of early Italy: a key to the language and writings of either people would make accessible vast stores of valuable material for interpreting the periods and races with which they are severally concerned.

Dr Cowley, in his Schweich Lectures for 1918 entitled *The Hittites*, concludes that this people was not of Indo-European race, thus opposing the theory upheld by Hrozny in *Die Sprache der Hethiter* (1917). He sums up the use of the term as follows: "The name Hittite was vaguely applied by the Assyrians to peoples of various states at various times. The main stock appears to consist of two strata, which may imply two distinct races. The linguistic affinities of the earlier stratum may perhaps be sought in western Asia Minor, those of the later stratum more probably in the east and south" (*op. cit.* p. 47).

It is most probable in view of the evidence at our disposal that the term Hittite was used to define a certain type of culture as well as to name a race. The origin of the people is lost in obscurity. "Were they an 'Asianic' people, who conquered with bronze imported from the Caucasus? Were they Alarodians from beyond the Caspian? Were they an Indo-European folk from Iran or beyond[1]?" They possibly formed part of the people of *Sabartu* who, having overturned the old Sumerian civilisation of Ashur, were driven back by Sargon of Agade (2872–2817 B.C.). Later Hatti or Hittites sacked Babylon in 1926 B.C. and brought to an end the First Babylonian Dynasty. This raid on Babylon was no doubt one of the manifestations of the activity of the Aryan race which from 2000 B.C. onwards began to move into Media, bringing horses with them. It was at any rate a period of great unrest witnessing the destruction of Cnossus and Phaestus and later the pressure exerted on the Syrians brought about the famous Hyksos invasion of Egypt (*c.* 1800 B.C.). Possibly after raiding Babylon the Hittites moved into Cappadocia and conquered the country with which their name is most closely associated. At any rate the

[1] D. G. Hogarth in *Camb. Anct. Hist.* II. 259.

earliest records of the Hatti themselves reveal to us the fact that before 1450 B.C. a Hittite kingdom was securely established, probably with its capital in N. Cappadocia, and that its influence spread into N. Syria and even across the Euphrates. The relations of this growing power with Egypt in the centuries which followed cannot here be entered into in any detail, it will suffice to say that they contended on equal terms, that a treaty was entered into between them in 1272, that the Hittite power gradually decayed owing to the presence of new peoples in north and west Asia Minor and that finally it collapsed in Cappadocia about 1175 B.C.

The later Hittite power, centred round Carchemish, may have arisen after the repulse of Hittite people from Babylon by Nebuchadrezzar I in 1140 B.C., for it is about this period that the first signs of this post-Hattic culture are discovered. "The whole body of evidence agrees," says Dr Hogarth, "in suggesting that Carchemish and its district experienced towards the close of the second millennium invasion by iron-using men who had acquired the full Hattic culture. Probably they came from eastern Asia Minor, and may have been either actual north Cappadocian Hatti forced southwards after the fall of their empire, or more southerly inheritors of the Hattic civilisation[1]."

The writers of O.T. are not exact in their use of the term Hittite, or at least those belonging or related to the Priestly school are not, for both P and Ezekiel include amongst Hittites all or any of the Canaanite peoples. A similar vagueness is however observable in Assyrian inscriptions, as Ammonites, and even the Israelites themselves, are sometimes spoken of under the name: see Sayce *Early Israel &c.* p. 80.

The earlier biblical writers use the name with two different connotations: (*a*) The great people referred to above, whose rule stretched from Asia Minor to Carchemish on the Euphrates and beyond, who fought with powerful Egyptian Pharaohs on equal terms (1 K. x. 29, xi. 1; 2 K. vii. 6: the last two references suggest that the Hittites were not very far from Syria).

(*b*) Hittites further south, perhaps settlements left behind by the above peoples, when compelled to retreat from Palestine after the great 'Philistine' migration which passed through Asia Minor and down to the borders of Egypt in 1192 B.C. and so weakened the Hittites that Ramses III was able to drive them still further north[2] (Jud. i. 26, iii. 3; Jos. xi. 3). These Hittites would be the children of Heth, the child of Canaan (Gen. x. 15), and the fact of their having ever been part of a great nation could hardly be gathered from the nature of the references[3].

Chapter XIV. 1–38.

The despair and punishment of the congregation.

The congregation in a panic over the evil report of the majority of the spies think of returning to Egypt. On the Lord expressing His indignation Moses intercedes for the people. The people are pardoned but none of those who have proved themselves rebellious are to enter into the promised land.

(*a*) *The despair of the congregation.* xiv. 1–10.
(*b*) *The intercession of Moses.* 11–19.
(*c*) *The punishment of the people.* 20–25.
(*d*) *Another account of their punishment.* 26–38.

---

[1] *Camb. Anct. Hist.* III. p. 162.
[2] Cf. Meyer *Gesch. des Alterthums* I. §§ 263 ff.
[3] It is a remarkable fact that the pre-Islamic Arabs were ignorant of the comparatively important Nabataeans: see Nöldeke *Amalekiter* pp. 25 f.

XIV. 1 And all the congregation lifted up their voice, and *P* cried; and the people wept that night. 2 And all the children of Israel murmured against Moses and against Aaron: and the whole congregation said unto them, Would God that we had died in the land of Egypt! or would God we had died in this wilderness! 3 And wherefore doth the LORD bring us unto this *JE* land, to fall by the sword? Our wives and our little ones shall be a prey: were it not better for us to return into Egypt? 4 And they said one to another, Let us make a captain, and let us

XIV. 1–10. The congregation in despair over the evil report of the spies wish to return to Egypt. By those who have no sure trust in God the terrors of the unknown are always exaggerated. Caleb and Joshua endeavour to bring the people to a better mind by assuring them of the divine protection and aid.

1. *all the congregation.* "Terror is more contagious than courage, for a mob is always more prone to base than to noble instincts" (Maclaren *Exodus &c.* p. 341).

the people wept. See on xi. 4. In a similar situation the Roman soldiers wept in terror on hearing reports of the huge stature of the Germans: see Caesar *De Bell. Gall.* I. 39.

2. *murmured*[1]. Used by JE in Ex. xv. 24, xvii. 3, elsewhere it is found in P only.

against Moses. Moses had an experience which is the lot of every leader whose ideals are above those of his followers.

in the land of Egypt. Cf. xx. 4 (P); Ex. xiv. 11 f. (J), xvi. 3 (P). In xi. 20 Moses reproaches the people because of a similar expression of opinion. The continual emphasis on the folly and wickedness of the desire to return to Egypt may be aimed at the later pro-Egyptian party of the time of Isaiah.

in this wilderness. Cf. *v.* 29; Ex. xiv. 11 (J).

3. *the LORD.* The people recognise that Jehovah is the real leader of the expedition, and in consequence their rebellion is deliberately against Him: cf. Dt. i. 27.

to fall by the sword. The people are afraid of the supposed military superiority of the Canaanites.

4. *one to another.* The previous suggestions had been made openly to Moses and Aaron; the proposal to replace Moses was discussed in secret.

make a captain. This incident is referred to in Neh. ix. 17. The vague murmurings and complaints of the people threaten on this occasion to result in action, in a definite denial of the leadership of Moses (cf.

---

[1] Heb. לוּן *to murmur* may be connected with Sumerian LIL *wind*, so called from its wailing: cf. Ball *Job* p. 282.

return into Egypt. 5 Then Moses and Aaron fell on their faces *P* before all the assembly of the congregation of the children of Israel. 6 And Joshua the son of Nun and Caleb the son of Jephunneh, which were of them that spied out the land, rent their clothes: 7 and they spake unto all the congregation of the children of Israel, saying, The land, which we passed through to spy it out, is an exceeding good land. 8 If the LORD delight in *JE* us, then he will bring us into this land, and give it unto us; a land which floweth with milk and honey. 9 Only rebel not against the LORD, neither fear ye the people of the land; for they are bread for us: their [1]defence is removed from over them,

[1] Heb. *shadow.*

xii. 1 ff.). For the dejection of the people and the resolve to appoint a fresh leader cf. Xenophon *Anab.* III. i.

return into Egypt. Cf. Dt. xvii. 16 where a return under a king is regarded as a future possibility. That passage, however, probably refers, not to a literal return of the nation (though cf. Jer. xlii f.) but to closer relationship with Egypt.

5. *fell on their faces.* Holzinger points out that Moses and Aaron repeatedly adopt this course in moments of crisis.

6. *rent their clothes.* "The rending of the clothes was an expression of extraordinary uncontrollable emotion, chiefly of grief, of terror, or of horror." Pusey on Joel ii. 13.

7. *an exceeding good land.* Cf. Dt. i. 25; Enoch lxxxix. 40 "a pleasant and glorious land."

8. *delight in us.* Used of God's favour in 2 S. xxii. 20 (to David); 1 K. x. 9 (to Solomon); and the classical passage, Is. lxii. 4 where Israel is to be *Hephzi-bah.*

9. *bread for us.* Cf. xiii. 32, xxiv. 8; Dt. vii. 16; Jer. x. 25; Ps. xiv. 4.

defence is removed: lit. *shadow.* The figure is probably taken from the value of shade in a hot country (cf. Is. xxxii. 2)[1]; it is of frequent occurrence in O.T. and is found also in the Code of Hammurabi. The meaning of the use here is that the Canaanite gods have deserted their worshippers or become powerless to help them. To depreciate the power of a nation's deities was a favourite way of undermining its courage (cf. Is. xxxvi. 18 ff.)[2]; here the intention is to give new zeal to those attacking them. In Jud. viii. 5 the name Zalmunna means *shadow withheld* and is, as Burney thinks, in all probability a jesting perversion of some other name.

---

[1] Frazer thinks that there is some reference to the ancient and widespread idea that a man's shadow has some close connexion with his power and fortune (*Taboo* pp. 86 ff.).

[2] It was not unusual for the early Romans to tempt the gods of besieged cities to withdraw their protection and so to allow the stronghold to be captured; an interesting form of evocation is given by Macrob. *Saturnalia* III. ix.

and the LORD is with us: fear them not. 10 But all the congregation bade stone them with stones. And the glory of the LORD appeared in the tent of meeting unto all the children of Israel. *P*

11 And the LORD said unto Moses, How long will this people despise me? and how long will they not believe in me, for all the signs which I have wrought among them? 12 I will smite them with the pestilence, and disinherit them, and will make of thee a nation greater and mightier than they. 13 And Moses said unto the LORD, Then the Egyptians shall hear it; for thou broughtest up this people in thy might from among them; *R^JE*

10. *the glory of the* LORD. Caspari thinks that this was originally connected with some meteorological condition, the presence of storm and clouds: see *Die Bedeutung der Wortsippe* כבד *in Heb.* p. 104. Vollers thinks that the brilliance of the sun is meant: *Archiv für Relig.* IX. pp. 176 ff. In P the glory first appears on Mount Sinai (Ex. xxiv. 16 ff.) but is subsequently attached to the tabernacle. See also xvi. 19, 42.

11–19. The LORD threatens to destroy the people and to make of Moses a new nation. Moses intercedes for the people urging Jehovah to pardon them (*a*) because of His reputation amongst the nations (*vv.* 13–16), and (*b*) His character as merciful and gracious (*vv.* 17–19).

11. *How long.* Cf. Ex. xvi. 28 (P); Hos. viii. 5; Jer. xxiii. 26, xlvii. 6.

despise. Cf. *v.* 23; and the *Fragments of a Zadokite Work* I. 3 (*Oxford Apoc.* II. p. 799) "He...will execute judgement upon all who despise Him."

not believe. Contrast Abraham (Gen. xv. 6). The unbelief of Israel was the cause of their failure to enter into God's rest (Heb. iii. 19, iv. 11 &c.).

signs. The emphasis on signs as evidence is typical of O.T. (cf. Ex. xiv. 31); it is however found in the fourth gospel in N.T. (e.g. Jn. xii. 37). Signs, as Westcott says, "are more properly in their highest form the substance than the proofs of revelation" (*The Gospel of Life* p. 206).

12. *pestilence.* Cf. 2 S. xxiv. 13, 15; Jer. xiv. 12, xxi. 9.

disinherit them. Probably the exact meaning of the Heb. verb should not be pressed, *root them out, annihilate them*: cf. Ex. xv. 9 with Baentsch's note.

of thee. LXX and Sam. add *and thy father's house.* The carrying out of this plan would have involved a long delay in the fulfilment of God's purposes; incidentally it would have carried the process of selection, by which Isaac was chosen rather than Ishmael, Jacob than Esau, a stage further: cf. Ex. xxxii. 9–14.

13 f. The text of these *vv.* is very corrupt; the meaning can, however, be clearly gathered from the context.

13. *the Egyptians shall hear.* Cf. Ex. xxxii. 12; Dt. ix. 23 f.; Jos. vii. 9; Ps. lxxiv., lxxix., cxv.; Ez. xx. 9.

14 and they will tell it to the inhabitants of this land: they have heard that thou LORD art in the midst of this people; for thou LORD art seen [1]face to face, and thy cloud standeth over them, and thou goest before them, in a pillar of cloud by day, and in a pillar of fire by night. 15 Now if thou shalt kill this people as one man, then the nations which have heard the fame of thee will speak, saying, 16 Because the LORD was not able to bring this people into the land which he sware unto them, therefore he hath slain them in the wilderness. 17 And now, I pray thee, let the power of the Lord be great, according as thou hast spoken, saying, 18 The LORD is slow to anger, and plenteous in mercy, forgiving iniquity and transgression, and that will by no means clear *the guilty*; visiting the iniquity of the fathers upon the children, upon the third and upon the fourth generation. 19 Pardon, I pray thee, the iniquity of this people according unto the greatness of thy mercy, and according as thou hast forgiven this people, from Egypt even until now. 20 And R^{JE}

[1] Heb. *eye to eye.*

14. *this land.* Presumably Canaan.

face to face: lit. *eye to eye.* Cf. Is. lii. 8 with Wade's note.

pillar of cloud. See note on ix. 15 ff.

15. *as one man.* Cf. Jud. vi. 16.

16. For the sentiment of this *v.* cf. Dt. ix. 28.

17. *the power of the Lord.* Power "is always strength residing in the person, whether it be the *power* (Ex. xv. 6, xxxii. 11 &c.) or *might of wisdom* (Job xxxvi. 5) of Almighty God Himself, or *power* which He imparts (Dt. viii. 18; Jud. xvi. 5, 9, 19) or implants." Pusey on Mic. iii. 8.

18. The quotation is from Ex. xxxiv. 6 f. and it finds echoes in many other passages in O.T. (see McNeile *ad loc.*). It is also used by the pseudo-Ezra (4 Ezra vii. 152 ff.).

iniquity: lit. *twisting*, Lat. *iniquitas.* "The crooked wandering ways in which we live" (George Herbert).

transgression. Better *rebellion, apostasy,* even *defiance.* In Ex. xxxiv. 6 sin is added (so LXX, Syr. here), it means failure, missing the mark.

19. *from Egypt &c.* The record of the wanderings is a record of man's rebellion and God's forbearance.

20–25. The prayer of Moses is heard and the pardon of the people is pronounced: those however who had shewn their lack of faith will not be allowed to enter into the promised land. "In answer to this importunate prayer, the Lord promised forgiveness, namely, the preser-

the LORD said, I have pardoned according to thy word: 21 but *R^JE* in very deed, as I live, and as all the earth shall be filled with the glory of the LORD; 22 because all those men which have seen my glory, and my signs, which I wrought in Egypt and in the wilderness, yet have tempted me these ten times, and have not hearkened to my voice; 23 surely they shall not see the land which I sware unto their fathers, neither shall any of them that despised me see it: 24 but my servant Caleb, because he had another spirit with him, and hath followed me fully, him will I bring into the land whereinto he went; and his seed shall possess it. 25 Now the Amalekite and the Canaanite dwell in *R*

vation of the nation, but not the remission of the well-merited punishment" (Keil on *v.* 20).

20. *according to thy word.* Later ages loved to dwell on Moses' power of intercession: cf. Ps. cvi. 23; Jer. xv. 1 (with the present writer's note); *Assumpt. Moses* XI. 14.

21. *as I live.* Cf. Is. xlix. 18; Jer. xxii. 24, xlvi. 16; Zeph. ii. 9.

all the earth &c. "The glory of the Lord is the manifestation of His external majesty and dominion, of which the sphere is the whole world as contrasted with the limited area over which the authority of a mere national god was supposed to extend (1 S. xxvi. 19)" (Wade on Is. vi. 3).

22. *tempted me.* In old English *tempt* was a neutral word (cf. Lat. *tentare*) meaning "to *test* or *prove* a person, to see *whether* he would act in a particular way, or *whether* the character which he bore was well established" (Driver *Genesis* p. 217). Cf. our Lord's rebuke to Satan (Mt. iv. 7).

ten times. Used as a round number as in Gen. xxxi. 7 (Jacob's wages); Lev. xxvi. 26; Zech. viii. 23; and Job xix. 3. The Talmud has compiled a list of ten temptations (*'Arakhin* 15 *a b*). A list of various groups of ten has been collected in *Pirke Aboth* v. 1–9: cf. also the ten temptations of Abram: see Charles *Book of Jubilees* pp. 120 f.

23. *they shall not see.* The people had shewn their unfitness for the task laid upon them, a new and hardier generation were now to undertake it. LXX adds after *their fathers* "but their children which are with me here, as many as know not good nor evil, every young and inexperienced one, to them will I give the land."

despised. See on *v.* 11.

24. *Caleb.* See Jos. xiv. 6–15; Jud. i. 20 for the fulfilment of the promise. There is here no mention of Joshua as in Dt. i. 36: cf. xiii. 30 above.

followed me fully. Complete obedience and complete confidence: cf. xxxii. 11; Dt. i. 36.

25. *the Amalekite and the Canaanite.* See on xiii. 29.

the valley: to-morrow turn ye, and get you into the wilderness *R* by the way to the Red Sea.

26 And the LORD spake unto Moses and unto Aaron, saying, *P* 27 How long *shall I bear* with this evil congregation, which murmur against me? I have heard the murmurings of the children of Israel, which they murmur against me. 28 Say unto them, As I live, saith the LORD, surely as ye have spoken in

the valley. In *v*. 45 the two peoples are said to be in the mountain. The two statements are not however inconsistent, as a valley in the hill-country would fit both. G. A. Smith *Hist. Geog.* p. 384 indeed goes so far as to say that the Heb. word here used עמק "is never applied to any extensive plain away from hills, but always to wide avenues running up into mountainous country." This ruling though accepted by Gray can hardly be justified in view of the usage in Jud. i. 19, 34, v. 15 *c*; 1 K. xx. 28 &c.: see Burney *Judges* pp. 203 f. In Dt. i. 44 which is parallel to *v*. 45 Amorites are substituted for Amalekite and Canaanite.

to-morrow. Cf. xi. 18.

the way to the Red Sea. Clay Trumbull (*Kadesh-Barnea* pp. 7 f., 352 ff.) regards this as the name of a specific highway *The Red Sea Road*, a road which ran from Elah to the top of the Gulf of Suez, and may be identified with a track still used by pilgrims. But this road would be too far away and the context requires something less definite. The Red Sea is in Heb. יַם סוּף *sea of rushes*; the name in E.VV. comes eventually from LXX ἡ ἐρυθρὰ θάλασσα. The term is used rather loosely: here and in xxi. 4; Dt. i. 40; Jer. xlix. 21 it seems to mean the Gulf of Akaba; in xxxiii. 10 f.; Ex. xl. 19 &c. and originally it meant the upper end of the Gulf of Suez: see McNeile *Exodus* pp. xcvii. and 81, W. Max Müller *As. u. Eur.* pp. 42 f.

26–38. The Lord swears that Israel shall wander for forty years in the wilderness until the faithless generation, excepting Caleb *and Joshua* (*v*. 30), has passed away. The punishment which befell the people was no merely arbitrary act: the unbelief and disobedience which they had repeatedly exhibited shewed their unsuitability for the conquest of Canaan. The tradition of the forty years wandering is early (Am. ii. 10, v. 25) though Meyer (*IN* p. 140: cf. Steuernagel *Die Einwanderung &c.* pp. 70 ff.) thinks that it formed no part of J[1]. The present passage is parallel to *vv*. 11–25 and probably was unknown to D since Dt. i. 40 = *v*. 25 and Dt. i. 41 = *v*. 40: see Chapman *Introd. Pent.* p. 95.

28. *saith the LORD*. The phrase so common in the prophets נאם יהוה *oracle of Yahweh* appears here and Gen. xxii. 16 only in Pent.: see also note on xxiv. 3.

---

[1] The tradition in the prophets seems often to pre-suppose that the wilderness period instead of being a time of disobedience and punishment was a time of purity both of conduct and worship: cf. Am. ii. 9 f., v. 25 f.; Hos. ii. 14; Jer. ii. 2 f., vii. 22 f. (contrast *vv*. 24 f.).

mine ears, so will I do to you: 29 your carcases shall fall in this *P* wilderness; and all that were numbered of you, according to your whole number, from twenty years old and upward, which have murmured against me, 30 surely ye shall not come into the land, concerning which I lifted up my hand that I would make you dwell therein, save Caleb the son of Jephunneh, and Joshua the son of Nun. 31 But your little ones, which ye said should be a prey, them will I bring in, and they shall know the land which ye have rejected. 32 But as for you, your carcases shall fall in this wilderness. 33 And your children shall be [1]wanderers in the wilderness forty years, and shall bear your whoredoms, until your carcases be consumed in the wilderness. 34 After the number of the days in which ye spied out the land, even forty days, for every day a year, shall ye bear your iniquities, even forty years, and ye shall know [2]my alienation. 35 I the LORD have spoken, surely this will I do unto all this evil congregation, that are gathered together against me: in this wilderness they shall be consumed, and there they shall die. 36 And the men, which Moses sent to spy out the land, who returned, and made all the congregation to murmur against him, by bringing up an

[1] Heb. *shepherds*. [2] Or, *the revoking of my promise*

29. *your carcases*. The Heb. word may be used of the bodies of men or of animals; R.V. rendering reproduces the contemptuous tone of the original.

from twenty &c. Probably the Levites were excluded from this sentence according to P: e.g. Eleazar who was certainly over twenty at Sinai (iii. 3 f., 32, iv. 16) is amongst those who enter Canaan: cf. also Jos. xxiv. 33 (E).

30. *lifted up my hand*. That is *I swore*: cf. Gen. xiv. 22; Ex. v. 8; common in Ez. xx. 5 &c.; the phrase is extended in Dt. xxxii. 40 by the addition of *to heaven* which gives an exact parallel to Virgil *Aen.* XII. 196 *tenditque ad sidera dextram*.

31. *be a prey*. Cf. *v.* 3; Dt. i. 39; Jer. ii. 14.

33. *wanderers*: lit. *shepherds*.

whoredoms. Common in the prophets for unfaithfulness to God.

be consumed. Better *be completed*. The meaning is not that the wanderings are to continue until the individual corpses have rotted away, but until the toll of those condemned has been taken in full.

34. *forty days...forty years*. Round numbers are used in either case: cf. the similar pronouncement to Ezekiel (iv. 6).

my alienation. That is the withdrawal of God's favour will be known by the disasters which will ensue.

evil report against the land, 37 even those men that did bring up an evil report of the land, died by the plague before the LORD. 38 But Joshua the son of Nun, and Caleb the son of Jephunneh, remained alive of those men that went to spy out the land. *P*

CHAPTER XIV. 39–45.

The defeat at Hormah.

In spite of the divine sentence the people attempt to force their way into the promised land. Moses and the ark remain in the camp and the people are repulsed and driven back. "It is human nature, to neglect to serve God, when He wills it, and then to attempt to serve Him when He forbids it" (Pusey on Hos. ix. 4). Nöldeke thinks that this account is a 'less accurate version' of Ex. xvii. 8 ff. (*Enc. Bib.* 128). The narrative in Dt. i. 41 ff. is parallel except for certain differences which will be noticed below.

39 And Moses told these words unto all the children of Israel: and the people mourned greatly. 40 And they rose up early in the morning, and gat them up to the top of the mountain, saying, Lo, we be here, and will go up unto the place which the LORD hath promised: for we have sinned. 41 And Moses said, Wherefore now do ye transgress the commandment of the LORD, seeing it shall not prosper? 42 Go not up, for the LORD is not among you; that ye be not smitten down before your enemies. 43 For there the Amalekite and the Canaanite are before you, and ye shall fall by the sword: because ye are turned back from following the LORD, therefore the LORD will not be with you. 44 But they presumed to go up to the top of the mountain: nevertheless the ark of the covenant of the LORD, *JE*

40. *to the top of the mountain.* Cf. Ex. xvii. 9. There is no mention of this in Dt. i.

hath promised. Cf. x. 29.

we have sinned. So in Dt. i. 41.

42. This *v.* = Dt. i. 42 except that the words are there spoken by the Lord to Moses as a message for the people.

the LORD. That is the ark was not with them according to *v.* 44: cf. 1 S. iv. 5 ff.

43. *the Amalekite...the Canaanite.* In Dt. i. 44 'the Amorites' is read.

not be with you. This and similar phrases (e.g. Dt. xxxi. 8, 23; Jos. i. 5, iii. 7, vii. 12) are taken by some scholars as references to the meaning of the divine personal name Yahweh *I will be*: see Hehn *BBG* p. 215.

44. *the ark.* See on x. 33. There is no reference to the ark in Dt. i. 41 ff.

and Moses, departed not out of the camp. 45 Then the Amalekite came down, and the Canaanite which dwelt in that mountain, and smote them and beat them down, even unto Hormah. *JE*

45. *Hormah.* See on xxi. 1–3. Buhl (*Geog.* p. 184) identifies it with *Sebaiṭa* on the ground of its resemblance to *Zephath* the old name of Hormah according to Jud. i. 17. This identification is now generally abandoned as the resemblance is not close and *Sebaiṭa* was probably not known before Christian times (see Lawrence *P.E.F. Annual* III. 91). Gressmann suggests *Naḳb es-Ṣafâ* (*Mose* p. 296).

CHAPTER XV.

VARIOUS LAWS AND REGULATIONS.

This section is similar to that contained in chh. v. and vi. in that it consists of a number of miscellaneous regulations which have but little apparent connexion one with another, and further, the whole collection has no definite relation with its context. Sayce indeed goes so far as to say that the ch. is "an interpolation which is singularly out of place in the narrative, and seems to have been substituted for a description of the disasters which followed on the abortive attempt of the Israelites to invade Canaan" (*EHH* p. 207).

Sacrificial directions. 1–16.
The cake of the heave offering. 17–21.
Unconscious trespasses. 22–31.
The punishment of the Sabbath-breaker. 32–36.
The wearing of fringes. 37–41.

CHAPTER XV. 1–16.

Sacrificial directions.

The regulations here set forth state the proper quantities of meal, oil, and wine to be offered with burnt offerings or 'peace' offerings. The attempt to systematise voluntary offerings points to a late date in the developement of Israelite sacrificial law. Three separate groups of regulations deal with the matter of the meal offering: (*a*) in Lev. ii. 1 ff. the offering of independent gifts is considered and no fixed amounts are required; (*b*) in Ez. xlvi. 5 ff. there is a scale appointed for meal offerings such as are dealt with in the present passage (i.e. those offered with other sacrifices); the main difference between them is that Ezekiel concerns himself with public offerings only and still allows room for an optional element; (*c*) the present passage which fixes the amounts for all sacrifices, public and private, and eliminates the optional element; the scale too is different from that fixed in Ezekiel.

The three articles of which the meal offering is to be made up have all been subjected to some process of manufacture, they are not the pure natural products. They were chosen probably as the staple articles of the diet of the people (Ps. cv. 15; Hos. ii. 22; Joel ii. 19; Neh. x. 39). In a similar way the Phoenicians offered milk and fat in their corresponding sacrifice: see *NSI* No. 42 *l.* 14.

XV. 1 And the LORD spake unto Moses, saying, 2 Speak unto the children of Israel, and say unto them, When ye be come into the land of your habitations, which I give unto you, 3 and will make an offering by fire unto the LORD, a burnt offering, or a sacrifice, [1]to accomplish a vow, or as a freewill offering, or in your set feasts, to make a sweet savour unto the LORD, of the herd, or of the flock: 4 then shall he that offereth his oblation offer unto the LORD a meal offering of a tenth part *P*

[1] Or, *in making a special vow*

XV. 2. *When ye be come.* It is important to notice that this legislation does not apply to the wilderness period.

land of your habitations. The phrase appears here only.

3. *offering by fire.* This type of sacrifice is found in P only (with the exception of Dt. xviii. 1; Jos. xiii. 14; 1 S. ii. 28 all D). The word in the original is אִשֶּׁה and has been connected with אֵשׁ *fire*, hence the rendering of E.VV.; but this derivation is by no means certain as it may be connected with an Arabic root signifying an offering of any kind. LXX render variously by ὁλοκαύτωμα which supports the connexion with *fire*, and by κάρπωμα or κάρπωσις: these two last words by their use had also come to be applied to sacrifices by *fire*: see Deissmann *Bibelstudien* pp. 134 f.; E. L. Hicks in *Journal of Hellenic Studies* IX. pp. 323 ff., and Kittel *Studien zur hebr. Arch.* pp. 96 ff. The use of *fire* in sacrifice was of course to spiritualise the material offering[1].

burnt offering...sacrifice. These two forms of sacrifice are distinguished by the fate of the offering; in the former the flesh is entirely consumed, in the latter the offerer himself partook of it. There is no mention here of the later types of offering known as the sin and guilt offerings.

a vow. See on vi. 2.

a sweet savour. Ancient peoples imagined that the deity took a delight in the fumes of burning sacrifices: cf. the well known instance in the Babylonian Deluge Story when "the gods gathered like flies over the sacrifices" (Rogers *CP* p. 98), and in the similar story in O.T. itself where Jehovah "smelled the sweet savour" and was propitiated (Gen. viii. 21 f.). In later usage the anthropomorphic origin of the term was forgotten: cf. Eph. v. 2; Phil. iv. 18.

herd...flock. The sacrifices of the primitive nomads would generally be animal (cf. W. Robertson Smith *Rel. Sem.*[2] p. 222), the additional offerings of *vv.* 5 f. are agricultural and belong to a later stage.

4. *he that offereth.* Notice the sudden change to the singular.

meal offering. Heb. מִנְחָה. In earlier times the word, which means

[1] "Fire destroys the material part of sacrifices, it purifies all things that are brought near it, releasing them from the bonds of matter and, in virtue of the purity of its nature, making them meet for the communion of the gods." Jamblichus *De Mysteriis* v. 12.

of an ephah of fine flour mingled with the fourth part of an hin P of oil: 5 and wine for the drink offering, the fourth part of an hin, shalt thou prepare with the burnt offering or for the sacrifice, for each lamb. 6 Or for a ram, thou shalt prepare for a meal offering two tenth parts *of an ephah* of fine flour mingled with the third part of an hin of oil: 7 and for the drink offering thou shalt offer the third part of an hin of wine, of a sweet savour unto the LORD. 8 And when thou preparest a bullock for a burnt offering, or for a sacrifice, [1]to accomplish a vow, or for peace offerings unto the LORD: 9 then shall he offer with the bullock a meal offering of three tenth parts *of an ephah* of fine flour mingled with half an hin of oil. 10 And thou shalt offer for the drink offering half an hin of wine, for an offering made

[1] Or, *in making a special vow*

present and sometimes *tribute*, was used of any kind of sacrifice, even as in Gen. iv. 4 f.; 1 S. xxvi. 19, of animal sacrifices. In later usage it came to be limited to non-animal sacrifices[1]. The rendering of A.V. *meat offering* may have been suggested by parallelism with drink offering. LXX usually renders *θυσία* (142 times), the more correct *δῶρον* being employed only 32 times.

the fourth part of an hin. Rather more than two and a half pints, see Benzinger *Arch.* pp. 182 ff.

oil. Oil was used in Babylonian sacrifices, but apparently not by the early Egyptians: see Sayce *HCM* p. 279.

5. *drink offering.* Cf. Gen. xxxv. 14; Hos. ix. 4; Jer. vii. 18 &c. Libations were not so common in Hebrew religion as in that of the Arabs: see W. Robertson Smith *Rel. Sem.*[2] pp. 229 ff. The root נסך means *to pour out*, and is used of casting metal in Is. xl. 19 and נֶסֶךְ of a *graven image* is found in Jer. x. 14, li. 17; Is. xli. 29, xlviii. 5.

shalt thou. Change to second person, cf. Lev. ii. 2 ff.

7. *wine, of a sweet savour.* The same combination is found in Ecclus. l. 15. The usual reference of *sweet savour* is to the smoke of a burning sacrifice (see on *v.* 3); some scholars have suggested that the libation was originally poured over the sacrifice, as in the Greek and Roman ritual, though in the later use of the Jewish people it was poured at the foot of the altar (Ecclus. l. 15; Joseph. *Ant.* III. ix. 4; cf. Nowack *Arch.* II. p. 246).

---

[1] There is much looseness in the use of sacrificial terms in all religions, both by way of restriction and amplification; the very word 'sacrifice' itself is an illustration of the former process, since strictly speaking it refers to anything made sacred; an illustration of the latter process may be found in the extension of זבח *slaughter* to include vegetable sacrifices, as in the Phoenician lists *CIS* Nos. 165, 167. Cf. also Arabic نسك *pour a libation* which is used of sacrificing in general.

by fire, of a sweet savour unto the LORD. 11 Thus shall it be done for each bullock, or for each ram, or for each of the he-lambs, or of the kids. 12 According to the number that ye shall prepare, so shall ye do to every one according to their number. 13 All that are homeborn shall do these things after this manner, in offering an offering made by fire, of a sweet savour unto the LORD. 14 And if a stranger sojourn with you, or whosoever be among you throughout your generations, and will offer an offering made by fire, of a sweet savour unto the LORD; as ye do, so he shall do. 15 For the assembly, there shall be one statute for you, and for the stranger that sojourneth *with you*, a statute for ever throughout your generations: as ye are, so shall the stranger be before the LORD. 16 One law and one ordinance shall be for you, and for the stranger that sojourneth with you. *P*

13. *homeborn.* LXX αὐτόχθων, the native Israelite.

14. *a stranger.* See on ix. 14. In the later law the Israelite and the sojourner were in an almost identical position "in respect of civic, moral, and religious rights and duties" (Gray).

CHAPTER XV. 17–21.

The cake of the heave offering.

The whole subject of firstfruits is regulated by the laws in ch. xviii., the provision here is an anticipation of the more general treatment. Unfortunately the exact meaning of the word עֲרִיסָה *'arīsah* which is rendered *dough* is by no means certain. Most scholars following the usage of the later post-biblical Heb. which has a corresponding word *'arsān* for a kind of barley paste (cf. also Syr. *'arsana* 'hulled barley') render *coarse meal.* In the passage in Ez. xliv. 30 where it also occurs both Smend and Cornill prefer *kneading-trough.*

According to later custom if a Jewish woman failed to set apart the first of the dough her husband was justified in divorcing her (*Kethuboth* VII. 6).

17 And the LORD spake unto Moses, saying, 18 Speak unto the children of Israel, and say unto them, When ye come into the land whither I bring you, 19 then it shall be, that, when ye eat of the bread of the land, ye shall offer up an heave offering unto the LORD. 20 Of the first of your [1]dough ye shall offer up

[1] Or, *coarse meal*

18. *When ye come.* Cf. *v.* 2.

19. *offer...heave offering.* See on v. 9.

a cake for an heave offering: as ye do the heave offering of the *P* threshing-floor, so shall ye heave it. 21 Of the first of your dough ye shall give unto the LORD an heave offering throughout your generations.

20. *cake.* Cf. Ex. xxix. 2; Lev. ii. 4.
the threshing-floor. See on xviii. 27.

CHAPTER XV. 22–31.

Unconscious trespasses.

The subject of unconscious trespasses is dealt with in Lev. iv. and v. The laws here seem to be older because simpler and less developed. Whereas in the present passage two classes only are distinguished, (*a*) the congregation (*vv.* 22–26), and (*b*) the individual (*vv.* 27 f.), in Lev. the offerings of the high-priest and of the prince are separately provided for. The Rabbis endeavoured to distinguish the laws here from those in Lev. by making the former apply to sins of omission, the latter to sins of commission; but Lev. v. 2 refers to a sin of omission, and Num. xv. 24, 29 f. have in view sins of commission.

It should be noticed that sins committed deliberately were not capable of being atoned for: see further on *v.* 30. It is interesting to compare the idea of Socrates that sin consisted in ignorance, that the man who had knowledge of what was right would not do other than perform it[1].

The Romans made a similar distinction between the *impurus* and the *impius* (see Dussaud *Les origines canan. du sacrifice israël.*[2] p. 118).

22 And when ye shall err, and not observe all these commandments, which the LORD hath spoken unto Moses, 23 even all that the LORD hath commanded you by the hand of Moses, from the day that the LORD gave commandment, and onward throughout your generations; 24 then it shall be, if it be done [1]unwittingly, without the knowledge of the congregation, that

[1] Or, *in error*

22. *all these commandments.* This section is evidently out of its context; its original place would seem to have been at the close of a long list of laws.
23. *by the hand of Moses.* See iv. 37.
24. *unwittingly.* Mg. *in error.* That is sins done in ignorance or defilement contracted without the wish of the one incurring it.
without the knowledge of. Cf. Lev. iv. 13 Heb. is literally *from the eyes of*: see *G-K*[28] § 119 *w*.

---

[1] Cf. Aristotle *Eth. Nicom.* VII. 3 (1145 *b* 23 f.): *δεινὸν γὰρ ἐπιστήμης ἐνούσης, ὡς ᾤετο Σωκράτης, ἄλλο τι κρατεῖν καὶ περιέλκειν αὐτὴν ὥσπερ ἀνδράποδον.*

all the congregation shall offer one young bullock for a burnt *P* offering, for a sweet savour unto the LORD, with the meal offering thereof, and the drink offering thereof, according to the ordinance, and one he-goat for a sin offering. 25 And the priest shall make atonement for all the congregation of the children of Israel, and they shall be forgiven; for it was an error, and they have brought their oblation, an offering made by fire unto the LORD, and their sin offering before the LORD, for their error: 26 and all the congregation of the children of Israel shall be forgiven, and the stranger that sojourneth among them; for in respect of all the people it was done unwittingly. 27 And if one person sin unwittingly, then he shall offer a she-goat of the first year for a sin offering. 28 And the priest shall make atonement for the soul that erreth, when he sinneth unwittingly, before the LORD, to make atonement for him; and he shall be forgiven. 29 Ye shall have one law for him that doeth aught unwittingly, for him that is homeborn among the children of Israel, and for the stranger that sojourneth among them. 30 But the soul that doeth aught with an high hand, whether he be homeborn or a stranger, the same blasphemeth the LORD; and that soul shall be cut off from among his people. 31 Because he hath despised the word of the LORD, and hath broken his commandment;

for a burnt offering. This is not required in Lev. iv.

sin offering. In most contexts this sacrifice comes before the burnt offering; another exception is Lev. xii. 8.

25. *make atonement*. Heb. כִּפֶּר. Two primary meanings have been suggested for the word: (*a*) that of covering (cf. the Arabic) and (*b*) that of wiping away (cf. the Syriac). From early times some idea of ritual purgation seems to have been attached to the word: see Driver in *HERE* under *Atonement* (*Hebrew*) and *Expiation*, and for a more elaborate study Herrmann *Die Idee der Sühne im A.T.*

27–29. In Lev. iv. a he-goat is required from a prince (*vv.* 23 f.), a she-goat (*vv.* 28 f.) or a female lamb (*v.* 32) from a commoner.

30. *an high hand*. Cf. Dt. xvii. 12; Ps. xix. 13; and see note on xi. 23.

blasphemeth. The Heb. word appears here only in Pent. and is regarded by Holzinger as an Aramaism.

shall be cut off. For deliberate sins the Hebrew sacrificial system provided no atonement (cf. Davidson *Theology of O.T.* pp. 316 ff.). The true Israelite would never think of sinning deliberately against Jehovah: so too the Christian is expected to avoid all sin (1 Jn. iii. 9). See further on ix. 13.

31. *despised the word*. The same condemnation falls upon David

that soul shall utterly be cut off, his iniquity shall be upon him. *P*

for the murder of Uriah the Hittite (2 S. xii. 9). Cf. Prov. xiii. 13, xix. 16[1].

Chapter XV. 32–36.

The punishment of the Sabbath-breaker.

The punishment of the Sabbath-breaker is an instance of the fate of those who commit sin with a high hand. A parallel to this method of illustrating the breach of the law by quoting an actual case is to be found in Lev. xxiv. 10 ff. The story, although a very late one, is valuable as shewing the conception which the Jews themselves had of the manner in which their laws grew up.

The instance here recorded may be compared with the saying of our Blessed Lord preserved in Codex D (Lk. vi. 5): τῇ αὐτῇ ἡμέρᾳ θεασάμενός τινα ἐργαζόμενον τῷ σαββάτῳ εἶπεν αὐτῷ· ἄνθρωπε, εἰ μὲν οἶδας τί ποιεῖς, μακάριος εἶ· εἰ δὲ μὴ οἶδας, ἐπικατάρατος καὶ παραβάτης εἶ τοῦ νόμου.

32 And while the children of Israel were in the wilderness, they found a man gathering sticks upon the sabbath day. 33 And they that found him gathering sticks brought him unto Moses and Aaron, and unto all the congregation. 34 And they put him in ward, because it had not been declared what should be done to him. 35 And the Lord said unto Moses, The man shall surely be put to death: all the congregation shall stone him with stones without the camp. 36 And all the congregation brought him without the camp, and stoned him with stones, and he died; as the Lord commanded Moses. *P*s

32. *were in the wilderness.* This statement seems to be the sign of a later date.

gathering sticks. Cf. 1 K. xvii. 12. According to the law fires were not to be kindled (Ex. xxxv. 3) on the Sabbath.

34. *been declared.* Heb. פֹּרַשׁ: perhaps connected with the Assyr. *pirishtu* meaning *oracular decision* (see Paterson in *SBOT*).

what should be done. The penalty was death (Ex. xxxi. 14 f., xxxv. 2); but the exact form under which it was to be inflicted had not yet been made clear.

36. *all the congregation.* Robertson Smith considers that in the execution of a member of the tribe if possible "every member of the kindred should not only be a consenting party but a partaker in the act, so that whatever responsibility it involves may be equally distributed over the whole clan" (*Rel. Sem.*[2] p. 285).

---

[1] According to the Rabbis he who could occupy himself with the Torah and fails to do so offends in this way (*Sanhed.* 99 *a*).

CHAPTER XV. 37–41.

The wearing of fringes.

The origin of wearing fringes or tassels on the garments is obscure. Robertson Smith makes reference to the passage in Herodotus (IV. 189) in which the sacrificial customs of the Libyan women are described, and amongst them the wearing of goat skins with fringes made of thongs of leather (*Rel. Sem.*[2] p. 437). Similar customs are found, according to the testimony of the monuments, among many of the nations of antiquity (see *Enc. Bib.* col. 1565). How the custom first arose among the Hebrews, whether borrowed from the Canaanites or from elsewhere, is quite unknown, but the habit when once adopted was never allowed to drop, traces of it are to be found in N.T. (Mt. ix. 20, xiv. 36, xxiii. 5; Mk. vi. 56), and to the present day every orthodox Jew over the age of thirteen fulfils the command by wearing the *ṭallith*, an oblong cloth with a hole in the middle through which the head is inserted and from whose four corners a tassel hangs.

The wearing of the fringe was to the ordinary Israelite what the long hair was to the Nazirite, a mark of his separation; the danger of this and all similar distinctions is that they tend to become signs of privilege rather than memorials of duty.

A parallel to this regulation is found in Dt. xxii. 12, and a law of similar intention in Ex. xiii. 9 where extracts from the law are commanded to be worn on the arm and between the eyes. The present passage shews signs, especially in *v.* 41, of coming from H.

37 And the LORD spake unto Moses, saying, 38 Speak unto *H* the children of Israel, and bid them that they make them [1]fringes in the borders of their garments throughout their generations, and that they put upon the fringe of each border a cord of blue: 39 and it shall be unto you for a fringe, that ye may

[1] Or, *tassels in the corners*

38. *fringes in the borders.* Read with mg. *tassels in the corners.* The word for tassels ציצת occurs elsewhere in Ez. viii. 3 only, and there has the meaning of *locks of hair*; it is perhaps connected with Assyr. *ṣîṣu* which means *something twisted or platted*, others connect it with the word ציץ *flower* (Is. xl. 6 &c.). See further S. A. Cook's article in *Enc. Bib.* col. 1565, Driver on Dt. xii. 12 (*ICC*), and an article "On the law of fringes in Num. and Dt." in *Bib. Sac.* 1894 pp. 705 ff.

garments. The word used is a general one, but the reference must be to the outer garment: see Benzinger *Arch.* p. 98.

a cord of blue. The colour, which is not mentioned in Dt. xxii. 12, may have been chosen because it is the colour of the sky. In Ecclus. vi. 30 the fetters of Wisdom are said to be a cord of blue (the words are the same in both Heb. and Gk.)[1].

39. *for a fringe.* We should expect 'for a *sign*': cf. Dussaud *Les Origines*[2] p. 44.

[1] In later times white threads were also allowed: see *Menaḥoth* IV. 1.

look upon it, and remember all the commandments of the LORD, *H*
and do them; and that ye [1]go not about after your own heart
and your own eyes, after which ye use to go a whoring: 40 that
ye may remember and do all my commandments, and be holy
unto your God. 41 I am the LORD your God, which brought
you out of the land of Egypt, to be your God: I am the LORD
your God.

[1] Heb. *spy not out.*

may look...and remember. There is in man's heart a pathetic desire for reminders of God's ways and commandments, and so for safeguards against temptation: in a similar manner a cross or a crucifix is worn by Christians.

after your own heart. Cf. Ez. vi. 9.

your own eyes. Cf. 1 Jn. ii. 16.

40. *be holy.* Cf. Lev. xi. 44 f.

41. *to be your God.* This is a characteristic thought of Jeremiah and of Ezekiel: see Driver on Gen. xvii. 7.

CHAPTERS XVI. AND XVII.

THE STORY OF KORAH, DATHAN, AND ABIRAM.

The position of the various elements which went to make up the Israelite people, and their relative privileges and rank, were matters upon which much doubt seems to have existed and over which struggle and protest were aroused. These quarrels are in the present division read back into the time of the wilderness wanderings, though so vague is the situation that it is impossible to localise it. The two chh. into which the text is divided by E.VV. give a convenient arrangement of the subject matter.

The rebellion and its punishment. xvi.
The rod that budded. xvii.

CHAPTER XVI.

The rebellion and its punishment.

The narrative in its present form gives an account of a rebellion against Moses and Aaron by two distinct groups of people, the Levites under Korah, and a body of laymen under the Reubenites Dathan and Abiram (On is to be ignored: see note on *v.* 1). Acting apparently independently and inspired by different motives, the one body having as its object the recognition of the 'full orders' of Levites, the other wishing to protest against the exalted position of Moses, they instigate rebellions. The divine power is exerted in favour of the state of things against which they agitated, and those taking part in the movements are punished; Dathan and Abiram by the opening of the earth beneath them, and the company of Korah by an outbreak of fire; in the latter case appeal was first made by a kind of ordeal to Jehovah to declare who were His rightful representatives.

That two bodies of men with entirely different grievances should choose the same moment to press for their removal is not unknown (e.g. in connexion with industrial disputes), and in itself would not be enough to discredit the narrative, as it is possible to discover traces of what might be regarded as common action—on the one hand the band of two hundred and fifty men who were associated with Korah were themselves probably non-Levites (see on *v.* 2) and might therefore be acting in the interest of the lay protest; on the other hand the protest of Dathan and Abiram has some affinity with that of Korah since the question of a religious offering comes in (*v.* 15)[1]. If the narrative as it stands is substantially accurate it must from any point of view have been clumsily worked over by a later editor—the fate of Korah and his men, for example, cannot be as stated, for according to *v.* 32 they were swallowed up, according to *v.* 35 they were burned with fire, and still more to confuse matters in another passage the "sons of Korah" themselves survived (xxvi. 11)[2].

Recent scholars have seen in the story a combination of two, or better still, of three sources; the revolt of Dathan and Abiram, which on linguistic and other grounds has been assigned to JE, forms almost a complete whole; the other sources deal with the revolt of Korah and belong to the school of P.

The original story in P recorded a revolt, not of Levites against the separation of the priests, but of the representatives of the whole congregation against the separation of the Levites. If the institution of the Levites goes back to the time of Moses, an unlikely supposition, it may have had a basis in real fact: more probably it represents a reaction in later times against the claims of the Levites and the story of the punishment of the objectors in the days of Moses was composed by the Priestly writer to silence such rebels in his own day. A still later writer changed Korah and his associates into Levites, and made their protest to be directed against the superior position of the priests. The latter addition makes the narrative exceedingly confusing.

The references to the story in other places give some slight clue to the date of the composition of the various sources. In Dt. xi. 6 Dathan and Abiram alone are referred to, but the same limited reference occurs in 4 Macc. ii. 17; in Num. xxvii. 3, as in Jude 11, Korah alone is mentioned. Both stories are combined in Num. xxvi. 9 f.; Ps. cvi. 16 ff.; Ecclus. xlv. 18.

The following is an analysis of the story as it stands at present (for its division into sources see Introd. pp. xxxi f.):

(*a*) *The test of holiness.* 1–7.
(*b*) *Moses rebukes the Levites.* 8–11.
(*c*) *Moses is defied.* 12–15.
(*d*) *The assembly before the tent of meeting.* 16–24.
(*e*) *The punishment of the rebels.* 25–35.
(*f*) *The memorial of the censers.* 36–40.
(*g*) *The outbreak of plague.* 41–50.

---

[1] This is admitted by *CH*: "Dathan and Abiram defy the authority of Moses on the ground that he has failed to fulfil his promise, and he replies by entreating Yahweh to pay no attention to their offering. The basis of ver. 15 is clearly some religious act, culminating in sacrifice, and having affinity rather with Korah's protest than with the rebellion of Dathan and Abiram" (II. p. 212).

[2] The text says nothing definite about the fate of Korah's sons, only about those of Dathan and Abiram (*v.* 27).

XVI. 1 Now Korah, | the son of Izhar, the son of Kohath, the son of Levi, | with Dathan and Abiram, the sons of Eliab, and On, the son of Peleth, sons of Reuben, took *men*: 2 and they rose up before Moses, | with certain of the children of Israel, two hundred and fifty princes of the congregation, called to the *P–Ps* *JE* *P*

XVI. 1–7. Certain of the children of Israel rebel against the position of isolation above the congregation taken up by Moses and Aaron. Moses challenges them to the ordeal of the censers.

1. *Korah...the son of Levi.* The Korahites were a branch of the Levites (Ex. vi. 16 ff.; 1 Chr. vi. 37 f.), and were especially associated with the temple choirs (see the titles of Pss. xlii.–xlix.). Another Korah was an Edomite clan which became part of Judah (see W. E. Addis in *Enc. Bib.* cols. 2686 ff.). It is very probable that the same person or clan is intended by the Edomite and the Levite: cf. the similar transformation which has taken place in the instance of Samuel, who was in reality an Ephraimite (1 S. i. 1, 19 f.), but regarded as a Levite by later tradition (1 Chr. vi. 33)[1].

Dathan and Abiram. The name *Dathan* does not occur elsewhere. Abiram is of course closely related to Abram and the Assyr. *Abī-rāmu.*

and On, the son of Peleth. Beyond the bare mention here *On* takes no part in the rebellion; Keil and other conservative commentators think that he must therefore have withdrawn from the conspiracy. A better explanation is to follow Graf (*Gesch. Bücher* p. 89) and to omit *and On* (ואון) as a dittography of (El)*iab* (יאב), and to read *Pallu* for *Peleth* (so LXX), thus making the genealogy agree with xxvi. 8 f. and other passages. Bacon (*Triple Trad.* p. 190), however, retains the present text and takes *Peleth* as being Philistine; the story then relates the unsuccessful attempt of *Korah the Edomite* and *On the Philistine* to enter the sanctuary.

sons of Reuben. That members of the tribe of Reuben should resent the superior position of Moses would be natural in view of the diminished glory of that tribe (cf. Gen. xlix. 3 f.). Blunt (*Undesigned Coincidences* Pt. I. § xx.) points out that the Levites marched after the camp of Reuben (cf. ii. 10 ff.) and suggests that the conspiracy grew out of their neighbourhood. Whatever value might be attached to this theory is much diminished when it is noticed that the actual neighbours of the Levites in the camp were not the Reubenites themselves but the tribe of Gad (ii. 14 ff.).

took men. The object here supplied is not convincing, perhaps offerings was the original reading (cf. *v.* 15).

2. *princes of the congregation.* See notes on iv. 34 and vii. 2. These *princes* are in P called elders (cf. *v.* 25) or captains in JE: they repre-

---

[1] In Mohammedan tradition Korah (Kārūn) is sometimes identified with Croesus: see D. B. Macdonald *Aspects of Islam* pp. 225 f.

assembly, men of renown: 3 and they assembled themselves *P* together against Moses and against Aaron, and said unto them, [1]Ye take too much upon you, seeing all the congregation are holy, every one of them, and the LORD is among them: wherefore then lift ye up yourselves above the assembly of the LORD? 4 And when Moses heard it, he fell upon his face: 5 and he spake unto Korah and unto all his company, saying, In the morning the LORD will shew who are his, and who is holy, and [2]will cause him to come near unto him: even him whom he shall choose will he cause to come near unto him. 6 This do; take you

[1] Heb. *It is enough for you.*
[2] Or, *whom he will cause to come near*

sented evidently other tribes besides that of Levi; cf. the statement in xxvii. 3 that Zelophehad the Manassite was not amongst them.

called to the assembly. A similar phrase is used in i. 16; it would appear to be a technical term like 'counsellor' but its exact meaning has been lost.

men of renown: lit. *men of name.* Cf. similar phrases in Gen. vi. 4; 1 Chr. v. 24, xii. 30, and contrast Job xxx. 8 where 'children of base men' is literally 'children of nameless men.' For a full discussion of the significance of 'names' see Giesebrecht *Die alttest. Schätzung des Gottesnamens* pp. 13 ff.

3. *Ye take too much upon you.* The meaning of the Heb. phrase רַב־לָכֶם is hardly represented by this rendering: a better would be *We have had enough of you (and your pretensions)*: cf. Dt. i. 6, ii. 3, iii. 26. The phrase perhaps underlies our Lord's utterance in Lk. xxii. 38 in connexion with St Peter's production of the two swords.

all...holy. The interpolator, who represented Korah as a Levite, apparently did not realise the force of this expression denying as it does the special status of the Levites.

the LORD is among them. Cf. the promise of Ex. xxix. 45.

the assembly of the LORD. Cf. xx. 4 and see Cornill in *ZAW* XI. 23 ff.

4. *he fell upon his face.* Cf. xiv. 5, xx. 6, and Hezekiah's treatment of the letter of Sennacherib (2 K. xix. 14). Gressmann thinks that Moses was afraid for his life (*Auswahl* p. 100).

5. *the LORD will shew.* The appeal is to the highest tribunal. In 2 Tim. ii. 19 the words are quoted in the form *The LORD knoweth them that are his*: see E. F. Brown *Pastoral Epp.* p. 71 in the present series of commentaries.

cause...to come near. This phrase suggests the service of the altar, although it is not confined to such a connotation: cf. iii. 6 where the Levites are brought near to the priests (see Baudissin *Priesterthum* pp. 29 f., 116); cf. also Pss. cxlv. 18, cxlviii. 14.

censers, Korah, and all his company; 7 and put fire therein, *P* and put incense upon them before the LORD to-morrow: and it shall be that the man whom the LORD doth choose, he *shall be* holy: ye take too much upon you, ye sons of Levi. 8 And Moses *P*s said unto Korah, Hear now, ye sons of Levi: 9 *seemeth it but* a small thing unto you, that the God of Israel hath separated you from the congregation of Israel, to bring you near to himself; to do the service of the tabernacle of the LORD, and to stand before the congregation to minister unto them; 10 and that he hath brought thee near, and all thy brethren the sons of Levi with thee? and seek ye the priesthood also? 11 Therefore thou and all thy company are gathered together against the LORD: and Aaron, what is he that ye murmur against him? 12 And *JE* Moses sent to call Dathan and Abiram, the sons of Eliab: and they said, We will not come up: 13 is it a small thing that thou hast brought us up out of a land flowing with milk and honey,

6. *censers.* In Ex. xxvii. 3 rendered *fire-pans.* Holzinger points out that the test was to be made with the least material form of offering.

7. *to-morrow.* Perhaps in order to give time for repentance. From *v.* 18 however no interval seems to have taken place: see Gressmann *Auswahl* p. 97.

8–11. Moses reproves Korah and the Levites for their pride, after Jehovah had separated them from the rest of the congregation, in seeking the priesthood also. The section cannot be reconciled with that which goes before, for there Korah is demanding the right to draw near to the LORD, here he and his companions have the right, and claim something more.

9. *a small thing.* Cf. *v.* 13 and Is. vii. 13.

to stand before. The phrase usually means either 'to serve' or 'to represent': see Driver on Dt. x. 8.

10. *the priesthood also.* The distinction between priests and Levites is generally considered to have been a late one: see Introd. pp. liv f. In regard to the whole attitude of Korah Hooker's comment may be recalled: "It behoveth generally all sorts of men to keep themselves within the limits of their own vocation" (*Eccles. Pol.* v. lxii. 13).

11. *against the LORD.* Cf. Ex. xvi. 8; 1 S. viii. 7; Acts v. 3 f.

Aaron. On the whole Aaron plays a very insignificant part in the incident: cf. *vv.* 2, 4, 8 &c.

12–15. Moses sends for Dathan and Abiram who reply by an insulting refusal to come.

13. *a land flowing &c.* On the phrase see xiii. 27. It is used of Egypt here only.

to kill us in the wilderness, but thou must needs make thyself *JE*
also a prince over us? 14 Moreover thou hast not brought us into a land flowing with milk and honey, nor given us inheritance of fields and vineyards: wilt thou [1]put out the eyes of these men? we will not come up. 15 And Moses was very wroth, and said unto the LORD, Respect not thou their offering: I have not taken one ass from them, neither have I hurt one of them.
16 And Moses said unto Korah, Be thou and all thy congrega- *P*[s]
tion before the LORD, thou, and they, and Aaron, to-morrow: 17 and take ye every man his censer, and put incense upon them, and bring ye before the LORD every man his censer, two hundred and fifty censers; thou also, and Aaron, each his censer.
18 And they took every man his censer, and put fire in them, *P*
and laid incense thereon, and stood at the door of the tent of meeting with Moses and Aaron. 19 And Korah assembled all the congregation against them unto the door of the tent of meeting: and the glory of the LORD appeared unto all the congregation.

20 And the LORD spake unto Moses and unto Aaron, saying,

[1] Heb. *bore out.*

to kill us. Cf. Ex. xiv. 11, xvii. 3.

a prince over us. The same question is asked in Ex. ii. 14.

14. *thou hast not.* Probably the word rendered *not* is a sign of a question as in Jud. xvi. 21; 1 S. xi. 2; 2 K. xxv. 7): so Ehrlich who suggests the pointing לֻא (= לוּ) instead of לֹא.

put out the eyes. The words are used in a literal sense in Jud. xvi. 21, and Ruskin would so understand them here (*St Mark's Rest* § 78). Probably the meaning is merely *to hoodwink.*

15. *very wroth.* His meekness was not proof against the ingratitude of the rebels.

Respect not. Cf. Gen. iv. 4 f.

I have not taken. Cf. Samuel's similar protest (1 S. xii. 3).

their offering. If a specific offering is referred to no reference to it remains in the narrative as it stands: the words can, however, be explained quite adequately as a general request to God to disregard their sacrifices.

16–24. Moses once more issues his challenge to Korah, and the latter assembles his allies against Moses and Aaron. The glory of the LORD appears and the congregation are bidden to depart from the neighbourhood of the rebels.

16 f. = 6 f.

19. This was the second time of its appearing: see on xiv. 10.

21 Separate yourselves from among this congregation, that I may consume them in a moment. 22 And they fell upon their faces, and said, O God, the God of the spirits of all flesh, shall one man sin, and wilt thou be wroth with all the congregation? 23 And the LORD spake unto Moses, saying, 24 Speak unto the congregation, saying, Get you up from about the tabernacle of Korah, Dathan, and Abiram. 25 And Moses rose up and went unto Dathan and Abiram; and the elders of Israel followed him. 26 And he spake unto the congregation, saying, | Depart, I pray you, from the tents of these wicked men, and touch nothing of

P (v. 21) *JE* (v. 25) R^P–*JE* (v. 26)

21. *Separate yourselves.* Cf. Gen. xix. 17, 22 (of Lot); Jer. li. 9.

22. *God of the spirits of all flesh.* Cf. xxvii. 16; Job xii. 10; Eccles. xii. 7. The phrase is very common in the post-biblical literature, occurring in *Enoch* alone more than 100 times; see also Jub. x. 3; 2 Macc. iii. 24, and xiv. 46 where the patriot Razis dies "calling on Him who is the Lord of life and spirit[1]." From a theological point of view the expression is important as exhibiting an advance from merely tribal conceptions of Jehovah.

one man...all the congregation. A recognition of different degrees of guilt, and of individual, as opposed to collective, responsibility.

24. *the tabernacle of Korah &c.* The word is never used in prose of a human dwelling, and in any case the singular would be strange. Read *the tabernacle of the LORD* as in xvii. 13. The necessity of this change is admitted by conservative critics like Strack, and practically by Orr *Problem of O.T.* p. 280 note 2.

25–35. Moses and the elders of Israel go to the tents of Dathan and Abiram. Having warned the congregation to flee from around them, and having staked his own divine appointment on the manner of death which should meet the rebels, the earth opens asunder and swallows them up[2]. The two hundred and fifty men also meet with a violent death.

25. *the elders.* In this account as Moses has the support of the official leaders of the people, the rebellion might seem to be limited to a small group of discontented Reubenites.

26. *these wicked men.* Moses addresses the people and takes no notice of the rebels.

touch nothing. Cf. Achan (Jos. vii. 1 ff.).

---

[1] Ball would derive רוּחַ *spirit* from Sum. RI (from RIG) *to blow*: he considers that *air, breath,* is its primary meaning: cf. the similar usage in Greek (*Job* p. 138).

[2] With the Greeks the swallowing up by the earth might shew the divine favour: cf. *Oedipus at Colonus* 1661 f.

ἢ τὸ νερτέρων
εὔνουν διαστὰν γῆς ἀλύπητον βάθρον.

theirs, lest ye be consumed in all their sins. 27 So they gat them *RP* up from the tabernacle of Korah, Dathan, and Abiram, on every side: | and Dathan and Abiram came out, and stood at the door *JE* of their tents, and their wives, and their sons, and their little ones. 28 And Moses said, Hereby ye shall know that the LORD hath sent me to do all these works; for *I have* not *done them* of mine own mind. 29 If these men die the common death of all men, or if they be visited after the visitation of all men; then the LORD hath not sent me. 30 But if the LORD [1]make a new thing, and the ground open her mouth, and swallow them up, with all that appertain unto them, and they go down alive into [2]the pit; then ye shall understand that these men have despised the LORD. 31 And it came to pass, as he made an end of

[1] Heb. *create a creation.* [2] Heb. *Sheol.*

consumed. Better *swept away*: so Gen. xviii. 23 and xix. 15 of the men of Sodom.

27. *came out.* Better *had come out.* The normal place for an Oriental household is outside the tent which is used merely for shelter and sleep.

their little ones. The word comes from a root meaning *to take quick steps, to trip*, and refers to young children a stage beyond our 'toddlers': cf. the use in 2 Chr. xx. 13, xxxi. 18, and Ez. ix. 6.

28. *Hereby ye shall know.* Moses proposes a test which will settle the question of his authority once and for all: for similar tests see Gen. xxiv. 14, xlii. 33; Ex. vii. 16 f.

mine own mind. Heb. *heart* since there is no word for *mind* in the language. Cf. Jer. xxiii. 16, 21 (of a true prophet); Jub. ii. 35; 2 Bar. xiv. 11.

29. *the LORD hath not sent me.* The position of the negative in the original, before *LORD* instead of before *sent*, is unusual and is meant to emphasise the source of Moses' authority: *it is not Jehovah who has sent me.* Cf. for a similar usage Gen. xlv. 8; 1 S. vi. 9; Ps. cxv. 17.

30. *make a new thing.* Heb. *create a creation* as in Jer. xxxi. 22 where see the present writer's note.

into the pit. Heb. *Sheol.* The unseen regions beneath the earth. Charles distinguishes three stages in the conception of *Sheol*, of which this is the earliest corresponding to the Homeric Hades, see *The Doctrine of the Future Life* passim. Peters has collected and compared a large number of passages in both biblical and post-biblical literature on the subject: see *The Rel. of the Hebs.* p. 451. For the beliefs regarding the underworld in classical literature see R. S. Conway's essay on "The Growth of the Underworld" in his volume *New Studies of a Great Inheritance.*

despised the LORD. Cf. xiv. 23.

speaking all these words, that the ground clave asunder that *JE* was under them: 32 and the earth opened her mouth, and swallowed them up, and their households, | and all the men that R^P appertained unto Korah, and all their goods. 33 So they, and *JE* all that appertained to them, went down alive into [1]the pit: and the earth closed upon them, and they perished from among the assembly. 34 And all Israel that were round about them fled at the cry of them: for they said, Lest the earth swallow us up. 35 And fire came forth from the LORD, and devoured *P* the two hundred and fifty men that offered the incense.

[2]36 And the LORD spake unto Moses, saying, 37 Speak unto P^s

[1] Heb. *Sheol.* [2] [Ch. xvii. 1 in Heb.]

32. *her mouth.* This *mouth*, like the mouth of Balaam's ass (xxii. 28), and the mouth of the well (xxi. 16 ff.), was according to Rabbinic tradition one of the last things to be made at the original creation (*Pirke Aboth* v. 9).

all the men...unto Korah &c. According to *v.* 35 these men were consumed by fire; the narrative is much simplified by the entire omission of the words. Gray regards them as "an unskilful attempt of the editor to unite in death the two sets of rebels who, even in his form of the story, had in life been constantly divided."

33. *from...the assembly.* "The seditious, separating themselves from the society ordained by God, were by the earth swallowed up quick, to invisible pains for a visible example." Aug. *de Civ. Dei*, IX. 8.

34. The people always responded to manifestations of Jehovah's power and holiness, but as quickly forgot them.

35. *fire came forth.* Korah and his men who offered incense (*vv.* 6 f.) have already been punished by the opening of the earth's mouth (*v.* 32); the compiler has retained two contradictory accounts of their end, or else it was he who supplied *v.* 32 *b* confounding their fate with that of Dathan and Abiram (see note above). Gressmann (*Mose* p. 263) thinks that one narrative underlies the present account and that of the similar punishment of Nadab and Abihu (Lev. x. 2).

36–40. The censers of the rebels, since they had been offered before Jehovah, are holy and must be rescued from any profane use. Eleazar at the divine command makes of them a covering for the altar. This passage exhibits in a striking way the priestly conception of holiness as being contagious. The censers partake of the holiness of Jehovah since they have been brought near to Him, they are therefore incapable of being used for any common purpose, and even the coals which had been laid upon them (xvi. 7, 18) have to be scattered in order to prevent their being used in any unworthy way (*v.* 37) since they too were holy. In its effects holiness was just as dangerous and as infectious as uncleanness (see on ch. xix.). See further Frazer *Taboo* p. 224, *Spirits of the Corn* II. 29 &c.

Eleazar the son of Aaron the priest, that he take up the censers out of the burning, and scatter thou the fire yonder; for they are holy; 38 even the censers of [1] these sinners against their own [2] lives, and let them be made beaten plates for a covering of the altar: for they offered them before the LORD, therefore they are holy: and they shall be a sign unto the children of Israel. 39 And Eleazar the priest took the brasen censers, which they that were burnt had offered; and they beat them out for a covering of the altar: 40 to be a memorial unto the children of Israel, to the end that no stranger, which is not of the seed of Aaron, come near to burn incense before the LORD; that he be not as Korah, and as his company: as the LORD spake unto him by the hand of Moses. P^s

41 But on the morrow all the congregation of the children of P

[1] Or, *these men who have sinned at the cost of their lives* [2] Or, *souls*

37. *Eleazar*. He was also chosen to perform the rite of the Red Heifer (xix. 3), perhaps because the high-priest was considered too sacred to have any contact, even an indirect one, with the dead. LXX adds *Moses*.

out of the burning. The priest was not to wait for the extinguishing of the fire; LXX, Syr. read *that which is burnt*.

scatter thou the fire. Some commentators consider that the task of extinguishing the flames was left to Moses as a piece of merely secular work. The suggestion made in the note above however is much more in accordance with Israelite ideas. LXX adds τὸ ἀλλότριον τοῦτο to τὸ πῦρ evidently reading זרה twice over.

38. *sinners against their own lives*. Better *at the cost of*: cf. Hab. ii. 10; Prov. xx. 2.

beaten plates &c. It is hard to know which altar is here intended. The altar of incense was of gold (Ex. xxx. 3, xxxvii. 26) and seems to be excluded. The altar of burnt offerings, however, was overlaid with bronze when it was first made (Ex. xxvii. 2). In Ex. xxxviii. 22 (= xxxviii. 2) LXX makes an ingenious attempt to reconcile the two passages by stating that the covering was made by Bezaleel himself from these very censers; the fact that the rebellion of Korah took place long after the making of the altar is apparently forgotten.

a sign. So Aaron's rod (xvii. 10).

40. *no stranger*. For a breach of this rule Uzziah is represented as having been smitten by leprosy (2 Chr. xxvi. 16 ff.).

41–50. The people murmur against Moses and Aaron on account of the death of their comrades and are punished by an outbreak of plague. Aaron seizes a censer and makes atonement for them, and so the plague is stayed.

Israel murmured against Moses and against Aaron, saying, Ye *P* have killed the people of the LORD. 42 And it came to pass, when the congregation was assembled against Moses and against Aaron, that they looked toward the tent of meeting: and, behold, the cloud covered it, and the glory of the LORD appeared. 43 And Moses and Aaron came to the front of the tent of meeting. 44 And the LORD spake unto Moses, saying, 45 Get you up from among this congregation, that I may consume them in a moment. And they fell upon their faces. 46 And Moses said unto Aaron, Take thy censer, and put fire therein from off the altar, and lay incense thereon, and carry it quickly unto the congregation, and make atonement for them: for there is wrath gone out from the LORD; the plague is begun. 47 And Aaron took as Moses spake, and ran into the midst of the assembly; and, behold, the plague was begun among the people: and he put on the incense, and made atonement for the people. 48 And he stood between the dead and the living; and the plague was stayed. 49 Now they that died by the plague were fourteen thousand and seven hundred, besides them that died about the matter of Korah. 50 And Aaron returned unto Moses unto the door of the tent of meeting: and the plague was stayed.

41. *Ye have killed.* The pronoun in the original is emphatic. The basis of the accusation is that Moses and Aaron in order to vindicate their own position had caused the death of those who had opposed them.

the people of the LORD. A frequent expression: cf. xxi. 29; also Jer. xlviii. 46 (the people of Chemosh).

42. *the cloud.* This is the last mention of *the cloud* since it belonged to the wilderness period only and does not occur in Jos.

44. *unto Moses.* LXX adds *Aaron* correctly.

46. *from off the altar.* Cf. Is. vi. 6.

make atonement. Atonement without bloodshed is unusual though not unknown elsewhere: cf. Ex. xxx. 15.

there is wrath. The wrath of God is almost personified: cf. 2 Chr. xix. 2.

the plague. See viii. 19.

48. *was stayed.* Better *having been stayed* (see Driver *Tenses* p. 16). In Gen. viii. 21 f. burnt offerings turn away God's wrath for the future; the parallel Babylonian story, however, makes the gods smell "reed, (*kanâ*) and cedar and myrtle" i.e. *incense* as here. Gressmann (*Mose* p. 277) compares the incident narrated in Herod. III. 107, but not very happily since there winged serpents (he calls them *Dämonen*) are driven away by smoke in order that incense may be collected.

CHAPTER XVII.

The rod that budded.

This story is concerned with the strife between the Levites and the secular tribes, it has nothing to do with any question between Priests and Levites. The test in the previous ch. was a negative one, the rejection of the offerings of the followers of Korah; here the test is positive, the budding of the rod belonging to the chosen tribe. The story is used by Clement in his Epistle to the Corinthians XLIII.

Gressmann thinks that the story arose as an explanation of a rod ornamented with almond decorations (as Babylonian staffs were ornamented with apple, rose, lily, and other tokens: Herod. I. 195) laid up before the ark (*Mose* pp. 281 ff.).

Stories of budding or blossoming sticks are very common in Jewish, Classical and Christian legend. Amongst the first may be mentioned the terebinth at Hebron which grew from the stick of the angel who appeared to Abraham (see Reland *Pal.* p. 712), also perhaps the legend that the trees in Solomon's temple bore fruit every year (see G. Salzberger *Salomos Tempelbau u. Thron* p. 20). Amongst Greek legends the story of the sprouting of Hercules' club as preserved by Pausanias (*Description of Greece* II. xxxi. 13) is often cited by commentators as is also the Latin parallel of Romulus' spear (see Ovid *Met.* XV. 560 ff.). Amongst Christian legends the sacred thorn of Glastonbury which grew out of the staff of Joseph of Arimathea, the terebinth of Smyrna from the staff of Polycarp, and the stick of Tannhäuser are but a few out of many similar stories: see further H. Günther *Die christliche Legende des Abendlandes* pp. 97 f.

[1] **XVII.** 1 And the LORD spake unto Moses, saying, 2 Speak unto the children of Israel, and take of them rods, one for each fathers' house, of all their princes according to their fathers' houses, twelve rods: write thou every man's name upon his rod. 3 And thou shalt write Aaron's name upon the rod of Levi: for there shall be one rod for each head of their fathers' houses. 4 And thou shalt lay them up in the tent of meeting before the testimony, where I meet with you. 5 And it shall come to pass, that the man whom I shall choose, his rod shall bud: and I will make to cease from me the murmurings of the children of Israel, which they murmur against you. 6 And Moses spake unto the children of Israel, and all their princes gave him rods, for each prince one, according to their fathers' houses, even twelve rods: and the rod of Aaron was among their rods. 7 And Moses laid *P*

[1] [Ch. xvii. 16 in Heb.]

XVII. 2. *write thou.* So in Ez. xxxvii. 16 the prophet writes "For Judah" on one stick, "For Joseph" on the other.

6. *among their rods.* McNeile translates *in the midst* arguing that Aaron's rod was the middle one.

up the rods before the LORD in the tent of the testimony. 8 And *P* it came to pass on the morrow, that Moses went into the tent of the testimony; and, behold, the rod of Aaron for the house of Levi was budded, and put forth buds, and bloomed blossoms, and bare ripe almonds. 9 And Moses brought out all the rods from before the LORD unto all the children of Israel: and they looked, and took every man his rod. 10 And the LORD said unto Moses, Put back the rod of Aaron before the testimony, to be kept for a token against the children of rebellion; that thou mayest make an end of their murmurings against me, that they die not. 11 Thus did Moses: as the LORD commanded him, so did he.

12 And the children of Israel spake unto Moses, saying, Behold, we perish, we are undone, we are all undone. 13 Every one that cometh near, that cometh near unto the tabernacle of the LORD, [1]dieth: shall we perish all of us?

[1] Or, *shall die*

7. *before the LORD.* Cf. *v.* 4 *before the testimony.*

8. *was budded &c.* The flowering of an almond blossom became a symbol, as in Jer. i. 11.

10. *before the testimony.* Cf. Ex. xvii. 33 f. (also a memorial of a murmuring). In Heb. ix. 4 the rod is said to be within the ark.

for a token. Cf. xvi. 40.

children of rebellion. Cf. Is. xxx. 9 "people of rebellion" and the phrase common in Ezekiel "house of rebellion."

CHAPTERS XVIII. AND XIX.

FURTHER LAWS AND REGULATIONS.

The laws and regulations of these two chh. are not closely connected, though an attempt has sometimes been made to link them up by suggesting that the heavy mortality which followed the rebellion of Korah was the occasion of bringing up the question of defilement by the dead. This attempt is too artificial to merit real consideration. The regulations of xviii. have a close connexion with the preceding chh. and are often taken with them. What follows xix. is related neither to that ch. nor to xviii.

The duties and revenues of Levi. xviii.
Rules for purification from defilement by the dead. xix.

CHAPTER XVIII.

The duties and revenues of Levi.

This ch. opens with a reference to the holiness and danger of the sanctuary, an obvious connexion with xvii. 12 f., and then goes on to define the duties of the Levites, introducing them almost as if they had not previously been mentioned. There are close parallels between *vv.* 1–7 and i. 50 ff., iii. 5–10, 38; and between the rest of the ch. and Lev. ii. 3, 10, vi. 16 ff.

Certain peculiarities in the style and manner of this ch. have been pointed out in the Oxford Hexateuch. The customary formula 'spake...saying' is not employed in *vv.* 1, 8, 20 (cf. *v.* 25), and the laws are addressed to Aaron directly and not to Moses. The normal method is for communications for Aaron to come through Moses (e.g. vi. 23, viii. 2), the only other exception being Lev. x. 8.

(*a*) *The duties of Levi.* xviii. 1–7.
(*b*) *The revenues of the priests.* 8–20.
(*c*) *The revenues of the Levites.* 21–24.
(*d*) *The priests' tithe.* 25–32.

XVIII. 1 And the LORD said unto Aaron, Thou and thy sons *P* and thy fathers' house with thee shall bear the iniquity of the sanctuary: and thou and thy sons with thee shall bear the iniquity of your priesthood. 2 And thy brethren also, the tribe of Levi, the tribe of thy father, bring thou near with thee, that they may be [1]joined unto thee, and minister unto thee: but thou and thy sons with thee shall be before the tent of the testimony. 3 And they shall keep thy charge, and the charge

[1] See Gen. xxix. 34.

XVIII. 1–7. In order that there may be no more disasters through unauthorised persons approaching the sanctuary the Levites are to have charge of it; the altar itself and its vessels, as being especially holy, are to be in the charge of the priests only.

1. *Thou and thy sons.* That is the priests as distinguished from the rest of the tribe of Levi.

thy fathers' house. Here used of the rest of the tribe: cf. xvii. 2.

the iniquity of the sanctuary. The consequences of anyone approaching too near to it, and possibly also shortcomings in the matter of ritual and worship.

2. *may be joined.* The verb contains a play on the name Levi as in Gen. xxix. 34; and Jub. xxxi. 16. Hommel (*AHT* pp. 278 f.) thinks that Levite is to be identified with *lavi'u* used for a priest of the god Wadd in Minaean inscriptions, but this usage is itself questioned by Grimme *Le Muséon* XXXVII. pp. 169–199.

3. The penalty for a breach of the prohibition is not merely the death of the offenders (as in iv. 15), but apparently of the lawful guardians also.

of all the Tent: only they shall not come nigh unto the vessels *P* of the sanctuary and unto the altar, that they die not, neither they, nor ye. 4 And they shall be joined unto thee, and keep the charge of the tent of meeting, for all the service of the Tent: and a stranger shall not come nigh unto you. 5 And ye shall keep the charge of the sanctuary, and the charge of the altar: that there be wrath no more upon the children of Israel. 6 And I, behold, I have taken your brethren the Levites from among the children of Israel: to you they are a gift, given unto the LORD, to do the service of the tent of meeting. 7 And thou and thy sons with thee shall keep your priesthood for every thing of the altar, and for that within the veil; and ye shall serve: I give you the priesthood as a service of gift: and the stranger that cometh nigh shall be put to death.

8 And the LORD spake unto Aaron, And I, behold, I have given thee the charge of mine heave offerings, even all the hallowed things of the children of Israel, unto thee have I given them [1]by reason of the anointing, and to thy sons, as a due for ever. 9 This shall be thine of the most holy things, *reserved*

[1] Or, *for a portion*

4. *a stranger*. Here a non-Levite; in *v.* 7 anyone who was not a priest.

5. *the altar*. Since one altar only is referred to the passage must come from the earlier stratum of P: see Introd. p. xx.

wrath. Cf. xvi. 46; Lev. x. 6.

7. *within the veil*. As a rule this refers to the most holy place into which the high-priest alone entered (Lev. xvi. 2 ff.): perhaps within the screen (cf. Ex. xxvi. 36 f.) is intended. There is a certain looseness of expression in this section, e.g. the wide meaning of *sanctuary* in *v.* 5.

8–20. Jehovah informs Aaron that certain offerings given to Himself are to be the property of the priests on account of their having no landed possessions in Canaan. A distinction is made in regard to the manner of use; certain offerings may be eaten by male or female members of the priestly households (*v.* 11), but others are to be consumed by males only (*v.* 10).

8. *the charge of*. Better *that which is retained of*. The reference is not to priestly duties but to the disposal of those parts of the sacrifices which had not been consumed.

by reason of the anointing. Better as mg. *for a portion*. See P. Haupt *JBL* xix. p. 80.

9. *the most holy things*. A distinction between holy and *most holy things* is definitely drawn in Lev. xxi. 22, perhaps because the latter offerings "obtained a higher consecration." According to Lev. vi. 27

from the fire: every oblation of theirs, even every meal offering *P* of theirs, and every sin offering of theirs, and every guilt offering of theirs, which they shall render unto me, shall be most holy for thee and for thy sons. 10 As the most holy things shalt thou eat thereof: every male shall eat thereof; it shall be holy unto thee. 11 And this is thine; the heave offering of their gift, even all the wave offerings of the children of Israel: I have given them unto thee, and to thy sons and to thy daughters with thee, as a due for ever: every one that is clean in thy house shall eat thereof. 12 All the [1]best of the oil, and all the [1]best of the vintage, and of the corn, the firstfruits of them which they give unto the LORD, to thee have I given them. 13 The firstripe fruits of all that is in their land, which they bring unto the LORD, shall be thine; every one that is clean in thy house shall eat thereof. 14 Every thing devoted in Israel shall be

[1] Heb. *fat.*

anyone touching *most holy* flesh became infected by it, but such was not the case apparently with holy flesh (Hag. ii. 10). It is probable as Gray suggests that the two terms were not always used very strictly (cf. *v.* 10 *a* and 10 *b*).

10. *As the most holy things.* Better *In a most holy place*: cf. Lev. vi. 16, 26; Ez. xlii. 13.

11. *the heave offering of their gift.* Better *the contribution* (see on v. 9) *from their gift.* That is the parts of the peace offering, here strangely called by the vague term *gift*, which were given to the priest, i.e. in a normal sacrifice the breast and right thigh (Lev. vii. 31 ff.).

thy daughters. As women were not admitted into the sanctuary the portion might be eaten outside.

12. *the best.* Heb. *fat* as mg.

oil...vintage...corn. These terms represent the new produce before undergoing any process of manufacture. Driver (on Gen. xxvii. 28) rejects the rendering *vintage* as "altogether incorrect"; he cites two meanings, *fresh, unfermented fruit* (as here), or *a light kind of wine* (cf. Jud. ix. 13; Hos. iv. 11).

firstfruits. Probably not first in time, but in quality: cf. Ex. xxiii. 19. The term used is ראשית *rē'shîth* which is used of quality in a Phoenician inscription mentioned by Kennedy in *Cent. Bib.*

13. *the firstripe fruits.* Heb. בִּכּוּרִים *bikkûrîm.* The distinction between this and *rē'shîth* above is not as a rule marked by E.VV. Whether the words were used with different meanings is by no means certain.

they bring unto &c. Cf. *vv.* 12 and 24 where no *bringing* is mentioned. In these cases the offerings were probably paid "direct to the priests and Levites without ritual at the Temple": see Gray *Sacrifice* p. 28.

14. *devoted.* This appears to refer to voluntary offerings dedicated to

thine. 15 Every thing that openeth the womb, of all flesh which they offer unto the LORD, both of man and beast, shall be thine: nevertheless the firstborn of man shalt thou surely redeem, and the firstling of unclean beasts shalt thou redeem. 16 [1]And those that are to be redeemed of them from a month old shalt thou redeem, according to thine estimation, for the money of five shekels, after the shekel of the sanctuary (the same is twenty gerahs). 17 But the firstling of an ox, or the firstling of a sheep, or the firstling of a goat, thou shalt not redeem; they are holy: thou shalt sprinkle their blood upon the altar, and shalt burn their fat for an offering made by fire, for a sweet savour unto the LORD. 18 And the flesh of them shall be thine, as the wave breast and as the right thigh, it shall be thine. 19 All the heave offerings of the holy things, which the children of Israel offer unto the LORD, have I given thee, and thy sons and thy daughters with thee, as a due for ever: it is a covenant of salt for ever before the LORD unto thee and to thy seed with thee. 20 And *P*

[1] Or, *And as to their redemption money, from a month old shalt thou redeem them*

God and therefore as irredeemable (cf. Mk. vii. 11) as enemy property placed under a ban (cf. xxi. 2 f.).

15 ff. All firstborn are to belong to the priests, but two classes are to be redeemed with money, the unclean animals which are not suitable for sacrifice, and the offspring of human parents against whose sacrifice the conscience of a later day protested. There is a similar law in Dt. xii. 18 f., xiv. 27, xv. 19 ff. but it refers to clean animals only; these are to be eaten by the owner at the central sanctuary.

15. *the firstborn of man.* See note on iii. 12. Whether the *firstborn* were originally sacrificed to Jehovah is uncertain; the view is rejected by W. Robertson Smith *Rel. Sem.*[2] p. 464 and Kamphausen *Das Verhältniss des Menschenopfer zur isr. Rel.* pp. 63 ff.

16. See on iii. 47.

17 f. The ritual here prescribed follows that of the peace offering except in the treatment of the flesh, which here belongs to the priests.

19. *a covenant of salt.* Here and 2 Chr. xiii. 5. The origin of the term no doubt goes back to the nomadic custom of regarding those who have taken salt together as being joined by a bond: cf. Robertson Smith *Rel. Sem.*[2] p. 270, Lagrange *Études sur les rel. sém.*[2] p. 421, Valeton *ZAW* (1892) p. 6, and Kraetzschmar *Die Bundesvorstellung im AT* p. 46. It is probable that *salt* formed part of every sacrifice (cf. Lev. ii. 13; Ez. xliii. 24; Mk. ix. 49)[1].

[1] Dussaud regards "alliance de sel" as synonymous with "alliance perpétuelle" (*Les origines*[2] p. 218).

the LORD said unto Aaron, Thou shalt have no inheritance in *P* their land, neither shalt thou have any portion among them: I am thy portion and thine inheritance among the children of Israel.

21 And unto the children of Levi, behold, I have given all the tithe in Israel for an inheritance, in return for their service which they serve, even the service of the tent of meeting. 22 And henceforth the children of Israel shall not come nigh the tent of meeting, lest they bear sin, and die. 23 But the Levites shall do the service of the tent of meeting, and they shall bear their iniquity: it shall be a statute for ever throughout your generations, and among the children of Israel they shall have no inheritance. 24 For the tithe of the children of Israel, which they offer as an heave offering unto the LORD, I have given to the Levites for an inheritance: therefore I have said unto them, Among the children of Israel they shall have no inheritance.

25 And the LORD spake unto Moses, saying, 26 Moreover thou shalt speak unto the Levites, and say unto them, When ye take of the children of Israel the tithe which I have given you from them for your inheritance, then ye shall offer up an heave offering of it for the LORD, a tithe of the tithe. 27 And

20. *Thou.* Aaron here represents the whole priesthood: cf. 1 Chr. xii. 27, xxvii. 17.

no inheritance. A similar proviso is made in Ez. xliv. 28 and the law is frequently referred to elsewhere. It was calculated to have a twofold effect: on the priests, of devotion to Jehovah alone (cf. Dt. x. 9); and on the people, of generosity towards those who had not had provision made for them (cf. Dt. xii. 12). See further notes on xxxv. 1–8.

21–24. The Levites are to have a tithe of all agricultural produce (cf. *vv.* 27 and 30; Dt. xiv. 22 ff., xxvi. 12 ff.): in Lev. xxvii. 30 ff. a tithe of cattle seems also to be included.

22. *they bear sin and die.* For the sin unto death cf. Jub. xxi. 22, xxxviii. 18; 1 Jn. v. 16. LXX *λαβεῖν ἁμαρτίαν θανατηφόρον* is interesting as containing the word which occurs in Jas. iii. 8 of the tongue as full of *deadly* poison: see Knowling *ad loc.*

25–32. The tithe paid to the Levites is itself subject to a tithe which they must pay to the priests. The style of this section is more regular, the law is addressed to Moses and not Aaron (cf. *vv.* 1, 8, 20) and the phrase *spake...saying* once more comes in.

26. *tithe of the tithe.* Cf. Neh. x. 38.

your heave offering shall be reckoned unto you, as though it were the corn of the threshing-floor, and as the fulness of the winepress. 28 Thus ye also shall offer an heave offering unto the LORD of all your tithes, which ye receive of the children of Israel; and thereof ye shall give the LORD's heave offering to Aaron the priest. 29 Out of all your gifts ye shall offer every heave offering of the LORD, of all the [1]best thereof, even the hallowed part thereof out of it. 30 Therefore thou shalt say unto them, When ye heave the [1]best thereof from it, then it shall be counted unto the Levites as the increase of the threshing-floor, and as the increase of the winepress. 31 And ye shall eat it in every place, ye and your households: for it is your reward in return for your service in the tent of meeting. 32 And ye shall bear no sin by reason of it, when ye have heaved from it the [1]best thereof: and ye shall not profane the holy things of the children of Israel, [2]that ye die not. *P*

[1] Heb. *fat*. [2] Or, *neither shall ye die*

27. *heave offering*. Better *contribution*.

shall be reckoned. Cf. Lev. vii. 18. The same word is used in Gen. xv. 6 of the faith of Abraham.

31. *your reward*. Cf. Mt. x. 11; Lk. x. 7; 1 Cor. ix. 4 ff.; 1 Tim. v. 17 f.

CHAPTER XIX.

Rules for purification from defilement by the dead.

The subject of this ch. seems to have no obvious connexion with what immediately precedes it nor with what follows.

The question of defilement by the dead is not here approached for the first time in Pent. previous mentions of it having been in v. 2, vi. 6 ff., ix. 6 f., 10 f.; Lev. v. 2, xi. 8, 24 ff., xxi. 1 ff.

That pollution or danger came from contact with the dead is a very ancient and widespread belief (see Tylor *Prim. Cult.*[3] II. pp. 433 ff., Frazer *Taboo* pp. 165 ff.). Its origin is not known, perhaps there is some connexion with ancestor worship (see *JBL* XXIV. 41 ff. and cf. *Enc. Bib.* 1335 ff., Kittel *Gesch. Isr.* I. p. 231), or the danger may come from the spirits of the departed hovering round the corpse (Frazer *Taboo* pp. 14, 138 ff.), or again death may have been the mark of divine displeasure. For the presence of the belief amongst the Greeks see Euripides *Alcest.* 98 ff., Thucyd. III. 104, and amongst the Romans Virgil *Aen.* VI. 228 ff., Plutarch *Sulla* 35.

The ch. although it deals with a single subject is probably not a unity, and sections (*a*) and (*b*) below may come from a different hand from section (*c*), since they are parallel but make use of different phraseology.

(*a*) *The ashes of the red heifer.* 1–10.
(*b*) *General rules as to purification.* 11–13.
(*c*) *Special rules of purification.* 14–22.

XIX. 1 And the LORD spake unto Moses and unto Aaron, P^x^ saying, 2 This is the statute of the law which the LORD hath commanded, saying, Speak unto the children of Israel, that they bring thee a red heifer [1]without spot, wherein is no blemish, *and* upon which never came yoke: 3 and ye shall give her unto Eleazar the priest, and he shall bring her forth without the camp, and one shall slay her before his face: 4 and Eleazar the priest shall take of her blood with his finger, and sprinkle of her blood toward the front of the tent of meeting seven times:

[1] Or, *perfect*

XIX. 1–10. The Israelites are commanded to bring a red heifer upon which no yoke has been placed to Eleazar who is to slay it without the camp. From its ashes when burnt a mixture for cleansing from pollution by the dead is to be prepared. All taking part in the ceremony become unclean. This rite of cleansing finds many parallels, though such as have been discovered suggest that it prevailed most widely among Aryan peoples. Dillmann compares Ovid *Fasti* IV. 639, 725, 733, others cite the purifying value of the cow in Hindoo religious ideas (see Oldenberg *Die Rel. des Veda* p. 490): see further on *v.* 2, Dussaud *Les Origines*[2] pp. 192 ff., H. P. Smith in *JBL* XXVII. pp. 153 ff., and *AJT* XIII. pp. 207 ff., and J. Scheftelowitz in *ZAW* (1921) pp. 113 ff.

2. *thee.* Aaron (cf. *v.* 1) is ignored.

a red heifer. The colour is perhaps chosen as being that of blood or fire[1]. *Red* oxen were offered by the Egyptians perhaps because *red* was a shade in the golden corn (cf. Frazer *Spirits of the Corn &c.* I. pp. 261 f.). The Lithuanians used to sacrifice a *black* heifer, a black he-goat, and a black cock to the thunder-god in time of drought (Frazer *Magic Art* II. p. 237).

never came yoke. The same limitation occurs in the case of the heifer of Dt. xxi. 1–9 (cf. also the oxen of 1 S. vi. 7). For similar provisions among the Greeks cf. *Iliad* X. 291 f., *Odyss.* III. 282 f., and among the Romans Virgil *Georg.* IV. 540, 550 f., Ovid *Fast.* III. 376, IV. 336, Horace *Epod.* IX. 22.

3. *Eleazar.* Aaron is not to defile himself: cf. on xvi. 37.

without the camp. Cf. Ex. xxix. 14; Lev. iv. 12; Heb. xiii. 11. The Mishnah says it was sacrificed on the Mount of Olives (*Pārāh* III. 6).

he shall. Better *one shall,* a form of the passive is intended, see *G-K*[28] 144 *d.*

4. *toward &c.* Robertson Smith thinks that the blood was sprinkled *towards* the sanctuary to indicate that that was the appropriate place for the sacrifice (*Rel. Sem.*[2] p. 376).

seven times. So in the peace offering (Lev. iv. 6, 17).

---

[1] Theodoret *Qu. in Num.* 35 says that: "Red is to shadow forth the earthly body of man, just as the name Adam suggests the red earth out of which that body was formed."

5 and one shall burn the heifer in his sight; her skin, and her flesh, and her blood, with her dung, shall he burn: 6 and the priest shall take cedar wood, and hyssop, and scarlet, and cast it into the midst of the burning of the heifer. 7 Then the priest shall wash his clothes, and he shall bathe his flesh in water, and afterward he shall come into the camp, and the priest shall be unclean until the even. 8 And he that burneth her shall wash his clothes in water, and bathe his flesh in water, and shall be unclean until the even. 9 And a man that is clean shall gather up the ashes of the heifer, and lay them up without the camp in a clean place, and it shall be kept for the congregation of the children of Israel for a water of [1]separation: it is a sin offering. 10 And he that gathereth the ashes of the heifer shall wash his clothes, and be unclean until the even: and it shall be unto the children of Israel, and unto the stranger that sojourneth among *Px*

[1] Or, *impurity*

5. *her skin.* That this should be burnt is unusual.

blood. The burning of blood is unique.

dung. Better *what is found inside the slain beast*: the word in the original like the cognate roots in Assyr. and Arab. is not used of excrement (see Pusey on Mal. ii. 3).

6. *cedar wood, and hyssop, and scarlet.* These ingredients are also used in cleansing the leper (Lev. xiv. 4). The Babylonians added fragrant woods to water to make it 'holy' (Jastrow *Die Rel. Bab.* II. p. 202). *Cedar* was perhaps chosen on account of its being a longlived tree, or perhaps because of its medicinal properties (see Pliny *Hist. Nat.* XVI. 21, 76, XXIV. 11; Herod. II. 87). *Hyssop* is some species of wild marjoram: see also Ex. xii. 22; Lev. xix. 4; 1 K. iv. 33. The *scarlet* was a thread of that colour chosen to match the red of the heifer.

7 f. Both the priest and he who burns the heifer become unclean, that is taboo, through coming in contact with purifying or holy substance (see above p. 126).

9. *ashes...water.* The *ashes* of the golden calf were mixed with *water* (Ex. xxxii. 20); is there any connexion between the two rites?

it shall be kept. In order that it may be available on any sudden emergency.

water of separation. Better with mg. *impurity.*

sin offering: lit. *sin.* Kennedy suggests expiation (cf. viii. 7); the intensive of the verb is used with the meaning *purify* in Lev. viii. 15. As he says "the red cow was not a sin-offering or indeed a sacrifice of any kind; for P there is only one legitimate place of sacrifice, the altar in the court of the tabernacle, and the cow was slaughtered and burnt elsewhere."

them, for a statute for ever. 11 He that toucheth the dead body of any man shall be unclean seven days: 12 the same shall purify himself therewith on the third day, [1]and on the seventh day he shall be clean: but if he purify not himself the third day, [2]then the seventh day he shall not be clean. 13 Whosoever toucheth the dead body of any man that is dead, and purifieth not himself, defileth the tabernacle of the LORD; and that soul shall be cut off from Israel: because the water of separation was not sprinkled upon him, he shall be unclean; his uncleanness is yet upon him. 14 This is the law when a man dieth in a tent: every one that cometh into the tent, and every one P[x]

[1] Or, *and on the seventh day*, so *shall he be clean* [2] Or, *and*

11–13. Anyone who touches a dead body becomes unclean for seven days, unless he make use of the water of impurity. Any unclean person is to be cut off from the congregation.

The Rabbis regarded uncleanness arising from contact with the dead as the greatest of all defilements (*Kelim* I.). Even Jehovah Himself was unclean after burying Moses and had to be purified by fire: see on xxxi. 23.

11. *the dead body of any man*. The use of נפשׁ for an actual corpse which could be touched seems strange (but cf. *v.* 2 &c.) especially in view of Gen. ii. 7 where the man only becomes a living creature (נפשׁ) after God has breathed into him. For various uses of the word see *BDB* and Peters *Rel. of Hebs*. p. 448.

12. *purify*. That is lit. *unsin*: see on viii. 21.

third...seventh. See xxxi. 19.

13. *defileth the tabernacle*. Cf. Ex. xxv. 8; Lev. xv. 31. God dwells in the midst of the camp (*v.* 3) and the *tabernacle* would be defiled also.

the water of separation. Better *impurity* as in *v.* 9 mg. In Ps. Sol. VIII. 23 Pompey is said to have poured out blood like the water of uncleanness.

14–22. Further regulations are given in regard to the defiling powers of a dead body. The main point to notice is that actual contact is not necessary to produce defilement, those under the same 'tent' are affected as much as if they had actually touched the body. This rule may have caused friends to desert a dying man: cf. Ecclus. xxxviii. 16 which Smend regards as referring to this law.

14. *in a tent*. Green *The Higher Crit. of the Pent*. p. 41 says: "The law of purification provides simply for death in tents and in the open fields (*vv.* 14, 16). The peculiarity of these laws carries with it the evidence that they were not only enacted during the sojourn in the wilderness, but that they were then committed to writing." LXX renders οἰκία.

that is in the tent, shall be unclean seven days. 15 And every *P*[x] open vessel, which hath no covering bound upon it, is unclean. 16 And whosoever in the open field toucheth one that is slain with a sword, or a dead body, or a bone of a man, or a grave, shall be unclean seven days. 17 And for the unclean they shall take of the ashes of the burning of the sin offering, and [1]running water shall be put thereto in a vessel: 18 and a clean person shall take hyssop, and dip it in the water, and sprinkle it upon the tent, and upon all the vessels, and upon the persons that were there, and upon him that touched the bone, or the slain, or the dead, or the grave: 19 and the clean person shall sprinkle upon the unclean on the third day, and on the seventh day: and on the seventh day he shall purify him; and he shall wash his clothes, and bathe himself in water, and shall be clean at even. 20 But the man that shall be unclean, and shall not purify himself, that soul shall be cut off from the midst of the assembly, because he hath defiled the sanctuary of the LORD: the water of separation hath not been sprinkled upon him; he is unclean. 21 And it shall be a perpetual statute unto them: and he that sprinkleth the water of separation shall wash his clothes; and he that toucheth the water of separation shall be unclean until even. 22 And whatsoever the unclean person toucheth shall be unclean; and the soul that toucheth it shall be unclean until even.

[1] Heb. *living*.

15. *every open vessel*. Cf. Lev. xi. 32. There is a widespread idea that such vessels collect infection; this may have arisen through experience of actual infection carried in such a way. Bender *JQR* VII. pp. 106 ff. cites an ancient Jewish belief that the angel of death cleanses his sword in the liquid.

16. *the open field*. Cf. 2 S. xi. 11.

a bone of a man. Josephus records the story of a Samaritan who succeeded in entering the Temple at Jerusalem secretly and scattering human bones in it (*Ant.* XVIII. ii. 2, *Bell. Jud.* II. xii. 3).

a grave. Hence the need for whitewashing them: cf. Mt. xxiii. 27; Lk. xi. 44.

17. *sin offering*. See on *v.* 9.

running water: lit. as mg. *living*.

18. *hyssop*. In *v.* 6 the use is different. The use of *hyssop* for sprinkling is referred to in Ex. xii. 22; Lev. xiv. 4 &c. Amongst the Greeks and Romans the laurel was used (see Bötticher *Baumkultus der Hellenen u. Römer* pp. 369 f.) and also the olive (see Virgil *Aen.* VI. 230).

20. *defiled the sanctuary*. Cf. *v.* 13 the tabernacle.

Chapters XX.—XXII. 1.

Incidents on the way to Moab.

The incidents contained in the two chh. which make up this division of the book are full of difficulties both chronological and geographical; these difficulties, moreover, are many of them of such a nature as to admit of no certain conclusion in regard to them.

The last note of time and place (xiv. 33) saw the Israelites at the beginning of their wanderings. The interval of some forty years contains practically no traditions, unless stories such as that of the rebellion of Korah and his companions belong to it. The Israelites in Egypt were a people without annals, and so it was during the wanderings in the desert. When they were at Kadesh in the wilderness of Paran the command was given to them to go back by the Red Sea to the wilderness (xiv. 25), now (xx. 1) they are back once more at Kadesh. Whether the intervening period was spent in wandering about Edom as is suggested by Dt. ii. 1, or at Kadesh itself, is quite uncertain; what, however, does seem certain in regard to the whole question is that no one distinct and authoritative tradition of the wilderness period and its journeyings has survived amongst the Israelites.

Events at Kadesh. xx. 1–21.
The journey to Moab. xx. 22–xxii. 1.

Chapter XX. 1–21.

Events at Kadesh.

Three events are grouped together here, presumably because according to the view of the editor there was a connexion of place and time between them. The chief incident, the striking of the rock, raises many difficulties since a similar incident is narrated in Ex. xvii. 1–7 (E) as taking place much earlier in the wanderings (see below).

(*a*) *The death of Miriam.* xx. 1.
(*b*) *The incident at Meribah.* 2–13.
(*c*) *Edom's refusal.* 14–21.

XX. 1 And the children of Israel, even the whole congregation, came into the wilderness of Zin in the first month: | and the people abode in Kadesh; and Miriam died there, and was buried *P* *E*

XX. 1. The congregation arrive at Kadesh in an unspecified year and there Miriam dies and is buried.

in the first month. The omission of the year is strange and may be due to deliberate suppression (see below).

Miriam died. No details are given, and perhaps the writer had but little interest in her fate. The lips which had led the triumph songs of Israel (Ex. xv. 20), and had murmured bitter and unworthy reproaches against the prophet of Jehovah and her own brother (xii. 1–15) at length were hushed in death.

buried. Eusebius *Onomasticon* says that her sepulchre was shewn near

there. 2 And there was no water for the congregation: and they *P*
assembled themselves together against Moses and against Aaron.
3 And the people strove with Moses, and spake, saying, | Would *R*ᴾ–*P*
God that we had died when our brethren died before the LORD!
4 And why have ye brought the assembly of the LORD into this
wilderness, that we should die there, we and our cattle? 5 And *J*

Petra, and Josephus (*Ant.* IV. iv. 6) in a mountain named Zin; he also adds that the rite of the Red Heifer was instituted at her death. It may be noticed incidentally that Josephus has recorded many traditions connected with Miriam: e.g. that she was the wife of Hur (*Ant.* III. ii. 4).

2–13. The children of Israel once more murmur against Moses on account of the shortage of water. Moses by the command of Jehovah takes his rod and smites the rock in the presence of the people, whereupon water flows forth. For some reason Moses offends against God in the manner of his performing this command and in consequence is excluded from the promised land. The place receives the name Meribah, that is *strife.* A similar story is given in Ex. xvii. 1–7 which seems almost certainly a variant tradition of the same incident: cf. especially the explanation of the name Meribah in Ex. xvii. 2 and Num. xx. 3[1]. Cornill in his discussion of the relation of the passages in *ZAW* XI. pp. 20 ff., to which reference was made in the Introd. p. xxxiii, thinks that in J the story was connected with the arrival at Kadesh, in P with the close of the wanderings: the editor follows P in placing the story in its present context—J's story being combined with one from E placed at Rephidim (Ex. xvii. 1 ff.)—but in order to avoid too great divergence he omits in xx. 1 the actual year in which the event took place. This explanation although worked out with great skill, and although it has been accepted by Gray and other scholars, is very complicated. It seems best to suppose that the year of xx. 1 has dropped out by mistake, or been omitted on more general grounds.

The reason for the exclusion of Moses and Aaron from the land of promise is exceedingly obscure and from the present story no real clue can be discovered: there is no lack of faith, no disobedience, or rebellion against Jehovah. It looks as if the sources, if they contained originally some sin of the two leaders, had been toned down and the real reason lost. In Dt. i. 37, iii. 26, iv. 21 the cause is due to the anger of Jehovah with Moses because of the people's disobedience.

3. *our brethren.* In the matter of Korah, Dathan, and Abiram.

4. *why have ye brought.* Cf. xiv. 3.

the assembly. Heb. קָהָל *qâhâl* here rendered in LXX by συναγωγή instead of the usual ἐκκλησία (see on i. 2).

we and our cattle. In Ex. xvii. 3 (JE) a different word is used for *cattle* and *our children* is added.

---

[1] Burney *Judges* p. 110 regards them as undoubtedly duplicates of the same tradition.

wherefore have ye made us to come up out of Egypt, to bring *J* us in unto this evil place? it is no place of seed, or of figs, or of vines, or of pomegranates; neither is there any water to drink. 6 And Moses and Aaron went from the presence of the assembly *P* unto the door of the tent of meeting, and fell upon their faces: and the glory of the LORD appeared unto them. 7 And the LORD spake unto Moses, saying, 8 Take the rod, and assemble the congregation, thou, and Aaron thy brother, and speak ye unto the rock before their eyes, that it give forth its water; and thou shalt bring forth to them water out of the rock: so thou shalt give the congregation and their cattle drink. 9 And Moses took the rod from before the LORD, as he commanded him. 10 And Moses and Aaron gathered the assembly together before the rock, and he said unto them, Hear now, ye rebels; shall we bring you forth water out of this rock? 11 And Moses lifted up his hand, and smote the rock with his rod twice: and water came forth abundantly, and the congregation drank, and

5. *out of Egypt*. This speech suits the beginning of the wanderings, but not the time immediately before the entry into Canaan, when the survivors from Egypt were nearly all dead.

8. *the rod*. Probably the rod of Aaron which blossomed and was afterwards placed "before the testimony" (xvii. 10). No instructions are given as to the way in which it is to be used. A rod formed part of the equipment of a magician or worker of wonders[1]: cf. Ex. vii. 9 ff., viii. 5 &c.

thou shalt. In Neh. ix. 15 the miracle is attributed to Moses, in Is. xlvii. 20, xlviii. 21 more properly to Jehovah Himself.

9. *from before the LORD*. This should have been a reminder of the danger of rebellion (xvii. 2).

10. *Hear now, ye rebels*. Moses forgets that the revolt of the people is not against himself only but also against Jehovah. Personal motives are oft-times mixed, like a base alloy, with the pure zeal for God's service. Cornill thinks that these words were in P's original account addressed to Moses and Aaron after a refusal on their part to make the attempt to bring water out of the rock.

11. *smote the rock*. Nothing was said in the command of *v*. 8 about striking the rock; this may have constituted the offence of Moses, but even so Aaron was guiltless. For the striking cf. Ps. lxxiv. 15, lxxviii. 15 f., 20; Is. xlviii. 21; also Ex. vii. 17, 25, xiv. 15 ff.; Jud. vi. 21.

water came forth. Similar stories are told of springs rising in response

[1] In early examples of Christian art our Lord when changing the water into wine is represented as holding the rod of Moses in His hand: see Trench *Miracles*[11] p. 125 note 3.

their cattle. 12 And the LORD said unto Moses and Aaron, Because ye believed not in me, to sanctify me in the eyes of the children of Israel, therefore ye shall not bring this assembly into the land which I have given them. 13 These are the waters of [1]Meribah; because the children of Israel strove with the LORD, and he [2]was sanctified in them. *P*

14 And Moses sent messengers from Kadesh unto the king of Edom, Thus saith thy brother Israel, Thou knowest all the travail that hath befallen us: 15 how our fathers went down *E*

[1] That is, *Strife*. [2] Or, *shewed himself holy*

to the stroke of a god or goddess: according to Antoninus Liberalis *Transform.* 4 Hercules on one occasion produced water by striking a rock with his club (quoted by Frazer *Adonis &c.* I. p. 209), cf. also the story of Dionysus (Pausanias IV. xxxvi. 7) and of Atalanta (Pausanias III. xxiv. 2)[1].

12. *ye believed not.* There is no trace in the story as it now stands of want of faith, though perhaps of haste and ill-temper in the utterance to the rebels (cf. Ps. cvi. 32 f.).

sanctify. A play on the name Kadesh.

13. *Meribah.* Possibly the well of Kadesh-Meribah was originally the scene of judgements (cf. Gen. xiv. 7 En-mishpat): see Meyer *IN* pp. 54 ff.

14–21. Moses requests permission from the king of Edom to go through his territory but is refused. Edom was a land of narrow defiles and passes, and to introduce a large body of foreigners into it, revealing to them the secret ways, would have been highly dangerous. The wide promises of Moses would have been difficult to carry out with a large and badly disciplined host like the Israelites. According to Dt. ii. 1–9; 2 Chr. xx. 10, Israel was forbidden to enter Edom or Moab without the permission of its inhabitants. On the relation of this request to the situation in Dt. ii. 4 ff. see above p. 130.

14. *the king of Edom.* "Edom was in advance of Israel, both in the possession of settled territory, and in attaining monarchical government...in this respect, also, Esau was the 'firstborn,' though in the end, Israel won from him his supremacy (2 S. viii. 14)." Driver on Gen. xxxvi. 31 ff.

thy brother Israel. Even the refusal did not embitter the heart of Israel against Esau (Dt. ii. 4 f., but cf. Am. i. 11).

all the travail. The labours of Israel were evidently as notorious as those of the Trojans (Virgil *Aeneid* I. 5 f.).

---

[1] It is possible that a natural explanation underlies the miracle. Miss Lina Eckenstein says of this neighbourhood: "wherever water percolates the soil with hard rock beneath it in the desert, it is possible to reach and raise it by cutting into the soil to the surface of the rock. The practice is still resorted to by the Bedawin who are adepts at striking water when they are on the march" (*A Hist. of Sinai* p. 72).

into Egypt, and we dwelt in Egypt a long time; and the Egyptians *E* evil entreated us, and our fathers: 16 and when we cried unto the LORD, he heard our voice, and sent an angel, and brought us forth out of Egypt: and, behold, we are in Kadesh, a city in the uttermost of thy border: 17 let us pass, I pray thee, through thy land: we will not pass through field or through vineyard, neither will we drink of the water of the wells: we will go along the king's *high* way, we will not turn aside to the right hand nor to the left, until we have passed thy border. 18 And Edom said unto him, Thou shalt not pass through me, lest I come out with the sword against thee. 19 And the children of Israel said *J* unto him, We will go up by the high way: and if we drink of thy water, I and my cattle, then will I give the price thereof: let me only, without *doing* any thing *else*, pass through on my feet. 20 And he said, Thou shalt not pass through. And Edom came out against him with much people, and with a strong hand. 21 Thus Edom refused to give Israel passage through *E* his border: wherefore Israel turned away from him.

16. *sent an angel.* Cf. Gen. xxiv. 7; Ex. xxiii. 20, xxxiii. 2.

17. *let us pass.* In the present day similar requests are made by one tribe to cross the territory of another: see von Alois Musil *Arabia Petraea* III. pp. 369 f. The Israelites in order to enter Canaan from E. of Jordan needed either to cross the territory of Edom or to make a long detour to the S. and then to march northwards. The present incident is important as shewing that Edomite territory extended W. of the Arabah: see Buhl *Gesch. der Edomiter* pp. 22 ff.

vineyard. There are still traces of terraces for vines in Edom and remains of its former fertility are numerous.

the wells. Strabo XVI. iv. 21 speaks of the abundant fountains of Petra, the capital of Edom. These wells have become choked up and ruined.

the king's high *way.* Gressmann connects this with Molech (= *king*) and cites parallels from Egypt and Babylon of roads belonging to the gods (*Mose* p. 301)[1]. Ancient routes evidently ran through Edom: see Buhl *op. cit.* p. 44; Von Mülinen *ZDPV* XXXI. pp. 25 ff.; and *Enc. Bib.* cols. 5162 f.

19. *water...the price.* Cf. Is. lv. 1. Water had often to be purchased in the East, and even in the present day the water-seller is a familiar figure.

on my feet. That is, as speedily as possible; cf. 1 Macc. v. 48.

---

[1] Against this theory may be cited the modern custom of naming certain roads *darb es-sultân* 'the Sultan's way.'

CHAPTERS XX. 22—XXII. 1.

The journey to Moab.

This portion of the book contains a number of narratives collected from the various sources (see Introd. p. xxxiii). Imbedded in the sources are interesting fragments of ancient song.

(*a*) *The death of Aaron.* xx. 22–29.
(*b*) *The victory of Hormah.* xxi. 1–3.
(*c*) *The bronze serpent.* 4–9.
(*d*) *The journey.* 10–20.
(*e*) *The defeat of Sihon and Og.* 21–xxii. 1.

22 And they journeyed from Kadesh: and the children of *P* Israel, even the whole congregation, came unto mount Hor. 23 And the LORD spake unto Moses and Aaron in mount Hor, by the border of the land of Edom, saying, 24 Aaron shall be gathered unto his people: for he shall not enter into the land

22–29. The people arrive at Mount Hor where Aaron dies and his son Eleazar is appointed priest in his room.

22. *mount Hor.* The site of this mountain is unknown. An ancient tradition, which first appears in Josephus *Ant.* IV. iv. 7, would identify it with *Jebel Nebi Hārûn* near Petra; this contradicts the biblical data since it is not on the *border* (*v.* 23, xxxiii. 37) but in the midst of Edom. A notable Arab mosque covers the supposed site of the tomb and it is the object of pilgrimages to the present day. For a description of this mountain see Palmer *Desert of the Exodus* pp. 433 f., 520. The Talmud has the impossible identification with Mount Amanus i.e. *Alma Dagh* N. of the Orontes. Most modern scholars favour *Jebel Madurah* a hill situated some miles S. of the Dead Sea: see Clay Trumbull *Kadesh-Barnea* pp. 127 ff. Lagrange however suggests *Jebel Murweile* N.W. of Kadesh: see *Rev. bibl.* IX. p. 280[1].

24. *gathered unto his people.* This exact phrase is peculiar to the Pent. (P) being used in Gen. xxv. 8 (of Abraham), xxv. 17 (Ishmael), xxxv. 29 (Isaac), xlix. 33 (Jacob), and Num. xxvii. 13, xxxi. 2; Dt. xxxii. 50 (all of Moses). A similar phrase "gathered to their fathers" is used in Jud. ii. 7, 10; 1 K. i. 21; 2 K. xxii. 20 &c. "The original reference is to the family sepulchre, in which, as in a common abode, the members of the family dwell together, and perpetuate in that shadowy existence the relations of the former life. By a natural extension the phrases are applied also to the nether world, in which, by their clans, and tribes, and nations, all the dead dwell." Moore *Judges* (*ICC*) p. 66.

---

[1] Conder thinks that the name Hor is possibly connected with Khar or Har which designates the Phoenicians and their land in Egyptian monuments: see *Heth and Moab* p. 7.

which I have given unto the children of Israel, because ye rebelled against my word at the waters of Meribah. 25 Take Aaron and Eleazar his son, and bring them up unto mount Hor: 26 and strip Aaron of his garments, and put them upon Eleazar his son: and Aaron shall be gathered *unto his people*, and shall die there. 27 And Moses did as the LORD commanded: and they went up into mount Hor in the sight of all the congregation. 28 And Moses stripped Aaron of his garments, and put them upon Eleazar his son; and Aaron died there in the top of the mount: and Moses and Eleazar came down from the mount. 29 And when all the congregation saw that Aaron was dead, they wept for Aaron thirty days, even all the house of Israel. *P*

ye rebelled. The sin of Aaron is not described in any of the accounts that have come down to us.

26. *strip Aaron of his garments*[1]. These garments are described in Lev. viii. 7 ff., and the regulation for their transfer is given in Ex. xxix. 29.

Eleazar. Eleazar appears frequently in P, but twice only in JE (Dt. x. 7; Jos. xxiv. 33): these passages are of importance as shewing that JE as well as P recognised Aaron as "the founder of a hereditary priesthood": Driver *Deut.* p. 121. Herodotus says of the Egyptian priesthood "if any die, his son is appointed in his place" (II. 37).

28. *died there.* In Dt. x. 6 the scene of his death is not Mt. Hor but Moserah, an unknown site which may of course have been in the neighbourhood of this mountain. Gressmann thinks that the whole story is an imitation of the death of Moses to which it has close parallels: the place, a mountain top; the successor appointed; no account is given of the disposal of the body: see *Mose* p. 343.

29. *saw that Aaron was dead.* They realised this from Eleazar's wearing his garments.

XXI. 1–3. The Canaanites of the Negeb attack Israel but are defeated at a place called Hormah. This passage is a fragment which has got out of its context. In ch. xx. the Israelites were moving S. in order to go round Edom and to enter Canaan from the E.; here they are represented as fighting a victorious battle far to the North. In Jud. i. 17 a city named Zephath is destroyed by Judah and Simeon, and then called Hormah; the present passage may be an anticipation of that destruction. Burney, however, thinks that the present position is the more correct and that it represents a movement N. by Judah and its allied clans (*Schweich Lectures* pp. 28 ff.): this movement was afterwards described as taking place S. from Jericho, perhaps in order to

---

[1] Jirku suggests that some magic power would cling to the garments: see *ZAW* (1917/8) pp. 109 ff.

XXI. 1 And the Canaanite, the king of Arad, which dwelt in the South, heard tell that Israel came by the way [1]of Atharim; and he fought against Israel, and took some of them captive. 2 And Israel vowed a vow unto the LORD, and said, If thou wilt indeed deliver this people into my hand, then I will [2]utterly destroy their cities. 3 And the LORD hearkened to the voice of *J*

[1] Or, *of the spies* [2] Heb. *devote.*

represent the conquest as being carried out at one time and by the whole people[1].

It has been suggested that the narrative here should be placed before xiv. 45 (see Wiener *Essays in Pent. Crit.* pp. 121 ff.), and that the attempt to invade Canaan by way of the Negeb was thus frustrated. If this were so the need for re-conquest (as narrated in Jud. i. 17) would be explained. The theory receives additional support from the fact that whilst xxi. 3 gives an explanation of the name Hormah, xiv. 45 refers to it as already well known.

1. *the king of Arad.* Here and Jos. xii. 14 (with the king of Hormah). The position of these words after the name of the nation is awkward, and Moore would reject them as a gloss (see his note on Jud. i. 17 which he considers to have no real connexion with the present passage), a suggestion which is favoured by Holzinger. *Arad* lies some 50 miles N. of Kadesh its name being still preserved in *Tell ʿArād*. In the list of names placed by Sheshonk I on the S. wall of the great temple at Karnak *Arad* occurs twice (nos. 108 and 110) but since the arrangement of the list is not geographical no clue is given to the situation of the town: at the same time it suggests the possibility that another place of this name may have been found further S. and therefore nearer to the position of the Israelites in the previous ch.

the South. That is the Negeb: see on xiii. 17.

the way of Atharim. The rendering of A.V. and mg. *of the spies* follows the Targums and Vg., but is to be rejected both on philological and grammatical grounds[2].

2. *vowed a vow.* Cf. Gen. xxviii. 20 ff. (Jacob); Jud. xi. 30 f.; 1 S. i. 11; 2 S. xv. 8.

utterly destroy. The rendering of mg. *devote* means *to place under a ban* or *taboo* and represents the original Heb. חֵרֶם (*ḥerem*). The effect of

---

[1] The theory that there was a successful invasion of Canaan from the S. immediately after the return of the spies has been urged with much skill by Steuernagel *Einwanderung* pp. 76 f.; see also S. A. Cook *NOTH* pp. 81 ff.; and the remarks of Lagrange *Rev. bibl.* (1902) pp. 124 ff.

[2] Philologically it rests on a supposed identification of אתרים and תרים for which there is no justification. Grammatically the use of דרך *way* followed by the users of the road and not by a proper name is not found elsewhere.

Israel, and delivered up the Canaanites; and they [1]utterly destroyed them and their cities: and the name of the place was called [2]Hormah. *J*

4 And they journeyed from mount Hor | by the way to the Red Sea, to compass the land of Edom: and the soul of the people [3]was much discouraged [4]because of the way. 5 And the people spake against God, and against Moses, Wherefore have ye brought us up out of Egypt to die in the wilderness? for there is no bread, and there is no water; and our soul loatheth this [5]light bread. 6 And the LORD sent fiery serpents among the *R^P–*

[1] Heb. *devoted.* [2] From the same root as *herem*, a devoted thing.
[3] Or, *was impatient* Heb. *was shortened.* [4] Or, *in* [5] Or, *vile*

the ban was that the thing so devoted had to be destroyed: cf. Dt. vii. 1 f.; Jos. vi. 17, 21 &c.[1]

3. *Hormah*. A play on *ḥerem* 'a devoted thing.' A similar explanation is given in Jud. i. 17. The city or district is referred to in xiv. 45; Dt. i. 44; Jos. xii. 14 (where it is distinguished from Arad), xv. 30 &c.

4–9. The people once more murmur against the manna and because of the shortage of water. As a punishment serpents are sent amongst them. Moses makes a bronze serpent and sets it up on a pole; those who look at it are healed of their bites. For a discussion of various points arising from this narrative see Additional Note pp. 139–141.

4. *the way to the Red Sea*. On this road see xiv. 25.

to compass. This use of סבב should be noticed, it does not mean to make a complete, but only a partial circuit (see König on Gen. ii. 11).

was much discouraged. Heb. *was shortened*. Used of Samson (Jud. xvi. 16); the opposite phrase *length of spirit* is used in Job vi. 11 &c.

5. *no water*. The writer has no knowledge of the Rabbinic tradition referred to in 1 Cor. x. 4 that the Rock followed them.

this light bread. Heb. word for *light* does not occur elsewhere but its meaning is plain: *contemptible, worthless*. The *Speaker's Commentary* quotes as an illustration Horace *De Arte Poetica* 423 "Et spondere levi pro paupere."

6. *fiery serpents*. Heb. *the serpents, the fiery ones*. If as seems probable the connexion with burning is to be maintained the reference must be to the serpent's bite and the inflammation which follows it: cf. the use, exactly similar, of πρηστήρ for a species of serpent with a

---

[1] The slaughter of the Canaanites (*v.* 3) was justified, according to a legend preserved in Epiphanius *Ancoratus* CXIV., on the ground that Noah after dividing up the world amongst his three sons made them swear to respect the territories of their brethren. By seizing Canaan Ham violated the oath. Lanchester cites a similar story from the Ethiopian *Kebra Nagast*: see *Oxford Apoc.* II. p. 381.

people, and they bit the people; and much people of Israel died. *E*
7 And the people came to Moses, and said, We have sinned, because we have spoken against the LORD, and against thee; pray unto the LORD, that he take away the serpents from us. And Moses prayed for the people. 8 And the LORD said unto Moses, Make thee a fiery serpent, and set it upon a standard: and it shall come to pass, that every one that is bitten, when he seeth it, shall live. 9 And Moses made a serpent of brass, and set it upon the standard: and it came to pass, that if a serpent had bitten any man, when he looked unto the serpent

poisonous bite by Dioscorides VII. 14 and Aelian *Nat. An.* VI. 51[1]. The word for *fiery* is *seraphim* as in Is. vi. 2, but in spite of the fact that the Arabs in times past believed, as they do to-day, that the desert is full of demons and spirits (cf. Wellhausen *Reste Arab. Heid.* pp. 153 ff., von Alois Musil *Arabia Petraea* III. pp. 320 ff.) the reference is hardly to anything but actual serpents. That these abound in the deserts S. of Palestine is testified by travellers, and as far back as the expedition of Esarhaddon they were known there (see *TB* I. 124: and cf. Herod. II. 73, III. 109; Strabo XVI. 759)[2].

7. *from us.* The expression in Heb. is particularly strong, it might almost be read *from oppressing us*[3].

8. *a fiery serpent.* See Additional Note below.

9. *when he looked.* For parallels to healing coming from a look see Weinreich *Antike Heilungswunder* pp. 169 f.

ADDITIONAL NOTE ON XXI. 9.

The Bronze Serpent.

According to the story in 2 K. xviii. 4 the children of Israel burned incense to this serpent in the time of Hezekiah, and in consequence it was destroyed[4]. It is possible that the serpent was a symbol of Jehovah Himself though the

---

[1] The Jerusalem Targum makes God say: "Now shall the serpent who has not complained of his food (cf. *v.* 5) come and bite the people who complain. So the Word of the Lord sent fiery serpents among the people." Quoted by Deane on Wisd. xvi. 6.

[2] Bronze serpents have actually been found by Glaser in Arabia: see Nielsen *Die altarab. Mondreligion* pp. 189 and D. H. Müller *Südarab. Altertümer im Kunsthist. Hofmuseum* (*Wien*) No. 137. Also for Palestine Macalister *PEFQS* (1903) p. 222, Vincent *Canaan* p. 175.

[3] מֵעַל is used instead of מִן as in 1 S. vi. 20; 1 K. xv. 19 &c.

[4] Aeneas Sylvius tells us that serpents had been worshipped in Lithuania from ancient times even up to his own day (*De Statu Europae* ch. 20), see also Alexander Guagninus in *Resp. Poloniae* (Elz. p. 276). I owe these references to Ranke *Deutsche Gesch. im Zeitalt der Ref.*[4] I. p. 151.

narrative makes no statement to this effect[1]. The present story may be an attempt to explain the origin and early significance of the symbol.

It was once suggested by Robertson Smith that David belonged to a 'serpent' clan and that the bronze serpent was the old sacred emblem of his tribe[2]. Other references to serpents as presumably sacred are perhaps contained in the 'serpent stone' of 1 K. i. 9 and the 'serpent spring' of Neh. ii. 13. Cheyne connects the serpent with the Babylonian dragon myth which has left traces on Hebrew mythology[3].

An interesting suggestion is made by Ed. Meyer *IN* pp. 42, 116 that the serpent is connected in some way with the rod of Moses (cf. Ex. iv. 3); this theory is also upheld by Gressmann *Auswahl* p. 106 who compares the serpent staff of Gudea of Lagash (B.C. 2300)[4], and has in addition worked out a number of parallels in his article "Der Zauberstab des Mose u. die eherne Schlange" in *Zeit. des Vereins für Volkskunde* 1913.

The connexion of serpents with the preservation or restoration of life is a commonplace of pagan mythology, perhaps the most noted example being Asklepios who sometimes assumed the form of a serpent[5]. The use of the image of a serpent to cure serpent bites is perhaps a piece of sympathetic magic. Frazer refers to the device of the Philistines of making an image of mice when their land was infested with such vermin (1 S. v. 6 LXX). He also quotes other examples: "Apollonius of Tyana is said to have cleared Antioch of scorpions by making a bronze image of a scorpion, and burying it under a small pillar in the middle of the city....Gregory of Tours tells us that the city of Paris used to be free of dormice and serpents, but that in his lifetime, while they were cleaning a sewer, they found a bronze serpent and a bronze dormouse, and removed them" with disastrous results: see *Spirits of the Corn* II. pp. 280 f. For other similar illustrations see G. Jacob *Studien in Arab. Dichtern* IV. pp. 11 f. and Weinreich *Antike Heilungswunder* pp. 163 ff.

The general relation of serpents to divine beings is too wide a subject to be discussed here, it may however be mentioned that the Sumerian goddess KA.DI had the form of that reptile, and that there may be some connexion between Serapis and the Heb. שָׂרָף (*sarāph*) used for *serpent*: see Baudissin *Studien zur semit. Rel. Gesch.* I. pp. 257 ff., and Hehn *BBG* pp. 310 ff.[6]

The writer of the book of Wisdom tries to spiritualise the whole incident by making the serpent a mere token of salvation to remind the people of the law: "he that turned towards it was not saved because of that which he beheld, But because of thee, the Saviour of all" (xvi. 6 f.). This explanation

---

[1] Hehn *BBG* p. 313 denies that the serpent represented Jehovah: "Dass der Neḥuštān einmal Jahwe selbst dargestellt habe, ist zweifellos zu verneinen. Ihn stellte man als Stier dar, nicht als Schlange." It may have been, however, that whilst Jehovah was undoubtedly represented as a bull in North Israel, His symbol in Judah was a serpent. Gressmann regards the serpent as being the rod which Moses received at Sinai (Ex. iv. 17), and a symbol of Jehovah: see *op. cit.* pp. 456 f.

[2] See "Ancestor worship and ancestor tribes" in *Journal of Philology* (1880) pp. 99 f. and further Frazer *The Dying God* p. 86 and *Enc. Bib.* col. 3388.

[3] See *Enc. Bib.* 3388 and cf. Gunkel *Schöpfung u. Chaos* on the general subject of the dragon myth.

[4] An illustration of this staff will be found in *T.B.* II. No. 170.

[5] See Pausanias *Description of Greece* II. x. 3 and for various parallels Frazer *Adonis, Attis, and Osiris* I. pp. 80 ff. The goddess Ea, patroness of physicians among the Babylonians, is represented with a serpent's head.

[6] The Greeks regarded the serpent as the representative of Ge, the prototype of Demeter: see Farnell *The Cults of the Greek States* III. pp. 9 f.

is accepted by Baudissin *Adonis u. Esmun* p. 326, but as Gressmann points out (*Mose* p. 286) it was much too subtle for the early Israelites.

For various allegorical interpretations of the incident see Philo *De Alleg.* II. 20 (p. 80) and *De Agricul.* 22 (p. 315), and also our Lord's reference in Jn. iii. 14. In *Ep. Barnabas* XII. 5 there is a reference to Eve's serpent (a thought found also in Philo), and St Augustine combines the natural and the allegorical systems of interpretation when he says that the serpent was set up on the pole "being both a present help for the hurt, and a type of future destruction of death by death in the passion of Christ crucified" (*De Civ. Dei* Bk. IX. ch. 8).

of brass, he lived. 10 And the children of Israel journeyed, and *P* pitched in Oboth. 11 And they journeyed from Oboth, and pitched at Iye-abarim, | in the wilderness which is before Moab, *E* toward the sunrising. 12 From thence they journeyed, and pitched in the valley of Zered. 13 From thence they journeyed, and pitched on the other side of Arnon, which is in the wilder-

10–20. The people continue their journey by stages until they reach Mount Pisgah between the Arnon and the Jabbok. The geographical problems raised by the itinerary are explained by its coming in part from P, and in part from JE.

10. *Oboth.* This site is "somewhere on the flinty plateau to the east of Edom, the *Ard Suwwan* or Flint Ground, Arabia Petraea," G. A. Smith *Hist. Geog.* p. 557 where a further reference is given to Doughty *Arabia Deserta* I. pp. 28 f. Von Alois Musil suggests *'Ain el-Weybeh* a meeting point for caravans from Petra and Akaba on the way to Gaza (*Arabia Petraea* II. ii. pp. 202 ff.).

11. *Iye-abarim.* Heb. *the ruins of the 'Abarim* is so called to distinguish it from the Iyim of Jos. xv. 29. The *'Abarim* means the *places on the other side*, but Sayce *EHH* p. 226 would render it *Hebrews.* The site is unknown, unless the identification with *Khirbet 'Ai* be adopted (see Lagrange *Rev. bibl.* IX. pp. 287, 443).

12. *the valley of Zered.* The word נחל *naḥal* translated *valley* is really a *wady* and includes both the stream and its dried-up bed in the hot season: see the use in 1 K. xvii. 3 f. The *Zered* is mentioned in Dt. ii. 13 f. and seems there to be identified with the *Wady el-Aḥsā*; but the present context requires a situation further N. such as the *Wady 'Ain-Franji* or the *Seil S'aideh,* a branch of the Arnon (Dillmann).

13. *on the other side of Arnon.* Strictly speaking this should mean, from the point of view of an Israelite, S. of the Arnon: so Dillmann &c. But the expression should probably be interpreted from the point of view of those engaged in the march, as in Jud. xi. 18 (on which see Moore), and will therefore be to the N. The *Arnon* is the present *Wady Mojib* "an enormous trench across the plateau of Moab. It is about 1700 feet deep, and two miles broad from edge to edge of the cliffs which bound it" (G. A. Smith *Hist. Geog.* p. 558).

in the wilderness. This wilderness is named Kedemoth in Dt. ii. 26 f.

ness, that cometh out of the border of the Amorites: for Arnon *E* is the border of Moab, between Moab and the Amorites.
14 Wherefore it is said in the book of the Wars of the LORD,

Vaheb [1]in Suphah,
And the valleys of Arnon,
15 And the slope of the valleys
That inclineth toward the dwelling of Ar,
And leaneth upon the border of Moab.

16 And from thence *they journeyed* to [2]Beer: that is the well *J* whereof the LORD said unto Moses, Gather the people together, and I will give them water.

[1] Or, *in storm* [2] That is, *A well.*

and the message to Sihon is inserted here, a much more suitable place than Pisgah: see on *v.* 21.

Arnon is the border of Moab. The *Arnon* was the N. border of Moab in the time of Omri according to the Moabite Stone, though previously territory to the N. had been possessed by it and was again recovered by Mesha himself. At the time of the Israelite invasion Moab had been forced S. of the Arnon by Sihon (*v.* 26; Jud. xi. 22).

14. *Wherefore it is said.* That is to prove the position of the border of Moab. The same phrase is found in Gen. x. 9 &c.

the book of the Wars of the LORD. A similar collection of songs was the Book of Jashar (Jos. x. 13; 2 S. i. 18) which in their earliest form no doubt were preserved orally. Among the Arabs such collections were well known: see Brockelmann *Gesch. der arab. Litt.*² pp. 13 ff., e.g. the *Ḥamāsa* of Abû Temmâm and the *Mu'allakât*. The poem here cited is a mere fragment without any beginning or ending.

Vaheb in Suphah. LXX τὴν Ζωὸβ ἐφλόγισεν. These places are both unknown, though possibly as Sayce thinks Ζωὸβ may equal *zâhâb* cf. Dt. i. 1 *Di-zahab*, and *Suphah* may be connected with *Suph* of the same passage: see *EHH* p. 222.

the valleys of Arnon. The *Arnon* is divided up into a number of branches (see G. A. Smith *op. cit.* p. 558).

15. *the slope.* The word appears here only in the singular (elsewhere Dt. iii. 17, iv. 49; Jos. xii. 3, xiii. 30) and it is possible that the text is corrupt: see Gressmann *Mose* p. 347.

Ar. The word means *city* and is evidently akin to Heb. *'ir*, both going back to Sum. URU: the full form is presumably *'Ir Moab* (xxii. 36; cf. Dt. ii. 18). The site is uncertain and it may be the same place as the *Ma'ab* of Arabic geographers (Buhl *Geog.* pp. 269 f.). *Ar* is sometimes wrongly identified with Rabbah, a quite unsuitable locality. Driver thinks the mistake arises from the use by Eusebius of Ἀρεόπολις for Rabbah.

16. *Beer.* The word means *well* and perhaps originally a defining word was attached to it: it may have been the *Beer Elim* of Is. xv. 8.

17 Then sang Israel this song: *J*
Spring up, O well; sing ye unto it:
18 The well, which the princes digged,
Which the nobles of the people delved,
[1]With the sceptre, *and* with their staves.
And from the wilderness *they journeyed* to Mattanah: 19 and from Mattanah to Nahaliel: and from Nahaliel to Bamoth:

[1] Or, *By* order of *the lawgiver*

17. Wells were very important in the life of ancient peoples[1] and their discovery matter enough to give fame (cf. Gen. xxxvi. 24 "Anah who found the hot springs in the wilderness"): at the same time their possession was an occasion for disputing (Gen. xxvi. 18 ff.; Jud. i. 15 ff.). The song here preserved refers not to the discovery of a specific well, but is rather a popular song addressed to a well by the women who gathered round it. Such songs are still used by modern Bedawin: see Seetzen *Reisen* II. p. 223; Dalman *Palästinen Diwan* p. 45, and Nöldeke *ZDMG* LXI. p. 232.

W. Robertson Smith regards the song as a sign of the worship of wells, since the well is addressed as a living being (*Rel. Sem.*[2] p. 135, see further on sacred wells pp. 165 ff.): but so is the vineyard in Is. xxvii. 2. The Rabbis said that the mouth of the well was one of the ten things made by God at the end of the original creation (*Pirke Aboth* v. 9): see further on xvi. 32.

18. *the sceptre*. The same word is used in Gen. xlix. 10. The reference is to the staff or baton of the ruler or commander. The rendering of R.V. mg. *By* order of *the lawgiver* which follows A.V. makes the word refer to the commander or leader himself, a possible interpretation. Kennedy in *Cent. Bib.* mentions Budde's suggestion "that the reference is to a custom according to which, after a well has been discovered, it was temporarily covered over, and afterwards formally opened by the authorities with some such symbolic action as is described in the text."

from the wilderness. LXX reads *Beer*. The Targum of Onkelos says that the well journeyed with them: cf. 1 Cor. x. 4.

Mattanah. The site is unknown. Budde regards the whole phrase as part of the song and renders *From the wilderness a gift*.

19. The stations mentioned in this *v.* are interpreted allegorically in *Pirke Aboth* VI. 2 being connected with the law: thus the law is a gift (*Mattanah*) and by it God leads (*Nahaliel*) man to the heights (*Bamoth*).

Nahaliel. The name means *wady of God* and it is identified with the *Wady Zerḳā Maʿīn* by G. A. Smith *op. cit.* p. 562.

Bamoth. Lit. *high places*. Perhaps a proper name followed or preceded probably the *Bamoth-baal* of xxii. 41; Jos. xiii. 17, or the *Beth*

---

[1] Even a great sovereign like an Egyptian Pharaoh could attend personally to fixing the sites of wells: *Camb. Anct. Hist.* II. pp. 44, 138.

20 and from Bamoth to the valley that is in the field of Moab, *J* to the top of Pisgah, which looketh down upon [1]the desert.

21 And Israel sent messengers unto Sihon king of the Amorites, *E*

[1] Or, *Jeshimon*

Bamoth of the Moabite stone. Various sites have been suggested, but, since high places were very common in Moab and cromlechs are still so, no definite locality can safely be fixed upon. The identification with *Bamoth-baal* would demand a wide view over the plains of Moab (xxii. 41; Jos. xiii. 17).

20. *the valley.* The word here used is not *naḥal* as in *vv.* 12 ff. but *gai'* and the reference is not to a torrent valley but what G. A. Smith calls a glen. Perhaps the *Wady 'Ayûn Mûsā* is meant.

the field of Moab. So in Gen. xxxvi. 35; Ruth i. 1, 2 &c. (though rendered 'country' by R.V.)[1].

to the top of Pisgah. The *to* is to be omitted, the expression is in apposition to the previous phrase and is probably a scribal gloss limiting the somewhat wide description. The head of Pisgah is one of the projections from the Moabite Plateau from which a wide view across the whole of Western Palestine is to be obtained: see G. A. Smith *op. cit.* pp. 562 f.[2]

the desert. Mg. *Jeshimon.* The word is usually applied to the desolate country on the opposite side of the Dead Sea (1 S. xxiii. 19, 24, xxvi. 1, 3). Here and in xxiii. 28 it is used of the E. side.

21–**XXII.** 1. The Israelites send a peaceful message to Sihon, king of the Amorites, similar in content to that sent to Edom (xx. 14 ff.), requesting permission to march through his territories. As in the case of Edom the request is not acceded to, but on this occasion war is the result and the Amorites are defeated and their land overrun by the Israelites. Further advance brings them into conflict with Og, king of Bashan, who is overthrown at Edrei. The stories of these victories are often alluded to by writers of the Deuteronomic school (e.g. Dt. i. 4, ii. 24–iii. 13, iv. 47, xxix. 7; Jos. ix. 10, xii. 4; Jud. xi. 19 ff. &c. There is also a reference in xxxii. 33 (Og only) and Jos. xiii. 27–31 both P).

21. *Israel.* Cf. xx. 14.

Sihon. The derivation of the name is uncertain; it may be connected with the later Heb. סְיָח *ass's foal* and so be a totemistic name (cf. Strack). Other critics think that it is derived from a place name (see Kittel's note *Gesch. des Volkes Isr.* I. p. 545).

king of the Amorites. Sihon is called variously by this title, by that

---

[1] The word in Heb. is שָׂדֶה *sâdeh*. It may be only a coincidence that the sign KUR is used in Assyr. for both *mâtu* = *land* and *šâdu*; the meaning of the latter is not of course *field* but *mountain*.

[2] The root *psg* means *to cleave* in Aram. and late Heb. The name seems to be due to the broken appearance of the mountain range: cf. the Apennines and our own Crinkle Crags.

saying, 22 Let me pass through thy land: we will not turn aside *E* into field, or into vineyard; we will not drink of the water of the wells: we will go by the king's *high* way, until we have passed thy border. 23 And Sihon would not suffer Israel to pass through his border: but Sihon gathered all his people together, and went out against Israel into the wilderness, and came to Jahaz: and he fought against Israel. 24 And Israel smote him with the edge of the sword, and possessed his land from Arnon unto Jabbok, | even unto the children of Ammon: for the border *J*

of king of Heshbon (Dt. ii. 26, 30 &c.), or by a combination of the two (Dt. i. 4, iii. 2 &c.).

22. For the contents of the message cf. xx. 14 ff. The message must have been sent before the arrival at Pisgah which was on the far side of the Amorite territory.

border. Read *territory*.

23. *Jahaz*. The exact site is unknown but presumably it lay somewhere on the E. border of Sihon's territory as that would be the most likely place for the encounter. The name is sometimes spelled *Jahzah* as in Jer. xlviii. 21. It formed part of the territory of Reuben but like many of the neighbouring cities fell into the hands of Mesha.

24. *Israel smote him*. According to Josephus the victory was largely due to the skill of the Israelite slingers and archers (*Ant*. IV. v. 2); the tradition may have originated from *v*. 30.

Arnon. See on *v*. 13. It formed the S. boundary of Sihon's kingdom.

Jabbok. This river here forms the N. border of the Amorites as in Jud. xi. 22 (cf. *v* 13). It is usually identified with the *Nahr ez-Zerkā* which flows into the Jordan some 25 m. N. of the Dead Sea. G. A. Smith *Hist. Geog*. pp. 583 f. (see Smend *ZAW* (1902) pp. 137 ff.).

Ammon. The Ammonites had been driven into the desert by the Amorites, and this formed the boundary of their territory to the E.

for the border...was strong. This statement would account for the limitation of the Amorite power, or for the failure of the Israelites to pursue their conquests further. There are however difficulties in the way of this reading since the boundary to the E. was not strong by nature and the Heb. עז *strong* does not elsewhere mean *fortified*. Most critics follow the reading of LXX and render *at Jazer was the border &c*. (cf. Jos. xiii. 25)[1]. The exact position of this place is not quite certain, it was however some ten (Roman) m. from Philadelphia (*Rabbath-'Ammon*)—see Eusebius *Onom*. 264. 98 ff., Jerome *Onom*. 86. 23 f.—and is probably the modern *Ṣâr*[2].

---

[1] The change in the Heb. is very slight ביעזר being read for כיעז.

[2] The sibilants in the two names do not agree, but instances of such confusion are given in Burney *Judges* p. 306.

of the children of Ammon was strong. 25 And Israel took all *J* these cities: and Israel dwelt in all the cities of the Amorites, in Heshbon, and in all the [1]towns thereof. 26 For Heshbon was *E* the city of Sihon the king of the Amorites, who had fought against the former king of Moab, and taken all his land out of his hand, even unto Arnon. 27 Wherefore they that speak in proverbs say,

[1] Heb. *daughters.*

25. *all these cities.* As no *cities* have been mentioned a portion of the text must have fallen out or been displaced.

Heshbon. The name of this city has survived in the modern *Ḥeshbân* which rises nearly 3000 ft. above sea-level, it lies some 18 m. E. of the Jordan at Jericho and 5 m. N.E. of Mt. Nebā.

towns. Heb. *daughters* as mg.: so in xxxii. 42; Jer. xlix. 2; Ez. xvi. 46 &c.

27–30. An ancient poem is here introduced describing a conquest of Moab either by the Amorites or possibly by the Israelites themselves. The poem may originally have been written by an Amorite to celebrate the victory of Sihon (Sayce *EHH* p. 136), but this is improbable. Since Herder's ingenious suggestion many scholars have adopted the view that the song is satiric. Accordingly *vv.* 27 f. must be taken as addressed by the Israelites to the Amorites, *v.* 29 to the Moabites, and the last *v.* of the poem describes Israel's own victory over the Amorites themselves. This theory seems too subtle and complicated for an ancient poem, and nothing in the text itself clearly supports it although it is quite compatible with such an interpretation. Other critics are more drastic (e.g. Ed. Meyer *ZAW* I. pp. 129 ff., V. pp. 36 ff.) and regard the song as celebrating a victory by Israel over Moab, probably in the days of Omri as described in Mesha's inscription. This last theory receives the support of Baentsch, and substantially of Kennedy; it is rejected by Dillmann, and by Kittel *Gesch. des Volkes Isr.* I. pp. 490, 545. Perhaps Gray's summing up is as near to the truth as we can get: "The one thing that is clear is that the poem celebrates a victory over Moab. Everything else is more or less uncertain."

27. *they that speak in proverbs.* The writer evidently got this song from an oral source since he gives no reference to one of the great collections (see on *v.* 14)[1]. The reciters of proverbs (better here ballads) were seemingly a special class, the ballad-singers or minstrels of an older generation. See further on xxiii. 7 and Budde *Gesch. der altheb. Literatur* p. 9.

---

[1] In a similar way William of Malmesbury tells us that an account of the birth of Athelstan is derived not from books but from *cantilenae* (ballads). See *De Gestis Regum Anglorum* II. (I. p. 155 in Rolls Series).

E

Come ye to Heshbon,
Let the city of Sihon be built and established:
28 For a fire is gone out of Heshbon,
A flame from the city of Sihon:
It hath devoured Ar of Moab,
The lords of [1]the high places of Arnon.
29 Woe to thee, Moab!
Thou art undone, O people of Chemosh:
He hath given his sons as fugitives,
And his daughters into captivity,
Unto Sihon king of the Amorites.

[1] Or, *Bamoth*

Come ye to Heshbon. The people addressed are either the conquered Amorites or else the Israelites themselves exulting in their victory.

28. *the city of Sihon.* That is Heshbon: see on *v.* 21. The name may have clung to the city even after the Moabites reconquered their territory, otherwise Meyer's theory is difficult unless it be supposed that originally Sihon was a *Moabite* king.

be built. That is *re-built*, as often.

28 f. These *vv.* are quoted with slight alterations in Jer. xlviii. 45 f.

28. *a fire.* A frequent metaphor for war: see Am. i. 4 &c.; Ps. lxviii. 63.

Ar of Moab. See note on *v.* 15. The flame of conquest is spreading to the S. which would be quite consistent with the conquest of the country by a foe from across the Jordan, either the Amorites under Sihon, or the Israelites themselves in the days of Omri.

lords of the high places (mg. *Bamoth*). The Targum takes this phrase to mean the heathen priests, a quite possible interpretation, though it is not necessary to regard *the high places* as necessarily religious (cf. Dt. xxxii. 13; 2 S. i. 19 &c.). The text is difficult and possibly corrupt since LXX read it slightly differently[1]. The *lords* would be the proprietors of the land specified (cf. Jud. ix. 2, xx. 5; 2 S. xxi. 12 &c.).

29. *O people of Chemosh. Chemosh* was the god of Moab as we know from Mesha's inscription, in addition to a number of biblical passages (Jer. xlviii. 8; 1 K. xi. 7 &c.).

He hath given. That is Chemosh was angry with his people, as in Mesha's inscription, just as Jehovah was with Israel according to the writer of passages such as Jud. ii. 14. Gray points out that in the citation of the poem in Jer. xlviii. 46 later thought has altered *Chemosh* into *Moab* and omitted any reference to his being an agent in the defeat of the Moabites.

Sihon king of the Amorites. The Heb. is unusual and the phrase may be a gloss; as the poem now stands it has no line parallel to it, and in Jer. xlviii. 46 it does not appear, either because the writer of that passage

---

[1] *κατέπιεν* probably represents a reading ותבלע instead of בעלי.

30 We have shot at them; Heshbon is perished even unto Dibon, *E*
And we have laid waste even unto Nophah,
[1]Which *reacheth* unto Medeba.

31 Thus Israel dwelt in the land of the Amorites. | 32 And Moses *J* sent to spy out Jazer, and they took the towns thereof, and drove out the Amorites that were there. 33 And they turned *D* and went up by the way of Bashan: and Og the king of Bashan went out against them, he and all his people, to battle at Edrei. 34 And the LORD said unto Moses, Fear him not: for I have delivered him into thy hand, and all his people, and his land; and thou shalt do to him as thou didst unto Sihon king of the Amorites, which dwelt at Heshbon. 35 So they smote him, and his sons, and all his people, until there was none left him remaining: and they possessed his land.

XXII. 1 And the children of Israel journeyed, and pitched *P* in the plains of Moab beyond the Jordan at Jericho.

[1] Some ancient authorities have, *Fire* reached *unto*.

did not find it in his original or because he broke off the quotation immediately before it.

30. This *v.* is corrupt and the attempts of various scholars to emend it are not very convincing.

We have shot at them. A sudden change of person. Gray follows LXX and reads *their posterity* taking *is perished* with it[1].

Dibon. The modern *Diban* situated some 5 m. N. of the Arnon: see Jer. xlviii. 18, 22.

Nophah. This should perhaps be read *Nobah* (cf. Jud. viii. 11).

Medeba. The modern *Mâdeba* between Ḥeshbân and Maʿīn, it appears in the Moabite stone under the form *Mehedeba*.

32. *Jazer.* Cf. xxxii. 1, 3; Jer. xlviii. 32.

33. *Og the king of Bashan.* Josephus states that he was in alliance with Sihon, but arrived too late to take part in the battle of Jahaz (*Ant.* IV. v. 3).

Edrei. Now *'Edraʿat* or *Derʿat* some 22 m. N.W. of Bosra.

35. *and his sons.* These words do not appear in Dt. iii. 3.

XXII. 1. The narrative of xxi. 11 seems to be continued.

the plains of Moab. This term occurs in P only. It signifies the open plain or steppes to the N. of the Dead Sea on the E. of Jordan and corresponds to the steppes of Jericho on the opposite side.

beyond the Jordan at Jericho. The obvious meaning is that the Israelites had crossed the river to Jericho. Such, however, was not the meaning of the original in which *beyond Jordan* represents the point of view of one already in Canaan, i.e. the E. bank. So also *at Jericho* is lit. *of Jericho*, that portion of the river flowing by the town.

---

[1] M.T. reads וַנִּירָם; LXX *καὶ τὸ σπέρμα αὐτῶν* represents וְנִינָם.

PART III.

EVENTS IN MOAB.

CHAPTERS XXII. 2—XXXVI.

This final part of the book of Numbers stretches from xxii. 2 to xxxvi., and its contents make up a miscellaneous collection of narratives, laws, and regulations, bound together on the supposition that they all took place, or were formulated, during the residence of the Israelites in Moab. The striking episode of Balaam, the gentile seer who spoke at the inspiration of Jehovah, appears in the opening chh.; at the close, various statements of a geographical or topographical nature concerning either the route through the wilderness, or the proposed division of the promised land, have been grouped together. The contents come from the three great sources J, E, and P.

(*a*) The story of Balaam. xxii. 2–xxiv. 25.
(*b*) Various laws and incidents. xxv.–xxxi.
(*c*) Miscellaneous topographical narratives. xxxii.–xxxvi.

CHAPTERS XXII. 2—XXIV. 25.

THE STORY OF BALAAM.

The story of Balaam is one of the most puzzling, and at the same time one of the most striking, in the whole of the O.T. "There are few incidents," as Conder says, "more dramatic than the tale of the wild seer of Pethor, restrained from cursing and compelled to bless, standing amid the smoke of the sacrifices, and gazing on the black camp in the white gorge below while the rude dolmen tables ran red with the blood of oxen and rams, and the words of his chant came without thought to his lips" (*Heth and Moab* p. 137).

Attempts to explain the motives of Balaam, and to account for the inconsistency of his character have been many; amongst them contributions of an exegetical nature from some of the greatest preachers of the Church of England. Dr Lock has collected a number of such studies in the introduction to a University sermon, now published in *The Bible and Christian Life* pp. 141 ff. (reprinted from *J.Th.S.* II. pp. 161 ff.); and the names which he cites consist of Bishop Butler, Newman, Arnold, Keble, Maurice, and F. W. Robertson. He ends his introduction with an apt quotation from Archbishop Benson: "It was an almost inconceivable character, one dramatist only has ever lived who could have traced all the windings of a spirit so lofty and so depraved, through light so intense and through shadow so deadly" (*Fishers of Men* p. 136).

Modern critics have in part accounted for some of the inconsistencies of the character of Balaam as it is portrayed in Numbers, and still more for the undoubted difficulties of the narrative in which the story has been preserved, by analysing the text into its component parts (see Introd. pp. xxxiv. f.). A casual reading of R.V. tells us that the account consists of a prose narrative in which a number of poems have been imbedded. In the opinion of the majority of critics the poems are of greater antiquity than their setting (see

Gray pp. 313 f.). But they have been incorporated into it with no little art and literary skill. The tradition which is embodied in them no doubt existed among the Israelite people in many different forms, and in all probability had its beginning in some actual incident in connexion with the entry into Canaan. For the poems obvious parallels can be found in the so-called Blessing of Jacob (Gen. xlix.) and the so-called Blessing of Moses (Dt. xxxiii.: cf. also xxxii.).

Our conceptions of the story, and of the character of the principal actor in it, are apt to be influenced, if not controlled, by later estimates of Balaam's character with which we are familiar: these estimates are almost certainly inconsistent with the story as it is contained in the present passage (see below), and when the compiler of JE had worked his two sources into one another he left little in either of them which was contradicted by the other, except in matters of detail. The character of the prophet is by no means despicable, rather is it admirable; for whilst he is anxious to do his best for his employer (a reasonable attitude of mind), "the outstanding fact to be kept in view is," as Gray points out, "that nothing suffices to seduce him from carrying out the will of Yahweh."

Later writers, unwilling to conceive the possibility of a heathen prophet acting as Balaam is represented as doing, added condemnation to condemnation (the passage in Micah vi. 4 f. is earlier than such unfavourable conceptions, or else the prophet deliberately ignores them). In Dt. xxiii. 4 f. (cf. Jos. xxiv. 9 f.) the writer in emphasising one of his favourite thoughts, the loving protection of Jehovah, may have unconsciously given a start to the less pleasing view of Balaam's character: in P, however, no fate is too bad for Balaam, and no means of working evil against Israel too abominable to be used by him (see xxxi. 8, 16; Jos. xiii. 22)[1].

Later writers, with very few exceptions, take up the same attitude: e.g. Philo *De Vit. Mos.* I. 48 (Mang. II. 123); 2 Pet. ii. 13 ff.; Jude 11; Rev. ii. 14; Joseph. *Ant.* IV. vi. 2–6, 13. Gray notices one favourable passage, the comment of *Siphrê* (ed. Friedmann, 150 *a*) on Dt. xxxiv. 10, "*There hath not arisen in Israel a prophet,*" to the effect that Balaam among the heathen was in many respects a greater prophet even than Moses himself (see further notes on xxiv. 4 below).

Balaam has been identified or connected with various figures known to the Oriental world: with Laban (*Sanhedrin* 105 *b*: cf. also Steuernagel *Die Einwanderung* pp. 104 f. where various parallels are worked out); with the famous Arabic writer of fables Lokman, son of Baʿur (this identification was first made I believe by Ewald: cf. also Meyer *IN* pp. 376 ff.); and some of the more bitter of the Rabbis saw in him a figure of our Blessed Lord (see Herford *Christianity in Talmud and Midrash* pp. 64 ff.).

The writers of the Priestly school, and their followers, failed to realise that the original story was not concerned mainly with the character of Balaam, or even with the use by Jehovah of a heathen prophet; it was rather an illustration of the inevitability of His plans, of the blessedness of those who worked with them, and of the madness of those who opposed them: for this latter thought cf. Cicero *In Cat.* III. ix. The whole story is intended to demonstrate the truth that nothing can avail to protect Jehovah's enemies, nothing

---

[1] An interesting theory has recently been propounded by Samuel Daiches in the *Hilprecht Anniversary Volume* pp. 60 ff. He considers that Balaam was a *bārū*, a sorcerer pure and simple, and instances a number of parallels between passages in the biblical account and Babylonian religious-magical texts which support his contention (these are referred to in the notes on the text). Moreover the very name Balaam may be a good Babylonian one *Bēl ʿammu* (see on xxii. 5), and if Pethor is on the Euphrates further evidence in favour of the suggestion is available.

can rob His chosen of their destined reward. This fact, however, must not blind us to the equally important truth that "The Jewish nation is selected that it may be trained to be a source of blessing to all the nations of the earth. And meanwhile we have glimpses of true religion and of real virtue in those nations. In Melchizedek we have an illustration of the heathen priesthood and its power of blessing; in Balaam, of heathen prophecy, and its power of reaching, however blindly and unconsciously, to truth; of heathen virtue in Job, praised both by God and man as 'a perfect and an upright man, one that feareth God and escheweth evil,' and winning from God a special power of intercession for others. The very title of the Lord's anointed, the Messiah, is applied to the heathen Cyrus; and the prophets always imply that all the surrounding nations are under Jehovah's control, and look forward to the time when they will consciously acknowledge His rule" (Lock *op. cit.* p. 50).

The negotiations between Balak and Balaam. xxii. 2–41.
The first Oracle. xxiii. 1–12.
The second Oracle. 13–26.
The third Oracle. 27–xxiv. 13.
The farewell message. xxiv. 14–25.

Chapter XXII. 2–41.

The negotiations between Balak and Balaam.

Balak, king of Moab, sends for Balaam to curse the Israelites who threaten his borders. After some negotiations the prophet agrees to come and sets out on his way. During the journey he is opposed by the angel of Jehovah.

There are in this section several discrepancies and uncertainties, such as the place from which Balaam came (*v.* 5), but chiefly the impossibility of reconciling *vv.* 20 f. with *vv.* 22 ff. In the first God's permission has been given, in the second it has *not* been given. This difficulty is not denied even by so strong an upholder of the conservative position as H. M. Wiener (see *Essays in Pent. Crit.* p. 147, where he refuses to make any guesses as to a solution in the absence of aid from the Versions).

(*a*) *The first invitation.* 2–6.
(*b*) *Balaam's first refusal.* 7–14.
(*c*) *The renewal of the invitation.* 15–20.
(*d*) *Balaam's journey.* 21–35.
(*e*) *Balak receives the prophet.* 36–41.

XXII. 2–6. Balak sends messengers to Balaam the son of Beor in order that he may curse his enemies. The custom of cursing an enemy before battle is very ancient and widespread: it was found amongst the ancient Germans (cf. Tacitus *Ann.* XIII. 57), the pre-Muhammadan Arabs (cf. Goldziher *Abhandlungen zur arab. Phil.* I. pp. 1–121), and even in the Middle Ages soothsayers and astrologers were often consulted by popes and monarchs alike, and accompanied generals to battle. It is recorded by Roger of Wendover that at the siege of Jerusalem in 1099 A.D. the 'Turks' brought up two witches to enchant one of the military machines of the Crusaders: they were, however, both struck dead by a large stone cast by the very machine which they were supposed to render useless.

2 And Balak the son of Zippor saw all that Israel had done to the Amorites. 3 And Moab was sore afraid of the people, because they were many: | and Moab [1]was distressed because of the children of Israel. 4 And Moab said unto the elders of Midian, Now shall [2]this multitude lick up all that is round about us, as the ox licketh up the grass of the field. And Balak the son of Zippor was king of Moab at that time. 5 And he sent messengers unto Balaam the son of Beor, | to Pethor, which is by — *E* *J* *E*

[1] Or, *abhorred* [2] Heb. *the assembly.*

2. *Balak.* Mentioned also Jos. xxiv. 9; Mic. vi. 5; and Jud. xi. 25 (in the last passage without Balaam). The meaning of the name is *the ravager.*

Zippor. This name is not found elsewhere in O.T. in its masc. form, unless Ball's conjecture that *Zophar* in Job ii. 11 is really *Zippor* be accepted, but the fem. form *Zipporah* was the name of Moses' wife. The name is found on a papyrus in the British Museum coming from the time of Meneptah II (see Brugsch *Egypt under the Pharaohs*, E.T.[2] II. p. 126), and the fem. also occurs in a Palmyrene inscription (*NSI* No. 120 *l.* 2). The meaning is *small bird* or *sparrow*, and the origin of the name may be totemistic: cf. Robertson Smith *Rel. Sem.*[2] pp. 124 ff.

to the Amorites. See above xxi. 21 ff.

3. The two halves of this *v.* seem to be derived from two different sources as they are tautologous.

was distressed. Cf. Ex. i. 12 of Egypt. In Ex. xv. 15 the terror of Moab is anticipated by the writer.

4. *Moab said.* Such personifications are not uncommon: cf. Jud. i. 3.

elders of Midian. The mention here and in *v.* 7 may be due to a gloss suggested by xxxi. 16. It is noteworthy that Balaam makes no reference to Midian in xxiv. At the same time Midian was used with some looseness, if we can trust Gen. xxxvii. 25 ff. where Midianites are confused with their kinsmen the Ishmaelites. A detached notice in Gen. xxxvi. 35 speaks of Midian being smitten in the field of Moab. Ehrlich suggests the possible reading *children of Ammon*: cf. *v.* 5.

ox licketh. The same figure is used in *Testaments of the Twelve Patriarchs*, Test. Gad. II. 2.

5. *sent messengers.* The recognition of a prophet belonging to another people, and the attempt to obtain his assistance, finds a parallel in 2 K. v. 5 ff. (Naaman).

Balaam the son of Beor. Nöldeke long ago pointed out the resemblance to Bela son of Beor king of Edom (Gen. xxxvi. 32); in the original both names are derived from the same root (בלע *to swallow up*)[1], the difference being the addition of a single letter to the Heb. Some connexion be-

---

[1] Neubauer, followed by Sayce *HCM* p. 275, divides up בלעם into בל and עם and reads *Bel-Ammi.*

the River, | to the land of the children of his people, to call him, *J* saying, Behold, there is a people come out from Egypt: behold, they cover the [1]face of the earth, and they abide over against me: 6 come now therefore, I pray thee, curse me this people; for they are too mighty for me: peradventure I shall prevail, that we may smite them, and that I may drive them out of the land: for I know that he whom thou blessest is blessed, and he whom thou cursest is cursed. 7 And the elders of Moab and

[1] Heb. *eye*.

tween them is found by many scholars, e.g. Ball, Gray, Hommel *AHT* p. 153, &c., but Driver questions the justice of the identification in view of the different accounts given in Israelite and Edomite traditions: see on Gen. xxxvi. 32.

Pethor...the River. Since *the River* can hardly mean anything else than the Euphrates (cf. Ex. xxiii. 31; Jos. xxiv. 2 f., 14 f.) some site near that river must be sought. The identification with *Pitru* near Carchemish which appears on an inscription of Shalmaneser III, the Egyptian form of which *pe-d-rui* is found in the lists of Thutmose III, seems an obvious one. The difficulty involved in supposing that Balaam lived so far from Moab, however, is very great in view of the number of journeys required by the narrative and the length of time which they would occupy. In Dt. xxiii. 4 *Pethor* is said to be in Aram-naharaim, a location which is not inconsistent with the above identification: see *Enc. Bib.* 287. The contention by certain scholars that *the River* here means the river of Egypt (cf. Gen. xxxvi. 37), though it has not received much support, ought perhaps to be mentioned: see *Enc. Bib.* 3685 f.

the children of his people (Heb. בְּנֵי עַמּוֹ)[1]. The addition of a single letter gives the reading *the children of Ammon*, a reading which is found in several Heb. MSS. as well as in Sam., Syr., Lucian, and Vulg. The final letter may have slipped out by accident, or it may have deliberately been omitted, as inconsistent with a residence in Pethor.

there is a people. Those who live on the edge of the desert must always be prepared for the sudden appearance of raiding tribes coming perhaps from a far distance: see G. Lowthian Bell *Syria &c.* p. 66.

6. *curse me this people*. On the power of curses see above and notes on *v.* 23 f. and cf. Lock *The Bible and Christian Life* pp. 150 ff.

7–14. Balak sends messengers to Balaam offering rewards in return for his assistance. Balaam however cannot fall in with their plans as Jehovah refuses permission.

---

[1] Glaser states that the Katabani, a south Arabian people, call themselves *walad 'Amm* i.e. children of 'Amm: see Hommel *AHT* p. 48 who connects them with the Benî Ammon. Is the form here really early?

the elders of Midian departed with the rewards of divination in their hand; and they came unto Balaam, and spake unto him the words of Balak. 8 And he said unto them, Lodge here this night, and I will bring you word again, as the LORD shall speak unto me: and the princes of Moab abode with Balaam. 9 And God came unto Balaam, and said, What men are these with thee? 10 And Balaam said unto God, Balak the son of Zippor, king of Moab, hath sent unto me, *saying*, 11 Behold, the people that is come out of Egypt, it covereth the face of the earth: now, come curse me them; peradventure I shall be able to fight against them, and shall drive them out. 12 And God said unto Balaam, Thou shalt not go with them; thou shalt not curse the people: for they are blessed. 13 And Balaam rose up in the morning, and said unto the princes of Balak, Get you into your land: for the LORD refuseth to give me leave to go with you. 14 And the princes of Moab rose up, and they went unto Balak, and said, Balaam refuseth to come with us. 15 And Balak sent yet again princes, more, and more honourable than they. 16 And

J
E
J
E

7. *elders*. Cf. *vv.* 8, 13 ff. *princes*, and for *Midian* see on *v.* 4.

rewards. To the ancient mind there was nothing degrading in such a practice: cf. 1 S. ix. 7 f. (Samuel); 1 K. xiv. 3 (Ahijah); 2 K. viii. 8 f. (Elisha). Later writers saw in this offer of rewards the temptation to which Balaam fell (2 Pet. ii. 15).

divination. See on xxiii. 23 and cf. Is. ii. 6 with Wade's notes.

8. *this night*. Revelations by means of dreams are characteristic of E: see on xii. 6.

as the LORD. The use of divine names in this story is very perplexing. On the use of Jehovah by heathen see König *Neue kirch. Zeitschrift* x. pp. 705 f.

12. Balaam is presumed to be ignorant of the Israelites (cf. *v.* 5), and of their peculiar relationship to Jehovah.

13. The negotiations seem definitely to be closed, though oriental methods of bargaining may have led Balaam—taking the lowest view of his character—to anticipate fresh efforts to re-open them; Balak evidently took this view of the matter.

15–20. Balak refuses to accept Balaam's rejection of his invitation, and sends a still more important embassy to wait upon him. Once more the prophet consults Jehovah and from Him obtains a conditional permission to return with the ambassadors.

15. *more, and more honourable*. The composition of an embassy gives an important clue to the regard felt for the person to whom it is sent. At the Congress of Mantua in 1459 Pius II refused to recognise the

they came to Balaam, and said to him, Thus saith Balak the *E*
son of Zippor, Let nothing, I pray thee, hinder thee from coming
unto me: 17 for I will promote thee unto very great honour, *J*
and whatsoever thou sayest unto me I will do: come therefore,
I pray thee, curse me this people. 18 And Balaam answered and
said unto the servants of Balak, If Balak would give me his house
full of silver and gold, I cannot go beyond the word of the LORD
my God, to do less or more. 19 Now therefore, I pray you, tarry *E*
ye also here this night, that I may know what the LORD will
speak unto me more. 20 And God came unto Balaam at night,
and said unto him, If the men be come to call thee, rise up, go
with them; but only the word which I speak unto thee, that
shalt thou do. 21 And Balaam rose up in the morning, and
saddled his ass, and went with the princes of Moab. 22 And *J*

representatives of Frederick III on the ground that they were not of sufficiently high rank: see Creighton *History of the Papacy* III. p. 221.

17. For the greatness of the promises cf. Dan. ii. 6, v. 7.

18. *his house &c.* Cf. the refusal of the prophet in 1 K. xiii. 8.

the LORD my God. This use by a heathen is difficult: cf. Jos. ii. 9 ff. (Rahab).

less or more. Heb. *small or great*: cf. xxiv. 13; Gen. xxiv. 50; *good or bad.* The idiom is meant to be exhaustive; see my note on Jer. x. 5.

19. The writer does not tell us that Balaam took any steps to obtain any further communication from God. Dean Stanley, however, regards him as persisting after God's first refusal and so bringing ruin upon himself; he compares Herod. I. 158, VI. 86: see *Jewish Church* I. p. 163. In a similar way the philosopher Maximus on receiving an invitation from Julian to come to his court refused to abide by the results of divination until they were favourable (Eunapius *Vitae Sophistorum &c.* p. 77).

21–35. The journey which Balaam undertakes is, in this passage, undertaken without the permission of God (*vv.* 22 and 34). In consequence of this the angel of the LORD makes three attempts to stop his progress; on each occasion the prophet's ass is aware of the angel, but Balaam requires to be informed by his beast of the presence of the divine messenger. Permission is at length given for Balaam to proceed on the same terms as those already laid down in *v.* 20. The persistence of Balaam in going on his prophetic mission may be contrasted with the equal persistence of Jonah in trying to avoid his (Jon. i. 3).

21. *saddled his ass.* In nearly every instance in O.T. the mention of this simple operation is connected with some tragic event: cf. 2 S. xvii. 23 (Ahithophel); 1 K. ii. 40 (Shimei), xiii. 13 ff. (the old prophet).

God's anger was kindled because he went: and the angel of the LORD placed himself in the way for an adversary against him. Now he was riding upon his ass, and his two servants were with him. 23 And the ass saw the angel of the LORD standing in the way, with his sword drawn in his hand: and the ass turned aside out of the way, and went into the field: and Balaam smote the ass, to turn her into the way. 24 Then the angel of the LORD stood in a hollow way between the vineyards, a fence being on this side, and a fence on that side. 25 And the ass saw the angel of the LORD, and she thrust herself unto the wall, and crushed Balaam's foot against the wall: and he smote her again. 26 And the angel of the LORD went further, and stood in a narrow place, J

22. *God's anger.* This statement cannot possibly be reconciled with *v.* 20 in which full permission was given to go to Balak.

the angel of the LORD. Cf. Ex. iv. 24 where Jehovah Himself is said to attack Moses on a journey. The angel is "a temporary appearance of Yahweh in human form" (Gray): cf. xx. 16.

an adversary. Heb. *a Satan.* In later literature the name was used of a definite individual opponent of God and man; in 1 S. xxix. 4; 2 S. xix. 22; 1 K. v. 4 &c. and probably here also it is used indefinitely: see further Peters *Rel. of Hebs.* pp. 332, 396; Gibson on Job i. 6.

two servants. There is no mention in this story of the princes of Moab. The two servants are as Holz. says "two mute figures" who perform no function in the narrative, they do not even help their master to control his ass. According to the Talmud they were none other than Johannes and Jambres, the magicians of Pharaoh (Buxtorf *Lex. Talmud.* p. 945).

23. *the ass saw.* The ass was regarded with respect by the Semites and quite possibly worshipped by them in early times: see Ball *The Ass in Sem. Mythology* in *PSBA* (1910) pp. 64 ff. Gressmann quotes an ancient story from Central Asia, of a horse which stood still on seeing an evil spirit, who remained unperceived by its rider, and, also, a Bosnian story of a horse which, in spite of repeated attempts to persuade or compel it, refused to take its master into a place where he would have been threatened by supernatural dangers. The superior instinct of the ass may be compared with that of the cattle who brought back the ark from the Philistines (1 S. vi. 7). Amongst the Arabs there is a belief that animals possess a certain power of clairvoyance: see Wellhausen *Arab. Heid.*[2] p. 151. Professor Giles states that according to the Chinese the ass is not alarmed at the sight of a spirit as a horse would be (*Chinese-Eng. Dict.* p. 667; quoted by Ball).

his sword drawn. Cf. Gen. iii. 24; Jos. v. 13.

24. *between the vineyards.* The journey is evidently through cultivated country and not through the desert.

where was no way to turn either to the right hand or to the left. *J*
27 And the ass saw the angel of the LORD, and she lay down under Balaam: and Balaam's anger was kindled, and he smote the ass with his staff. 28 And the LORD opened the mouth of the ass, and she said unto Balaam, What have I done unto thee, that thou hast smitten me these three times? 29 And Balaam said unto the ass, Because thou hast mocked me: I would there were a sword in mine hand, for now I had killed thee. 30 And the ass said unto Balaam, Am not I thine ass, upon which thou hast ridden all thy life long unto this day? was I ever wont to do so unto thee? And he said, Nay. 31 Then the LORD opened the eyes of Balaam, and he saw the angel of the LORD standing in the way, with his sword drawn in his hand: and he bowed his head, and fell on his face. 32 And the angel of the LORD said unto him, Wherefore hast thou smitten thine ass these three times? behold, I am come forth for an adversary, because thy way is [1]perverse before me: 33 and the ass saw me, and

[1] Heb. *headlong.*

28. Instances of animals being made to speak with a human voice are found in many ancient stories (see Bochart *Hierozoicon*[2] pp. 197 f. for examples). Perhaps the favourite parallel is the warning given to Achilles by his horse Xanthus that he was about to be slain (*Iliad* XIX. 400 ff.). Stories of speaking oxen are common in Livy (e.g. XXXV. 21). The only other example in the Bible is the serpent of Gen. iii. which Frazer thinks, from the analogy of the serpent in the Gilgamesh Epic, was originally lent the gift of speech only in his capacity of ambassador from God (*Folk-Lore in O.T.* p. 51): such a theory would make the parallel with the present story much closer, but it has little to support it in the text of Gen. iii. as it is now extant. There was a common Jewish belief that before man's fall the beasts and he had a common speech (cf. Jub. iii. 28)[1].

the mouth of the ass. See on xvi. 32.

29. *mocked me. Made a plaything of.* Used of God in Ex. x. 2: see further Driver *Samuel* p. 228.

30. The writer shews a touching insight into the relation of a man and his beast: cf. 2 Sam. xii. 3.

31. *opened the eyes.* Cf. Elisha's servant (2 K. vi. 17).

32. *perverse.* The meaning of the Heb. ירט is 'headlong': its only

---

[1] Authorities are not agreed as to what this speech was; some not unnaturally favour Hebrew (Jub. xii. 25 &c.), some Syriac (Theodoret) or Aramaic (*Sanh.* 38 *b*, though *Shabb.* 21 *b* says angels do not understand Aramaic), and some even Greek (2 Enoch xxx. 13; Sibyll. Orac. III. 24 ff.).

turned aside before me these three times: unless she had turned *J* aside from me, surely now I had even slain thee, and saved her alive. 34 And Balaam said unto the angel of the LORD, I have sinned; for I knew not that thou stoodest in the way against me: now therefore, if it displease thee, I will get me back again. 35 And the angel of the LORD said unto Balaam, Go with the *E* men: but only the word that I shall speak unto thee, that thou shalt speak. So Balaam went with the princes of Balak. 36 And *J* when Balak heard that Balaam was come, he went out to meet him unto the City of Moab, | which is on the border of Arnon, *E* which is in the utmost part of the border. 37 And Balak said unto Balaam, Did I not earnestly send unto thee to call thee? | wherefore camest thou not unto me? am I not able indeed to *J* promote thee to honour? 38 And Balaam said unto Balak, Lo, *E* I am come unto thee: have I now any power at all to speak any thing? the word that God putteth in my mouth, that shall I speak. 39 And Balaam went with Balak, and they came unto *J* Kiriath-huzoth. 40 And Balak sacrificed oxen and sheep, and *E* sent to Balaam, and to the princes that were with him. 41 And

other occurrence is in Job xvi. 11 where the reading is doubtful. Ehrlich's suggestion, that רע (*evil*) should be read, has much to commend it.

35. The last part of the *v.* is copied from 21 *b*, and the mention of the princes comes in rather harshly. Wellhausen thinks that in the original ending Balaam may have been told to return home.

the word &c. Balaam is to be a mere passive instrument: cf. Philo *De Vit. Mos.* I. 49 (Mang. II. 124).

36–41. Balak comes to meet Balaam upon his arrival, and complains of his delay: Balaam in reply tells the king that even now he can only utter the words which are given him by Jehovah. Balak offers sacrifices, and then in the morning shews the prophet the camp of his enemies.

36. *the City of Moab.* Cf. xxi. 15 with note. The position of this meeting place would fit in with Balaam's approach from either the Euphrates or from Ammon.

38. *putteth in my mouth.* Cf. xxiii. 5, 12, 16 and for a similar usage in Aramaic the Zenjirli inscription (*NSI* No. 61 *l.* 29).

that shall I speak. Cf. Micaiah (1 K. xxii. 14).

39. *Kiriath-huzoth.* The meaning of the name is *city of streets*; its situation is quite unknown, unless it be the same place as *Kiriathaim* (xxxii. 37).

40. *sent to Balaam.* The only explanation of the phrase seems to be that the object of *sent* has fallen out, or was intended to be supplied: the incident will then find a parallel in Samuel's treatment of Saul (1 S. ix. 23 f.).

it came to pass in the morning, that Balak took Balaam, and *E*
brought him up into [1]the high places of Baal, and he saw from
thence the utmost part of the people.

[1] Or, *Bamoth-baal*

41. *in the morning.* Daiches *Hilprecht Anniversary Volume* pp. 61 f. produces a number of passages from Babylonian ritual tablets according to which sacrificing and divining had to be done before sunrise.

the high places of Baal. There can be but little doubt that this is a place-name *Bamoth-baal*, probably identical with *Bamoth* in xxi. 19 where see note.

the utmost part. It is not quite certain whether the meaning of this is 'the nearest part of the Israelites' only, as Gray takes it; or *the uttermost part* and therefore by implication the whole: see Burney on 1 K. xii. 31.

Chapter XXIII. 1–12.

The first Oracle.

Balak, having brought Balaam to Bamoth-baal, at the prophet's request builds for him seven altars; upon each of which he sacrifices a bullock and a ram. Balaam receives an oracle from Jehovah which he proceeds to declare. The oracle, however, instead of cursing Israel declares that no curse can harm them, since God Himself has not cursed them; and ends by declaring the magnitude of Israel's numbers.

XXIII. 1 And Balaam said unto Balak, Build me here seven altars, and prepare me here seven bullocks and seven rams.

1. *Build me here.* That is on the high places of Baal, or better at Bamoth-baal (xxii. 41). The place itself was a sanctuary, and the neighbourhood even in the present day is full of remains (see G. A. Smith *Hist. Geog.* p. 566). Conder is of the opinion, though without much evidence, that "New altars were built apparently whenever an important sacrifice was to be offered, and sacred centres would thus in time become crowded with such structures" (*Heth and Moab*, p. 234)[1].

seven. The sacredness of the number *seven* goes back to very ancient times, and its significance has been repeatedly investigated[2]: cf. *HDB* III. p. 565; *Enc. Bib.* 3436; Burney in *JThS* XII. pp. 118 f.; *KAT* pp. 620 ff.; Hehn *Siebenzahl.* Burney suggests that 'Seven' may have

---

[1] Vincent is more definite: "Ces trois groupes d'autels localisés par le récit à Bamôth Ba'al, à Sophîm, sur la crête du Pisgah et au sommet du Pe'or, ont bien l'air de coincider avec les divers centres mégalithiques les plus importants, d'el-Mekheyît, du Ṣiâgha et du Nebo." *Canaan* p. 424.

[2] Seven is especially connected with sacrifices: see Ex. xxiii. 8 and cf. Jeremias *ATLAO* p. 89.

2 And Balak did as Balaam had spoken; and Balak and Balaam offered on every altar a bullock and a ram. 3 And Balaam said unto Balak, Stand by thy burnt offering, and I will go; peradventure the LORD will come to meet me: and whatsoever he sheweth me I will tell thee. And he went to a bare height. 4 And God met Balaam: and he said unto him, I have prepared the seven altars, and I have offered up a bullock and a ram on every altar. 5 And the LORD put a word in Balaam's mouth, and said, Return unto Balak, and thus thou shalt speak. 6 And he returned unto him, and, lo, he stood by his burnt offering, *E*

been a divine title (*op. cit.* and *Judges* pp. 44 and 251), he instances the Babylonian deity (*ilu*) *Sibitti* and the Israelite names Elisheba 'God is seven,' and Jehosheba 'Yahweh is seven.'

2. *Balak and Balaam.* These words are omitted by several MSS., LXX, Copt. &c., and most critics regard them as a gloss. Daiches points out, however, that in the Babylonian ritual both the diviner and the person enquiring are to take part in the sacrifices (*op. cit.* p. 62).

3. *Stand &c.* This command is in accordance with the Babylonian practice.

he went to a bare height. Daiches thinks that Balaam's 'going' was part of the magic rites (*op. cit.* pp. 63 ff.). The mention of *a bare height* (Heb. שפי) raises difficulties as the word is always used, with the doubtful exception of Job xxxiii. 21, in the plural. A comparison with the versions also points to a corruption of the text. Daiches makes two interesting suggestions based on the statement in *Sota* 10 *a* and *Sanhed.* 105 *a* that Balaam was lame[1]. He connects שפי (*a*) with שופי *quietly*, and so with directions in Babylonian ritual that the diviner is to act quietly, or (*b*) with Assyr. *šēpu, step by step* or *with hindered step*, an expression also found in ritual tablets (see *op. cit.* pp. 65 f.).

4. *I have prepared &c.* As the text stands at present Balaam evidently thinks that Jehovah will be moved by his elaborate preparations in much the same way that he himself had been moved by the promises of Balak. Another view of God's attitude towards the multiplying of altars is found in Hos. xii. 11. Possibly the words should be transferred to a position between *vv.* 2 and 3, and be referred to Balak, not Balaam.

5. *put a word.* The mark of a true prophet: cf. Dt. xviii. 18; Jer. i. 9. Origen points out that the word was put into Balaam's mouth not into his heart, a refinement of criticism which does perhaps represent the truth (see Lock *The Bible and Christian Life* p. 149).

7–10. Balaam's oracle is in the form of a poem of seven couplets after the manner of Hebrew parallelism, the second line merely repeating, in different language, the thought of the first.

---

[1] "Balaam was lame on one leg, because it is written וילך שפי."

he, and all the princes of Moab. 7 And he took up his parable, *E*
and said,

From Aram hath Balak brought me,
The king of Moab from the mountains of the East:
Come, curse me Jacob,
And come, [1]defy Israel.
8 How shall I curse, whom God hath not cursed?
And how shall I defy, whom the LORD hath not defied?
9 For from the top of the rocks I see him,
And from the hills I behold him:

[1] Heb. *be wroth against.*

7. *parable.* Heb. מָשָׁל *māshāl.* The root meaning of the word is *likeness*: cf. Assyr. *mašālu* 'to be like' which according to Ball (*Job* p. 326) is connected with Sum. MASH *twin* triliteralised by the addition of LI *in* or *into.* The word is used of many different types of discourse, aphorisms (1 S. x. 12, xxiv. 14; Ez. xii. 22), lamentations (see Is. xiv. 4; Hab. ii. 6 and cf. Dt. xxviii. 37), and utterances which more nearly approach the later parables (Ez. xvii. 2: cf. L. E. Browne *The Parables of the Gospel* pp. 27 f.). The underlying idea seems to be the use of figurative or representative language. The most striking use, in view of the present passage, is that in Proverbs (i.e. *mĕshālim*) where it is applied to "didactic and artistically constructed sentences" such as are not unlike the utterances of Balaam. Similar oracles may be found in Enoch xxxvii. 5 &c.

From Aram. It is possible that the original reading was 'Edom,' which is practically identical in the Heb. Edom was the home of wisdom (Obad. 8; Jer. xlix. 7 with the present writer's note), and as such a place suitable for the home of a magician. *Aram* itself was not mountainous in any special sense (cf. Pusey *Amos* pp. 70 f.), though the loose use of the term makes it difficult to define its limits.

the mountains of the East[1]. Meyer (*IN* pp. 244, 378) thinks the mountains of Edom are meant (cf. Gen. xxv. 6). Von Gall would translate *the ancient mountains* (*Bileam-Perikope* p. 19). The reference can hardly be to Pethor which lay to the north of Moab, and was not mountainous.

Jacob...Israel. This usage is frequent in all the Balaam oracles. It is found elsewhere in the Pent. only in Ex. xix. 3; and in the Blessing of Moses (Dt. xxxiii. 4, 10, 28). Other writers who use it are Micah (four times) and Isaiah xl.–lv. (seventeen times).

---

[1] Skinner considers that 'East' (קֶדֶם) often denotes the region E. and S.E. of the Dead Sea: *Genesis* p. 351. A recently discovered fragment of the Egyptian romance of Sinuhe shews that the country E. of Byblos was known as Qedem: see Clay *Empire of the Amorites* p. 79 n. 8.

E

Lo, it is a people that dwell alone,
And shall not be reckoned among the nations.
10 Who can count the dust of Jacob,
[1]Or number the fourth part of Israel?
Let [2]me die the death of the righteous,
And let my last end be like his!

11 And Balak said unto Balaam, What hast thou done unto me? I took thee to curse mine enemies, and, behold, thou hast blessed them altogether. 12 And he answered and said, Must I not take heed to speak that which the LORD putteth in my mouth?

[1] Heb. *Or, by number, the &c.* [2] Heb. *my soul.*

9. *dwell alone.* The passage in the Blessing of Moses (Dt. xxxiii. 28) couples isolation with security (cf. Mic. vii. 14; Jer. xlix. 31). The parallelism of the present passage, however, suggests the possession of special privileges.

not be reckoned. Cf. Ex. xxxiii. 16; 1 K. viii. 53.

10. *count...number.* In the original these verbs are perfects, which tense is used "to express astonishment at what appears to the speaker in the highest degree improbable" (Driver *Tenses* § 19).

the dust. Cf. Gen. xiii. 16, xxviii. 14.

the fourth part. LXX δήμους. Probably רבע should be read as רבבת *ten thousands.*

the death of the righteous. According to P the prophet's fate was far different: see xxxi. 8.

my last end (Heb. אחריתי). The old idea that this referred to a future life is no longer held, rather it is taken as meaning the closing years of life. I am disposed to think, however, that it should be taken as a reference to the prophet's posterity, as this exact use is found in a seventh century Aramaic inscription found at Nērab (*NSI* No. 65):

"(9) May Sahar and Nikal and Nusk make miserable
(10) his death and may his posterity (אחרתה) perish."

The same meaning seems to be demanded in several Nabataean inscriptions (see *NSI* No. 79 *l.* 2, 82 *l.* 3 &c.).

12. Cf. xxii. 38, xxiii. 5.

CHAPTER XXIII. 13–26.

The second Oracle.

Balak still hopes that a curse may be pronounced by finding some other spot from which God may be persuaded to do this service: again, however, Balaam utters blessings and not curses. The main contents of the oracle are a declaration of Jehovah's unchanging purpose for Israel, His favourable regard towards the nation in which He dwells, and the impossibility of interrupting Israel's march of conquest.

13 And Balak said unto him, Come, I pray thee, with me unto *E* another place, from whence thou mayest see them; thou shalt see but the utmost part of them, and shalt not see them all: and curse me them from thence. 14 And he took him into the field of Zophim, to the top of Pisgah, and built seven altars, and offered up a bullock and a ram on every altar. 15 And he said unto Balak, Stand here by thy burnt offering, while I meet *the* *LORD* yonder. 16 And the LORD met Balaam, and put a word in his mouth, and said, Return unto Balak, and thus shalt thou speak. 17 And he came to him, and, lo, he stood by his burnt offering, and the princes of Moab with him. And Balak said unto him, What hath the LORD spoken? 18 And he took up his parable, and said,

Rise up, Balak, and hear;
Hearken unto me, thou son of Zippor:
19 God is not a man, that he should lie;
Neither the son of man, that he should repent:

13. *another place.* For Balak's persistence cf. xxii. 19.

14. *the field of Zophim.* That is *the field of the watchers* (or even *prophets*: cf. Is. lii. 8, lvi. 10). Dillmann thinks that it may have been a position from which approaching danger could be seen, or else from which the flight of birds could be viewed for purposes of divination. The rendering of שָׂדֶה by *field* is in accordance with its usual meaning in Heb. The Bab. *šâdû*, however, means *mountain*, and it is possible that in this passage, and perhaps also in 2 S. i. 21 *a*; Jer. xviii. 14, something of this meaning is found: cf. Burney *Judges* pp. 111 f.

the top of Pisgah. See on xxi. 20.

15. Balaam is willing to fall in with Balak's suggestions, though there is no reason for supposing that he felt that the change of scene would have any influence upon Jehovah.

here...yonder. Heb. כה in each case. The usual meaning of the word is *thus*, and Daiches would so translate it here. "Balaam shows Balak *how* to stand by his burnt-offering...he also tells him *how* he will try to get his 'decision' this time" (*op. cit.* p. 67).

18–24. The poem consists of eleven couplets, though in several places the structure is not quite clear, owing possibly to later interpolations.

18. *Rise up...Hearken.* Cf. Gen. iv. 23; Ex. xv. 26; Jud. v. 3.

19. *not a man.* Cf. 1 S. xv. 29 which seems closely connected with this half verse: *Test. Twelve Patriarchs* Test. Jos. II. 5.

son of man. The meaning here is clearly a human being, and no trace of later ideas can be read into it.

repent. "There is only one simple Good, and therefore one alone Unchangeable, which is God" (Augustine *De Civ. Dei* XI. 10). Cf. Jer.

Hath he said, and shall he not do it? *E*
Or hath he spoken, and shall he not make it good?
20 Behold, I have received *commandment* to bless:
And he hath blessed, and I cannot reverse it.
21 He hath not beheld iniquity in Jacob,
Neither hath he seen perverseness in Israel:
The LORD his God is with him,
And the shout of a king is among them.
22 God bringeth them forth out of Egypt; *J*
He hath as it were the [1]strength of the [2]wild-ox.

[1] Or, *horns* [2] Or, *ox-antelope* Heb. *reem.*

xviii. 8, xxvi. 3; Mal. iii. 6; Slav. Enoch xxxiii. 4; Rom. xi. 29; Jas. i. 17.

20. *he hath blessed.* This hardly represents the Heb., LXX reads the first person singular, and should be followed, *I will bless and will not reverse it.*

reverse it. God does reverse even His most definite promises of blessing if those who receive them are unworthy: cf. 1 S. ii. 30.

21. *iniquity...perverseness* (און...עמל). Cf. Hab. i. 13; Is. xxvi. 2; Ps. xliv. 17 f. for the conception of Israel as ethically superior to other nations. LXX however renders μόχθος and πόνος taking the passage to denote Israel's freedom, not from moral offences, but from material disasters: this interpretation is followed by Dillmann, Gray, Baentsch (who renders the words as *Unheil* and *Mühsal*) &c. Since עמל almost if not quite always means some kind of labour or sorrow, and און can be used with the sense of *calamity* (Jer. iv. 15; Prov. xii. 21, xxii. 8: and cf. Bevan in *Journal of Philol.* XXVI. pp. 300 f.), the latter meaning should be adopted, especially in view of the double usage in Hab. i. 3: the rendering of R.V. is based on Syr. and the Rabbinic commentators.

the shout of a king. Ewald, Wellhausen, and other leading critics take this as a reference to an earthly *king*: the parallelism is against this, and the plain reference is to Jehovah as the divine king (Dt. xxxiii. 5; 1 S. viii. 7, xii. 12). Cf. Targ. *the Shekhinah of their King.*

22. This *v.* is repeated as xxiv. 8.

strength (Heb. תּוֹעֲפוֹת: *to'ăphoth*). The meaning of the word is obscure, in Ps. xcv. 4 it apparently refers to the peaks of mountains. There may be some connexion with Assyr. *appu* (*top*). The usual rendering here is *horns* (of wild-ox: cf. Dt. xxxiii. 17) for which Sum. SAG = *rēšu* (*top*)—which is also used for *qarnu* (*horn*)—would give a parallel. Horns were a sign of strength and even of deity amongst the Babylonians (cf. Hehn *BBG* pp. 205, 299 &c.) and other Semitic peoples (cf. the representation of Hadad in the Zenjirli inscriptions). In an inscription Assurbanipal describes Beltis as knocking down his foes with her mighty horns (quoted by Ball *Job* p. 429), and in another inscription the actual

23 Surely there is no enchantment [1]with Jacob, *J*
Neither is there any divination [1]with Israel:
[2]Now shall it be [3]said of Jacob and of Israel,
What hath God wrought!
24 Behold, the people riseth up as a lioness, *E*

[1] Or, *against* [2] Or, *At the due season*
[3] Or, *told to...what God hath wrought*

reference to the horns of a wild-ox is made (Rawlinson *Cuneiform Inscriptions of Western Asia* IV. No. 2 *ll.* 20 f.). The present passage does not, however, refer to the strength of Jehovah except in so far as it is manifested in the prowess of Israel.

the wild-ox (רְאֵם *re'ēm*). Tristram suggested a relation to the *bos urus* of Caesar *De Bell. Gall.* VI. 28[1]. The meaning of the Heb. was lost (cf. LXX μονοκέρως; A.V. *unicorn*) until the decipherment of the Assyrian inscriptions revealed the existence of the animal called *rīmu*, a huge species of bison. A late Jewish tradition informs us that this animal was so large that it could not be got into the ark but had to be tied on behind. See further W. Max Müller in *Mitteilungen der Vorderasiat. Gesell.* (1904) 2 pp. 50 ff.

23. This *v.* raises a double problem. It does not fit in well in its context, and if it were omitted the smoothness of the poem would be increased: the two parts which compose it are hard to connect. McNeile would omit the first half of the *v.* as a mistaken gloss on *v.* 21 *a*, and read the second half as a comment on the deliverance from Egypt in *v.* 22 *a*. Other critics would omit the whole *v.*

with Jacob...with Israel. Israel, having Jehovah for its God, has no need to employ oracles or omens in order to know the future. The reading of mg. *against* was the common interpretation of the older commentators (in spite of LXX ἐν), but it hardly suits the meaning of the words used (see following note).

enchantment...divination (Heb. נַחַשׁ...קֶסֶם). The former word appears here and xxiv. 1 only, though the verb from the same root is common in the sense *practise divination, observe signs* (e.g. Gen. xliv. 5; Lev. xix. 26 &c.). It refers to "divination from natural omens, of which the most familiar example is divination by the flight of birds" (Driver *Deut.* p. 225): it should be noted that no use of magic for purposes of injuring another seems to be implied. *Divination* means *to obtain an oracle*, especially by means of lots (cf. Ez. xxi. 21 f.), though the use is wide enough to include any kind of divination. Such practices are forbidden by Dt. xviii. 10 f.; Hos. iv. 12; Jer. xxvii. 9; Ez. xiii. 6 ff.; and even as late as Zech. x. 2.

What hath God wrought! Cf. Ps. xliv. 1.

24. *as a lioness.* The attribution of the qualities of animals to men

---

[1] Gregory of Tours noted that in his day (sixth century) large horned cattle were still hunted in the Vosges and the Ardennes (x. x. 369).

And as a lion doth he lift himself up: *E*
He shall not lie down until he eat of the prey,
And drink the blood of the slain.

25 And Balak said unto Balaam, Neither curse them at all, nor bless them at all. 26 But Balaam answered and said unto Balak, Told not I thee, saying, All that the LORD speaketh, that I must do?

and nations is common in O.T.: cf. xxiv. 9; Gen. xlix. 9 and 27; Mic. v. 8; Jer. xlix. 19 &c.

25 f. These *vv.* read like the close of the narrative, and the insertion of further oracles comes as an anti-climax. In E's account of Balaam it seems probable that xxiv. 25 should follow immediately; the editor, however, having further matter, perhaps from J, inserted it here and introduced it by a fresh heading.

26. Cf. *v.* 12, xxii. 20.

CHAPTERS XXIII. 27—XXIV. 13.

The third Oracle.

This third oracle is introduced by matter which is apparently borrowed from elsewhere (see on xxiii. 25 f.). The contents have parallels with the previous utterances, yet at the same time an individuality of their own. Emphasis is laid on the fertility of Israel's possessions, the greatness of its rulers, the strength of the nation, and the folly of those who oppose it. Daiches accepts this third oracle as genuine, and points out the importance of doing certain actions (e.g. reciting incantations) three times in Bab. ritual.

27 And Balak said unto Balaam, Come now, I will take *JE* thee unto another place; peradventure it will please God that thou mayest curse me them from thence. 28 And Balak took Balaam unto the top of Peor, that looketh down upon [1]the

[1] Or, *Jeshimon*

27. Cf. *v.* 13, xxii. 6, xxiv. 1.

28. Cf. *v.* 14.

the top of Peor &c. Cf. xxi. 20 where Pisgah takes the place of Peor. The site of this mountain is unknown though places of similar name are found—Beth-peor (Dt. iii. 29, iv. 46, xxxiv. 6; Jos. xiii. 20) and Baal-peor (xxv. 3). Eusebius mentions an ὄρος φογώρ (so LXX) to the north of Nebo (*Onomast.* 213): Buhl *Geog.* p. 123 identifies it with the mountain called *el-Mushaḳḳar*, between *Wady ʿajūn Mūsā* and *Wady Ḥeshbān*, which has ruins of an ancient town near by, and a road going to Livias. In Gen. xxxvi. 39 a city named *Pau* is mentioned as belonging to Hadad II of Edom which LXX renders as φογώρ (= *Peor*); as Hadad's father was named Baal-hanan there may be a reference to the Baal of Peor: cf. Ed. Meyer *IN* p. 374.

desert. 29 And Balaam said unto Balak, Build me here seven *JE* altars, and prepare me here seven bullocks and seven rams. 30 And Balak did as Balaam had said, and offered up a bullock and a ram on every altar. **XXIV.** 1 And when Balaam saw *J* that it pleased the LORD to bless Israel, he went not, as at the other times, to meet with enchantments, but he set his face toward the wilderness. 2 And Balaam lifted up his eyes, and he saw Israel dwelling according to their tribes; and the spirit of God came upon him. 3 And he took up his parable, and said,

Balaam the son of Beor saith,

29 f. Cf. *vv.* 1 f.

XXIV. 1. *the other times.* As the seeking of omens was not Balaam's method according to the previous stories, there must here be a reference to some different tradition.

enchantments. (LXX οἰωνοῖς: cf. *Il.* XII. 237, *Od.* XV. 532). The word is used in xxiii. 23 where see note.

2. *he saw Israel &c.* He saw, as Keble puts it in one of the grandest of all his poems,

"the bannered lines,
Where by their several signs
The desert-wearied tribes in sight of Canaan sleep."
The Christian Year: the Second Sunday after Easter.

the spirit of God. In other places God came in a dream (xxii. 9, 20), or by His angel (xxii. 32), or a word was put in the prophet's mouth (xxiii. 5, 16): here by a more spiritual conception the whole man is inspired: cf. Mic. iii. 8; Is. xlviii. 16, lxi. 1.

3–9. The poem is in a much worse state of preservation than those which have already been considered, perhaps a sign of greater age or greater popularity, and much room is given for conjectural emendation. The former poems consisted of a number of couplets, in the present poem, *v.* 4 is a tristich, and another seems to come in *v.* 8.

3. *Balaam the son of Beor saith.* Cf. *v.* 15 and for the egotistical point of view xxiii. 7. The structure and expression used in this *v.* are found also in 2 Sam. xxiii. 1; unless there is a dependence of one passage on the other the form may be conventional. Daiches points out that the other two oracles are addressed to Balak, in accordance with the custom that the *bārū* must give his answer to the person for whom he is divining. In the present oracle he no longer tries to divine, but rises to a state of prophecy, hence he does not address Balak.

saith. Heb. נְאֻם *oracle of.* The word, as a rule, is restricted to utterances of Jehovah; an exception is found here, also in 2 S. xxiii. 1; Ps. xxxvi. 1 (where however the text is very uncertain); and Prov. xxx. 1. In post-biblical Heb. נוּם means *to speak*, and in Sum. NIM is found in certain combinations I-NIM, E-NIM, with the meaning of *word.*

And the man whose eye [1]was closed saith: *J*
4 He saith, which heareth the words of God,
Which seeth the vision of the Almighty,
Falling down, and having his eyes open:
5 How goodly are thy tents, O Jacob,
Thy tabernacles, O Israel!
6 As valleys are they spread forth,

[1] Or, *is opened*

the man. Heb. הַגֶּבֶר. Here, *v.* 15; Ex. x. 11, xii. 37 (J); and Dt. xxii. 5 in the Pent.

whose eye was closed: mg. *is opened.* The meaning of Heb. שְׁתֻם which occurs here only is uncertain, and probably the text is corrupt. The rendering of R.V. is that of Vulg. and the Rabbinic commentators, and depends for its force on referring the statement here to the eye of the body as distinguished from that of the soul (see *v.* 4): the objection to it lies in its too great subtilty, and as Gray points out a much simpler way of making the distinction was available (cf. Job x. 4). The R.V. mg. follows Syr. and agrees with *v.* 4 but at the same time renders it unnecessary. LXX ὁ ἀληθινῶς ὁρῶν presupposes the same consonantal text, but a different division of the words. Enoch i. 2, which is probably derived from this passage, seems to favour the rendering *open.* The *bārū* was by Bab. custom a person of good eyesight in order that he should read the *omina* aright.

4. *seeth the vision.* The original implies a continual, habitual enjoyment of this privilege. In a Bab. ritual tablet the *bārū* is called: "The wise man, the knower, who keeps the mystery of the gods" (cf. *v.* 16).

the Almighty (Heb. שַׁדַּי *Shaddai*). This may be the earliest appearance of the word in O.T. (cf. however Gen. xlix. 25). In P the Patriarchs knew God by no other name (Ex. vi. 3). The meaning of the word is not clear, two explanations have most to commend them (*a*) a derivation from שדד which would give the meaning *Destroyer*, suggesting that originally Jehovah was a storm god; (*b*) a derivation from Assyr. *šâdû mountain*; Asshur and Bel are called *šâdû rabû* (Sum. KUR-GAL). See further Driver *Genesis* pp. 404 ff., Hehn *BBG* pp. 265 ff., Baentsch on Ex. vi. 3. Loisy has the interesting suggestion that *Shaddai* may have been the original god of Hebron: *Rel. of Isr.* p. 117.

Falling down. No satisfactory explanation has been given of the meaning of the present text which probably is defective. To represent Balaam as fallen down in awe, or under the influence of the spirit, or in sleep, seem all alike unnatural interpretations of the language. Daiches suggests that 'falling down' was part of the divination ceremony, as with the Babylonians.

5. *thy tents, O Jacob.* Cf. Dt. xxxiii. 18; Ecclus. xlvi. 14.

6. This *v.* consists of a number of comparisons with objects in the natural world, intended to shew forth the luxuriance of Israel and its land.

As gardens by the river side, *J*
As lign-aloes which the LORD hath planted,
As cedar trees beside the waters.
7 Water shall flow from his buckets,
And his seed shall be in many waters,
And his king shall be higher than Agag,
And his kingdom shall be exalted.
8 God bringeth him forth out of Egypt;

gardens. Cf. Is. lviii. 11[1].
by the river side. Cf. Ps. i. 3; Jer. xvii. 8.
lign-aloes. The tree was not familiar to the Hebrews (see *Enc. Bib.* 122). This rendering, which is a hybrid (*lignum* ἀλόης), appears here only. Dillmann suggests an emendation which would give the reading *palms* (cf. Ex. xv. 27; Gen. xiv. 6), and Cheyne would read *poplars* (cf. Is. xliv. 4).
the LORD hath planted. For the thought cf. Is. lx. 21, lxi. 3; Ps. lxxx. 8, civ. 16.
cedar trees &c. Cf. Ecclus. xxxix. 13. These trees do not grow beside the water, perhaps as Cheyne suggested (*Exp. Times* x. p. 401) the trees in this, and the previous line, should be interchanged: cf. Ps. civ. 16.
7. The first two lines are obscure, and this obscurity has led to many suggested emendations[2]. R.V. translation represents the Heb., the first line of which seems to be a figurative description of Israel's overflowing prosperity; the second line, however, gives no meaning which makes sense. Dillmann and others find in it a promise of well watered fields, but to state that the seed will be in water is an unnatural mode of putting it: cf. Ps. lxv. 10 f.
his king. Here a mortal king: cf. xxiii. 21.
Agag. LXX and Sam. *Gog.* The name may have been of frequent occurrence amongst the Amalekites, otherwise the line must be later than the time of Samuel. In any case the power of Amalek does not ever seem to have been sufficiently notable to make the comparison likely[3].
8. The first half of the *v.* = xxiii. 22.

---

[1] Heb. word for garden exists in two forms גַּן and גַּנָּה (*gan* and *gannāh*), as does the corresponding word in Assyr. *ginû* (=*field*) and *gannatum* (=*garden*). The word comes ultimately from GAN (cf. Theis *Sum. in A.T.* p. 21) and is perhaps the origin of γάνος.
[2] Gray, following suggestions by Cheyne, renders:
"Let peoples tremble at his might,
And his arm be on many nations" (עמים for מים).
[3] The meaning of Agag is unknown. Is it possible that just as Magog comes from MA (=matum) *land* and KUG *darkness*: see van Hoonacker (*Zeitschrift für Ass.* XXVIII. p. 336), Agag comes from A.KUG *water of darkness*? *A-gi-gu* is cited by Ranke in his *Early Personal Names of the Hammurabi Dynasty* p. 61.

He hath as it were the [1]strength of the [1]wild-ox: *J*
He shall eat up the nations his adversaries,
And shall break their bones in pieces,
And smite *them* through with his arrows.
9 He couched, he lay down as a lion,
And as a lioness; who shall rouse him up?
Blessed be every one that blesseth thee,
And cursed be every one that curseth thee.

10 And Balak's anger was kindled against Balaam, and he smote his hands together: and Balak said unto Balaam, I called thee to curse mine enemies, and, behold, thou hast altogether blessed them these three times. 11 Therefore now flee thou to thy place: I thought to promote thee unto great honour; but, lo, the LORD hath kept thee back from honour. 12 And Balaam said unto Balak, Spake I not also to thy messengers which thou sentest unto me, saying, 13 If Balak would give me his house full of silver and gold, I cannot go beyond the word of the LORD, to do either good or bad of mine own mind; what the LORD speaketh, that will I speak?

[1] See ch. xxiii. 22.

break their bones. Cf. Jer. i. 17.

with his arrows. Heb. וחציו: Syr., however, evidently read חלציו *his loins*: the line would then read, in excellent parallelism with what goes before, *And shatters their loins*: cf. Dt. xxxiii. 11. Another emendation is that of Dillmann ולחציו *his oppressors*, this is adopted by Gray and gives quite a good sense; the previous reading, however, should be preferred as it has the support of a version.

9. *as a lion.* Cf. xxiii. 24; Gen. xlix. 9.

blessed &c. Cf. Gen. xii. 3, xxvii. 29.

10. *smote his hands.* As a sign of contempt: cf. Job xxvii. 23; Lam. ii. 15.

three times. An editorial addition to cover all the previous attempts.

11. *to thy place.* Cf. *v.* 25.

the LORD &c. A noble testimony to Balaam's character.

12 f. Cf. xxii. 18.

CHAPTER XXIV. 14–25.

The farewell message.

Without any request from Balak, Balaam foretells the fate of Moab in its conflict with Israel. The future of other nations is also included in the prophet's utterance.

14 And now, behold, I go unto my people: come, *and* I will

advertise thee what this people shall do to thy people in the *J*
latter days. 15 And he took up his parable, and said,

Balaam the son of Beor saith,
And the man whose eye [1]was closed saith:
16 He saith, which heareth the words of God,
And knoweth the knowledge of the Most High,
Which seeth the vision of the Almighty,
Falling down, and having his eyes open:
17 I see him, but not now:
I behold him, but not nigh:
There shall come forth a star out of Jacob,

[1] Or, *is opened*

14. *advertise thee.* So in Ruth iv. 4 (A.V.): *disclose to thee, announce to thee.* Van Hoonacker, following the Rabbinic commentators, connects the word with the advice given to Balak in xxxi. 16 (P).

in the latter days: lit. *in the end of the days.* "The expression...denotes the *closing period* of the future, so far as it falls within the range of view of the writer" (Driver *Genesis* p. 381).

15–19. The original poem would seem to end at *v.* 17, as the two losing *vv.*, though printed as poetry in R.V., are prosaic in style and ccontents.

15. Cf. *v.* 3. Balaam perhaps mentions his father because the profession of the *bārū* was hereditary (cf. Amos vii. 14).

16. Cf. *v.* 4.

Most High (LXX Ὑψίστου). This title for God occurs in Gen. xiv. 18 ff. (used by Melchizedek); and Dt. xxxii. 8 (Song of Moses) in the Pent. It is mostly used by non-Israelites (so Mic. vi. 6; Is. xiv. 10). See further Driver *Genesis* p. 165; Hehn *BBG* pp. 258 ff. Philo of Byblos knew of a god καλούμενος Ὕψιστος who was worshipped by the Phoenicians (Müller *Frag. Hist. Gr.* III. 566 *s*). Cumont compares *Jupiter summus exsuperantissimus* (*Oriental Rel.* p. 151).

17. *him.* This must refer to Israel, not by anticipation to the star.

not nigh. Gray takes this as temporal: cf. Jer. xlviii. 16; Ez. vii. 7; Joel i. 16. McNeile sees in the two statements a change of both time and situation.

a star. Used as a symbol of a monarch in Is. xiv. 12; Ez. xxxii. 7. The same usage is found in the hymn of praise addressed to Thutmose III and now preserved in the Cairo museum.

"I have made them see Thy Majesty as a Lord of shining splendour,
When thou shinest before them in my image.

* * * * *

I grant that they may see Thy Majesty as the comet,
Which rains down the heat of its flame, and sheds its dew."

Two parallels may also be adduced from Latin authors: *Ecce Dionaei*

And a sceptre shall rise out of Israel, *J*
And shall smite through the corners of Moab,
And break down all the sons [1]of tumult.
18 And Edom shall be a possession,
Seir also shall be a possession, *which were* his enemies;

[1] Or, *of Sheth*

processit Caesaris astrum (Virg. *Ecl.* IX. 47) and *Micat inter omnes Julium sidus* (Hor. *Od.* I. xii. 47). Even in pre-Christian times the star was given a Messianic reference: cf. Mt. ii. 2; Rev. xxii. 16, *Test. Twelve Patr.* Test. Levi. XVIII. 3, Test. Jud. XXIV. 1; Targ. Jon., *Taanith* IV. 8, *Deb. Rabba* § 1. It is, however, taken in a non-Messianic sense in the fragments of a Zadokite work which are given in the *Oxford Apocrypha &c.* II. p. 816. There is also the well-known case of the supposed Messiah in the time of Hadrian who was called Bar Kokba *son of a star* by R. Aqiba: see Schürer *Gesch. d. jüd. Volkes*[3] I. pp. 682 ff.

shall come forth. Heb. דרך means *trampled on* or possibly *marched forth* (cf. Jud. v. 21); most commentators suggest the reading זרח *is risen.*

a sceptre (שבט). Cf. Gen. xlix. 10; Zech. x. 11. Since the star is used of a ruler, the parallelism is exact. In later Hebrew שביט was the name of an actual star, perhaps through a mistaken reading of the present passage, and a desire to find in it a verbal parallelism[1].

the corners of Moab. Cf. Jer. xlviii. 45 *corner*. The plural represents the temples of the head (cf. Lev. xix. 27). The reference is probably to the conquests of David (2 S. viii. 2), or even to those of Omri (cf. Moabite Stone).

break down. By a very slight change in Heb., קדקד for קרקר, *the crown of the head* is read as in Jer. xlviii. 45.

the sons of tumult: mg. *Sheth* (שת). If the reading of the mg. is followed the reference is to the son of Adam, and his sons will be his descendants, that is all men (cf. Jub. xxii. 12). Sayce, *EHH* p. 230, takes it to mean the *Sutu*, Bedawin tribes appearing in both Babylonian and Egyptian records. The parallel passage in Jer. xlviii. 45 reads שאין which should perhaps be adopted here. The suggestion of Wellhausen that שת=שְׂאֵת *pride* is commended by Gray[2].

18. *Edom.* Cf. 2 S. viii. 14; Ps. lx. 8; and see on xx. 14. The later Jews used Edom as a synonym for Rome, and finally for the Christians: see Buxtorf *Lex. Talmud.* pp. 29 ff.

Seir (LXX Ἠσαῦ). A synonym for Edom as in Jud. v. 4, one denoting the people, the other their land[3].

his enemies. Something seems to have fallen out of M.T. Reuss thinks that these words formed the end of a lost line.

---

[1] In *ZAW* (1925) pp. 301 f. Gemser has worked out the use of שבט = *comet* or *star*.
[2] Hoffmann *ZAW* III. p. 97 suggested that שאין was the acropolis of Ar Moab.
[3] An inscription of Ramses III (B.C. 1200 *c.*) records a defeat of the *Sa-'a-ira*, i.e. the Seirites (Max Müller *A. u. E.* pp. 136 f.), which may be an equivalent for Edomites.

While Israel doeth valiantly. *J*
19 And out of Jacob shall one have dominion,
And shall destroy the remnant from the city.
20 And he looked on Amalek, and took up his parable, and said,
Amalek was the first of the nations;
But his latter end shall come to destruction.

doeth valiantly: lit. *maketh might*. Cf. 1 S. xiv. 48; Ps. lx. 12, cxviii. 15 f.

19. *from the city*. The meaning is obscure as no city is named. Several critics take the phrase as parallel to *out of Jacob*, and refer it to Zion.

20–24. Three short oracles deal with the fate of Amalek (*v.* 20), the Kenites (*vv.* 21 f.), and Asshur and Eber (*vv.* 23 f.). These oracles have no apparent connexion with what has gone before[1], and their position is probably due to accident: they can only be regarded as isolated fragments of unknown date and origin. Kuenen and Dillmann refer them to the seventh century, Von Gall and Winckler bring them down to much later times.

20. *he looked*. Either in vision, or as spread out before him in the desert (cf. xxii. 41, xxiii. 13 &c.).

Amalek. See on xiii. 29. In this passage *Amalek* may be taken as a type of the enemies of Israel (cf. Ps. lxxxiii. 7 with Duhm's note), possibly with some specific nation in view (cf. note on *Edom v.* 18).

the first of the nations. This can hardly mean the most powerful of the nations, though that is the obvious interpretation of the text. Meyer *IN* p. 392 thinks the context rules out this meaning, and simply emphasises the origin and end of the Amalekites: we should then have to suppose that they were the oldest of all the nations. But according to O.T. the Amalekites are descended from Esau (Gen. xxxvi. 12), and therefore cannot be the primeval nation; nor are they represented by Hebrew writers as being a powerful nation[2]. Keil and others see in the statement a reference to the first attack on Israel (Ex. xvii. 8 ff.).

latter end. See on xxiii. 10. Amalek was apparently almost annihilated in the time of the early monarchy (1 S. xv., xxx.). The emphasis laid on the extermination of Amalek in Dt. xxv. 17 ff. is interesting, and can hardly be explained merely as suitable to the supposed situation of the Israelites; there would seem to have been some definite tradition, to which at present we have no clue, representing Amalek as a contemporary enemy: see above.

---

[1] Later tradition, however, represented the Amalekites as being finally exterminated in Mt. Seir (1 Chr. iv. 42 ff.), and even as an Edomite tribe (Gen. xxxvi. 12).

[2] In this connexion Nöldeke points out "that neither Egyptian nor Assyrian records allude to their existence. Ancient Arabic authors, indeed, describe them as a mighty nation which dwelt in Arabia, Egypt, and other countries...these and other similar statements...have no historical value" (*Enc. Bib.* 129 f., and for proofs see *Die Amoriter*).

21 And he looked on the Kenite, and took up his parable, and said, *JE*

Strong is thy dwelling place,
And thy nest is set in the rock.
22 Nevertheless [1]Kain shall be wasted,
[2]Until Asshur shall carry thee away captive.
23 And he took up his parable, and said,

[1] Or, *the Kenites* [2] Or, *How long? Asshur &c.*

21. *the Kenite.* According to Jud. i. 16 (see Moore, Burney *ad loc.*), 1 S. xv. 6 *the Kenites* were connected in some way with the Amalekites (I cannot see that the evidence is sufficient for calling them 'a branch' of the Amalekites without qualification as is done by Nöldeke, Gray, &c.), the present passage suggests a similar connexion. They were also closely associated with Judah (Jud. i. 16, v. 24; 1 S. xxvii. 10, xxx. 29) and it is difficult to account for their inclusion here in a context of condemnation. Some critics connect the tribe with Cain, a connexion which is suggested by the Heb., and Stade has built up a number of theories on this basis[1]: see *Das Kainszeichen* in *ZAW* XIV. pp. 250 ff., XV. pp. 157 ff. In the sixth century B.C. a Bedawin tribe of *Kain* was settled in south-east Palestine: see Sprenger *Alte Geog. Arabiens* pp. 288 f. Ewald suggested that this tribe was descended from the Kenites (*Hist. Isr.* I. p. 271).

Strong (Heb. אֵיתָן). The original meaning of the word is *perennial, ever-flowing* (e.g. in Am. v. 24), and so it has the figurative sense of *permanent, enduring.*

thy nest. Heb. קִנֶּךָ *ḳinneka* which gives a pun upon Kenite. For the use of *nest* for a strong dwelling-place cf. Obad. 3 f.; Jer. xlix. 16.

22. *shall be wasted.* Klostermann by a slight re-arrangement of the Heb. obtains the reading *shall belong to Eber* (cf. *v.* 24).

Until. This does not really represent Heb. (עד־מה) which should be rendered with mg. *How long?* The text is corrupt, for what follows hardly makes sense. Perhaps מה is a fragment representing a place-name to which Asshur carried away the captives.

Asshur. That is according to the usual rendering Assyria. There may be a reference to the taking away captive of some desert tribe by the Assyrians. Hommel, who thinks that the passage is very early, sees in Asshur a reference to the land of Shur in south Palestine (*AHT* pp. 245 f.). Von Gall on the other hand would take it down to Seleucid times, and make Asshur refer to Syria. Ed. Meyer *IN* p. 320 suggests that the *Asshurim* of Gen. xxv. 3 are meant.

23. *he took up &c.* LXX prefixes καὶ ἰδὼν τὸν Ὢγ[2]: cf. the introduc-

---

[1] Nöldeke is sceptical both of the suggested relationship of the Kenites with the Cain of Gen. iv., and also of the speculations which Stade and others have based upon it: see *Enc. Bib.* 130 f.

[2] Lucian reads Γὼγ: cf. xxiv. 7. LXX^F omits altogether.

Alas, who shall live when God [1]doeth this? *JE*
24 But ships *shall come* from the coast of Kittim,
And they shall afflict Asshur, and shall afflict Eber,
And he also shall come to destruction.
25 And Balaam rose up, and went and returned to his place: *E* and Balak also went his way.

[1] Or, *establisheth him*

tory formula to *v.* 20 and to *v.* 21. The oracle which follows is so obscure that its meaning can hardly be discovered, and the various attempts to emend it are not satisfactory since they seem to depend very largely on the subjective ideas of their authors; Hommel's emendation, for example, takes the poem back to Mosaic times.

who shall live. Cf. Joel ii. 11; Mal. iii. 2.

24. *ships...of Kittim.* Vg. *venient in trieribus de Italia.* The phrase appears in Dan. xi. 30 where Professor Bevan points out that although Kittim[1] "originally...meant the inhabitants of Cyprus...among the later Jews it was used for all the western maritime countries (1 Macc. i. 1, viii. 5; Josephus *Antiq.* I. vi. 1). The allusion here is to the Romans, who sent Caius Popilius Laenas to Egypt, summarily demanding that Antiochus should quit the country." Hommel by a slight emendation renders *ships* as *wild cats*, and refers it to wild tribes of invaders from the North: see *AHT* pp. 245 ff. for fuller details.

Asshur. According to the reference to this *v.* in 1 Macc. i. 1, which applies it to the conquests of Alexander the Great, *Asshur* here means the Persian Empire (cf. Ezra vi. 22). If the reference be to Antiochus (as in Dan. xi. 30) *Asshur* will be Syria (cf. on *v.* 22).

Eber. LXX Ἑβραίους. The meaning here is quite unknown.

25. The actors depart and the stage is left empty, the last spoken word, as the text now stands, being not inappropriately *destruction.*

to his place. Cf. *v.* 11; Acts i. 25; Ignatius *ad Magn.* v. 1; Polycarp *ad Phil.* IX. 2.

CHAPTERS XXV.—XXXI.

VARIOUS LAWS AND INCIDENTS.

The various materials which go to form this division of the book are drawn from different sources, and the connexion between them is almost haphazard. The incidents include the sin of the Israelites in connexion with Baal-peor,

---

[1] W. Max Müller (*Asien u. Europa* p. 345) thinks that the Kittim were the Hittites: Hommel (*op. cit.* p. 247) also holds this view and regards the application to Cilicia and Cyprus as later. Winckler *Altorient. Forschungen* II. p. 422 thinks a site further W. is demanded. Jeremias *ATLAO* p. 154 suggests S. Italy, and especially Sicily.

the vengeance taken upon Midian, and the appointment of Joshua. The laws and regulations deal mainly with public offerings, but two passages give directions concerning the position of daughters in regard to their father's estate, and the validity of vows undertaken by women.

Baal-peor. xxv.
The second census. xxvi.
The inheritance of daughters. xxvii. 1–11.
Moses and his successor. 12–23.
Regulations concerning public worship. xxviii., xxix.
The vows of women. xxx.
The holy war against Midian. xxxi.

Chapter XXV.

Baal-peor.

This section is concerned with the sin of consorting with foreign women: it is composed of two unconnected and fragmentary stories, one from JE and the other from P. There is therefore a marked difference in point of view between them. "The interest of the former is prophetic, and is concerned with the struggle between the pure worship of Jehovah and the native local cults. The interest of the latter is ecclesiastical, and is concerned with the succession of the Aaronite priesthood" (McNeile). The first story lacks an ending, and the second presupposes circumstances which have not been related.

(*a*) *The sin of Baal-peor.* 1–5.
(*b*) *The zeal of Phinehas.* 6–9.
(*c*) *The reward of Phinehas.* 10–15.
(*d*) *The punishment of the Midianites.* 16–18.

XXV. 1 And Israel abode in Shittim, and the people began *JE* to commit whoredom with the daughters of Moab: 2 for they called the people unto the sacrifices of their gods; and the people

XXV. 1–5. The Israelites are seduced into idolatry by Moabite women. The Lord commands Moses to hang the chiefs of the people (!), and he thereupon orders the judges to slay each his man. The carrying out of the punishment is not recorded.

1. *Shittim.* The name has the article in Heb. and so can be translated *the Acacias.* It was from *Shittim* that Joshua sent the spies (Jos. ii. 1, iii. 1). The full name appears in xxxiii. 49 as *Abel-shittim* from which it has been identified with *Abila* stated by Josephus (*Ant.* IV. viii. 1) to be sixty stadia from the Jordan. In *Rev. bibl.* XI. p. 150 the interesting suggestion is made that the traditional site may have been *Betomarsea-Maiumas*, i.e. בת מרזח (Jer. xvi. 5) = Μαιουμας, a scene of licentious festivals which is mentioned on the mosaic map found at Madeba (*NSI* p. 122).

of Moab. Cf. *vv.* 6 and 16 where Midian is the offender.

2. *for they called.* R.V. does not represent Heb. which should be rendered *and they called* (cf. Solomon and Ahab similarly seduced into

did eat, and bowed down to their gods. 3 And Israel [1]joined *JE* himself unto [2]Baal-peor: and the anger of the LORD was kindled against Israel. 4 And the LORD said unto Moses, Take all the chiefs of the people, and hang them up unto the LORD before the sun, that the fierce anger of the LORD may turn away from Israel. 5 And Moses said unto the judges of Israel, Slay ye every one his men that have joined themselves unto Baal-peor. 6 And, *P*

[1] Or, *yoked* [2] Or, *the Baal of Peor* See ch. xxiii. 28.

foreign worship). It is, however, probable that the story was originally connected with religious prostitution as Gressmann supposes: he compares the case of Engidu in the Gilgamesh Epic.

did eat. A sacrificial meal: cf. Gen. xxxi. 54; Ex. xxxiv. 15.

their gods. The singular may be intended as in Jud. xi. 24; 1 K. xi. 33. The god of Moab was Chemosh: xxi. 29.

3. *Baal-peor.* (See on xxiii. 28.) Various localities were supposed by the Semites to have their local deity, or a local manifestation of the deity: cf. the different Madonnas, our Lady of Walsingham &c. By some *Peor* has been taken for the name of the deity himself: e.g. St Jerome on Is. xv. 2: *In Nebo erat Chamos idolum consecratum, quod alio nomine Baal-phegor appellatur*: cf. also Milton's description of Chemos:

> "*Peor* his other Name, when he entic'd
> *Israel* in *Sittim* on their march from *Nile*
> To do him wanton rites, which cost them woe."
>
> *Paradise Lost* I. *ll.* 412 ff.

4. *hang them up.* As the text now stands it is the chiefs who are to be executed, not the offenders; perhaps because they were the ringleaders (cf. *v.* 14), and their punishment would serve to terrify the rest (so St Thomas Aquinas *Summa Theol.* II. ii. Q. cviii. Art. I. § 5). In view of *v.* 5, however, it is probable that something has fallen out of the text. The punishment here to be inflicted is not quite clear from Heb.; if R.V. *hang* is correct, the word used is unusual. LXX and Syr. (*expose*) give no help, Aquila renders ἀνάπηξον *impale* (cf. Ezra vi. 11 with Siegfried's note). Driver thinks that *crucifixion* (so Targ.) is the probable punishment intended: *Samuel* p. 351.

before the sun. Cf. 2 S. xii. 12; Jer. viii. 2.

5. *the judges.* Cf. Ex. xviii. 12 ff. No record is preserved of the carrying out of the sentence.

every one his men. According to his jurisdiction (Ex. xviii. 25 f.): cf. the command to the Levites at the destruction of the Golden Calf (Ex. xxxii. 27).

6–9. The incident recorded in these *vv.* has only an apparent connexion with what has gone before. The congregation are weeping, not for a punishment inflicted upon certain of their number by human judges, but because of a divine chastisement (*vv.* 8 f.). The zeal of Phinehas here exhibited became proverbial (cf. Ps. cvi. 30; 1 Macc. ii.

behold, one of the children of Israel came and brought unto his *P*
brethren a Midianitish woman in the sight of Moses, and in the sight of all the congregation of the children of Israel, while they were weeping at the door of the tent of meeting. 7 And when Phinehas, the son of Eleazar, the son of Aaron the priest, saw it, he rose up from the midst of the congregation, and took a spear in his hand; 8 and he went after the man of Israel into the [1]pavilion, and thrust both of them through, the man of Israel, and the woman through her belly. So the plague was stayed from the children of Israel. 9 And those that died by the plague were twenty and four thousand.

[1] Or, *alcove*

24 ff., 54; 1 Cor. x. 8) and he was taken as a model by the Zealots (4 Macc. xviii. 12). According to a late tradition he was granted immortality (see Fabricius *Cod. Pseudep.* I. pp. 893 f.); at the end of Jos. xxiv., however, LXX states that he was buried in Gibeah[1].

6. *brought unto his brethren.* The wording of the original means that he took her to wife, an offence entirely different from the immorality condemned in the previous story. The point of view is that of the post-exilic community.

Midianitish. Cf. xxxi. 8, 16. Moses himself had married a Midianite woman.

while they were weeping. The reason for the weeping is not given, but presupposed.

7. *Phinehas.* The word seems to be Egyptian in origin *pe-nḥēsi*=*the negro.* In 1 Chr. ix. 20 he is said to have been ruler over the keepers of the gates, possibly because of this incident: see Curtis *ad loc.* in *ICC.* His action here is in striking contrast with that of his namesake in 1 S. iv. 4, 11.

8. *pavilion.* Heb. here only. The rendering of mg. *alcove* is derived from the cognate Arab. word with the article *al* prefixed, it has come down to us through Spanish.

the plague was stayed. In xvi. 46 f. by an equally dramatic act Aaron with his smoking censer stays a similar outbreak.

9. *twenty and four thousand.* In 1 Cor. x. 8 the number is reduced by a thousand.

---

[1] Mention should perhaps be made of the ingenious theory of Sellin that Moses, himself the possessor of a Midianite wife (Ex. ii. 21; Num. xii. 1), was slain at Shittim, and thus gave his life to save his people from plague (cf. Ex. xxxii. 32; Num. xiv. 12). Sellin finds a reference to his death in Hos. v. 2 (where שחטה שטים should be read as שחת השטים). Moses thus became the original of the suffering servant of Isaiah. See *Mose u. seine Bedeutung für die isr.-jüd. Religionsgesch.* pp. 44 ff.

10 And the LORD spake unto Moses, saying, 11 Phinehas, the son of Eleazar, the son of Aaron the priest, hath turned my wrath away from the children of Israel, in that he was jealous with my jealousy among them, so that I consumed not the children of Israel in my jealousy. 12 Wherefore say, Behold, I give unto him my covenant of peace: 13 and it shall be unto him, and to his seed after him, the covenant of an everlasting priesthood; because he was jealous for his God, and made atonement for the children of Israel. 14 Now the name of the man of Israel that was slain, who was slain with the Midianitish woman, was Zimri, the son of Salu, a prince of a fathers' house among the Simeonites. 15 And the name of the Midianitish woman that was slain was Cozbi, the daughter of Zur; he was head of the people of a fathers' house in Midian. *P*

16 And the LORD spake unto Moses, saying, 17 Vex the Midianites, and smite them: 18 for they vex you with their wiles, wherewith they have beguiled you in the matter of Peor, and in the matter of Cozbi, the daughter of the prince of Midian, their sister, which was slain on the day of the plague in the matter of Peor. *P*s

10–15. The zeal of Phinehas is rewarded by the priesthood being made perpetual in his house; the point of view is that of the post-exilic priesthood by which the Zadokite priesthood of Ezekiel (xliv. 10 ff. &c.) is linked up with Phinehas: cf. 1 Chr. vi. 3 ff., 50 ff.; Ezra vii. 1 ff.

11. *my jealousy.* "His jealousy was so deep and real that it adequately expressed the jealousy of Jehovah, rendering it unnecessary for Jehovah to express it further by consuming Israel" (McNeile). Cf. 1 K. xviii. 19 ff. with xix. 10; 2 K. x. 16.

12. *my covenant of peace.* Cf. Mal. ii. 5 *life and peace.*

13. *the covenant of an everlasting priesthood.* The whole tribe of Levi was the original beneficiary under God's covenant promise (Jer. xxxiii. 21; Mal. ii. 4 f., 8), perhaps because of their zeal on a similar occasion (Ex. xxxii. 9). *Covenant* here means promise only, as in Is. lxi. 8.

made atonement. See on xvi. 47.

14. *Zimri, the son of Salu.* Cf. 1 K. xvi. 9; 1 Chr. viii. 36. In 1 Macc. ii. 26 *Salu* becomes *Salom* (cf. LXX Σαλμών)

15. *Cozbi, the daughter of Zur.* Cf. xxxi. 8 where *Zur* is one of the five kings of Midian (cf. Jos. xiii. 21).

16 ff. These *vv.* are an editorial addition combining the above narratives, and leading up to xxxi. 1. Possibly the omitted portion of the second (P) story contained an account of Balaam's advice to lead the Israelites into sin.

Chapter XXVI.

The second census.

The object of this second census is to know the numbers for the purpose of allotting the territory of Canaan, and also the strength of the army of invasion. The previous census recorded in chh. i. and iii. is known to the writer, though his order is not quite the same, Manasseh coming before Ephraim in the list of tribes (cf. *v.* 28 with i. 32 ff.). Some close connexion also exists between this ch. and Gen. xlvi., the names being mostly common to the two, and in the Hebrew text used by LXX the order of the tribes was the same. The use of a fixed formula shews the style of P.

(*a*) *The command to Moses and Eleazar.* 1–4.
(*b*) *The result of the census.* 5–51.
(*c*) *The allotment of territory.* 52–56.
(*d*) *The census of the Levites.* 57–62.
(*e*) *An editorial conclusion.* 63–65.

XXVI. 1 And it came to pass after the plague, that the LORD *Ps* spake unto Moses and unto Eleazar the son of Aaron the priest, saying, 2 Take the sum of all the congregation of the children of Israel, from twenty years old and upward, by their fathers' houses, all that are able to go forth to war in Israel. 3 And Moses and Eleazar the priest spake with them in the plains of Moab by the Jordan at Jericho, saying, 4 *Take the sum of the people*, from twenty years old and upward; as the LORD commanded Moses and the children of Israel, which came forth out of the land of Egypt.

XXVI. 1–4. Moses and Eleazar are commanded to take the numbers of the people. The command is much the same as that given to Moses alone in i. 1, but here the actual carrying out is done by him and Eleazar, instead of Aaron who was now dead.

1. *after the plague.* A note of time: cf. Amos i. 1 "two years before the earthquake." M.T. and LXX include in previous ch. as *v.* 19.

2. *to war.* For service against Midian, and also for the invasion of Canaan.

3. *the plains of Moab.* The first census took place in the wilderness of Sinai (i. 1).

saying. No speech follows, and something has fallen out as the opening words of *v.* 4 have no MS. authority, being supplied to make sense.

5–51. The numbers of the various secular tribes are given in order; as in the first census, Levi receives separate treatment. Gray thinks that the two passages *vv.* 8–11 and 30–33 may be interpolated as the exact formulas of the other notices are varied in them. When compared with the numbers of the previous census there is a decrease of 1820 due perhaps in the mind of the writer to the losses (over 40,000) by

5 Reuben, the firstborn of Israel: the sons of Reuben; *of* Hanoch, the family of the Hanochites: of Pallu, the family of the Palluites: 6 of Hezron, the family of the Hezronites: of Carmi, the family of the Carmites. 7 These are the families of the Reubenites: and they that were numbered of them were forty and three thousand and seven hundred and thirty. 8 And the sons of Pallu; Eliab. 9 And the sons of Eliab; Nemuel, and Dathan, and Abiram. These are that Dathan and Abiram, which were called of the congregation, who strove against Moses and against Aaron in the company of Korah, when they strove against the LORD: 10 and the earth opened her mouth, and swallowed them up together with Korah, when that company died; what time the fire devoured two hundred and fifty men, and they became a sign. 11 Notwithstanding the sons of Korah died not. P^s

12 The sons of Simeon after their families: of [1]Nemuel, the family of the Nemuelites: of Jamin, the family of the Jaminites: of [2]Jachin, the family of the Jachinites: 13 of [3]Zerah, the family of the Zerahites: of Shaul, the family of the Shaulites.

[1] In Gen. xlvi. 10, Ex. vi. 15, *Jemuel.* [2] In 1 Chr. iv. 24, *Jarib.*
[3] In Gen. xlvi. 10, *Zohar.*

plague and visitation (on the artificial character of the numbers see above on ch. i.). This decrease is more than accounted for by the large falling off in the tribe of Simeon (37,100), which perhaps suffered especially at Baal-peor (cf. xxv. 14).

5. *Reuben, the firstborn.* So in i. 20; Gen. xlvi. 8; Ex. vi. 14.

the sons of Reuben. The names are as given in Gen. xlvi. 9; Ex. vi. 14; 1 Chr. v. 3.

8. *the sons of.* Only one name is given in spite of the use of the plural; the formula had to be used although it did not fit the details: see also *v.* 36; Gen. xxxvi. 25, xlvi. 23; 1 Chr. i. 41, ii. 7 &c.

9–11. The story of Korah, Dathan, and Abiram as it stands in the present text after the combination of J, E, and P is presupposed.

10. *a sign.* Cf. xvi. 38; 1 Cor. x. 6; 2 Pet. ii. 6. The Heb. נֵס means *standard* and it is here used instead of אות or some such word: in later Heb., however, *sign* became the more usual meaning especially in the sense of a miracle.

11. *the sons of Korah died not.* See on *v.* 58.

12. *Nemuel.* So 1 Chr. iv. 24: in Gen. xlvi. 10 and Ex. vi. 15 *Jemuel.* After *Jamin* another son, Ohad, appears in Gen., Ex., and Jub. xliv. 13.

13. *Zerah.* In Gen. xlvi. 10; Ex. vi. 15; Jub. xliv. 13 *Zohar* (with a different initial letter in the Heb.).

Shaul. In Gen. xlvi. 10 he is described as the son of the Canaanitish

14 These are the families of the Simeonites, twenty and two P^s thousand and two hundred.

15 The sons of Gad after their families: of [1]Zephon, the family of the Zephonites: of Haggi, the family of the Haggites: of Shuni, the family of the Shunites: 16 of [2]Ozni, the family of the Oznites: of Eri, the family of the Erites: 17 of [3]Arod, the family of the Arodites: of Areli, the family of the Arelites. 18 These are the families of the sons of Gad according to those that were numbered of them, forty thousand and five hundred.

19 The sons of Judah, Er and Onan: and Er and Onan died in the land of Canaan. 20 And the sons of Judah after their families were; of Shelah, the family of the Shelanites: of Perez, the family of the Perezites: of Zerah, the family of the Zerahites. 21 And the sons of Perez were; of Hezron, the family of the Hezronites: of Hamul, the family of the Hamulites. 22 These are the families of Judah according to those that were numbered of them, threescore and sixteen thousand and five hundred.

23 The sons of Issachar after their families: *of* Tola, the family of the Tolaites: of Puvah, the family of the Punites: 24 of [4]Jashub, the family of the Jashubites: of Shimron, the family

[1] In Gen. xlvi. 16, *Ziphion*. [2] In Gen. xlvi. 16, *Ezbon*.
[3] In Gen. xlvi. 16, *Arodi*. [4] In Gen. xlvi. 13, *Iob*.

woman; Jub. xliv. 13 goes still further into detail "the son of the Zephathite woman" (cf. Jud. i. 17).

15. *Zephon*. Appears as *Ziphion* in Gen. xlvi. 16 (cf. LXX); Jub. xliv. 20.

16. *Ozni*. In Gen. xlvi. 16; Jub. xliv. 20; and also in 1 Chr. vii. 7, which as a rule agrees with Num., *Ezbon*. For the name cf. Bab. *A-a-uzni* (Tallquist *Namenbuch* p. 301).

19–22. Various traditions relating to the clans of Judah are to be found in Gen. xxxviii., all of which derive them from Canaanite mothers (see Driver *ad loc.* and cf. Luther *IN* pp. 202 ff.).

19. *died in the land of Canaan*. Their deaths are described in Gen. xxxviii. 7, 10.

20. *Shelah*. The son of Judah by the daughter of Shua (Gen. xxxviii. 5).

Perez...Zerah. The twin sons of Judah by Tamar (Gen. xxxviii. 29 f.).

23. *Tola...Puvah*. Both these names, strangely enough, are those of dye-stuffs: *Tola* (= *worm*) being the cochineal insect from which scarlet dye is obtained, and *Puvah* being a species of madder (*Rubia tinctorum*) explained by Eusebius as ἐρυθρά: see Burney *Schweich Lectures* p. 57.

24. *Jashub*. In Gen. xlvi. 13 mistakenly *Job* (cf. LXX).

of the Shimronites. 25 These are the families of Issachar according to those that were numbered of them, threescore and four thousand and three hundred. P^s

26 The sons of Zebulun after their families: of Sered, the family of the Seredites: of Elon, the family of the Elonites: of Jahleel, the family of the Jahleelites. 27 These are the families of the Zebulunites according to those that were numbered of them, threescore thousand and five hundred.

28 The sons of Joseph after their families: Manasseh and Ephraim. 29 The sons of Manasseh: of Machir, the family of the Machirites: and Machir begat Gilead: of Gilead, the family of the Gileadites. 30 These are the sons of Gilead: *of* [1]Iezer, the family of the Iezerites: of Helek, the family of the Helekites: 31 and *of* Asriel, the family of the Asrielites: and *of* Shechem, the family of the Shechemites: 32 and *of* Shemida, the family of the Shemidaites: and *of* Hepher, the family of the Hepherites. 33 And Zelophehad the son of Hepher had no sons, but daughters: and the names of the daughters of Zelophehad were Mahlah, and Noah, Hoglah, Milcah, and Tirzah. 34 These are the families

[1] In Josh. xvii. 2, *Abiezer*. See Judg. vi. 11, 24, 34.

26. *Elon*. *Elon* the Zebulonite is numbered amongst the Judges (Jud. xii. 11).

29. *Machir begat Gilead*. In xxxii. 39 *Gilead* is given by Moses to *Machir*, the same fact seems to be represented here in the language of genealogy.

30–32. In Jos. xvii. 1 f. Machir is said to be the firstborn of Manasseh and the other male children *of Manasseh* Abiezer, Helek, Asriel, Shechem, Hepher, and Shemida. In Jos. xvii. 3 however Hepher is the son of Gilead. Still further differences can be discovered in 1 Chr. ii. 21 ff., vii. 14 ff.: see Driver on 'Manasseh' in *HDB*.

30. *Iezer*. In Jos. xvii. 2 *Abiezer*: cf. Jud. vi. 11 ff.[1]

31. *Shechem*. The spelling here and in Jos. xvii. 2 is slightly different from the well-known town of this name: Gray would connect them.

32. *Shemida*. This name appears last in Jos. xvii. 2. The meaning is *The name* (of God) *knoweth*: cf. Arab. *Sumîda'a* and see Hommel *AHT* p. 100[2].

33. *the daughters of Zelophehad*. See on xxvii. 1.

---

[1] Hommel *AHT* p. 116 thinks that the *I*- is an ancient collateral form of Yahweh: cf. Ithamar (Ex. vi. 23), Ichabod (1 S. iv. 21).

[2] Parallels to the name are found in early Arabic inscriptions: see *CIS* IV. 37.

of Manasseh: and they that were numbered of them were fifty and two thousand and seven hundred. *P*s

35 These are the sons of Ephraim after their families: of Shuthelah, the family of the Shuthelahites: of [1]Becher, the family of the Becherites: of Tahan, the family of the Tahanites. 36 And these are the sons of Shuthelah: of Eran, the family of the Eranites. 37 These are the families of the sons of Ephraim according to those that were numbered of them, thirty and two thousand and five hundred. These are the sons of Joseph after their families.

38 The sons of Benjamin after their families: of Bela, the family of the Belaites: of Ashbel, the family of the Ashbelites: of [2]Ahiram, the family of the Ahiramites: 39 of [3]Shephupham, the family of the Shuphamites: of Hupham, the family of the Huphamites. 40 And the sons of Bela were [4]Ard and Naaman: *of Ard*, the family of the Ardites: of Naaman, the family of the Naamites. 41 These are the sons of Benjamin after their families: and they that were numbered of them were forty and five thousand and six hundred.

42 These are the sons of Dan after their families: of [5]Shuham, the family of the Shuhamites. These are the families of Dan after their families. 43 All the families of the Shuhamites, ac-

[1] In 1 Chr. vii. 20, *Bered*.
[2] In Gen. xlvi. 21, *Ehi* in 1 Chr. viii. 1, *Aharah*.
[3] In Gen. xlvi. 21, *Muppim, and Huppim*.
[4] In 1 Chr. viii. 3, *Addar*.
[5] In Gen. xlvi. 23, *Hushim*.

35. *Becher*. In Gen. xlvi. 21; 2 S. xx. 1 this clan belongs to Benjamin and LXX omits it here. Probably it should be transferred to *v*. 38 (so *IN* p. 515). In 1 Chr. vii. 20 a clan *Bered* appears in its place, either correctly, being omitted here, or perhaps in order to avoid the apparent inclusion of a Benjamite clan.

Tahan. Perhaps to be equated with *Tohu* in 1 S. i. 1: see Meyer *IN* p. 432.

38–41. The genealogies of the tribe of Benjamin present as many difficulties as those of Manasseh, names appearing sometimes as sons, sometimes as grandsons, and LXX having different traditions from M.T.: see Driver on Gen. xlvi. 21.

39. *Shephupham...Hupham*. In Gen. xlvi. 21 *Muppim and Huppim*, in 1 Chr. vii. 12 *Shuppim and Huppim* and in 1 Chr. viii. 5 *Shephuphan and Huram*.

42. *Shuham*. In Gen. xlvi. 23 *Hushim*. Jub. xliv. 28 gives six sons to Dan though five only are named.

cording to those that were numbered of them, were threescore P^s and four thousand and four hundred.

44 The sons of Asher after their families: of Imnah, the family of the Imnites: of Ishvi, the family of the Ishvites: of Beriah, the family of the Beriites. 45 Of the sons of Beriah: of Heber, the family of the Heberites: of Malchiel, the family of the Malchielites. 46 And the name of the daughter of Asher was Serah. 47 These are the families of the sons of Asher according to those that were numbered of them, fifty and three thousand and four hundred.

48 The sons of Naphtali after their families: of Jahzeel, the family of the Jahzeelites: of Guni, the family of the Gunites: 49 of Jezer, the family of the Jezerites: of Shillem, the family of the Shillemites. 50 These are the families of Naphtali according to their families: and they that were numbered of them were forty and five thousand and four hundred.

51 These are they that were numbered of the children of Israel, six hundred thousand and a thousand seven hundred and thirty.

52 And the LORD spake unto Moses, saying, 53 Unto these the land shall be divided for an inheritance according to the number of names. 54 To the more thou shalt give the more inheritance, and to the fewer thou shalt give the less inheritance: to every one according to those that were numbered of him shall his inheritance be given. 55 Notwithstanding the land shall be divided by lot: according to the names of the tribes of

45. *Heber...Malchiel.* In the Tell el-Amarna Letters a certain Milki-el is prominently associated with the Ḥabiru: Hommel thinks that the coupling together of these names here may be a reminiscence of the fact: see *AHT* p. 235.

52–56. The promised land is divided up amongst the tribes. Two systems seem to be confused in the account, division according to number, and division according to lot: the same apparent confusion is found in xxxiii. 54, and from the material at our disposal we are unable to discover what was really in the writer's mind. Here Moses is to make the allotments, as he does in Jud. i. 1–3, but not in Jos. xiii. 15 ff., xiv. 1 ff. (both P).

53. *Unto these.* That is excluding the Levites, whose census has not yet been carried out.

55. *by lot.* A favourite means of deciding difficult or complicated questions in ancient times: the method is not unknown even in N.T.,

their fathers they shall inherit. 56 According to the lot shall their inheritance be divided between the more and the fewer. *P*[s]

57 And these are they that were numbered of the Levites after their families: of Gershon, the family of the Gershonites: of Kohath, the family of the Kohathites: of Merari, the family of the Merarites. 58 These are the families of Levi: the family of the Libnites, the family of the Hebronites, the family of the Mahlites, the family of the Mushites, the family of the Korahites. And Kohath begat Amram. 59 And the name of Amram's wife was Jochebed, the daughter of Levi, who was born to Levi in Egypt: and she bare unto Amram Aaron and Moses, and Miriam their sister. 60 And unto Aaron were born Nadab and

cf. Acts i. 24 ff. The purpose of the *lot* was perhaps to decide the situation of the land divided off to the several tribes. The division of the territory before its actual conquest seems ideal; a parallel can be drawn from our own history in the partition of Ireland by Henry II in 1177: see Stubbs *Constit. Hist.* I. p. 599. According to tradition Argos, Laconia, and Messenia were divided by lot after the Dorian Conquest: see Holm *Hist. of Greece* I. p. 138.

57–62. The census of the Levites is taken separately, as at the first census. There are signs of compilation in this small section, *vv.* 58–61 may perhaps be an intrusion here, certainly *vv.* 57 and 58 cannot have stood together, in view of their contradictory traditions of Levite genealogy.

57. *after their families.* The threefold division of Levi is the usual one, but is not followed in the next *v.*

58. The names of the various Levite families are derived from persons mentioned in Ex. vi. 16 ff., where Libni (and also Shimei) appears as a son of Gershon; Hebron as a son of Kohath (together with Amram, Izhar, and Uzziel), to whom Korah is a grandson, being the offspring of Izhar; Mahli and Mushi are sons of Merari.

the Libnites. Probably connected with Libnah in S. Judah.

the Hebronites. It is difficult to avoid connecting this clan with the place name. Hebron was not far from Libnah.

the Mahlites. In *v.* 33 a daughter or clan of Zelophehad is named Mahlah.

the Mushites. That is the descendants of Moses (*Mosheh* in Heb.).

the Korahites. Cf. *v.* 11. They are mentioned frequently in later times: e.g. 1 Chr. ix. 19 as doorkeepers; 2 Chr. xx. 19 as choristers (cf. the headings of Pss. xlii., xliv.–xlix., lxxxiv., lxxxv., and lxxxvii.).

Amram. As *Amram* was the nephew of Jochebed their marriage was incestuous according to the law of Lev. xviii. 12. Frazer suggests that the exposure of Moses was perhaps partly due to the irregularity of his parents' union (*FLOT* II. p. 454).

Abihu, Eleazar and Ithamar. 61 And Nadab and Abihu died, *P*[s] when they offered strange fire before the LORD. 62 And they that were numbered of them were twenty and three thousand, every male from a month old and upward: for they were not numbered among the children of Israel, because there was no inheritance given them among the children of Israel.

63 These are they that were numbered by Moses and Eleazar the priest; who numbered the children of Israel in the plains of Moab by the Jordan at Jericho. 64 But among these there was not a man of them that were numbered by Moses and Aaron the priest; who numbered the children of Israel in the wilderness of Sinai. 65 For the LORD had said of them, They shall surely die in the wilderness. And there was not left a man of them, save Caleb the son of Jephunneh, and Joshua the son of Nun.

61. *Nadab and Abihu.* See on iii. 4.

63–65. The second census was taken in order to form a basis for the division of the land (*v.* 54), and incidentally to prove that none of the former generation were left, save the two permitted exceptions.

64. Cf. i. 44; Dt. ii. 14 f.

65. *the LORD had said.* See xiv. 28.

Caleb...Joshua. In addition Moses and Eleazar were survivors from the previous numbering.

CHAPTER XXVII. 1–11.

The inheritance of daughters.

The position of women—legal, social and economic—has always apparently been a subject of uncertainty and dispute. This section is an attempt to work it out in connexion with the inheritance of land[1]. Amongst the Arabs women received no portion of their family inheritance before the time of Muhammed. The Babylonians treated them a little more generously, though the references to their powers in the Code of Hammurabi are rather vague (see S. A. Cook *Laws of Moses &c.* pp. 145 f.). In Athens the sons shared equally in the father's property, the daughters were left to the generosity of their brothers. The early Romans divided the inheritance equally amongst sons and daughters, though restrictions were placed on the ability of a female to hand on her rights to her descendants.

In Dt. xxv. 5–10 the sons alone inherit, but land is prevented from leaving the family by the custom of levirate marriage; presumably the present law was unknown to the compiler. Job is represented as placing his daughters on the same level as sons (xlii. 15): see Gibson *ad loc.*

[1] It must not, however, be supposed that this was the writer's real object: the point of interest was the saving of the family inheritance from passing into alien hands.

XXVII. 1 Then drew near the daughters of Zelophehad, the son of Hepher, the son of Gilead, the son of Machir, the son of Manasseh, of the families of Manasseh the son of Joseph: and these are the names of his daughters; Mahlah, Noah, and Hoglah, and Milcah, and Tirzah. 2 And they stood before Moses, and before Eleazar the priest, and before the princes and all the congregation, at the door of the tent of meeting, saying, 3 Our father died in the wilderness, and he was not among the company of them that gathered themselves together against the LORD in the company of Korah: but he died in his own sin; and he had no sons. 4 Why should the name of our father be taken away from among his family, because he had no son? Give unto us a possession among the brethren of our father. 5 And Moses brought their cause before the LORD. 6 And the LORD spake unto Moses, saying, 7 The daughters of Zelophehad speak right: thou shalt surely give them a possession P^s

XXVII. 1. The daughters of Zelophehad are perhaps townships to judge from their names: so Kuenen *Th. Tijd.* XI. p. 488.

Mahlah. Cf. 1 Chr. vii. 18 the daughter of Hammolecheth.

Noah. Perhaps the same as *Neah* a town in Zebulon (Jos. xix. 13).

Hoglah. In Jos. xv. 6 a town in Judah *Beth-hoglah* is mentioned.

Milcah. A name which occurs more frequently than the others; it is hard to avoid connecting it with the Phoenician deity מלכת as Nöldeke suggests (*ZDMG* XLII. p. 484)[1]. The town name would then be *Beth-Milcah.*

Tirzah. The capital of Israel in the reigns of Baasha and his immediate successors (1 K. xv. 21).

2. *Eleazar.* According to 1 Chr. xxiii. 22 *Eleazar* himself died without male issue leaving only daughters. See below on *v.* 7.

3. *the company of Korah.* The possibility of Zelophehad, who was a Manassite, being amongst this company shews quite clearly that it was not a purely Levite body.

4. *because he had no son.* Cf. 2 S. xviii. 18 (Absalom's pillar).

a possession. That is a landed possession (see *BDB*).

5. *before the LORD.* Cf. ix. 8, xv. 34; Ex. xviii. 19.

7. The case came up again, according to Jos. xvii. 3 f., after the entry into Canaan, when Eleazar and Joshua were appealed to: the wording seems to imply that Eleazar was not one of those who gave the original decision.

right (כֵּן). So used in Is. xvi. 6; Prov. xi. 19 &c. It is used by Joseph's brethren in Gen. xlii. 11 &c. with the sense *honest.*

---

[1] Nöldeke would also derive Zelophehad from the name of a deity פחד: cf. Gen. xxxi. 42, 53 Heb. (*Untersuchungen* p. 89; see also Holz. on xxvii. 1).

of an inheritance among their father's brethren; and thou shalt P^s cause the inheritance of their father to pass unto them. 8 And thou shalt speak unto the children of Israel, saying, If a man die, and have no son, then ye shall cause his inheritance to pass unto his daughter. 9 And if he have no daughter, then ye shall give his inheritance unto his brethren. 10 And if he have no brethren, then ye shall give his inheritance unto his father's brethren. 11 And if his father have no brethren, then ye shall give his inheritance unto his kinsman that is next to him of his family, and he shall possess it: and it shall be unto the children of Israel a statute of judgement, as the LORD commanded Moses.

8–11. Taking this case as a precedent a formal law is now drafted, and its clauses extended to cover further eventualities: as in the case of other laws these provisions required later supplements (see xxxvi. 1 ff.).

8. This rule is put on the lips of the Archbishop of Canterbury in *Henry V* Act I. Scene ii. when arguing against the Salic Law.

CHAPTER XXVII. 12–23.

Moses and his successor.

Two distinct, but related, events are recorded in this section; the viewing of the promised land and forecast of the death of Moses (*vv.* 12–14), and the choice and appointment of Joshua (*vv.* 15–23).

12 And the LORD said unto Moses, Get thee up into this R^P mountain of Abarim, and behold the land which I have given

12–14. Moses is commanded to view the Promised Land from which he is himself excluded on account of his 'rebellion against God's word.' It would be easy to criticise the representation of the character of God contained in this narrative: according to which a lifetime of faithful service is apparently wiped out by a single lapse. But the divine majesty had to be vindicated, and a public failure atoned for, by a striking and impressive punishment: moreover there was another Land of Promise from which Moses was not excluded by his offence.

The event which is foreshadowed here is not narrated until Dt. xxxiv. (P), and then only after a fresh and longer command has been given (Dt. xxxii. 40 ff.), a command based on the present passage (so Bacon *Triple Tradition* pp. 239 f., 268), and probably borrowed from it by the compiler who placed the final ch. of Deut. in its present position. Dillmann, however, thinks that Dt. xxxii. 48 ff. originally stood here, and on its removal the present abbreviated passage was inserted.

12. *this mountain of Abarim.* The range of *Abarim* (= *parts beyond*) was probably so called because situated 'beyond' Jordan (that is of

unto the children of Israel. 13 And when thou hast seen it, thou also shalt be gathered unto thy people, as Aaron thy brother was gathered: 14 because ye rebelled against my word in the wilderness of Zin, in the strife of the congregation, [1]to sanctify me at the waters before their eyes. (These are the waters of Meribah of Kadesh in the wilderness of Zin.) 15 And Moses spake unto the LORD, saying, 16 Let the LORD, the God of the spirits of all flesh, appoint a man over the congregation, 17 which may go out before them, and which may come in before them, and which may lead them out, and which may bring them in; that the congregation of the LORD be not as sheep which have no shepherd. 18 And the LORD said unto Moses, Take

*R*P

P

[1] See ch. xx. 12, 13.

course from the standpoint of an inhabitant of Palestine). In LXX as in the parallel passage in Dt. xxxii. 49 Mount Nebo is specified.

13. *be gathered &c.* A technical term on which see note on xx. 24.

as Aaron. See xx. 28 f.

14. *rebelled.* As described in xx. 1 ff. where see the discussion of their offence.

strife...sanctify. A play on the words Meribah and Kadesh.

15–23. Moses, having seen the land which Israel is to possess, is next informed of the name of his successor in leading them in thither. Joshua is appointed by Moses, at the divine command, in the presence of Eleazar his colleague as high-priest and of the congregation over whom he is to rule[1].

Different accounts of the choice of Joshua have apparently survived. According to D he was definitely announced as the successor of Moses at the time of the return of the spies (Dt. i. 37 f.: cf. iii. 21, xxxi. 3) In Dt. xxxi. 14 f., 23 (JE) the choice is only separated from the actual commission by a short interval: JE would thus agree with P against D, a somewhat rare occurrence. For a detailed discussion of these passages see Driver *Deut.* pp. 26 f., 337 f.

16. *the God of the spirits &c.* See note on xvi. 22. In Jub. x. 3 the same phrase is used by Noah when praying for his sons.

17. *sheep which have no shepherd.* Cf. 1 K. xxii. 17; Ez. xxxiv. 5; Judith xi. 19; and our Lord's use in Mk. vi. 34 (= Mt. ix. 36) also Jn. viii. 8 f. In Enoch lxxxix. 10 ff. the idea is worked out in an elaborate allegory.

---

[1] John of Salisbury, the famous medieval political thinker, points out the importance of the various stages in this election: the convoking of the people, the laying on of hands, the setting before Eleazar, and the giving of a public charge: see *Policraticus* v. 549 *a*.

thee Joshua the son of Nun, a man in whom is the spirit, and *P*
lay thine hand upon him; 19 and set him before Eleazar the priest, and before all the congregation; and give him a charge in their sight. 20 And thou shalt put of thine honour upon him, that all the congregation of the children of Israel may obey. 21 And he shall stand before Eleazar the priest, who shall inquire for him by the judgement of the Urim before the LORD:

18. *Joshua the son of Nun.* See note pp. 72 f.

the spirit. Omit *the.* In Dt. xxxiv. 9 Joshua is described as being full of the spirit of wisdom as a consequence of the laying on of the hands of Moses.

lay thine hand upon him. "The previous reception of the inner grace did not dispense with the outward sign; cf. the case of Cornelius, Acts x. 44–48; and St Paul's baptism after his miraculous conversion, Acts ix. 18." *Speaker's Commentary.* For the use of the rite see further Hooker *Eccles. Polity* Bk. v. lxvi. 1 ff.; Rackham *Acts* p. 85[1].

19. *set him before Eleazar.* The priest played but a small part in the ceremony, being merely a witness.

give him a charge. Cf. Dt. iii. 28, xxxi. 7 f.

20. *of thine honour.* Cf. xi. 17 (the elders); 2 K. ii. 9; Ecclus. xlv. 7 (God's gift to Aaron). The word for *honour* occurs here only in Pent., it is often used of kingly majesty, especially of God as the divine king.

21. The position of Joshua is practically that of a military commander under the direction of the high-priest; the high-priest himself gives direction through the use of the divine oracle. In pagan Rome the three great colleges of religion—the *pontifices, augurs,* and *duo-decem-quindecim-viri sacris faciundis*—likewise owed their power in state affairs to their authority to report or interpret omens: cf. Gwatkin *Knowledge of God* II. p. 132.

Hooker (*op. cit.* Bk. II. vi. 3) points out that Joshua failed to obtain the high-priest's direction in the matter of the Gibeonites (Jos. ix. 3 ff.)[2].

the Urim. Except in this passage and 1 S. xxviii. 6 *Thummim* accompanies *Urim*: see Ex. xxviii. 30; Lev. viii. 8; Ezra ii. 63; 1 S. xiv. 41 (LXX). In Dt. xxxiii. 8 *Thummim* comes first. The exact nature of the sacred lot is not known: see McNeile on Ex. xxviii. 30 and

---

[1] Gressmann points out that the hand is the member with which things are done, and therefore it fittingly represents human, and even divine, power (*Mose* p. 158). Representations of the 'divine' hand which were supposed to possess magic power have been found at Hagia Triada in Crete, in Babylon, South Arabia, and Phoenicia (see Weinreich *Antike Heilungswunder* p. 17; René Dussaud *Notes de Mythologie Syrienne* pp. 117 ff.).

[2] The subordination of the secular to the ecclesiastical head of the nation points to a period subsequent to the writing of Zech. vi. 9 ff. which in its original form treated the two as equal (see Merx *Die Bücher Moses und Joshua* pp. 109, 155).

at his word shall they go out, and at his word they shall come in, both he, and all the children of Israel with him, even all the congregation. 22 And Moses did as the LORD commanded him: and he took Joshua, and set him before Eleazar the priest, and before all the congregation: 23 and he laid his hands upon him, and gave him a charge, as the LORD spake by the hand of Moses. *P*

A. Jeremias *Urim und Thummim* in *Hilprecht Anniversary Volume* pp. 223 ff.[1]

CHAPTERS XXVIII., XXIX.

Regulations concerning public worship[2].

Sacred feasts formed part of the religion of Israel from the earliest times, and, in each stratum of the Pent., legislation is found for their regulation. The later codes, however, are not merely more elaborate in their requirements for the existing feasts, but also provide additional festivals. There is thus a wide gulf between the simplicity of the feasts described in JE (Ex. xii. 21 ff., xiii. 3 ff., xxiii. 14 ff., xxxiv. 18 ff.), and those of P contained in this passage and elsewhere. The gulf is partly bridged by the legislation of D (Dt. xvi. 1 ff.), and of H (Lev. xxiii.). The carrying out of these costly offerings would not of course have been possible in the wilderness: cf. Dt. xii. 8 f.

(*a*) *Introduction.* xxviii. 1 f.
(*b*) *The daily offerings.* 3–8.
(*c*) *The sabbath.* 9 f.
(*d*) *The first day of each month.* 11–15.
(*e*) *The feast of unleavened bread.* 16–25.
(*f*) *The feast of weeks.* 26–31.
(*g*) *The feast of trumpets.* xxix. 1–6.
(*h*) *The Day of Atonement.* 7–11.
(*i*) *The feast of Booths.* 12–38.
(*j*) *General offerings.* 39 f.

XXVIII. 1 f. A general command introducing the whole section. The main interest in it is the recognition that offerings are to be made at a set time. In the early days the agricultural feasts depended for their observance on the progress of the necessary operations which would vary in different parts of the country: in these chh. a fixed date is insisted upon (cf. *v.* 16, xxix. 12).

---

[1] The old rendering for *Urim* and *Thummim* 'Lights and Perfections' should probably be abandoned since the words are scarcely from אור and תם, but may be connected with Ass. *ûrû*=*oracle* and *tamû*=*to speak*: see G. R. Driver in *The People and the Book* pp. 90 f.

[2] See further Gray *Sacrifice* pp. 271 ff. Similar tables of sacrifices and dues have been found on Phoenician Inscriptions (see *NSI* Nos. 42 to 44) and amongst the Greeks (see the Sacrificial Calendar from Cos in Michel *Recueil d'Inscriptions Grecques*, pp. 716 ff.). Cooke points out that whilst the Hebrews sacrificed domestic animals only, the Phoenicians offered wild animals (*NSI* p. 117).

XXVIII. 1 And the LORD spake unto Moses, saying, 2 Command the children of Israel, and say unto them, My oblation, my [1]food for my offerings made by fire, of a sweet savour unto me, shall ye observe to offer unto me in their due season. 3 [2]And thou shalt say unto them, This is the offering made by fire which ye shall offer unto the LORD; he-lambs of the first year without blemish, two day by day, for a continual burnt offering. 4 The one lamb shalt thou offer in the morning, and the other lamb shalt thou offer [3]at even; 5 and the tenth part of an ephah of fine flour for a meal offering, mingled with the fourth part of an hin of beaten oil. 6 It is a continual burnt offering, which was ordained in mount Sinai for a sweet savour, *P*[s]

[1] Heb. *bread*. [2] See Ex. xxix. 38–42.
[3] Heb. *between the two evenings*.

1. *My oblation.* The use of קרבן (*ḳorbān*) is limited to P and Ezek., its root meaning is *to bring near* and it is used of offerings in general. Cf. Mk. vi. 11.

my food. An anthropomorphic expression which represents the primitive idea that the gods actually ate the sacrifices offered to them: cf. Lev. xxi. 6 ff., xxii. 25; Jud. ix. 13: and contrast Ps. xxx. 1, 12 ff. The same idea is found amongst the Greeks (cf. *Iliad* IX. 531), and the Babylonians (Herod. I. 181, 183; *KAT*[3] pp. 594 f.). See further Robertson Smith *Rel. Sem.*[2] pp. 223 ff.

by fire. See on xv. 3.

a sweet savour. See on xv. 3.

3–8. A daily, or continual, offering is to be made every morning and every evening: this is to consist of a burnt offering and a meal offering. On the importance of this offering as the basis of the whole sacrificial system, and the various uses at different times see Introd. p. lii.

3. *ye shall offer.* That is the whole community: the writer is dealing with public offerings.

a continual burnt offering. Neh. x. 33 speaks of a *continual meal offering*, also referring to *v.* 4. Probably the meal offering was the earlier of the two, and even by the time of Elijah it had come to mean eventide (1 K. xviii. 29, 36), a usage which continued (Ezra ix. 4 f.; Dan. ix. 21). In Dan. viii. 11 &c. the word תמיד is alone used (see Bevan *Daniel* p. 32), and the tractate of the Mishnah is called simply *Tamid*, i.e. *continual*.

4. *in the morning.* Cf. Ps. v. 3 "In the morning will I order unto thee," which probably refers to a sacrifice (cf., however, Job xxxii. 14, xxxiii. 5 &c.).

at even. See ix. 3 with note.

5. *ephah...hin.* See on xv. 4.

6. This *v.* reads like a marginal gloss which has been copied into the text: the reference is to Ex. xxix. 38 ff.

an offering made by fire unto the LORD. 7 And the drink *Ps* offering thereof shall be the fourth part of an hin for the one lamb: in the holy place shalt thou pour out a drink offering of strong drink unto the LORD. 8 And the other lamb shalt thou offer at even: as the meal offering of the morning, and as the drink offering thereof, thou shalt offer it, an offering made by fire, of a sweet savour unto the LORD.

9 And on the sabbath day two he-lambs of the first year without blemish, and two tenth parts *of an ephah* of fine flour for a meal offering, mingled with oil, and the drink offering thereof: 10 this is the burnt offering of every sabbath, beside the continual burnt offering, and the drink offering thereof.

11 And in the beginnings of your months ye shall offer a burnt offering unto the LORD; two young bullocks, and one ram, seven he-lambs of the first year without blemish; 12 and three tenth parts *of an ephah* of fine flour for a meal offering, mingled with oil, for each bullock; and two tenth parts of fine flour for a meal offering, mingled with oil, for the one ram; 13 and a several tenth part of fine flour mingled with oil for a meal offering unto

7. *the holy place.* According to Ecclus. l. 15 libations were poured out at the base of the altar of burnt offerings which stood in the court.

of strong drink. See on vi. 3, xv. 4, 7. The use of *strong drink,* instead of wine, is without parallel in Jewish ritual (cf. however its use in Babylonian libations: *KAT*[3] p. 600) and possibly we are to understand wine here.

9 f. The sabbath is to be distinguished from other days by an additional offering of equal value to that made continuously; the priests on the sabbath have thus double labour (cf. Mt. xii. 5). This ordinance is new, and indeed is the only law relating to a sabbath offering in the Pent., though its observance is repeatedly insisted upon (Ex. xx. 8 ff. &c.). The reference in Is. i. 13 to new moon and sabbath seems to indicate the use of sacrifices on these festivals, but the first clear reference is Ez. xlvi. 4 f. In later times Ps. xcii. "a song for the sabbath day" was sung with the pouring out of the libation.

11–15. On the first day of each month large offerings are to be made. Although the observance of new moons was an old festival in Israel (cf. 1 S. xx. 5 ff.; 2 K. iv. 23; Am. viii. 5; Hos. i. 13; Is. i. 13), this is the first instance of any command to observe it: that it would be observed is however taken for granted in x. 10. The reason for this ignoring of a great festival by the earlier legislation is a little hard to understand, and the argument that would account for it on the grounds of the danger of moon-worship is hardly satisfactory. The normal way of dealing with popular superstitions, as in the medieval Church, is to

every lamb; for a burnt offering of a sweet savour, an offering made by fire unto the LORD. 14 And their drink offerings shall be half an hin of wine for a bullock, and the third part of an hin for the ram, and the fourth part of an hin for a lamb: this is the burnt offering of every month throughout the months of the year. 15 And one he-goat for a sin offering unto the LORD; it shall be offered beside the continual burnt offering, and the drink offering thereof. *P*[s]

16 And in the first month, on the fourteenth day of the month, is the LORD's passover. 17 And on the fifteenth day of this month shall be a feast: seven days shall unleavened bread be eaten. 18 In the first day shall be an holy convocation; ye shall do no servile work: 19 but ye shall offer an offering made by fire, a burnt offering unto the LORD; two young bullocks, and one ram, and seven he-lambs of the first year: they shall be unto you without blemish: 20 and their meal offering, fine flour mingled with oil: three tenth parts shall ye offer for a bullock, and two tenth parts for the ram; 21 a several tenth part shalt thou offer for every lamb of the seven lambs; 22 and one he-goat for a sin offering, to make atonement for you. 23 Ye shall offer these beside the burnt offering of the morning, which is for a continual burnt offering. 24 After this manner ye shall

adopt them, but to take measures for their regulation[1]. Originally the festival was a welcome to the returning moon (so Loisy *Rel. of Isr.* p. 86), but its later importance from a practical point of view was in connexion with the calendar.

16–25. The offerings for the feast of unleavened bread. This passage is based on Lev. xxiii. 5–8 and indeed *vv.* 16–19 *a* are simply copied from it. It should be noticed that in *v.* 16 no offerings are specified. The requirements of Ezek. for this festival are more onerous (xlv. 23).

17. *seven.* On the significance of *seven* as a sacred number see on xxiii. 1.

18. *servile work*: lit. *work of tillage.* The expression occurs mainly in H.

---

[1] That moon-worship was common amongst the Semites is undeniable, though traces of its influence amongst the Hebrews are practically non-existent (see *Enc. Bib.* 3197): cf. however Burney's note "Early Identification of Yahweh with the Moon-God" in *Judges* pp. 249 ff. In a fourth-century inscription from Kition there is a reference to certain (unknown) "gods of the new moon" which is of interest in the present connexion (*CIS* I. p. 86; *NSI* pp. 65 f.). Other evidence of the importance of the festival is to be found in the custom of naming children from it, e.g. Ben-Ḥodesh in the inscription given in *NSI* p. 63: Cooke compares the Christian Paschalis &c.

offer daily, for seven days, the [1]food of the offering made by fire, of a sweet savour unto the LORD: it shall be offered beside the continual burnt offering, and the drink offering thereof. 25 And on the seventh day ye shall have an holy convocation; ye shall do no servile work. *P*[s]

26 Also in the day of the firstfruits, when ye offer a new meal offering unto the LORD in your *feast of* weeks, ye shall have an holy convocation; ye shall do no servile work: 27 but ye shall offer a burnt offering for a sweet savour unto the LORD; two young bullocks, one ram, seven he-lambs of the first year; 28 and their meal offering, fine flour mingled with oil, three tenth parts for each bullock, two tenth parts for the one ram, 29 a several tenth part for every lamb of the seven lambs; 30 one he-goat, to make atonement for you. 31 Beside the continual burnt offering, and the meal offering thereof, ye shall offer them (they shall be unto you without blemish), and their drink offerings.

XXIX. 1 And in the seventh month, on the first day of the month, ye shall have an holy convocation; ye shall do no servile work: it is a day of blowing of trumpets unto you. 2 And ye shall offer a burnt offering for a sweet savour unto the LORD; one young bullock, one ram, seven he-lambs of the first year without blemish: 3 and their meal offering, fine flour mingled with oil, three tenth parts for the bullock, two tenth parts for the ram, 4 and one tenth part for every lamb of the seven lambs: 5 and one he-goat for a sin offering, to make atonement for you: 6 beside the burnt offering of the new moon, and the meal offering thereof, and the continual burnt offering and the

[1] Heb. *bread*.

26–31. The offerings for the day of firstfruits are here specified. The festival is the same as that called harvest (Ex. xxiii. 16) or weeks (*v.* 26; Ex. xxxiv. 22). The parallel law of H is found in Lev. xxiii. 15 ff. where several modifications occur. The feast does not occur in Ezekiel.

26. *the day of the firstfruits.* This phrase is unique.

XXIX. 1–6. The offerings for the feast of trumpets. The blowing of trumpets on various occasions has been already provided for (x. 10); the provision here is for a feast called especially by the name.

1. Cf. Lev. xxiii. 24 f. Some authorities regard this feast as a celebration of the New Year (see *Enc. Bib.*), though according to Ez. xl. 1 the New Year began on the 10th day of the month.

meal offering thereof, and their drink offerings, according unto their ordinance, for a sweet savour, an offering made by fire unto the LORD. *Ps*

7 And on the tenth day of this seventh month ye shall have an holy convocation; and ye shall afflict your souls; ye shall do no manner of work: 8 but ye shall offer a burnt offering unto the LORD for a sweet savour; one young bullock, one ram, seven he-lambs of the first year; they shall be unto you without blemish: 9 and their meal offering, fine flour mingled with oil, three tenth parts for the bullock, two tenth parts for the one ram, 10 a several tenth part for every lamb of the seven lambs: 11 one he-goat for a sin offering; beside the sin offering of atonement, and the continual burnt offering, and the meal offering thereof, and their drink offerings.

12 And on the fifteenth day of the seventh month ye shall have an holy convocation; ye shall do no servile work, and ye shall keep a feast unto the LORD seven days: 13 and ye shall offer a burnt offering, an offering made by fire, of a sweet savour unto the LORD; thirteen young bullocks, two rams, fourteen he-lambs of the first year; they shall be without blemish: 14 and their meal offering, fine flour mingled with oil, three tenth parts for every bullock of the thirteen bullocks, two tenth parts for each ram of the two rams, 15 and a several tenth part for every lamb of the fourteen lambs: 16 and one he-goat for a sin offering; beside the continual burnt offering, the meal offering thereof, and the drink offering thereof.

17 And on the second day *ye shall offer* twelve young bullocks, two rams, fourteen he-lambs of the first year without blemish:

7–11. The offerings for the Day of Atonement. The great day of the later Judaism, the crown of the whole sacrificial system. A tractate of the Mishnah *Yômā* was devoted to it (see also Lev. xvi., xxiii. 26 ff.).

7. *afflict your souls.* That is *fast*: cf. Ps. xxxv. 13; Is. lviii. 3, 5.

no manner of work. As on the sabbath: a stricter regulation than in xxviii. 18 &c.

11. *the sin offering of atonement.* The ceremony from which the festival got its special name.

12–38. The offerings for the feast of booths. Unlike the regulations in Ez. xlv. 25 the demands here made are much severer than those for the spring festival.

12. Cf. Lev. xxiii. 34 f.

18 and their meal offering and their drink offerings for the bullocks, for the rams, and for the lambs, according to their number, after the ordinance: 19 and one he-goat for a sin offering; beside the continual burnt offering, and the meal offering thereof, and their drink offerings. *Ps*

20 And on the third day eleven bullocks, two rams, fourteen he-lambs of the first year without blemish; 21 and their meal offering and their drink offerings for the bullocks, for the rams, and for the lambs, according to their number, after the ordinance: 22 and one he-goat for a sin offering; beside the continual burnt offering, and the meal offering thereof, and the drink offering thereof.

23 And on the fourth day ten bullocks, two rams, fourteen he-lambs of the first year without blemish: 24 their meal offering and their drink offerings for the bullocks, for the rams, and for the lambs, according to their number, after the ordinance: 25 and one he-goat for a sin offering; beside the continual burnt offering, the meal offering thereof, and the drink offering thereof.

26 And on the fifth day nine bullocks, two rams, fourteen he-lambs of the first year without blemish: 27 and their meal offering and their drink offerings for the bullocks, for the rams, and for the lambs, according to their number, after the ordinance: 28 and one he-goat for a sin offering; beside the continual burnt offering, and the meal offering thereof, and the drink offering thereof.

29 And on the sixth day eight bullocks, two rams, fourteen he-lambs of the first year without blemish: 30 and their meal offering and their drink offerings for the bullocks, for the rams, and for the lambs, according to their number, after the ordinance: 31 and one he-goat for a sin offering; beside the continual burnt offering, the meal offering thereof, and the drink offerings thereof.

32 And on the seventh day seven bullocks, two rams, fourteen

18. *their drink offerings.* These have been omitted in *v.* 15 though appearing in Sam. version.

32. *seventh day seven bullocks.* The offering of *bullocks* diminished day by day from the first day. Various suggestions have been advanced to account for this; such as the symbolism required by the waning moon,

he-lambs of the first year without blemish: 33 and their meal *P*s offering and their drink offerings for the bullocks, for the rams, and for the lambs, according to their number, after the ordinance: 34 and one he-goat for a sin offering; beside the continual burnt offering, the meal offering thereof, and the drink offering thereof.

35 On the eighth day ye shall have a [1]solemn assembly: ye shall do no servile work: 36 but ye shall offer a burnt offering, an offering made by fire, of a sweet savour unto the LORD: one bullock, one ram, seven he-lambs of the first year without blemish: 37 their meal offering and their drink offerings for the bullock, for the ram, and for the lambs, shall be according to their number, after the ordinance: 38 and one he-goat for a sin offering; beside the continual burnt offering, and the meal offering thereof, and the drink offering thereof.

39 These ye shall offer unto the LORD in your set feasts, beside your vows, and your freewill offerings, for your burnt offerings, and for your meal offerings, and for your drink offerings, and for your peace offerings. [2]40 And Moses told the children of Israel according to all that the LORD commanded Moses.

[1] See Lev. xxiii. 36. [2] [Ch. xxx. 1 in Heb.]

or a gradual working down to the number required on an ordinary day.

35. *a solemn assembly.* Heb. עֲצֶרֶת (*'ăẓereth*). In later Heb. the word came to be applied to the feast of weeks: see further Driver's note in *Deut.* p. 195.

39 f. The foregoing regulations are stated to be in addition to voluntary gifts and the fulfilments of vows (cf. Dt. xvi. 10, 17). The law provided for two classes of offerings "the one proceeding upon ordinary observance, the other upon a devout cheerfulness": Bacon *The Advancement of Learning* I. i. 1.

CHAPTER XXX.

The vows of women.

The greater part of this section (i.e. *vv.* 3–16) is concerned with vows made by women. Put shortly the rule is that a woman living under the protection of her father or husband can only make a binding vow with their knowledge and in the absence of any veto. A woman who is a widow or divorced, however, is free to make any vow she chooses, and is personally responsible.

Amongst other passages dealing with vows of various kinds see vi. 2 ff.; Dt. xxiii. 21 ff.; Pss. xxii. 25, l. 14, lxvi. 13 f., cxvi. 14, 18; Eccles. v. 4 f.; Mt. v. 32 and see the Tractate *Nedarim*.

XXX. 1 And Moses spake unto the heads of the tribes of the children of Israel, saying, This is the thing which the LORD hath commanded. 2 When a man voweth a vow unto the LORD, or sweareth an oath to bind his soul with a bond, he shall not [1]break his word; he shall do according to all that proceedeth out of his mouth. 3 Also when a woman voweth a vow unto the LORD, and bindeth herself by a bond, being in her father's house, in her youth; 4 and her father heareth her vow, and her bond wherewith she hath bound her soul, and her father holdeth his peace at her: then all her vows shall stand, and every bond wherewith she hath bound her soul shall stand. 5 But if her father disallow her in the day that he heareth; none of her vows, or of her bonds wherewith she hath bound her soul, shall stand: and the LORD shall forgive her, because her father disallowed her. 6 And if she be *married* to a husband, while her vows are upon her, or the rash utterance of her lips, wherewith she hath bound her soul; 7 and her husband hear it, and hold

P[s]

[1] Heb. *profane*.

XXX. 1. *Moses spake.* Though we are told that the command was from the LORD there is no direct mention of its having been given.

the heads of the tribes. Mentioned in i. 4, 16, vii. 2 &c. though the actual phrase is different.

2. *vow...bond.* Holz. distinguishes these as a vow of *performance* and a vow of *abstinence*. Ehrlich denies this and considers the *vow* to be a religious, the *bond* a secular obligation. The Heb. word for *vow* (נדר) is the general term employed for such undertakings: *bond* (אסר) is not found outside this ch., a verb, however, from the same root is in frequent use.

break his word: lit. *profane*: cf. Pss. lv. 20, lxxxix. 34; Mal. ii. 10.

all that proceedeth. Cf. xi. 23 (with note), xxxii. 24; Jud. xi. 35 f.

3. *in her youth.* The law seems to take it for granted that all women will marry.

4. *heareth her vow.* Better *cometh to hear of it*: not necessarily the hearing of the taking of the vow itself.

6. *while her vows.* The case of a woman married whilst unfulfilled vows are upon her. The *Speaker's Commentary* takes this provision to refer to the case of a betrothed woman still living at home—a common occurrence—under these circumstances the husband had rights over her property, and if she committed adultery death was the consequence, just as if the marriage had actually taken place (Dt. xxii. 23 f.).

the rash utterance. The noun is found only in this passage, but a verb from the same root is used Lev. v. 4; Ps. cvi. 33; cf. also Prov. xii. 18.

his peace at her in the day that he heareth it: then her vows shall stand, and her bonds wherewith she hath bound her soul shall stand. 8 But if her husband disallow her in the day that he heareth it; then he shall make void her vow which is upon her, and the rash utterance of her lips, wherewith she hath bound her soul: and the LORD shall forgive her. 9 But the vow of a widow, or of her that is divorced, *even* every thing wherewith she hath bound her soul, shall stand against her. 10 And if she vowed in her husband's house, or bound her soul by a bond with an oath, 11 and her husband heard it, and held his peace at her, and disallowed her not; then all her vows shall stand, and every bond wherewith she bound her soul shall stand. 12 But if her husband made them null and void in the day that he heard them; then whatsoever proceeded out of her lips concerning her vows, or concerning the bond of her soul, shall not stand: her husband hath made them void; and the LORD shall forgive her. 13 Every vow, and every binding oath to afflict the soul, her husband may establish it, or her husband may make it void. 14 But if her husband altogether hold his peace at her from day to day; then he establisheth all her vows, or all her bonds, which are upon her: he hath established them, because he held his peace at her in the day that he heard them. 15 But if he shall make them null and void after that he hath heard them; then he shall bear her iniquity. 16 These are the statutes, which the LORD commanded Moses, between a man and his wife, between a father and his daughter, being in her youth, in her father's house. P[s]

9. *that is divorced.* Lit. *driven out* in accordance with the regulations of Dt. xxiv. 1. There is no account of the origin of divorce in O.T., the right is taken for granted; in Dt. xxiv. 1 ff. the custom is regulated, and legal forms are applied to it.

13. *to afflict the soul.* The usual meaning of this expression is *to fast*: see on xxix. 7.

CHAPTER XXXI.

The holy war against Midian.

In xxv. 16 ff. Moses was commanded to vex Midian on account of the sin at Peor: this ch. seems to be a carrying out of the command (cf. the expedition against Amalek: 1 S. xv. 2 ff.). Three main subjects however find a place in the story or are built upon it: (i) the ideal method of carrying out a *jihâd* or holy war; (ii) the purification of the warriors (cf. xix.); (iii) the division of the spoil (cf. 1 S. xxx. 24 f.). Kennedy says of the ch. "The story of this wonderful crusade is not history—nor was it seriously intended to be taken for history, which from the apologetic standpoint is a distinct gain—but an illustration of the method by which the later Jewish authorities sought to invest certain laws with a more authoritative sanction by providing them with a Mosaic precedent."

(*a*) *The gathering to war.* 1–6.
(*b*) *The fate of the Midianites.* 7–12.
(*c*) *Further destruction ordered by Moses.* 13–18.
(*d*) *The purification of the army.* 19–24.
(*e*) *The division of the spoil.* 25–54.

XXXI. 1 And the LORD spake unto Moses, saying, 2 Avenge the children of Israel of the Midianites: afterward shalt thou be gathered unto thy people. 3 And Moses spake unto the people, saying, Arm ye men from among you for the war, that they may go against Midian, to execute the LORD's vengeance on Midian. 4 Of every tribe a thousand, throughout all the tribes of Israel, shall ye send to the war. 5 So there were delivered, out of the thousands of Israel, a thousand of every tribe, twelve thousand armed for war. 6 And Moses sent them, a thousand of every tribe, to the war, them and Phinehas the son *P*[s]

XXXI. 1–6. The organisation of the expedition of vengeance against Midian. A thousand warriors from each tribe are put under the command of Phinehas.

2. As the offence of the Midianites had taken place during the leadership of Moses, he is now to wipe it out before laying down his office.

the Midianites. A Bedawin tribe who are represented as inhabiting different districts from time to time (see *Enc. Bib.*). For their connexion with Balaam see above p. 152, and for their general history H. Winckler *Gesch. Isr.* I. pp. 46 ff.

3. *the LORD's vengeance.* Cf. xxv. 16 ff.

5. *delivered.* The word is late Heb. and is not found outside this passage in O.T. (the occurrence in *v.* 16 is probably due to a corruption of the text)[1].

twelve thousand. The same number occurs in Jud. xxi. 10: the whole passage is probably based on the present narrative (so G. F. Moore).

6. *Phinehas.* Whether he went as commander of the expedition, in place of Joshua, or as priest, instead of Eleazar, is not quite clear. He was also sent with the expedition against the east Jordan tribes (Jos. xxii. 13).

---

[1] The reading of LXX *ἐξηρίθμησαν* suggests that even here a corruption has taken place and וַיִּסָּפְרוּ has become וַיִּמָּסְרוּ.

of Eleazar the priest, to the war, with the vessels of the sanctuary and the trumpets for the alarm in his hand. 7 And they warred against Midian, as the LORD commanded Moses; and they slew every male. 8 And they slew the kings of Midian with the rest of their slain; Evi, and Rekem, and Zur, and Hur, and Reba, the five kings of Midian: Balaam also the son of Beor they slew with the sword. 9 And the children of Israel took captive the women of Midian and their little ones; and all their cattle, and all their flocks, and all their goods, they took for a *P*[s]

the vessels of the sanctuary. Better *the sacred vessels* (cf. iii. 31, iv. 15 &c.). The *Speaker's Commentary* would place this phrase in apposition to the next, and reads "holy instruments to wit the trumpets." The meaning is obscure.

7–12. The campaign is successful in every respect; though no details are given of the time or place of the battles, the names of the defeated leaders have been preserved.

7. *every male.* That this is unhistorical appears from the fact that Midian did not disappear as a tribe: possibly only a clan or division was attacked. In Jud. viii. 12 Midian is again destroyed.

8. *the kings of Midian.* The rulers of Midian are given different titles in different passages of O.T.: in xxii. 4 *elders*; in Jos. xiii. 21 (where the names of these five reappear) *chiefs* or *princes*, as also in Ps. lxxxiii. 11.

Evi. Here and Jos. xiii. 21.

Rekem. This name appears in 1 Chr. ii. 43 f., vii. 16 and has also been found in Nabataean inscriptions from Petra (see Brünnow and Domaszewski *Die Provincia Arabia* I. p. 285). Josephus derives the original name of Petra Ἀρεκέμη from him (see *Ant.* IV. vii. 1 and cf. Euseb. *Onom.* 228, 286 f. Ῥοκόμ), and the derivation is approved in *IN* pp. 388 f. A town in the tribe of Benjamin has the same name (Jos. xviii. 27) and Syr. habitually uses it for Kadesh.

Zur. See on xxv. 15.

Hur. Also the name of an Israelite chief (Ex. xvii. 10), and of a post-exilic Jew. In an Aramaic inscription (B.C. 482) at Memphis (*NSI* No. 71 *l.* 1) חור is found as a proper name (cf. Horus) and in Nabataean inscriptions the name חורו occurs frequently (e.g. *NSI* No. 87 *l.* 8, 90 *l.* 5).

Reba. Here and Jos. xiii. 21 only.

Balaam. According to the Samaritan Joshua viii. he was seized in the temple by Joshua (!) who tried to save him; the tribe of Simeon (cf. xxv. 14), however, had him put to death, being afraid of his enchantments.

9. *little ones.* The word used (טַף) is generally restricted to J and D: it is found here in a late passage from P.

cattle. There is no mention of camels, for which the Midianites were noted (Jud. vi. 5 &c.).

prey. 10 And all their cities in the places wherein they dwelt, P^s and all their encampments, they burnt with fire. 11 And they took all the spoil, and all the prey, both of man and of beast. 12 And they brought the captives, and the prey, and the spoil, unto Moses, and unto Eleazar the priest, and unto the congregation of the children of Israel, unto the camp at the plains of Moab, which are by the Jordan at Jericho.

13 And Moses, and Eleazar the priest, and all the princes of the congregation, went forth to meet them without the camp. 14 And Moses was wroth with the officers of the host, the captains of thousands and the captains of hundreds, which came from the service of the war. 15 And Moses said unto them, Have ye saved all the women alive? 16 Behold, these caused the children of Israel, through the counsel of Balaam, to commit trespass against the LORD in the matter of Peor, and so the plague was among the congregation of the LORD. 17 Now therefore kill every male among the little ones, and kill every woman that hath known man by lying with him. 18 But all the women children, that have not known man by lying with him, keep alive for yourselves. 19 And encamp ye without the camp seven

10. *their encampments.* A.V. *goodly castles.* The use of this word (טִירָה) is a little vague, its root (טוּר *ṭūr*) has the meaning *enclosure* (cf. DAR = bond, cord), and so it may be applied to an encampment as here (Gen. xxv. 16 &c.). The corresponding word in Syr. means *sheepfolds.*

13–18. Moses, like Samuel on the return of Saul from the slaughter of Amalek, insists on further destruction still.

13. *without the camp.* The warriors, because blood was upon them, were unclean.

15. *the women.* The Amalekite women fell in the original massacre (1 S. xv. 3).

16. *through the counsel of Balaam.* The original story (xxv. 1 ff.) knows nothing of any such counsel, the fact that it immediately follows the departure of Balaam may have led to the inference that he inspired the plan (see above p. 150).

17. This *v.* is very similar to Jud. xxi. 11 (see on *v.* 5 above)[1].

18. *for yourselves.* Later Jewish thought was strongly opposed to mixed marriages, which makes this provision a difficulty for those who

---

[1] The Heb. idiomatic use of יָדַע together with לְמִשְׁכַּב זָכָר is found in the Code of Hammurabi § 130 *zi-ka-ra-am la i-du-u-ma*: see Cook *Laws of Moses &c.* p. 101.

days: whosoever hath killed any person, and whosoever hath touched any slain, purify yourselves on the third day and on the seventh day, ye and your captives. 20 And as to every garment, and all that is made of skin, and all work of goats' *hair*, and all things made of wood, ye shall purify yourselves. 21 And Eleazar the priest said unto the men of war which went to the battle, This is the statute of the law which the LORD hath commanded Moses: 22 howbeit the gold, and the silver, the brass, the iron, the tin, and the lead, 23 every thing that may abide the fire, ye shall make to go through the fire, and it shall be clean; nevertheless it shall be purified with the water of [1]separation: and all that abideth not the fire ye shall make to go through the water. 24 And ye shall wash your clothes on the seventh day, and ye shall be clean, and afterward ye shall come into the camp. P^s

25 And the LORD spake unto Moses, saying, 26 Take the sum

[1] Or, *impurity*

date the passage late. On the other hand it "is in entire accord with the views and practice of the husband of Zipporah" (Wiener *Essays* p. 170).

19–24. The warriors and their belongings are to be purified. We must not imagine that there is here any recognition of the theory that the taking of life, even in a just cause, is of the nature of sin; those who have touched the slain are in exactly the same position as their slayers. For fuller details as to the question of uncleanness through the dead see on xix. above, also Frazer *Taboo* pp. 165 ff., Farnell *Evolution of Religion* p. 94.

19. *purify*: lit. *unsin* as in viii. 21 where see note.

22. *brass.* Heb. *nehōsheth.* *Copper* would be a more accurate rendering.

iron. Heb. *barzel* cf. Ass. *parzillu* perhaps borrowed from Sum. BAR-GAL: see Hommel *ZDMG* XLV. p. 340. The final letter of the Hebrew root is probably an affirmative (*G-K*[28] § 85). The original *barza* is thus akin to Latin *ferrum* (= *fersum*).

tin. Heb. *bĕdīl.* As with the Greeks and the Romans *tin* was not sharply distinguished from *lead.*

lead (Heb. *'ōphereth*) is seldom referred to in O.T., Jer. vi. 29 is one instance.

23. *fire...water.* In *'Aboda Zara* v. 12 still narrower distinctions are to be observed, as certain objects are not merely to be washed, but washed with hot water. Jewish tradition saw in this *v.* a baptism by fire (cf. Mt. iii. 11), by which even Jehovah Himself was purified after burying Moses: see Edersheim *Life and Times &c.* II. p. 16.

25–54. The spoil of the Midianites is divided between those who had

of the prey that was taken, both of man and of beast, thou, and Eleazar the priest, and the heads of the fathers' *houses* of the congregation: 27 and divide the prey into two parts; between the men skilled in war, that went out to battle, and all the congregation: 28 and levy a tribute unto the LORD of the men of war that went out to battle: one soul of five hundred, *both* of the persons, and of the beeves, and of the asses, and of the flocks: 29 take it of their half, and give it unto Eleazar the priest, for the LORD's heave offering. 30 And of the children of Israel's half, thou shalt take one drawn out of every fifty, of the persons, of the beeves, of the asses, and of the flocks, *even* of all the cattle, and give them unto the Levites, which keep the charge of the tabernacle of the LORD. 31 And Moses and Eleazar the priest did as the LORD commanded Moses. 32 Now the prey, over and above the booty which the men of war took, was six hundred thousand and seventy thousand and five thousand sheep, 33 and threescore and twelve thousand beeves, 34 and threescore and one thousand asses, 35 and thirty and two thousand persons in all, of the women that had not known man by lying with him. 36 And the half, which was the portion of them that went out to war, was in number three hundred thousand and thirty thousand and seven thousand and five hundred sheep: 37 and the LORD's tribute of the sheep was six hundred and threescore and fifteen. 38 And the beeves were thirty and six thousand; of which the LORD's tribute was threescore and twelve. 39 And the asses were thirty thousand and five hundred; of which the LORD's tribute was threescore and

*P*s

taken part in the battle and those who remained in the camp. The bringing of all the booty into a common stock is an important disciplinary measure, and as such was practised by the ancient Franks and other warlike tribes. Muhammed also regulated the division of booty (Koran viii. 1, 42) amongst his followers: see further Muir, *Mahomet*[3] pp. 221 f. The origin of the present passage is thought to be David's ruling after the defeat of the Amalekites recorded in 1 S. xxx. 24 f.

28. *a tribute.* The word occurs in this ch. only in O.T. The cognate word is found in Aram., and in particular, in the late Palmyrene Fiscal Inscription where its Greek equivalent is τέλος.

the beeves. Cf. Shakespeare *Merchant of Venice* I. iii. 166 ff.:

"A pound of man's flesh, taken from a man,
Is not so estimable, profitable neither,
As flesh of muttons, *beefs*, or goats."

one. 40 And the persons were sixteen thousand; of whom the LORD's tribute was thirty and two persons. 41 And Moses gave the tribute, which was the LORD's heave offering, unto Eleazar the priest, as the LORD commanded Moses. 42 And of the children of Israel's half, which Moses divided off from the men that warred, 43 (now the congregation's half was three hundred thousand and thirty thousand, seven thousand and five hundred sheep, 44 and thirty and six thousand beeves, 45 and thirty thousand and five hundred asses, 46 and sixteen thousand persons;) 47 even of the children of Israel's half, Moses took one drawn out of every fifty, both of man and of beast, and gave them unto the Levites, which kept the charge of the tabernacle of the LORD; as the LORD commanded Moses. 48 And the officers which were over the thousands of the host, the captains of thousands, and the captains of hundreds, came near unto Moses: 49 and they said unto Moses, Thy servants have taken the sum of the men of war which are under our charge, and there lacketh not one man of us. 50 And we have brought the LORD's oblation, what every man hath gotten, of jewels of gold, ankle chains, and bracelets, signet-rings, earrings, and [1]armlets, to make atonement for our souls before the LORD. *P*[s]

[1] Or, *necklaces*

40. *thirty and two persons.* What was their fate; death or slavery in the service of the tabernacle?

49. *not one man.* This circumstance in itself would not reduce the whole story to legend since the attack would be a surprise and if successful might be carried out without loss to the victors. Motley repeatedly remarks on the amazing disproportion of the losses of the Spaniards and their opponents during the fighting in the Netherlands: see *The Rise of the Dutch Republic* (passim).

50. This description agrees with that in Jud. vi. 5, viii. 24 ff. The Bedawin of the present day are still fond of jewels and other finery.

jewels of gold. This rendering is not quite exact: *vessels* or *objects* being nearer the original: cf. however Gen. xxiv. 53; Ex. iii. 22 &c.

ankle chains. Here and 2 S. i. 10[1]. Probably an ornament for the arm is meant according to Gray.

to make atonement. After a census such an atonement was considered necessary: cf. *v.* 49 and Introd. to ch. i.

---

[1] In both passages M.T. reads אצעדה (without the article): Wellhausen, followed by Driver, reads in 2 S. i. 10 וְהַצְּעָדָה (cf. Is. iii. 20). The same emendation should be made here also.

51 And Moses and Eleazar the priest took the gold of them, even all wrought jewels. 52 And all the gold of the heave offering that they offered up to the LORD, of the captains of thousands, and of the captains of hundreds, was sixteen thousand seven hundred and fifty skekels. 53 ([1]*For* the men of war had taken booty, every man for himself.) 54 And Moses and Eleazar the priest took the gold of the captains of thousands and of hundreds, and brought it into the tent of meeting, for a memorial for the children of Israel before the LORD. P^s

[1] See ver. 32.

CHAPTERS XXXII.—XXXVI.

MISCELLANEOUS TOPOGRAPHICAL NARRATIVES.

The closing chh. of Num. are concerned with questions of topography; with the route taken by the people on their way from Egypt to the borders of Canaan, and with the settlement of the various tribes, some on the East of Jordan, the others on the West. Except for a few fragments the whole of this division comes from the source known as P, and probably from its later contributors (see Introd. pp. xxxvi ff.).

The East Jordan Territories. xxxii.
The journeyings from Egypt to Moab. xxxiii.
The West Jordan Territories. xxxiv.
The Levitical cities. xxxv.
The daughters of Zelophehad. xxxvi.

CHAPTER XXXII.

The East Jordan Territories.

The tradition that Reuben, Gad, and part of Manasseh, settled on the East side of Jordan before the entry into Canaan is continually referred to (e.g. Dt. iii. 12 f., iv. 43, xxix. 8; Jos. xii. 6, xiii. 29, 31, xiv. 3, xviii. 7). In this ch., however, the reference to the half tribe of Manasseh seems to be an interpolation, and if the mention of them in *v.* 33 be cut out, there is a story of the settlement of Reuben and Gad only, to which *vv.* 39–42 form an appendix relating the conquest of Gilead by the children of Machir. This last story would fit in very well with Jos. xvii. 14 ff., which Budde regards as referring to the Hill-country of Gilead (*Richter u. Samuel* pp. 32 ff.). In this case the original settlers East of Jordan were Reuben and Gad only, the half tribe of Manasseh or Machir conquered their portion from the West, being too large for the territory assigned to them by Joshua. See further *IN* pp. 516 ff.

(*a*) *The request of Reuben and Gad.* 1–5.
(*b*) *Moses' indignation.* 6–15.
(*c*) *The promise of Reuben and Gad.* 16–19.
(*d*) *The conditions imposed by Moses.* 20–38.
(*e*) *Machir conquers Gilead.* 39–42.

XXXII. 1 Now the children of Reuben and the children of *JED* Gad had a very great multitude of cattle: and when they saw the land of Jazer, and the land of Gilead, that, behold, the place was a place for cattle; 2 the children of Gad and the children of Reuben came and spake unto Moses, and to Eleazar the priest, and unto the princes of the congregation, saying, 3 Ataroth, and Dibon, and Jazer, and [1]Nimrah, and Heshbon, and Elealeh, and [2]Sebam, and Nebo, and [3]Beon, 4 the land which the LORD smote before the congregation of Israel, is a land for cattle, and thy servants have cattle. 5 And they said, If we have found grace in thy sight, let this land be given unto thy servants for a possession; bring us not over Jordan. 6 And

[1] In ver. 36, *Beth-nimrah.* [2] In ver. 38, *Sibmah.*
[3] In ver. 38, *Baal-meon.*

XXXII. 1–5. Reuben and Gad come to Moses with the request that they may be allowed to settle East of Jordan, since the country is well suited to their numerous flocks. The narrative has as its basis the recognition that the East Jordan tribes were different from those on the West, though why they should have accumulated cattle more than the other tribes in the desert we are not informed. The conditions of a later time are reflected back into the past.

1. *Reuben.* There are traces of this tribe having been originally on the West side of Jordan, though they are not conclusive: see Burney *Schweich Lectures* pp. 50 f. and *Enc. Bib.*

Gad. See *Enc. Bib.* for the origin of this tribe.

very great multitude. The Heb. phrase is found here, Ex. i. 9; Dt. vii. 1, ix. 14, only in Pent.

the land of Jazer. This description is unique, elsewhere we hear of the town of this name: see on xxi. 24.

the land of Gilead. This phrase is used with very different content: (*a*) for the whole of Israel, East of Jordan (Dt. iii. 12 f.; Jos. xii. 2, 5, xiii. 31); (*b*) for the territory north of the Jabbok (*vv.* 39 f.; Jos. xvii. 1); (*c*) for the territory south of the Jabbok (here and *v.* 29 &c.). The northern and southern parts of Gilead differ in character, the former being agricultural, the latter pastoral (cf. G. A. Smith *Hist. Geog.* XXVII.).

3. For notes on the towns here mentioned see on *vv.* 34 ff.

Beon. In the list in *v.* 38 Baal-meon appears. In Jub. xxix. 10 there is mention of Beon in Gilead which Charles (*Apoc. and Pseud.* II. p. 57) also identifies with the Baean (Βαιάν) in 1 Macc. v. 4 f.: but as this latter town is in Idumaea (Blau identifies it with *Bajjan* east of Hebron) this can hardly be correct.

6–15. The proposal of the two tribes is received by Moses with indignation, and he warns them of the consequences of discouraging Israel by the example of the spies.

Moses said unto the children of Gad and to the children of *JEDP* Reuben, Shall your brethren go to the war, and shall ye sit here? 7 And wherefore discourage ye the heart of the children of Israel from going over into the land which the LORD hath given them? 8 Thus did your fathers, when I sent them from Kadesh-barnea to see the land. 9 For when they went up unto the valley of Eshcol, and saw the land, they discouraged the heart of the children of Israel, that they should not go into the land which the LORD had given them. 10 And the LORD's anger was kindled in that day, and he sware, saying, 11 Surely none of the men that came up out of Egypt, from twenty years old and upward, shall see the land which I sware unto Abraham, unto Isaac, and unto Jacob; because they have not wholly followed me: 12 save Caleb the son of Jephunneh the Kenizzite, and Joshua the son of Nun: because they have wholly followed the LORD. 13 And the LORD's anger was kindled against Israel, and he made them wander to and fro in the wilderness forty years, until all the generation, that had done evil in the sight of the LORD, was consumed. 14 And, behold, ye are risen up

6. *Gad...Reuben.* The order varies in Heb. cf. LXX.

sit still. The same accusation is made in the Song of Deborah against Reuben and Gilead (= Gad). Cf. Ps. lxxviii. 9 (the children of Ephraim).

7. *discourage.* Moses has to think of the effect of their conduct on the rest of Israel; he seems to have feared that they might all wish to settle down where they were and refuse to enter Canaan.

8 ff. These *vv.* are based on the spy narratives in a form similar to that which they have reached in xiii.–xiv., elements from both JE and P being included.

8. *your fathers.* Not merely the ancestors of the two tribes.

Kadesh-barnea. Cf. xiii. 26 *b* (JE). The form is Deuteronomic.

9. *the valley of Eshcol.* Cf. xiii. 23 *a* (JE).

11. *I sware unto Abraham &c.* Characteristic of D: see Driver *Deut.* p. lxxix. No. 13.

12. *Caleb...the Kenizzite.* So named in Jos. xiv. 6, 14 (D). The word *Kenizzite* is spelt in a variety of ways (A.V. *Kenezite*), but is derived from Kenaz, a tribe with Edomite connexions (Gen. xxxvi. 11, 15, 42; 1 Chr. i. 36, 52). P regards Caleb as a member of the tribe of Judah (see on xiii. 6).

Joshua. The mention of Joshua is a sign of P.

13. *all the generation.* Cf. Ex. i. 6. A process ever going on unobserved, just as in a great wood the old trees die off and the saplings push up into their place.

in your fathers' stead, an increase of sinful men, to augment *JED* yet the fierce anger of the LORD toward Israel. 15 For if ye turn away from after him, he will yet again leave them in the wilderness; and ye shall destroy all this people. 16 And they came near unto him, and said, We will build sheepfolds here for our cattle, and cities for our little ones: 17 but we ourselves will be ready armed to go before the children of Israel, until we have brought them unto their place: and our little ones shall dwell in the fenced cities because of the inhabitants of the land. 18 We will not return unto our houses, until the children of Israel have inherited every man his inheritance. 19 For we will not inherit with them on the other side Jordan, and forward; because our inheritance is fallen to us on this side Jordan eastward. 20 And Moses said unto them, If ye will do this thing; if ye will arm yourselves to go before the LORD to the war, 21 and every armed man of you will pass over Jordan before the

14. *an increase of sinful men.* The Heb. word for *increase* is found here only, though the root from which it comes is of course very common. *BDB* regard the expression as contemptuous and render *brood.*

15. *all this people.* Cf. Jos. xxii. 18 where the building of an altar by these same tribes on their return home is regarded as likely to stir up God's wrath against the whole people.

16–19. Reuben and Gad promise to go before the people to the conquest of Canaan. Their families and cattle will be left in the new settlements. The difficulty of this promise lies in the fact that the new cities and sheepfolds would have required a very strong guard to protect them from the attacks of neighbouring tribes.

16. *sheepfolds.* Formed either from stakes planted in the ground, or of stones heaped upon one another (see Nowack *Heb. Arch.* I. p. 226). The word rendered *sheepfolds* in Jud. v. 16 is different in Heb., and in fact its real meaning can only be guessed at.

17. *ready armed.* The Heb. is awkward and a slight emendation first suggested by Knobel חֲמֻשִׁים for חֻשִׁים justifies the E.VV. rendering.

18 f. The fulfilment of this contract seems to be referred to in Dt. xxxiii. 21 where Gad after obtaining his 'first part' comes 'with the heads of the people.'

19. *the other side...this side.* The same Heb. word in each case is used: it really means *beyond*, the speaker in the latter half of *v.* places himself on the West of Jordan and looks back.

20–38. Moses accepts the offer of the two tribes, and charges Eleazar and Joshua to see that it is carried out. The two tribes thereupon build cities for their possessions.

21. *before the LORD.* Jehovah Himself takes part in the war: cf. xxi. 14; Jud. v. 23.

LORD, until he hath driven out his enemies from before him, *JEDP*
22 and the land be subdued before the LORD: then afterward ye shall return, and be guiltless towards the LORD, and towards Israel; and this land shall be unto you for a possession before the LORD. 23 But if ye will not do so, behold, ye have sinned against the LORD: and be sure your sin will find you out. 24 Build you cities for your little ones, and folds for your sheep; and do that which hath proceeded out of your mouth. 25 And the children of Gad and the children of Reuben spake unto Moses, saying, Thy servants will do as my lord commandeth. 26 Our little ones, our wives, our flocks, and all our cattle, shall be there in the cities of Gilead: 27 but thy servants will pass over, every man that is armed for war, before the LORD to battle, as my lord saith.

28 So Moses gave charge concerning them to Eleazar the priest, and to Joshua the son of Nun, and to the heads of the fathers' *houses* of the tribes of the children of Israel. 29 And Moses said unto them, If the children of Gad and the children of Reuben will pass with you over Jordan, every man that is armed to battle, before the LORD, and the land shall be subdued before you; then ye shall give them the land of Gilead for a possession: 30 but if they will not pass over with you armed, they shall have possessions among you in the land of Canaan. 31 And the children of Gad and the children of Reuben answered, saying, As the LORD hath said unto thy servants, so will we do. 32 We will pass over armed before the LORD into the land of Canaan, and the possession of our inheritance *shall remain* with us beyond Jordan. 33 And Moses gave unto them, even to the children of Gad, and to the children of Reuben, and unto the half tribe of Manasseh the son of Joseph, the kingdom

driven out. A phrase characteristic of D: see Driver *Deut.* p. lxxix. No. 10.

22. *guiltless.* Better *exempt* (cf. 1 K. xv. 22), *free from obligation.*

23. *be sure your sin &c.* The origin of the popular saying. Sin is conceived of as personal: cf. Gen. iv. 7 and the Νέμεσις of the Greeks.

24. *proceeded.* See on xxx. 2.

28. *Moses gave charge.* This was necessary because he himself was not to cross Jordan.

33. *the half tribe of Manasseh.* In view of the absence of any mention of Manasseh in the rest of the narrative this reference must be regarded as the work of a harmoniser.

of Sihon king of the Amorites, and the kingdom of Og king of *JEL*
Bashan, the land, according to the cities thereof with *their* borders, even the cities of the land round about. 34 And the children of Gad built Dibon, and Ataroth, and Aroer; 35 and Atroth-shophan, and Jazer, and Jogbehah; 36 and Beth-nimrah,

the kingdom of Sihon. See on xxi. 21 ff.

the kingdom of Og. See on xxi. 33 ff.

34–38. The list of cities here includes those contained in *v.* 3 with a few alterations. A still longer list of cities belonging to Gad and Reuben is to be found in Jos. xiii. 15 ff., where several important differences occur (see the following notes). Several of the cities below came into the possession of Moab (see the Moabite stone and Jer. xlviii. with the present writer's notes)[1].

34. *Dibon.* Here belonging to Gad; in Jos. xiii. 17 to Reuben; in the Moabite stone; xxi. 30; Is. xv. 2; Jer. xlviii. 18, 22; to Moab. This constant change of possessors may quite well be historical, at any rate as between Moab and Israel. The modern name is *Dhîbân*, 4 miles north of the Arnon.

Ataroth. Now *'Aṭṭârûs* some 7½ miles north of *Dhîbân* (see Tristram *Moab* pp. 271 ff.). The name is used of several other places, and is said to mean *crowns*, though Wellhausen renders *protected places* (*De Gentibus &c.* p. 15). According to the Moabite stone the men of Gad had held the town from ancient times, though it had been 'built' in the time of the monarchy; it was the seat apparently of the worship of a god Daudoh (*ll.* 10 ff.).

Aroer. A city of this name is found in Judah (1 S. xxx. 28), and in addition there is also the mysterious *Aroer* of Jos. xiii. 25 and Jud. xi. 33, situated in Ammon. As Jos. xiii. 16 gives an *Aroer* in the south to Reuben, the writer would seem to identify the city of the present passage with this latter (my note on Jer. xlviii. 19 accepted this identification). The position of *Aroer* in apparent close connexion with Dibon and Ataroth makes it almost certain that the Moabite city is here referred to. This city is now known as *'Ara'ir* and is situated about 3 miles south of *Dhîbân* close to and above the Arnon: see Burckhardt *Syria* p. 372, von Alois Musil *Arabia Petraea* p. 130.

35. *Atroth-shophan.* This site is unknown. *Shophan* may possibly be the same as the unknown שרן (SRN) of the Moabite stone (*l.* 13), as in the old characters ר (R) and פ (P) might easily be confused.

Jazer. See on xxi. 24.

Jogbehah. To be identified with *Khirbet el-Gubeihât* or *'Ajbêhât* about 9 miles due east of *es-Salṭ*: the name occurs elsewhere only in Jud. viii. 11.

36. *Beth-nimrah.* Now *Tell Nimrīn* on the *Wādy Nimrīn* about 6 miles East of the Jordan, and 8 miles north of the Dead Sea.

---

[1] The two excellent maps in *Enc. Bib.* illustrating the articles Moab and Gilead should be consulted.

and Beth-haran: fenced cities, and folds for sheep. 37 And the *JEDP* children of Reuben built Heshbon, and Elealeh, and Kiriathaim; 38 and Nebo, and Baal-meon, (their names being changed,) and

Beth-haran. In Jos. xiii. 27 spelt *Beth-haram.* Probably *Tell er-Rameh* about 6 miles south of Beth-nimrah.

folds for sheep. Mesha was a sheepmaster (2 K. iii. 4), and the country here said to belong to Gad was afterwards the territory of Moab. "Moab with its extensive grass-covered uplands is even now an essentially sheep-breeding country." Palmer *Desert of the Exodus* p. 497.

37. *Heshbon.* This city seems to have changed hands more even than the others in the present passage: in xxi. 25 it is an Amorite city, having been taken from Moab, here and in Jos. xiii. 17 it belongs to Reuben, in Jos. xxi. 39 to Gad, in Is. xv. 4, xvi. 9; Jer. xlviii. 2, to Moab, and finally in Jer. xlix. 3 to Ammon (see however the present writer's note *ad loc.*). *Heshbon* (modern *Ḥesbân*) was built on two hills about 3000 ft. above sea-level, the site is some 13 miles east of the northern extremity of the Dead Sea.

Elealeh. This town, the modern *el-ʿĀl,* was situated not far from Heshbon, and is never mentioned without it: *v.* 3; Is. xv. 4, xvi. 9; Jer. xlviii. 34.

Kiriathaim. The identification is somewhat uncertain, but it is usually regarded as being the modern *Kureyat* some 6 miles east of *Mkaur,* the site of Machaerus. It appears as *Ḳiryathēn* in the Moabite stone.

38. *Nebo.* Four distinct meanings are attached to this name in O.T. (*a*) the Babylonian deity (Is. xlvi. 1: where LXX ℵAQ have the interesting reading Δαγών); (*b*) the mountain: Dt. xxxii. 49 *b* &c.; (*c*) here and in Jer. xlviii. 1 an East Jordan city; (*d*) a city of Judah 'the other Nebo' mentioned in Neh. vii. 33; Ezra ii. 29. The name probably testifies, in each case, to some connexion with the worship of Nebo (i.e. *Nabû* the god of Borsippa), a testimony to the widespread influence of Babylonian religion[1]; though strangely enough when Mesha captured *Nebo* from Israel it was apparently a sanctuary of Jehovah with sacred vessels. This city according to Buhl (*Alt. Paläst. Geog.* pp. 266 f.) was on or near Mt. Nebo.

Baal-meon is the modern *Maʿin* situated about 5 miles south-west of Medeba. There are large ruins on the site which suggest that it must have been a place of considerable importance. In Jer. xlviii. 23 it is called *Beth-meon*; the full form was perhaps *Beth Baal Meon* as in Jos. xiii. 17 and the Moabite stone *l.* 30 (cf. *l.* 9 *Baal Meon*).

their names being changed. Better *to be changed in name.* A gloss directing the attention of the reader (cf. Mk. xiii. 14) to the necessity of not pronouncing the names of two heathen deities, *Nebo* and *Baal.*

---

[1] The connexion with the deity is not quite certain, as the name may come from an Arabic word = *the height* (cf. *NSI* p. 12); Jeremias, however, not only accepts it, but would also connect the priestly city of Nob with *Nabu* (*ATLAO* p. 280). Clay thinks that *Nebo* was originally an Amorite deity (*Origin of Biblical Traditions* p. 52).

Sibmah: and gave other names unto the cities which they builded. 39 And the children of Machir the son of Manasseh went to Gilead, and took it, and dispossessed the Amorites which were therein. 40 And Moses gave Gilead unto Machir the son of Manasseh; and he dwelt therein. 41 And Jair the son of Manasseh went and took the towns thereof, and called them *JEI*

Sibmah. According to Conder (*PEFQS* (1882) p. 9) to be identified with the modern *Sūmia,* a little to the west of Heshbon, whose ruins contain remains of wine-presses (cf. 'vine of Sibmah': Jer. xlviii. 32).

gave other names. This is a paraphrase, or rather an interpretation of the original, which runs *they called with names the names of.*

they builded. That is 're-built' 1 K. ix. 18; 2 Chr. xi. 6; Dan. iv. 27; cf. Moabite stone for the same usage, and in non-Semitic usage Pliny *Hist. Nat.* VI. xiv. 17 (of Ecbatana), xxvii. 31 (of Susa).

39–42. The children of Machir drive out the Amorites from Gilead. This fragment is quite evidently out of its context, since we are told nothing of what preceded the action of the children of Machir, and there is nothing in the preceding part of the ch. to link on to this section, save only the reference *v.* 33, which is itself in all probability a late addition. Budde thinks that the narrative in Jos. xvii. 14 ff. is the introduction to this fragment which has been ante-dated by an editor (*Richter u. Samuel* pp. 32 ff.), and his suggestion is accepted by Burney *Schweich Lectures* pp. 20 f., *Judges* pp. 47 ff.

39. *Machir.* See xxvi. 29 with note.

Gilead. See on *v.* 1. The northern part only is referred to. In Jos. xvii. 18 the *hill-country* is thought to refer to the hill-country of Gilead: in *v.* 1 of the same ch. Machir is said to be the father of Gilead, as in Num. xxvi. 29.

the Amorites. See xiii. 29 with note. The Amorite kingdom of Sihon stretching up to the Jabbok was conquered at an earlier period (see xxi. 24), the country north of the Jabbok is said however to belong to Ammon. Kittel suggests reading *the Syrians* (i.e. הארמי for האמרי).

40. This *v.* does not fit into its context and interrupts the sequence between *vv.* 39 and 41. It appears to be connected with Dt. iii. 15.

41. *Jair the son of Manasseh.* According to 1 Chr. ii. 21 ff. *Jair* was the son of Segub of the tribe of Judah, but his mother was a daughter of Machir. The explanation of this genealogical curiosity has been lost: cf. Jair the judge in Jud. x. 3 f. where see Moore. The Jairus of Mk. v. 22 ff.; Lk. viii. 41 ff. is possibly connected. The name afterwards lost favour as it is not found, according to Edersheim (*Life and Times &c.* I. p. 617), in Rabbinic literature till after the Middle Ages.

towns thereof. Lit. *their* towns, a reference back to the Amorites (though this is collective in the Heb.). The numbers of these towns at different periods varied considerably: in Jos. xiii. 30; 1 K. iv. 13 it is given as sixty, in Jud. x. 3 f. as thirty, in 1 Chr. ii. 22 as twenty-three (cf. however sixty in *v.* 23).

[1]Havvoth-jair. 42 And Nobah went and took Kenath, and the *JEDP*
[2]villages thereof, and called it Nobah, after his own name.

[1] That is, *The towns of Jair.* [2] Heb. *daughters.*

Havvoth-jair. Havvoth is probably connected with the Arabic *ḥiwâ'* "a cluster of tents": the Hivites may have got their name from living in such settlements.

42. *Nobah.* A chieftain. *Nobah* appears frequently in the Samaritan book of Joshua, and in xii. 24 he is appointed ruler over the East-Jordan tribes. In Jud. viii. 11 a place with the name of *Nobah* occurs; this was possibly an earlier seat of the clan (Dillmann, and Stade *Gesch. des Volkes Israel* I. p. 149), as it can hardly be the place named here.

Kenath. Probably the modern *el-Ḳanawāt* on the north-west slopes of the Hauran. Moore (*Judges* p. 222), following Dillmann, rejects the placing of *Havvoth-jair* in Bashan as erroneous, and would regard the site of *Kenath* as that of Nobah in Jud. viii. 11, in which case the identification with *el-Ḳanawāt* would have to be given up.

Chapter XXXIII.

The journeyings from Egypt to Moab.

This itinerary, which claims to have been compiled by Moses (see on *v.* 2), consists of forty-two stages, beginning with Rameses in Egypt and ending on the steppes of Moab. The same number of names is found in our Lord's genealogy in Mt. i. 1–17; though it is not possible in the present passage to divide up the stages, according to any rational system, into three sets of fourteen each, as is done in the gospel.

The names included in the list are not peculiar to any one of the documents from which the present Pentateuch was compiled—a fact which is held by some conservative critics (e.g. Green *The Higher Criticism of the Pent.* p. 38) to disprove the whole theory—but some come from P, and some from JE: in addition, a large number are entirely unknown[1]. A further peculiarity should be noticed; certain well-known places such as Massah, Meribah, and Taberah, are omitted; perhaps because included under other names, or possibly because of the unfortunate incidents connected with them.

---

[1] In connexion with the large number of unidentified sites the following passage from Miss G. Lowthian Bell's *Syria: the Desert and the Sown* is not without interest: "Though we were riding through plains which were quite deserted and to the casual observer almost featureless, we seldom travelled for more than a mile without reaching a spot that had a name. In listening to Arab talk you are struck by this abundant nomenclature. If you ask where a certain sheikh has pitched his tents you will at once be given an exact answer. The map is blank, and when you reach the encampment the landscape is blank also. A rise in the ground, a big stone, a vestige of ruin, not to speak of every possible hollow in which there may be water either in winter or in summer, these are marks sufficiently distinguishing to the nomad eye. Ride with an Arab and you shall realise why the pre-Mohammadan poems are so full of names, and also how vain a labour it would be to attempt to assign a definite spot to the greater number of them, for the same name recurs hundreds of times" (p. 49).

The general direction of the line of march can be traced; but, as most of the sites have not been located, any certainty in detail is not possible[1]. The list was probably based upon oral, or even written, traditions of the supposed route of the Exodus, supplemented by the compiler's knowledge of the conditions of his own day. The date of the composition is almost certainly very late: Guthe attributes it to a learned Jew of Jerusalem who lived about the end of the fifth century B.C.; but whether such exactitude is possible or not we have no means of deciding.

(*a*) *Introductory section.* 1–4.
(*b*) *From Egypt to Sinai.* 5–15.
(*c*) *The wanderings in the wilderness.* 16–36.
(*d*) *From Kadesh to Moab.* 37–49.
(*e*) *The fate of Canaan.* 50–56.

XXXIII. 1 These are the [1]journeys of the children of Israel, [2]when they went forth out of the land of Egypt by their hosts under the hand of Moses and Aaron. 2 And Moses wrote their goings out according to their journeys by the commandment of the LORD: and these are their journeys according to their goings out. 3 And they journeyed from Rameses in the first month, on the fifteenth day of the first month; on the morrow after the passover the children of Israel went out with an high hand *Ps*

[1] Or, *stages* [2] Or, *by which*

XXXIII. 1–4. This introductory section gives the date and the circumstances of the setting forth from Egypt: it also records that Moses himself was the compiler of the list[2].

1. *the journeys.* The reading of mg. *stages* is better, since it more nearly represents the Heb. lit. *pluckings up* i.e. the taking up of the tent-pegs before beginning the march.

by their hosts. A regular organisation is implied.

2. *Moses wrote.* The mention of Moses' authorship of a specific passage cannot but suggest that other portions of the Pent. are not by him, save such as are definitely attributed to him—see Ex. xvii. 14, xxiv. 4, xxxiv. 28 (JE); Dt. xxxi. 9, 22, 24 (D). Dillmann would find in such references the use of a written source.

3. *Rameses.* Cf. Ex. xii. 37. According to Flinders Petrie the site is to be found in the modern *Tell er-Retabeh* some 20 miles east of Ismailiyeh: see the passage from *Hyksos and Israelite cities* quoted in the Addenda to McNeile's *Exodus*.

an high hand. See xv. 30.

---

[1] See discussion by M. J. Lagrange *Rev. bibl.* IX. pp. 63 ff., 273 ff., 443 ff.; McNeile *Exodus* pp. xciv ff.; and Furrer 'Lager, Lagerstätten' in Riehm's *Bibl. Wörterbuch*[2].

[2] The date of the Exodus is still a matter of dispute. Some recent scholars such as Hall *The People and the Book* p. 3, Budge *Egypt* p. 110, and A. Gardiner *Journal Eg. Arch.* x. pp. 87 ff. place it as early as the beginning of the sixteenth century at the time of the Hyksos defeat and expulsion. Gardiner thinks that the Hebrews went out by the Gate of Pelusium and then along by Lake Serbonis. See further J. W. Jack *The Date of the Exodus*.

in the sight of all the Egyptians, 4 while the Egyptians were *P*s burying all their firstborn, which the LORD had smitten among them: upon their gods also the LORD executed judgements. 5 And the children of Israel journeyed from Rameses, and pitched in Succoth. 6 And they journeyed from Succoth, and pitched in Etham, which is in the edge of the wilderness. 7 And they journeyed from Etham, and turned back unto Pi-hahiroth, which is before Baal-zephon: and they pitched before Migdol. 8 And they journeyed from before Hahiroth, and passed through the midst of the sea into the wilderness: and they went three days' journey in the wilderness of Etham, and pitched in Marah. 9 And they journeyed from Marah, and came unto Elim: and in Elim were twelve springs of water, and threescore and ten

4. *upon their gods.* Cf. Ex. xii. 12; Is. xix. 1; Jer. xliii. 12.

5–15. This section, which is parallel to Ex. xii. 37–xix. 2, contains the names of stations between the starting point and the wilderness of Sinai. With the exception of Dophkah and Alush all the places named are well known.

5. *Succoth.* Called *Thku*(*t*) in Egyptian inscriptions (see W. Max Müller *As. u. Eur.* p. 20) and probably the same place as Pithom, the modern *Tell el-Maskhuta*: see Naville *Pithom*4 pp. 6 f. and McNeile *Exodus* p. xciv[1].

6. *Etham.* LXX Βουθαν includes the Egyptian article: contrast Ὀθαμ in Ex. xii. 20. Behind this name lies an Egyptian word *Khetem* signifying *a fortified place*, and since there were many such in the neighbourhood of the frontier, to identify it with any one of them is difficult: *Selle* (*Tell Abu-Sefeh*), which appears in Roman itineraries, is most favoured.

7. *Pi-hahiroth...Baal-zephon...Migdol.* The sites of these places, which all appear in Ex. xiv. 2, have not been identified. The two latter words are Semitic, the first Egyptian. See Driver *Exodus* pp. 122 f.

8. *from before Hahiroth.* Read *from Pi-hahiroth* with some Hebrew MSS. and most of the versions.

the wilderness of Etham. In Ex. xv. 22 *the wilderness of Shur* is mentioned, the present passage seems to define it more exactly as that part which was near to Etham. LXX omits *of Etham.*

Marah. Ex. xv. 23 ff. Another site about which there is much uncertainty.

9. *Elim.* Ex. xv. 27 ff. Heb. = Terebinths. Probably the same place as Elath, and Eloth (Dt. ii. 8; 2 K. xvi. 6).

---

[1] *Succoth* is usually said to mean *booths* from a root סכך = *weave*. Landersdorfer, however, points out that no parallel exists in other Semitic languages, and he suggests a connexion with Sumerian SUG = (1) *reedy* (2) *God's dwelling* (cf. Bab. *sukku*): see *Sum. Sprachgut im A.T.* p. 50. Incidentally this connexion would give a good meaning for סך in Ps. xlii. 5.

palm trees; and they pitched there. 10 And they journeyed *Ps* from Elim, and pitched by the Red Sea. 11 And they journeyed from the Red Sea, and pitched in the wilderness of Sin. 12 And they journeyed from the wilderness of Sin, and pitched in Dophkah. 13 And they journeyed from Dophkah, and pitched in Alush. 14 And they journeyed from Alush, and pitched in Rephidim, where was no water for the people to drink. 15 And they journeyed from Rephidim, and pitched in the wilderness of Sinai. 16 And they journeyed from the wilderness of Sinai, and pitched in Kibroth-hattaavah. 17 And they journeyed from Kibroth-hattaavah, and pitched in Hazeroth. 18 And they journeyed from Hazeroth, and pitched in Rithmah. 19 And they journeyed from Rithmah, and pitched in Rimmon-perez.

10. *by the Red Sea.* See on xiv. 25. There is no mention in Exodus of such a station. Palmer *Desert of the Exodus* pp. 274 f. suggests a suitable site for an encampment, but his suggestion is not convincing.

11. *the wilderness of Sin.* See on xiii. 21.

13. *Dophkah* (LXX Ῥαφακα)...*Alush* (LXX [B] Αἰλειμ, [AF] Αἰλους). Not mentioned elsewhere. The sites of these places are quite unknown: some attempts at identification have been made, but, as in the case of other sites, they depend on particular theories of the position of Sinai, and of the route taken by the Israelites: see Baentsch on the present passage, and Dillmann on Ex. xvii. 1.

14. *Rephidim.* Ex. xvii. 1, xix. 2: see McNeile *op. cit.* p. civ.

15. *the wilderness of Sinai.* Ex. xix. 2. The position of the wilderness here indicated will depend on the site of Sinai itself: see McNeile *op. cit.* pp. ci ff.

16–36. The great majority of the names in this section of the itinerary, which deals with the wanderings in the wilderness, are entirely unknown. Gray considers that they cannot be taken as indicating a route, but are "rather points scattered over a district of which ʽEẓion-geber and Ḳadesh may be taken as being respectively the southern and northern points."

16. *Kibroth-hattaavah.* See on xi. 34.

17. *Hazeroth.* See on xi. 35.

18–29. With the possible exception of *Libnah* (see on *v.* 20) none of the names here mentioned is found elsewhere.

18. *Rithmah.* This may be connected with *Wady Retemât* near to Kadesh: see Clay Trumbull *Ḳadesh-Barnea* pp. 150 ff. The plant *retem* which is very common in this locality may have given the name to the place.

19. *Rimmon-perez.* Combinations of place names with *perez* are not uncommon: cf. Perez-uzzah (2 S. vi. 8; 1 Chr. xiii. 11), and Baal-perazim (2 S. v. 20; 1 Chr. xiv. 11). The reference may be to the

20 And they journeyed from Rimmon-perez, and pitched in Libnah. 21 And they journeyed from Libnah, and pitched in Rissah. 22 And they journeyed from Rissah, and pitched in Kehelathah. 23 And they journeyed from Kehelathah, and pitched in mount Shepher. 24 And they journeyed from mount Shepher, and pitched in Haradah. 25 And they journeyed from Haradah, and pitched in Makheloth. 26 And they journeyed from Makheloth, and pitched in Tahath. 27 And they journeyed from Tahath, and pitched in Terah. 28 And they journeyed from Terah, and pitched in Mithkah. 29 And they journeyed from Mithkah, and pitched in Hashmonah. 30 And they jour- P^s

breaking forth of a fountain (cf. *HERE* II. p. 286 *a*). *Rimmon* may be derived from the Heb. for *pomegranate*, more probably it is the deity to whom reference is made: cf. En-rimmon (Neh. xi. 29)[1].

20. *Libnah.* May be a variant of *Laban* (Dt. i. 1). Its site is not known. A town of the name occurs in Jos. x. 29, xv. 42 &c.: cf. also *Lebonah* in Jud. xxi. 19. These names are derived from a root meaning *white*, as is Lebanon also, which would account for their frequency.

21. *Rissah.* Palmer suggests an identification with the *Rasa* of the Peutinger Tables; a place situated about 16 Roman miles from Ezion-geber.

22. *Kehelathah.* Lagrange connects with *Contellet Qureye* the *Gypsaria* of the Peutinger Tables: cf. Palmer *op. cit.* 341 f., 422.

23. *mount Shepher.* Hommel suggests a connexion with *Sephar*, the mountain of the east (Gen. x. 30). Possibly this mountain is to be identified with *Jebel Shuref*, to the south-west of Kadesh on the western borders of the wilderness of Sin.

24. *Haradah.* Palmer pointed out long ago that this name is etymologically the same as *Jebel ʻAradeh*, a mountain near the Gulf of Akaba (*op. cit.* pp. 314 f.).

25. *Makheloth.* The likeness of this word to *Kehelathah* (*v.* 22) suggests that they both represent the same place.

26. *Tahath* (LXX Κατααθ). Palmer identifies this with the *Wady Elt'hi* which runs between *Jebel ʻAradeh* and *ʻAin-Huderah.* Lagrange regards this place, and Terah in the following *v.*, as due to textual corruption.

28. *Mithkah.* The root from which this word is derived means *to become sweet*, and the verb is actually used in Ex. xv. 25 to describe the changing of the bitter waters of Marah.

29. *Hashmonah* (LXX Σελμωνα). Identified by Palmer with *Heshmon* in Jos. xv. 27 (*op. cit.* p. 509).

---

[1] It is possible that the Rimmon mentioned in Zech. xiv. 10 is Rimmon-perez, and not as is usually supposed En-rimmon.

neyed from Hashmonah, and pitched in Moseroth. 31 And they journeyed from Moseroth, and pitched in Bene-jaakan. 32 And they journeyed from Bene-jaakan, and pitched in Hor-haggidgad. 33 And they journeyed from Hor-haggidgad, and pitched in Jotbathah. 34 And they journeyed from Jotbathah, and pitched in Abronah. 35 And they journeyed from Abronah, and pitched in Ezion-geber. 36 And they journeyed from Ezion-geber, and pitched in the wilderness of Zin (the same is Kadesh). *P*[s]

30. *Moseroth.* According to Dt. x. 6, which reads Moserah, the scene of the death and burial of Aaron.

31. *Bene-jaakan.* In Dt. x. 6 *Beeroth Bene-jaakan* is mentioned as a station *before* Moserah, not, as here, *after* it. The Horite clan ‘Akan mentioned in Gen. xxxvi. 27 (= *Ja‘akan* in 1 Chr. i. 42) doubtless has some connexion with this place name.

32. *Hor-haggidgad.* Cf. *Gudgodah* in Dt. x. 7. LXX rendering τὸ ὄρος (Γαδγάδ) depends on a misreading of *Hor* the initial letter of which is ח (ḥ) not ה (h). Robinson's suggestion that the *Wady Ghudhāghidh*, south of *Contellet Qureye*, is meant, is not likely on etymological grounds. Furrer in Riehm's *Bibl. Wörterbuch*[2] suggests the *Wady Giddade* near the Gulf of Akaba.

33. *Jotbathah.* So in Dt. x. 7 which adds "a land of brooks of water." It may be the same place as the *Jotbah* mentioned in 2 K. xxi. 19. According to Reland *Pal.*[2] p. 397 a bishopric of Ἰωταβη in the neighbourhood of Gaza, Elusa, and Petra, is mentioned in the acts of the Council of Jerusalem in 536. I cannot, however, trace the name in the list of Sees taken from a MS. in the library of the Patriarchate of Jerusalem (given in Appendix D of Palmer *Desert of the Exodus*).

34. *Abronah.* This site is quite unknown.

35. *Ezion-geber.* Driver is disposed to accept Robinson's suggested identification of this place with *‘Ain-el-Ghudyan*, now situated about 15 miles north of the Gulf of Akaba, but originally on the sea itself which has here receded. Elsewhere *Ezion-geber* is mentioned in Dt. ii. 8; 1 K. ix. 26, xxii. 49; 2 Chr. viii. 17, xx. 36. In the *Onomastica* its original name is said to have been *Essia* (Ασια).

36. In order to avoid the statement that the Israelites visited Kadesh after Ezion-geber, a statement which "is contradicted by Deuteronomy, Judges xi. 16 ff., the indications of the JE narrative, and Numbers xxxii.," Wiener proposes to remove *vv.* 36 *b*–37 *a* to *v.* 18 immediately after Hazeroth (*Essays in Pent. Crit.* p. 127). The reading of LXX is interesting as it inserts between *Zin* and (*the same is Kadesh*) another stage *And they journeyed from the wilderness of Zin, and pitched in the wilderness of Paran.* The effect of this is to identify Kadesh and Paran. Lucian reads ἐπὶ τὴν πηγὴν τῆς κρίσεως, αὕτη ἐστὶν Καδής which is identical with Gen. xiv. 7 (LXX).

37 And they journeyed from Kadesh, and pitched in mount Hor, in the edge of the land of Edom. 38 And Aaron the priest went up into mount Hor at the commandment of the LORD, and died there, in the fortieth year after the children of Israel were come out of the land of Egypt, in the fifth month, on the first day of the month. 39 And Aaron was an hundred and twenty and three years old when he died in mount Hor. 40 And the Canaanite, the king of Arad, which dwelt in the South in the land of Canaan, heard of the coming of the children of Israel. 41 And they journeyed from mount Hor, and pitched in Zalmonah. 42 And they journeyed from Zalmonah, and pitched in Punon. 43 And they journeyed from Punon, and pitched in Oboth. 44 And they journeyed from Oboth, and pitched in Iye-abarim, in the border of Moab. 45 And they journeyed from Iyim, and pitched in Dibon-gad. 46 And they journeyed from Dibon-gad, and pitched in Almon-diblathaim. 47 And they journeyed from Almon-diblathaim, and pitched in the mountains of Abarim, before Nebo. 48 And they journeyed from the mountains of P^s

37–49. The list of the journeyings is continued from Kadesh to the plains of Moab. There is a change from the usual brief record of stages by the insertion of *vv.* 38–40 which are probably to be rejected as a gloss based on xx. 23–xxi. 1.

37. This *v.* agrees with xx. 22.

mount Hor. See on xx. 22.

39. Cf. Ex. vii. 7.

40. This *v.* is almost identical with xxi. 1 and should be omitted as a gloss. Lucian does not include it in his text of LXX.

41. *Zalmonah.* Cf. *mount Zalmon* (Jud. ix. 48) and *Zalmon* (Ps. lxviii. 14). The site is unknown.

42. *Punon* (LXX ^{B}Φεινω ^{AF}Φινω(ν)). Probably to be identified with the *Pinon* of Gen. xxxvi. 41 which was situated in Northern Edom. According to the *Onomastica* it was a place then called *Faenon*, where criminals were sent to work in the copper-mines. The site is almost certainly the modern *Khirbet Fenan*: see Lagrange *Rev. bibl.* IX. pp. 284 ff., von Alois Musil *Arab. Petraea* II. i. pp. 293 ff.

43. *Oboth.* See on xxi. 10.

44. *Iye-abarim.* See on xxi. 11.

45. *Dibon-gad.* See on xxi. 30, xxxii. 34.

46. *Almon-diblathaim.* The situation of this place suggests that it is to be identified with *Beth-diblathaim* of Jer. xlviii. 22 upon which see the present writer's note.

47. *Abarim.* See on xxvii. 12, and cf. Jer. xxii. 20.

Nebo. See on xxxii. 38.

Abarim, and pitched in the plains of Moab by the Jordan at Jericho. 49 And they pitched by Jordan, from Beth-jeshimoth even unto Abel-shittim in the plains of Moab. *P*ˢ

50 And the LORD spake unto Moses in the plains of Moab by the Jordan at Jericho, saying, 51 Speak unto the children of Israel, and say unto them, When ye pass over Jordan into the land of Canaan, 52 then ye shall drive out all the inhabitants of the land from before you, and destroy all their figured *stones*, and destroy all their molten images, and demolish all their high places: 53 and ye shall take possession of the land, and dwell therein: for unto you have I given the land to possess it. 54 And ye shall inherit the land by lot according to your families; to *D*(?*I* *P*

48. Cf. xxii. 1.

49. *Beth-jeshimoth.* Mentioned in Jos. xii. 3, xiii. 20; Ez. xxv. 9. Jerome describes a town *Isimuth* (*Onom. Sac.* 103. 9) situated some 10 Roman miles from Jericho which suggests the modern *Khirbet es-Suwême.* The second part of the name may come from *Yathîmât,* a district belonging to the ʻAkib, an Arabian tribe: see Hommel *AHT* p. 274.

Abel-shittim. See on xxv. 1. The proposed identifications for Beth-jeshimoth (*Suwême*) and Abel-shittim (*Kefrên*) are situated about five miles apart.

50–56. The Israelites are commanded to destroy all the idolatrous objects of worship in Canaan, and to divide up the land by lot. The style of this section is perplexing, as it combines characteristics of P, H, and D. To P belongs *v.* 54; *vv.* 51–53 seem to come from H; and the rest from D.

50. *the plains of Moab.* See on xxii. 1.

51. *When ye pass over.* Cf. xxxiv. 2, xxxv. 10; Dt. xi. 31, xviii. 9.

52. *drive out.* See on xxxii. 21.

figured stones. The exact meaning of the Heb. משכיתם, which also occurs Lev. xxvi. 1, is unknown, and the Versions do not support the present rendering[1]. There may possibly be an example of the use of the word in early Aramaic: see the Zenjirli Inscription *NSI* No. 62 *l.* 18 where for the meaningless משתי Halévy proposes to read משכי.

their molten images. This is the only place in Pent. where *images* (צלם) is used of heathen gods: cf. Am. v. 26; Ez. vii. 20, xvi. 17.

high places. Here and Lev. xxvi. 30 in Pent. in the sense of *sanctuary.* The word is very common in the historical books and the prophets.

54. *by lot.* See on xxvi. 55.

---

[1] See further Dussaud *Les Origines cananéennes du sacrifice israélite* pp. 222 f. who connects them with *maṣṣeba.*

the more ye shall give the more inheritance, and to the fewer *P* thou shalt give the less inheritance: wheresoever the lot falleth to any man, that shall be his; according to the tribes of your fathers shall ye inherit. 55 But if ye will not drive out the *D(?H* inhabitants of the land from before you; then shall those which ye let remain of them be as pricks in your eyes, and as thorns in your sides, and they shall vex you in the land wherein ye dwell. 56 And it shall come to pass, that as I thought to do unto them, so will I do unto you.

55. *pricks...thorns.* Cf. the similar language of Jos. xxiii. 13; Ez. xxviii. 24; and in a different connexion 2 Cor. xii. 7.

CHAPTER XXXIV.

The West Jordan Territories.

The representation of the boundaries of the Israelite possessions west of Jordan contained in this ch., and the manner of their distribution are evidently ideal. Not only is it exceedingly unlikely that their territories were at any time so extensive, but in addition, the division before the entry, although it has support from other passages (e.g. Jud. i. 3 'my lot'), reflects the mind of the writer, and what he considered fitting, rather than the actual course of events.

(*a*) *The boundaries of the land.* 1–15.
(*b*) *The superintendents of the division.* 16–29.

XXXIV. 1 And the LORD spake unto Moses, saying, 2 Com- *P* mand the children of Israel, and say unto them, When ye come into the land of Canaan, (this is the land that shall fall unto you for an inheritance, even the land of Canaan according to

XXXIV. 1–15. The boundaries of the West Jordan territory are laid down in some detail, but owing to our ignorance of some of the sites, and of the absence of clearly defined geographical features, except in the case of the western boundary, we are unable to trace the precise line of the frontier. Similar descriptions in Jos. xv.–xix.; Ez. xlvii. 13–20, xlviii. 28, invite comparisons. Ezekiel's vision puts into the ideal future, as Gray points out, that which P, in accordance with his habitual principles, has embodied in the ideal past.

3–5. In these *vv.* the southern border is defined. It ran from the southern end of the Dead Sea, along Edom to the south of Kadesh, and then in a north-westerly direction along the *Wady el-'Arīsh* to the sea. The definition of this boundary "is in strict accordance with the geographical limits of the country" (Palmer *op. cit.* p. 529), although we have lost any clue to the identification of several of the sites.

the borders thereof,) 3 then your south quarter shall be from the wilderness of Zin along by the side of Edom, and your south border shall be from the end of the Salt Sea eastward: 4 and your border shall turn about southward of the ascent of Akrabbim, and pass along to Zin: and the goings out thereof shall be southward of Kadesh-barnea; and it shall go forth to Hazar-addar, and pass along to Azmon: 5 and the border shall turn about from Azmon unto the brook of Egypt, and the goings out thereof shall be at the sea. 6 And for the western border, *P*

3. *your south quarter*. Heb. פְּאָה *pē'ah* (cf. the cognate Assyr. *pātu*) has the meaning of *side, edge,* or *border* as well as that of a *portion* or *corner*.

the side of Edom. Cf. Jos. xv. 1.

the Salt Sea. So called from its excessive saltness, which arises from the nature of the surrounding soil. Ezekiel calls it the east sea—in contrast with the Mediterranean or great sea (xlvii. 18)—whilst in Dt. iii. 17, iv. 49 &c., the additional name of *the sea of the Arabah* is given to it. It is now known as the Dead Sea.

4. *the ascent of Akrabbim*. Cf. Jos. xv. 3; Jud. i. 36. The meaning of *Akrabbim* is *scorpions*, and the neighbourhood in which the pass must be situated still swarms with them: see Guthe *Kurzes Bibelwörterbuch* pp. 23, 630. Many identify the pass with the *Naḳbeṣ-Ṣafâ* which ascends from the *Wady el-Fiḳreh* (e.g. Buhl *Geog. Pal.* pp. 16, 66): others favour the *Wady el-Fiḳreh* itself: see Burney *Judges* p. 33. In Jub. xxix. 14 there is a reference, almost certainly erroneous, to the *forest* of Akrabbim.

Zin. An unknown place (mentioned also in Jos. xv. 3) from which the wilderness of Zin presumably took its name. LXX reads Ἐννα(κ) which Lagarde argues may represent חצין (= *axe* in Aram. and Assyr., *iron* in Ethiopic). In the present passage Targ. Jer. has the rendering טור ברזלא (= *iron mountain*), which suggests a similar reading.

Hazar-addar. In Jos. xv. 3 *Hezron* and *Addar* are mentioned as separate places. Neither of the sites is known.

Azmon. Possibly *'Ain el-Ḳasaymeh*: see Trumbull *Kadesh-Barnea* pp. 117, 289 ff.

5. *the brook of Egypt*. This is generally identified with the *Wady el-'Arish*, which runs in a northerly direction from the middle of the Sinai peninsula into the Mediterranean some 50 miles below Gaza. Palmer remarks that "The appellation is singularly appropriate from the point of view of one dwelling in Palestine, for the only direct road from Judaea to Egypt was across the Desert of the Tíh by this very valley, and it might well be regarded as the River of Egypt, inasmuch as it separates that country from the Holy Land" (*op. cit.* pp. 286 f.). On the origin of the name and its possible derivation from a North Arabian district see *Enc. Bib.* 1249 f., 4529 f. and *Camb. Anct. Hist.* III., pp. 383 f.

ye shall have the great sea [1]and the border *thereof*: this shall be *P* your west border. 7 And this shall be your north border: from the great sea ye shall mark out for you mount Hor: 8 from mount Hor ye shall mark out unto the entering in of Hamath; and the goings out of the border shall be at Zedad: 9 and the border shall go forth to Ziphron, and the goings out thereof shall be at Hazar-enan: this shall be your north border. 10 And ye shall mark out your east border from Hazar-enan to Shepham:

[1] Or, *for a border*

6. *the great sea.* The Mediterranean was at no time the boundary of Israel, and indeed until the time of the Maccabees (1 Macc. xiv. 5) their territory did not touch it at any point so far as we know.

7–9. The north border is to extend from the Mediterranean to the unknown Hazar-enan. The same boundary line seems to be described in Ez. xlvii. 15–17. There is much difference of opinion as to the exact extent of the border, especially on the question of the inclusion of the greater part of the Lebanon. Though Dan, south of the mountains, is, as Gray says, "the proverbial northern town," the tide of Israelite conquest in the reigns of David (1 K. viii. 65) and of Jeroboam II (2 K. xiv. 25) seems to have flowed far beyond it.

7. *from the great sea.* No precise point of departure from the Mediterranean is indicated: room is therefore given for a wide difference of selection according to whether the selector favours the more, or the less, extensive border line.

mount Hor. Not to be confused with the mountain of the same name on the border of Edom (xx. 22). This site is unknown, but Furrer, who holds that the frontier extended into the Lebanon, sees in it *Jebel Akkar* the northern spur of Lebanon (*ZDPV* VIII. p. 27). Baedeker's *Palestine*[2] p. 451 also gives an extreme northern site, *Jebel el Aḳra,* to the south of the mouth of the Orontes. Van Kasteren, who upholds the theory of a less inclusive frontier, finds the site at the bend of the *Nahr el-Ḳâsimîyeh* (*Rev. bibl.* 1895 pp. 30 f.).

8. *the entering in of Hamath.* See on xiii. 21.

Zedad. LXX Σαραδακ. Furrer identifies this with the modern Jacobite village *Ṣadad* on the road from Riblah to *Ḳarjatên.* Advocates of the more southerly boundary, adopting the reading suggested by LXX, find the site in *Khirbet Serada* between *Merj ʿAyūn* and Hermon.

9. *Ziphron.* Furrer identifies this site with *Zeferāne,* between Emesa and Hamath; Wetzstein (*Hauran* p. 88) with *Zifran* to the north-east of Damascus. Possibly *Ziphron* is a corruption of *Sibraim* (Ez. xlvii. 16) which has been identified with *Khirbet Sanbarîye,* a little to the south of *Khirbet Serada.*

Hazar-enan. So in *v.* 10, Ez. xlviii. 1 (with Aramaic spelling): in Ez. xlvii. 17 *Hazar-enon.* The name means *the enclosure of the spring,* and on this and other grounds Buhl (*Geog. Pal.* p. 67) would identify

11 and the border shall go down from Shepham to Riblah, on *P* the east side of Ain; and the border shall go down, and shall reach unto the [1]side of the sea of Chinnereth eastward: 12 and the border shall go down to Jordan, and the goings out thereof shall be at the Salt Sea: this shall be your land according to the borders thereof round about. 13 And Moses commanded the children of Israel, saying, This is the land which ye shall inherit by lot, which the LORD hath commanded to give unto the nine tribes, and to the half tribe: 14 for the tribe of the children of Reuben according to their fathers' houses, and the tribe of the children of Gad according to their fathers' houses, have received, and the half tribe of Manasseh have received, their inheritance: 15 the two tribes and the half tribe have received

[1] Heb. *shoulder*.

it with *Bâniâs* situated at one of the sources of the Jordan. Van Kasteren places it at *el-Ḫadr* slightly to the north-east. Furrer's site is *Ḳaryatēn*, an oasis in the Syrian desert, some 60 miles to the south and west of Tudmur (Palmyra).

10–12. The east border leaves Hazar-enan, and travelling by Shepham and Riblah, reaches the Lake of Galilee, from which it follows the Jordan and the Dead Sea to the south-east corner of the latter.

10. *Shepham.* This place is otherwise unknown, though possibly it was the home of Zabdi the Shiphmite (1 Chr. xxvii. 27).

11. *Riblah.* The famous town of this name on the Orontes is excluded on geographical grounds. The name here has the article *the Riblah.* LXX reads Βηλα, and Sam. הארבלה, which suggests that the Heb. should be read (as is quite possible without any alteration of the text) *to Harbel*, i.e. *the mount of Bel.* This suggestion appears in the *Speaker's Commentary* with a proposed identification with *Har Baal-Hermon* (Jud. iii. 3), an identification which is hardly probable since this site (= *Baal Gad* = *Bâniâs*) is not suitable.

Ain. Since this is the common word for *spring* its identification is impossible, probably it had some word attached to it which has fallen out of the text.

the side. Heb. means *shoulder*, but there is a similar usage in Jos. xv. 8, 10 f., xviii. 12 f. &c.; Is. xi. 14.

the sea of Chinnereth. So called probably from Chinnereth (Dt. iii. 17; Jos. xix. 35), the later Γεννησαρ (1 Macc. xi. 67) or Γεννησαρετ (Mt. xiv. 34). As the name appears under the form *kn-na-ra-tu* in the list of places captured by Thutmose III (*c.* 1480) it had retained its identity during many centuries. Another derivation comes from the likeness of its shape to a harp (*kinnôr*).

12. *the Salt Sea.* See on *v.* 3.

13. *by lot.* See on xxvi. 55.

their inheritance beyond the Jordan at Jericho eastward, toward the sunrising. *P*

16 And the LORD spake unto Moses, saying, 17 These are the names of the men which shall divide the land unto you for inheritance: Eleazar the priest, and Joshua the son of Nun. 18 And ye shall take one prince of every tribe, to divide the land for inheritance. 19 And these are the names of the men: of the tribe of Judah, Caleb the son of Jephunneh. 20 And of the tribe of the children of Simeon, Shemuel the son of Ammihud. 21 Of the tribe of Benjamin, Elidad the son of Chislon. 22 And of the tribe of the children of Dan a prince, Bukki the son of Jogli. 23 Of the children of Joseph: of the tribe of the children of Manasseh a prince, Hanniel the son of Ephod: 24 and of the tribe of the children of Ephraim a prince, Kemuel the son of Shiphtan. 25 And of the tribe of the children of Zebulun a prince, Elizaphan the son of Parnach. 26 And of the

15. *at Jericho.* Cf. xxii. 1. In the present context the limitation is unsuitable and may well be a gloss or scribal error.

16–29. Moses is commanded to appoint ten princes whose names are given to him to assist Eleazar and Joshua in the division of the land. One prince is chosen from each of the tribes, ten in number, who are to receive territory west of Jordan: cf. i. 1 ff. Since none of the original fugitives from Egypt survived the wanderings (xiv. 26 ff.) except Caleb and Joshua, none of the other princes included in previous lists (i. 1 ff., xiii. 4 ff.) appears in this one.

The tribes are arranged geographically according to their actual situation in Canaan: it is noteworthy that Dan is placed in the south, between Simeon and Joseph.

20. *Shemuel.* Cf. 1 S. i. 20; 1 Chr. vii. 2, and see Hommel *AHT* p. 100.

Ammihud. See i. 10.

21. *Elidad.* LXX Ἐλδαδ: cf. xi. 26.

22. *Bukki.* Also in 1 Chr. v. 31; Ezra vii. 4 and cf. Bukkiah (1 Chr. xxv. 4, 13).

23. *Hanniel.* Here and 2 Chr. vii. 39. The form suggests that of well-known Phoenician names like Hannibal. The name itself is actually found in a Nabataean inscription (*CIS* II. 191).

24. *Kemuel.* The name of a son of Nahor (Gen. xxii. 21), and of a Levite (1 Chr. xxvii. 17).

25. *Elizaphan.* See on iii. 30.

Parnach. Wellhausen suggests that this is the Persian Φαρνάκης (Herod. VIII. 126). The name appears however in a Palmyrene inscription (*NSI* No. 135 *l.* 3), and is possibly connected with פרנוג = *Saturn.*

tribe of the children of Issachar a prince, Paltiel the son of *P* Azzan. 27 And of the tribe of the children of Asher a prince, Ahihud the son of Shelomi. 28 And of the tribe of the children of Naphtali a prince, Pedahel the son of Ammihud. 29 These are they whom the LORD commanded to divide the inheritance unto the children of Israel in the land of Canaan.

26. *Paltiel.* Here and 2 S. iii. 15. Several similar names also occur, e.g. *Palti* in the list of spies (xiii. 9), and *Piltai* (Neh. xii. 17). The form *Phaltiel* in 4 Ezra v. 16 represents the same Heb.

27. *Ahihud.* An ancient type of name: see *HPN* pp. 38 ff., 205. LXX Ἀχιωρ occurs in Judith v. 5 &c. as an Ammonite: Cowley thinks that it represents an original *Ahihud*: see *Oxford Apocrypha ad loc.*

28. *Pedahel.* Cf. the Assyr. *Pudu-ilu*, *Pudi-ilu* and the Phoenician בלעפדא: and see on Pedahzur (i. 10)[1].

CHAPTER XXXV.

The Levitical Cities.

Arrangements having been made for the division of the yet unconquered territory of the Canaanites amongst the tribes, the needs of the Levites now receive attention. Forty-eight cities are set aside for them of which six are to be cities of refuge. The cities of refuge are to be an asylum for those who, having slain another by accident, are in danger from the avenger of blood.

(*a*) *The provision for the Levites.* 1–8.
(*b*) *The cities of refuge.* 9–15.
(*c*) *Definition of manslaughter.* 16–25.
(*d*) *Various provisions and warnings.* 26–34.

XXXV. 1–8. Moses is commanded to make arrangements for the Levites to be put in possession of forty-eight cities with the land surrounding them, on the entry into Canaan being completed. In Jos. xxi. there is a minute account of the fulfilment of the command. According to the account there given, the priests received thirteen cities from Judah, Simeon, and Benjamin; the Kohathites, ten cities from Ephraim, Dan, and West Manasseh; the Gershonites, thirteen cities from Issachar, Asher, Naphtali, and East Manasseh; and the Merarites, twelve cities from Reuben, Gad, and Zebulon. These allocations of cities in the various tribes to different groups of Levites do not follow the arrangements of the camp in ii., iii. 21 ff.

According to D no provision was made for the Levites, who had to depend on the offerings made to the LORD (Dt. xviii. 1–5); a view which is also found in the older stratum of P (Num. xviii. 21 ff.). That certain

---

[1] A similar name occurs in an ancient Arabic inscription, the elements being reversed, אלפדי for פדהאל: see *CIS* IV. 335.

XXXV. 1 And the LORD spake unto Moses in the plains of Moab by the Jordan at Jericho, saying, 2 Command the children of Israel, that they give unto the Levites of the inheritance of their possession cities to dwell in; and [1]suburbs for the cities round about them shall ye give unto the Levites. 3 And the cities shall they have to dwell in; and their suburbs shall be for their cattle, and for their substance, and for all their beasts. 4 And the suburbs of the cities, which ye shall give unto the Levites, shall be from the wall of the city and outward a thousand cubits round about. 5 And ye shall measure without the city for the east side two thousand cubits, and for the south side two thousand cubits, and for the west side two thousand cubits, and for the north side two thousand cubits, the city being in the midst. This shall be to them the suburbs of the cities. 6 And the cities which ye shall give unto the Levites, they shall be the six cities of refuge, which ye shall give for the manslayer to flee thither: and beside them ye shall give forty *P^s^*

[1] Or, *pasture lands*

cities were peculiarly associated with the priests cannot be denied: e.g. Shiloh (1 S. i.–iv.), Nob (1 S. xxi. 1), Bethel (Am. vii. 10), but we have no information as to the ownership of such cities. In ancient Egypt lands were allotted to the priests for the support of the temples, and these included towns in Syria: see Sayce *EHH* p. 237, Erman *Life in Anct. Egypt* (E.T.) p. 299. Such provisions were however probably not intended for the residence of priests, but as endowments.

The geometrical arrangement of the proposed cities is further evidence in favour of the view that the whole conception is, like that of Ezekiel xlviii., ideal rather than actual.

2. *cities to dwell in.* Some critics see in this phrase a distinction between dwelling and owning: Lev. xxv. 32 ff. however makes it quite clear that the Levites were not merely to dwell in the cities but to own them.

suburbs. Mg. *pasture lands* is correct. The rendering of E.VV. comes from Vulg. *et suburbana earum.* Land belonging to the citizens as a body is evidently meant.

4. *a thousand cubits.* The pasture land is to extend some 1500 feet from the wall of the city.

5. The measurements here proposed are impossible, in view of *v.* 4, unless the city itself be omitted from the centre of the square. The defence of Van Hoonacker to the effect that the measurements are only approximate, and that the writer knew what he meant (*Sacerdoce lévitique* p. 433), is not satisfactory, for if the writer knew what he meant he has certainly not succeeded in conveying his meaning to his readers.

and two cities. 7 All the cities which ye shall give to the Levites *Ps* shall be forty and eight cities: them *shall ye give* with their suburbs. 8 And concerning the cities which ye shall give of the possession of the children of Israel, from the many ye shall take many; and from the few ye shall take few: every one according to his inheritance which he inheriteth shall give of his cities unto the Levites.

9 And the LORD spake unto Moses, saying, 10 Speak unto the children of Israel, and say unto them, When ye pass over Jordan into the land of Canaan, 11 then ye shall appoint you cities to be cities of refuge for you; that the manslayer which killeth any person [1]unwittingly may flee thither. 12 And the cities shall be unto you for refuge from the avenger; that the

[1] Or, *through error*

8. *many...few.* The same principle was adopted in arranging the original allotment of the land (xxvi. 54, xxxiii. 54).

9–15. From the Levitical cities six are to be selected as asylums for those who have unwittingly committed manslaughter. In the early days it is probable that all altars were sanctuaries (cf. Ex. xxi. 13 f.), though the more famous would be regarded as of special sanctity (cf. 1 K. i. 50, ii. 28). The centralisation of worship under Josiah, with its consequent abolition of sanctuaries, made necessary the provision of some other alternative asylums, hence the legislation of Dt. xix. 1–13.

The right of sanctuary is found in all ages and amongst almost all peoples, from the Greeks (cf. Herod. I. 35; Thuc. IV. 98) and Romans (cf. Tacitus *Ann.* III. 60 ff., IV. 14) down to the close of the Middle Ages and even later. In medieval times famous cathedrals and monasteries were liable to be turned into caravansaries owing to the right of sanctuary: see *Camb. Med. Hist.* I. p. 566.

11. *ye shall appoint.* Better *select.* The carrying out of this command is recorded in Jos. xx. (P).

unwittingly. In ignorance: see on xv. 24. The distinction is recognised in the earliest law (Ex. xxi. 12 ff.), and in Dt. xix. 4, though the term used is different. By limiting the right of sanctuary to the innocent, O.T. raises the practice from the level of magic or *taboo* upon which it began (cf. Robertson Smith *Rel. Sem.*[2] p. 148), and to which in many cases it relapsed in medieval times, and gives it a humanitarian and ethical complexion.

12. *the avenger.* Heb. *gō'ēl.* The exact meaning of the term is uncertain, and the duties to be performed by its holder were varied and numerous. In addition to avenging his kinsman's murder, they included recovering money owing (v. 8); the contracting of a levirate marriage (Ruth iii. 13); certain duties in regard to family property (Lev. xxv. 25; Ruth iv. 1–6; Jer. xxxii. 8–12); and also the redeeming of the kinsman

manslayer die not, until he stand before the congregation for judgement. 13 And the cities which ye shall give shall be for you six cities of refuge. 14 Ye shall give three cities beyond Jordan, and three cities shall ye give in the land of Canaan; they shall be cities of refuge. 15 For the children of Israel, and for the stranger and for the sojourner among them, shall these six cities be for refuge: that every one that killeth any person [1]unwittingly may flee thither. 16 But if he smote him with an instrument of iron, so that he died, he is a manslayer: the man- P^s

[1] Or, *through error*

from slavery (Lev. xxv. 47 ff.), a duty which suggested the figure of the divine redemption. The connexion between the right of sanctuary and blood-revenge is close, for where such a custom was non-existent, as amongst the Romans, the use of sanctuaries gradually became confined to slaves (see *Enc. Bib.* 377). The Koran tried to limit the vengeance to the person of the actual murderer, and then only in cases of deliberate homicide. In general the custom has done something to prevent bloodshed amongst the Arabs, because of the danger of starting a blood-feud (see Palmer *Desert of the Exodus* pp. 80 and 200). On the principles of blood-revenge, see Robertson Smith *Kinship*[2] pp. 25 ff.; Cook *The Laws of Moses &c.* pp. 51 f., 256 ff.; H. J. Treston *Poine: a Study in Anct. Gk. Blood-Vengeance.*

stand before. The phrase is used with a forensic sense, as in xxvii. 2; Dt. xix. 17; Jos. xx. 6; Zech. iii. 1; cf. the use in xvi. 9.

the congregation. Cf. Dt. xix. 12 "the elders of his city."

13. *six cities.* The number appointed in Dt. is not quite clear. Dt. iv. 41 ff. provides for three, three are mentioned in xix. 2, and three more in xix. 9; it is possible that the first three are included in the later mention.

14. The names of the cities are given in Jos. xx. 7 f., viz. Kedesh, Shechem, and Kiriath-arba, on the west of Jordan; Bezer, Ramoth, and Golan, on the east.

beyond Jordan. That is east of Jordan. According to Dt. iv. 41 Moses himself appointed these cities.

15. *stranger...sojourner.* For the former term see on ix. 14. The latter is found only in P in Pent., and his status and condition are a little uncertain. Driver and White think that "possibly he was a foreigner who gave his services to a particular patron or master in return for board and lodging" (note on Lev. xxv. 6 in *SBOT*). See further Baentsch on Ex. xii. 45.

16–25. A number of examples of unwitting murder are given for the guidance of those who have to distinguish between such acts, together with a statement of the procedure in the case of the proof of guilty intention.

16. *of iron.* As the two following instruments are qualified by the

slayer shall surely be put to death. 17 And if he smote him with a stone in the hand, whereby a man may die, and he died, he is a manslayer: the manslayer shall surely be put to death. 18 Or if he smote him with a weapon of wood in the hand, whereby a man may die, and he died, he is a manslayer: the manslayer shall surely be put to death. 19 The avenger of blood shall himself put the manslayer to death: when he meeteth him, he shall put him to death. 20 And if he thrust him of hatred, or hurled at him, lying in wait, so that he died; 21 or in enmity smote him with his hand, that he died: he that smote him shall surely be put to death; he is a manslayer: the avenger of blood shall put the manslayer to death, when he meeteth him. 22 But if he thrust him suddenly without enmity, or hurled upon him any thing without lying in wait, 23 or with any stone, whereby a man may die, seeing him not, and cast it upon him, so that he died, and he was not his enemy, neither sought his harm: 24 then the congregation shall judge between the smiter and the avenger of blood according to these judgements: 25 and the congregation shall deliver the manslayer out of the hand of the avenger of blood, and the congregation shall restore him to his city of refuge, whither he was fled: and he shall dwell therein until the death of the high priest, which was anointed with the holy oil. 26 But if the manslayer shall at any time go beyond

P[s]

phrase *likely to cause death* and this is not, presumably the use of any *iron* weapon was considered likely to be fatal; cf. also Ex. xxi. 18 f. where *iron* is not mentioned in the case of wounds only.

17. *whereby a man may die.* That is *likely to cause death.* The use of either a stone or a staff is referred to in Ex. xxi. 18 f. (see previous note).

19. This *v.* seems out of place.

20. *thrust him.* Cf. Ez. xxxiv. 21.

hurled at him. LXX adds πᾶν σκεῦος as in *v.* 22.

22 f. Cf. Dt. xix. 4 f.

24. *these judgements.* Cf. Ex. xxi. 1.

25. *restore him.* The trial does not take place in the city of refuge but elsewhere.

the high priest. Used of Jehoiada (2 K. xii. 10), Hilkiah (2 K. xxii. 4, 8), Joshua (Hag. i. 1 &c.; Zech. iii. 1), Eliashib (Neh. iii. 1 &c.). P uses 'the priest' as the normal term for Aaron and his successors. The term best suits the Persian period, for such a functionary was not known until the people, from a kingdom, had become a church: see Peters *Rel. of Hebs.* p. 369.

26–34. Various supplementary provisions are here made, in order that

the border of his city of refuge, whither he fleeth; 27 and the avenger of blood find him without the border of his city of refuge, and the avenger of blood slay the manslayer; [1]he shall not be guilty of blood: 28 because he should have remained in his city of refuge until the death of the high priest: but after the death of the high priest the manslayer shall return into the land of his possession. 29 And these things shall be for a statute of judgement unto you throughout your generations in all your dwellings. 30 Whoso killeth any person, the manslayer shall be slain at the mouth of witnesses: but one witness shall not testify against any person that he die. 31 Moreover ye shall take no ransom for the life of a manslayer, which is guilty of death: but he shall surely be put to death. 32 And ye shall take no ransom for him that is fled to his city of refuge, that he should come again to dwell in the land, until the death of the priest. *P*s

[1] Or, *there shall be no blood-guiltiness for him*

the procedure may be quite clear, and at the end of the section a solemn warning is uttered against the defilement of the land by the shedding of blood.

27. *not be guilty of blood.* Cf. Lev. xx. 9; Ez. xviii. 13.

29. This *v.* seems the natural close of the regulations, what follows has evidently been added by way of supplement.

30. *witnesses.* Cf. Mt. xviii. 16. Dt. xix. 15 requires two witnesses to establish any charge: the provision here, like that in reference to idolatry (Dt. xvii. 6), applies the general principle to a particular crime. According to ancient Teutonic law the number of witnesses required varied with the different nations: the Saxons and the Lombards required two at least; the Bavarians, three or more; the Franks, seven or twelve according to the importance of the matter in question (Stubbs *Constitutional Hist.* I. p. 654).

31. *no ransom.* The custom of paying compensation for murder is ancient and widespread: cf. ποινή of the Greeks (*Il.* v. 266, XVIII. 498 ff. &c.), and the *wergild* of the old Teutonic law (see Stubbs *op. cit.* I. p. 179). Muhammed was more merciful than the present law as he allowed compensation even for wilful murder: Koran II. 173 f. See further Ex. xxi. 12, 29 f.; Dt. xix. 1–13.

32. No ransom was allowed even for the innocent. The detention in the city of refuge was considered to be a punishment. Amongst the Greeks and Romans exile was the normal punishment for homicide: Heineccius in the preface to his *Elements of Germanic Law* comments upon this with favour contrasting the greater severity of capital punishment. In reply Gibbon points out that for a citizen of Rome or Athens exile was a *capital* punishment (*Decline and Fall* XXXVIII.).

33 So ye shall not pollute the land wherein ye are: for blood, *P*s it polluteth the land: and no expiation can be made for the land for the blood that is shed therein, but by the blood of him that shed it. 34 And thou shalt not defile the land which ye inhabit, in the midst of which I dwell: for I the LORD dwell in the midst of the children of Israel.

33. *pollute the land.* Cf. Enoch vii. 6 where the earth cries out against the evil deeds done upon it: cf. Gen. iv. 10 f.[1]

no expiation. Jub. xxi. 19 warns Israel against allowing gifts as compensation for murder, lest bloodshed should increase.

34. *I dwell.* Cf. v. 3, xxiii. 21; Ex. xxix. 45 f.; Zech. ii. 10; also 2 Cor. vi. 16; Rev. xxi. 3.

CHAPTER XXXVI.

The daughters of Zelophehad.

This ch. forms a supplement to xxvii. 1–11, and insists that women who inherit the family property under its provisions must not marry outside the tribe and so cause possessions to go from one tribe to another: cf. Lev. xxv. 10, 31, which seem to have in mind the preserving of tribal properties. By the laws of Solon if a man died leaving only an unmarried daughter the nearest relation might claim her hand in order to keep the property in the family (see Holm *Hist. of Greece* I. p. 393): and according to the Theodosian Code heiresses marrying outside their late father's *curia* had to forfeit a fourth part of their property (see *Camb. Med. Hist.* I. p. 557).

XXXVI. 1 And the heads of the fathers' *houses* of the family of the children of Gilead, the son of Machir, the son of Manasseh, of the families of the sons of Joseph, came near, and spake before Moses, and before the princes, the heads of the fathers' *houses* of the children of Israel: 2 and they said, The LORD commanded my lord to give the land for inheritance by lot to the children of Israel: and my lord was commanded by the LORD to give the inheritance of Zelophehad our brother unto his daughters. 3 And if they be married to any of the sons of the *other* tribes of the children of Israel, then shall their inheritance be taken away from the inheritance of our fathers, and shall be added to the inheritance of the tribe whereunto they shall belong: so shall it be taken away from the lot of our

XXXVI. 1. *fathers'* houses. See on i. 2.

---

[1] The Greeks held some similar belief as to the pollution of the earth by blood shed upon it: see Frazer *FLOT* I. p. 83 where the story of Alcmaeon is quoted (cf. Thucydides II. 102; Pausanias VIII. xxiv. 7–9).

inheritance. 4 And when the jubile of the children of Israel shall *P*[s] be, then shall their inheritance be added unto the inheritance of the tribe whereunto they shall belong: so shall their inheritance be taken away from the inheritance of the tribe of our fathers. 5 And Moses commanded the children of Israel according to the word of the LORD, saying, The tribe of the sons of Joseph speaketh right. 6 This is the thing which the LORD doth command concerning the daughters of Zelophehad, saying, Let them marry to whom they think best; only to the family of the tribe of their father shall they marry. 7 So shall no inheritance of the children of Israel remove from tribe to tribe: for the children of Israel shall cleave every one to the inheritance of the tribe of his fathers. 8 And every daughter, that possesseth an inheritance in any tribe of the children of Israel, shall be wife unto one of the family of the tribe of her father, that the children of Israel may possess every man the inheritance of his fathers. 9 So shall no inheritance remove from one tribe to another tribe; for the tribes of the children of Israel shall cleave every one to his own inheritance. 10 Even as the LORD commanded Moses, so did the daughters of Zelophehad: 11 for Mahlah, Tirzah, and Hoglah, and Milcah, and Noah, the daughters of Zelophehad, were married unto their father's brothers' sons. 12 They were married into the families of the sons of Manasseh the son of Joseph, and their inheritance remained in the tribe of the family of their father.

13 These are the commandments and the judgements, which the LORD commanded by the hand of Moses unto the children of Israel in the plains of Moab by the Jordan at Jericho.

4. *the jubile.* Heb. יֹבֵל (*jobel*) which gives its name to this feast means lit. *a ram*: it is however never used in its primary sense in O.T. being applied to the blowing of rams' horns: contrast the use in Phoenician inscriptions (*NSI* No. 42 *l.* 7).

be added. The provisions of the law of jubile (see Lev. xxv. 13 ff.) would not apply to an inheritance of property as distinguished from a sale.

11. The order here differs from the list of daughters in xxvii. 1, Noah and Tirzah having changed places.

father's brothers' sons. Another instance of the carrying out of this law is contained in 1 Chr. xxiii. 22, where the sons of Kish marry the daughters of their uncle Eleazar who died without male offspring.

13. A subscription to cover the whole book: cf. Lev. xxvii. 34.

INDEX

CAMBRIDGE: PRINTED BY W. LEWIS, M.A., AT THE UNIVERSITY PRESS

METHUEN'S GENERAL LITERATURE

A SELECTION OF

MESSRS. METHUEN'S PUBLICATIONS

This Catalogue contains only a selection of the more important books published by Messrs. Methuen. A complete catalogue of their publications may be obtained on application.

PART I. GENERAL LITERATURE

Allen (R. Wilberforce)
METHODISM AND MODERN WORLD PROBLEMS. *Crown 8vo* 7*s*. 6*d*. *net.*

Bain (F. W.)
A DIGIT OF THE MOON. THE DESCENT OF THE SUN. A HEIFER OF THE DAWN. IN THE GREAT GOD'S HAIR. A DRAUGHT OF THE BLUE. AN ESSENCE OF THE DUSK. AN INCARNATION OF THE SNOW. A MINE OF FAULTS. THE ASHES OF A GOD. BUBBLES OF THE FOAM. A SYRUP OF THE BEES. THE LIVERY OF EVE. THE SUBSTANCE OF A DREAM. *All Fcap. 8vo.* 5*s*. *net.* AN ECHO OF THE SPHERES. *Wide Demy 8vo.* 10*s*. 6*d*. *net.*

Baker (C. H. Collins)
CROME. Illustrated. *Quarto.* £5 5*s*. *net.*

Balfour (Sir Graham)
THE LIFE OF ROBERT LOUIS STEVENSON. *Twentieth Edition. In one Volume. Cr. 8vo. Buckram,* 7*s*. 6*d*. *net.*

Belloc (Hilaire)
PARIS. THE PYRENEES. *Each* 8*s*. 6*d*. *net.* ON NOTHING. HILLS AND THE SEA. ON SOMETHING. FIRST AND LAST. THIS AND THAT AND THE OTHER. ON. ON EVERYTHING. ON ANYTHING. *Each* 3*s*. 6*d*. *net.* MARIE ANTOINETTE. 18*s*. *net.* A HISTORY OF ENGLAND. In 4 vols. Vols. I and II. 15*s*. net each.

Birmingham (George A.)
A WAYFARER IN HUNGARY. Illustrated. *Crown 8vo.* 8*s*. 6*d*. *net.* SPILLIKINS: A BOOK OF ESSAYS. *Fcap. 8vo.* 5*s*. *net.*

Bowen (Frank C.)
THE KING'S NAVY. Illustrated. *Fcap. 4to.* 7*s*. 6*d*. *net.*

Bowles (George F. S.)
THE STRENGTH OF ENGLAND. *Demy 8vo.* 8*s*. 6*d*. *net.*

Brinton (Selwyn)
THE GOLDEN AGE OF THE MEDICI. Illustrated. *Demy 8vo.* 15*s*. *net.*

Bulley (M. H.)
ART AND COUNTERFEIT. Illustrated. *Demy 4to.* 15*s.* *net.* ANCIENT AND MEDIEVAL ART: A SHORT HISTORY. *Second Edition, Revised. Crown 8vo.* 10*s.* 6*d.* *net.*

Burns (Robert)
THE POEMS AND SONGS. Edited by ANDREW LANG. *Fourth Edition. Wide Demy 8vo.* 10*s.* 6*d.* *net.*

Campbell (Olwen Ward)
SHELLEY AND THE UNROMANTICS. Illustrated. *Second Edition, Revised. Demy 8vo.* 16*s.* *net.*

Chandler (Arthur), D.D., late Lord Bishop of Bloemfontein
ARA CŒLI. 5*s.* *net.* FAITH AND EXPERIENCE. 5*s.* *net.* THE CULT OF THE PASSING MOMENT. 6*s.* *net.* THE ENGLISH CHURCH AND REUNION. 5*s.* *net.* SCALA MUNDI. 4*s.* 6*d.* *net.*

Chesterton (G. K.)
THE BALLAD OF THE WHITE HORSE. ALL THINGS CONSIDERED. TREMENDOUS TRIFLES. FANCIES VERSUS FADS. CHARLES DICKENS. *All Fcap. 8vo.* 3*s.* 6*d.* *net.* ALARMS AND DISCURSIONS. A MISCELLANY OF MEN. THE USES OF DIVERSITY. THE OUTLINE OF SANITY. *All Fcap. 8vo.* 6*s.* *net.* A GLEAMING COHORT. *Fcap 8vo.* 2*s.* 6*d.* *net.* WINE, WATER, AND SONG. *Fcap. 8vo.* 1*s.* 6*d.* *net.*

Clutton-Brock (A.)
WHAT IS THE KINGDOM OF HEAVEN? ESSAYS ON ART. SHAKESPEARE'S HAMLET. *Each* 5*s.* *net.* ESSAYS ON BOOKS. MORE ESSAYS ON BOOKS. ESSAYS ON LIFE. ESSAYS ON RELIGION. ESSAYS ON LITERATURE AND LIFE. *Each* 6*s.* *net.* SHELLEY, THE MAN AND THE POET. 7*s.* 6*d.* *net.*

Cowling (George H.)
A PREFACE TO SHAKESPEARE. Illustrated. *Crown 8vo.* 5*s.* *net.*

Dolls' House (The Queen's)
THE BOOK OF THE QUEEN'S DOLLS' HOUSE. Vol. I. THE HOUSE, Edited by A. C. BENSON, C.V.O., and Sir LAWRENCE WEAVER, K.B.E. Vol. II. THE LIBRARY, Edited by E. V. LUCAS. Profusely Illustrated. A Limited Edition. *Crown 4to.* £6 6*s.* *net.*

EVERYBODY'S BOOK OF THE QUEEN'S DOLLS' HOUSE. An abridged edition of the above. Illustrated. *Crown 4to.* 5*s.* *net.*

Edwardes (Tickner)
THE LORE OF THE HONEYBEE. *Thirteenth Edition. Crown 8vo.* 7*s.* 6*d.* *net.* BEEKEEPING FOR ALL. *Crown 8vo.* 3*s.* 6*d.* *net.* THE BEE-MASTER OF WARRILOW. *Third Edition. Crown 8vo.* 7*s.* 6*d.* *net.* All Illustrated. BEE-KEEPING DO'S AND DON'TS. *Fcap. 8vo.* 2*s.* 6*d.* *net.*

Einstein (Albert)
RELATIVITY: THE SPECIAL AND GENERAL THEORY. 5*s.* *net.* SIDELIGHTS ON RELATIVITY. 3*s.* 6*d.* *net.* THE MEANING OF RELATIVITY. 5*s.* *net.* THE BROWNIAN MOVEMENT. 5*s.* *net.*
Other books on the **Einstein Theory.**
AN INTRODUCTION TO THE THEORY OF RELATIVITY. By LYNDON BOLTON. *Crown 8vo.* 5*s.* *net.*
THE PRINCIPLE OF RELATIVITY. By A. EINSTEIN, H. A. LORENTZ, H. MINKOWSKI and H. WEYL. With Notes by A. SOMMERFELD. *Demy 8vo.* 12*s.* 6*d.* *net.*
Write for Complete List

Forrest (H. Edward)
THE OLD HOUSES OF STRATFORD-UPON-AVON. Illustrated. *Crown 8vo.* 7*s.* 6*d.* *net.* Also an edition limited to 250 copies, *Fcap. 4to.* 21*s.* *net.*

Fyleman (Rose)
FAIRIES AND CHIMNEYS. THE FAIRY GREEN. THE FAIRY FLUTE. THE RAINBOW CAT. EIGHT LITTLE PLAYS FOR CHILDREN. FORTY GOOD-NIGHT TALES. FAIRIES AND FRIENDS. THE ADVENTURE CLUB. FORTY GOOD-MORNING TALES. *Each* 3*s.* 6*d.* *net.* A SMALL CRUSE, 4*s.* 6*d.* *net.* THE ROSE FYLEMAN FAIRY BOOK. Illustrated. 10*s.* 6*d.* *net.* LETTY. Illustrated. 6*s.* *net.* A CHRISTMAS BOOK. Illustrated. 2*s.* *net.*

Gibbon (Edward)
THE DECLINE AND FALL OF THE ROMAN EMPIRE. With Notes, Appendixes, and Maps, by J. B. BURY. Illustrated. Seven volumes. *Demy 8vo.* 15*s.* *net* each volume. Also, unillustrated. *Crown 8vo.* 7*s.* 6*d.* *net* each volume.

Glover (T. R.)
THE CONFLICT OF RELIGIONS IN THE EARLY ROMAN EMPIRE. POETS AND PURITANS. VIRGIL. *Each* 10*s.* 6*d.* *net.* FROM PERICLES TO PHILIP. 12*s.* 6*d.* *net.*

Gotch (J. A.)
OLD ENGLISH HOUSES. Illustrated. *Demy 8vo.* 16*s.* *net.* Also an edition limited to 50 copies, £2 2*s.* *net.*

Graham (Harry)
THE WORLD WE LAUGH IN: More Deportmental Ditties. Illustrated by "FISH." *Sixth Edition. Fcap.* 8*vo.* 5*s. net.* STRAINED RELATIONS. Illustrated by H. STUART MENZIES and HENDY. *Royal* 16*mo.* 6*s. net.*

Grahame (Kenneth)
THE WIND IN THE WILLOWS. *Nineteenth Edition. Crown* 8*vo.* 7*s.* 6*d. net.* Also, Illustrated by NANCY BARNHART. *Small* 4*to.* 10*s.* 6*d. net.* Also, Illustrated by H. STUART MENZIES. *Fcap.* 8*vo.* 5*s. net.*

Hadfield (J. A.)
PSYCHOLOGY AND MORALS. *Sixth Edition. Crown* 8*vo.* 6*s. net.*

Hall (H. R.)
THE ANCIENT HISTORY OF THE NEAR EAST. *Sixth Edition, Revised. Demy* 8*vo.* £1 1*s. net.* THE CIVILIZATION OF GREECE IN THE BRONZE AGE. Illustrated. *Demy* 8*vo.* 10*s.* 6*d. net.*

Hamer (Sir W. H.), and Hutt (C. W.)
A MANUAL OF HYGIENE. Illustrated. *Demy* 8*vo.* £1 10*s. net.*

Hewlett (Maurice)
THE LETTERS OF MAURICE HEWLETT. Edited by LAURENCE BINYON. Illustrated. *Demy* 8*vo.* 18*s. net.*

Hind (A. M.)
A CATALOGUE OF REMBRANDT'S ETCHINGS. Two Vols. Profusely Illustrated. *Wide Royal* 8*vo.* £1 15*s. net.*

Holdsworth (W. S.)
A HISTORY OF ENGLISH LAW. Nine Volumes. *Demy* 8*vo.* £1 5*s. net each.*

Hudson (W. H.)
A SHEPHERD'S LIFE. Illustrated. *Demy* 8*vo.* 10*s.* 6*d. net.* Also, unillustrated, *Fcap.* 8*vo.* 3*s.* 6*d. net.*

Hutton (Edward)
CITIES OF SICILY. Illustrated. 10*s.* 6*d. net.* MILAN AND LOMBARDY. THE CITIES OF ROMAGNA AND THE MARCHES. SIENA AND SOUTHERN TUSCANY. VENICE AND VENETIA. THE CITIES OF SPAIN. NAPLES AND SOUTHERN ITALY. Illustrated. *Each,* 8*s.* 6*d. net.* A WAYFARER IN UNKNOWN TUSCANY. THE CITIES OF UMBRIA. COUNTRY WALKS ABOUT FLORENCE. ROME. FLORENCE AND NORTHERN TUSCANY. Illustrated. *Each,* 7*s.* 6*d. net.*

Imms (A. D.)
A GENERAL TEXTBOOK OF ENTOMOLOGY. Illustrated. *Royal* 8*vo.* £1 16*s. net.*

Inge (W. R.), D.D., Dean of St. Paul's
CHRISTIAN MYSTICISM. (The Bampton Lectures of 1899.) *Sixth Edition. Crown* 8*vo.* 7*s.* 6*d. net.*

Jackson (H. C.)
OSMAN DIGNA. *Demy* 8*vo.* 12*s.* 6*d. net.*

Kipling (Rudyard)
BARRACK-ROOM BALLADS. 241*st Thousand.*

THE SEVEN SEAS. 180*th Thousand.*

THE FIVE NATIONS. 138*th Thousand.*

DEPARTMENTAL DITTIES. 111*th Thousand.*

THE YEARS BETWEEN. 95*th Thousand.*
Four Editions of these famous volumes of poems are now published, viz.:—*Crown* 8*vo. Buckram,* 7*s.* 6*d. net. Fcap.* 8*vo. Cloth,* 6*s. net. Leather,* 7*s.* 6*d. net.* Service Edition. Two volumes each book. *Square Fcap.* 8*vo.* 3*s. net* each volume.

A KIPLING ANTHOLOGY—Verse. *Fcap.* 8*vo. Cloth,* 6*s. net. Leather,* 7*s.* 6*d. net.*

TWENTY POEMS FROM RUDYARD KIPLING. 423*rd Thousand. Fcap.* 8*vo.* 1*s. net.*

A CHOICE OF SONGS. *Second Edition. Fcap.* 8*vo.* 2*s. net.*

Lamb (Charles and Mary)
THE COMPLETE WORKS. Edited by E. V. LUCAS. A New and Revised Edition in Six Volumes. With Frontispieces. *Fcap.* 8*vo.* 6*s. net each.*
The volumes are: I. MISCELLANEOUS PROSE. II. ELIA AND THE LAST ESSAYS OF ELIA. III. BOOKS FOR CHILDREN. IV. PLAYS AND POEMS. V. and VI. LETTERS.

SELECTED LETTERS. Chosen and Edited by G. T. CLAPTON. *Fcap.* 8*vo.* 3*s.* 6*d. net.*

THE CHARLES LAMB DAY BOOK. Compiled by E. V. LUCAS. *Fcap.* 8*vo.* 6*s. net.*

Lankester (Sir Ray)
SCIENCE FROM AN EASY CHAIR. SCIENCE FROM AN EASY CHAIR: Second Series. DIVERSIONS OF A NATURALIST. GREAT AND SMALL THINGS. Illustrated. *Crown* 8*vo.* 7*s.* 6*d. net.* SECRETS OF EARTH AND SEA. Illustrated. *Crown* 8*vo.* 8*s.* 6*d. net.*

Lodge (Sir Oliver)
MAN AND THE UNIVERSE (*Twentieth Edition*). THE SURVIVAL OF MAN (*Seventh Edition*). *Each Crown* 8*vo*. 7*s*. 6*d*. *net*. RAYMOND (*Thirteenth Edition*). *Demy* 8*vo*. 10*s*. 6*d*. *net*. RAYMOND REVISED. *Crown* 8*vo*. 6*s*. *net*. RELATIVITY (*Fourth Edition*). *Fcap*.8*vo*. 1*s*.*net*.

Lucas (E. V.)
THE LIFE OF CHARLES LAMB. 2 Vols. £1 1*s*. *net*. EDWIN AUSTIN ABBEY, R.A. 2 Vols. £6 6*s*. *net*. VERMEER OF DELFT. 10*s*. 6*d*. *net*. A WANDERER IN ROME. A WANDERER IN HOLLAND. A WANDERER IN LONDON. LONDON REVISITED (Revised). A WANDERER IN PARIS. A WANDERER IN FLORENCE. A WANDERER IN VENICE. *Each* 10*s*. 6*d*. *net*. A WANDERER AMONG PICTURES. 8*s*. 6*d*. *net*. E. V. LUCAS'S LONDON. £1 *net*. INTRODUCING LONDON. 2*s*. 6*d*. *net*. THE OPEN ROAD. 6*s*. *net*. Also, illustrated. 10*s*. 6*d*. *net*. Also, India Paper. *Leather*, 7*s*. 6*d*. *net*. THE FRIENDLY TOWN. FIRESIDE AND SUNSHINE. CHARACTER AND COMEDY. *Each* 6*s*. *net*. THE GENTLEST ART. 6*s*. 6*d*. *net*. *And* THE SECOND POST. 6*s*. *net*. Also, together in one volume 7*s*. 6*d*. *net*. HER INFINITE VARIETY. GOOD COMPANY. ONE DAY AND ANOTHER. OLD LAMPS FOR NEW. LOITERER'S HARVEST. CLOUD AND SILVER. A BOSWELL OF BAGHDAD. 'TWIXT EAGLE AND DOVE. THE PHANTOM JOURNAL. GIVING AND RECEIVING. LUCK OF THE YEAR. ENCOUNTERS AND DIVERSIONS. ZIGZAGS IN FRANCE. EVENTS AND EMBROIDERIES. 365 DAYS (AND ONE MORE). *Each* 6*s*. *net*. SPECIALLY SELECTED. 5*s*. *net*. URBANITIES, 7*s*. 6*d*. *net*. *Each* illustrated by G. L. STAMPA. YOU KNOW WHAT PEOPLE ARE. Illustrated by GEORGE MORROW. 5*s*. *net*. THE SAME STAR: A Comedy in Three Acts. 3*s*. 6*d*. *net*. THE BRITISH SCHOOL. 6*s*. *net*. LITTLE BOOKS ON GREAT MASTERS. *Each* 5*s*. *net*. ROVING EAST AND ROVING WEST. 5*s*. *net*. PLAYTIME AND COMPANY. 7*s*. 6*d*. *net*. See also **Dolls' House (The Queen's)** and **Lamb (Charles)**

Lynd (Robert)
THE MONEY BOX. THE ORANGE TREE. THE LITTLE ANGEL. *Each Fcap*. 8*vo*. 6*s*. *net*. THE BLUE LION. THE PEAL OF BELLS. *Each Fcap*. 8*vo*. 3*s*. 6*d*. *net*.

Marie Louise (H.H. Princess)
A CHOICE OF CAROLS. *Fcap*. 4*to*. 2*s*. 6*d*. *net*. LETTERS FROM THE GOLD COAST. Illustrated. *Demy* 8*vo*. 16*s*. *net*.

McDougall (William)
AN INTRODUCTION TO SOCIAL PSYCHOLOGY (*Twentieth Edition, Revised*). 10*s*. 6*d*. *net*. NATIONAL WELFARE AND NATIONAL DECAY. 6*s*. *net*. AN OUTLINE OF PSYCHOLOGY (*Second Edition*). 12*s*. *net*. AN OUTLINE OF ABNORMAL PSYCHOLOGY. 15*s*. *net*. BODY AND MIND (*Fifth Edition*). 12*s*. 6*d*. *net*. ETHICS AND SOME MODERN WORLD PROBLEMS (*Second Edition*). 7*s*. 6*d*. *net*.

Mackenzie-Rogan (Lt.-Col. J.)
FIFTY YEARS OF ARMY MUSIC. Illustrated. *Demy* 8*vo*. 15*s*. *net*.

Maeterlinck (Maurice)
THE BLUE BIRD. 6*s*. *net*. Also, illustrated by F. CAYLEY ROBINSON. 10*s*. 6*d*. *net*. MARY MAGDALENE. 5*s*. *net*. DEATH. 3*s*. 6*d*. *net*. OUR ETERNITY. 6*s*. *net*. THE UNKNOWN GUEST. 6*s*. *net*. POEMS. 5*s*. *net*. THE WRACK OF THE STORM. 6*s*. *net*. THE MIRACLE OF ST. ANTHONY. 3*s*. 6*d*. *net*. THE BURGOMASTER OF STILEMONDE. 5*s*. *net*. THE BETROTHAL. 6*s*. *net*. MOUNTAIN PATHS. 6*s*. *net*. THE STORY OF TYLTYL. £1 1*s*. *net*. THE GREAT SECRET. 7*s*. 6*d*. *net*. THE CLOUD THAT LIFTED and THE POWER OF THE DEAD. 7*s*. 6*d*. *net*.

Masefield (John)
ON THE SPANISH MAIN. 8*s*. 6*d*. *net*. A SAILOR'S GARLAND. 6*s*. *net*. SEA LIFE IN NELSON'S TIME. 5*s*. *net*.

Methuen (Sir A.)
AN ANTHOLOGY OF MODERN VERSE. 117*th Thousand*.
SHAKESPEARE TO HARDY: An Anthology of English Lyrics. 19*th Thousand*. *Each Fcap*. 8*vo*. *Cloth*, 6*s*. *net*. *Leather*, 7*s*. 6*d*. *net*.

Milne (A. A.)
NOT THAT IT MATTERS. IF I MAY. *Each* 3*s*. 6*d*. *net*. WHEN WE WERE VERY YOUNG. Illustrated by E. H. SHEPARD. *Fourteenth Edition*. 129*th Thousand*. 7*s*. 6*d*. *net*. *Leather*, 10*s*. 6*d*. *net*. WINNIE-THE-POOH. Illustrated by E. H. SHEPARD. 7*s*. 6*d*. *net*. Leather, 10*s*. 6*d*. *net*. FOR THE LUNCHEON INTERVAL. 1*s*. 6*d*. *net*.

Milne (A. A.) and Fraser-Simson (H.)
FOURTEEN SONGS FROM "WHEN WE WERE VERY YOUNG." (*Tenth Edition.*) TEDDY BEAR AND OTHER SONGS FROM "WHEN WE WERE VERY YOUNG." Words by A. A. Milne. Music by H. Fraser-Simson. Each *Royal 4to.* 7*s.* 6*d. net.* THE KING'S BREAKFAST. *Second Edition. Music 4to.* 3*s.* 6*d. net.*

Montague (C. E.)
DRAMATIC VALUES. *Cr. 8vo.* 7*s.* 6*d. net.*

Morton (H. V.)
THE HEART OF LONDON. 3*s.* 6*d. net.* (Also illustrated, 7*s.* 6*d. net.*) THE SPELL OF LONDON. THE NIGHTS OF LONDON. Each, 3*s.* 6*d. net.* THE LONDON YEAR. Illustrated. 7*s.* 6*d. net.*

Newman (Tom)
HOW TO PLAY BILLIARDS. *Second Edition.* Illustrated. *Cr. 8vo.* 8*s.* 6*d. net.* BILLIARD DO'S AND DON'TS. 2*s.* 6*d. net.*

Oman (Sir Charles)
A HISTORY OF THE ART OF WAR IN THE MIDDLE AGES, A.D. 378–1485. *Second Edition,* Revised and Enlarged. 2 Vols. Illustrated. *Demy 8vo.* £1 16*s. net.*

Oxenham (John)
BEES IN AMBER. *Small Pott 8vo.* 2*s. net.* ALL'S WELL. THE KING'S HIGHWAY. THE VISION SPLENDID. THE FIERY CROSS. HIGH ALTARS. HEARTS COURAGEOUS. ALL CLEAR! *Each Small Pott 8vo. Paper,* 1*s.* 3*d. net. Cloth,* 2*s. net.* WINDS OF THE DAWN. 2*s. net.*

Perry (W. J.)
THE ORIGIN OF MAGIC AND RELIGION. THE GROWTH OF CIVILIZATION (*Second Edition*). *Each* 6*s. net.* THE CHILDREN OF THE SUN. 18*s. net.*

Petrie (Sir Flinders)
A HISTORY OF EGYPT. In 6 Volumes.
Vol. I. FROM THE IST TO THE XVITH DYNASTY. *Eleventh Edition, Revised.* 12*s. net.*
Vol. II. THE XVIITH AND XVIIITH DYNASTIES. *Seventh Edition, Revised.* 9*s. net.*
Vol. III. XIXTH TO XXXTH DYNASTIES. *Third Edition.* 12*s. net.*
Vol. IV. PTOLEMAIC EGYPT. By EDWYN BEVAN. 10*s.* 6*d. net.*
Vol. V. EGYPT UNDER ROMAN RULE. J. G. MILNE. *Third Edition, Revised.* 12*s. net.*
Vol. VI. EGYPT IN THE MIDDLE AGES. STANLEY LANE POOLE. *Fourth Edition.* 10*s. net.*

Raleigh (Sir Walter)
THE LETTERS OF SIR WALTER RALEIGH. Edited by LADY RALEIGH. Two Vols. Illustrated. *Second Edition Demy 8vo.* £1 10*s. net.*

Ridge (W. Pett) and Hoppé (E. O.)
LONDON TYPES: TAKEN FROM LIFE. The text by W. PETT RIDGE and the 25 Pictures by E. O. HOPPÉ. *Large Crown 8vo.* 10*s.* 6*d. net.*

Smith (Adam)
THE WEALTH OF NATIONS. Edited by EDWIN CANNAN. 2 Vols. *Demy 8vo.* £1 5*s. net.*

Smith (C. Fox)
SAILOR TOWN DAYS. SEA SONGS AND BALLADS. A BOOK OF FAMOUS SHIPS. SHIP ALLEY. *Each,* illustrated, 6*s. net.* FULL SAIL. Illustrated. 5*s. net.* TALES OF THE CLIPPER SHIPS. 5*s. net.* THE RETURN OF THE "CUTTY SARK." Illustrated. 3*s.* 6*d. net.* A BOOK OF SHANTIES. 7*s.* 6*d. net.*

Sommerfeld (Arnold)
ATOMIC STRUCTURE AND SPECTRAL LINES. £1 12*s. net.* THREE LECTURES ON ATOMIC PHYSICS. 2*s.* 6*d. net.*

Stevenson (R. L.)
THE LETTERS. Edited by Sir SIDNEY COLVIN. 4 Vols. *Fcap. 8vo. Each* 6*s. net.*

Surtees (R. S.)
HANDLEY CROSS. MR. SPONGE'S SPORTING TOUR. ASK MAMMA. MR. FACEY ROMFORD'S HOUNDS. PLAIN OR RINGLETS? HILLINGDON HALL. *Each* illustrated, 7*s.* 6*d. net.* JORROCKS'S JAUNTS AND JOLLITIES. HAWBUCK GRANGE. *Each,* illustrated, 6*s. net.*

Taylor (A. E.)
PLATO: THE MAN AND HIS WORK. *Demy 8vo.* £1 1*s. net.*

Tilden (W. T.)
THE ART OF LAWN TENNIS. SINGLES AND DOUBLES. *Each,* illustrated, 6*s. net.* THE COMMON SENSE OF LAWN TENNIS. Illustrated. 5*s. net.*

Tileston (Mary W.)
DAILY STRENGTH FOR DAILY NEEDS. *32nd Edition.* 3*s.* 6*d. net. India Paper, Leather,* 6*s. net.*

Underhill (Evelyn)
MYSTICISM (*Eleventh Edition*). 15*s. net.* THE LIFE OF THE SPIRIT AND THE LIFE OF TO-DAY (*Sixth Edition*). 7*s.* 6*d. net.* CONCERNING THE INNER LIFE. (*Second Edition*). 2*s. net.*

Vardon (Harry)
HOW TO PLAY GOLF. Illustrated. 19*th Edition. Crown* 8*vo.* 5*s. net.*

Waterhouse (Elizabeth)
A LITTLE BOOK OF LIFE AND DEATH. 22*nd Edition. Small Pott* 8*vo.* 2*s.* 6*d. net.*

Wilde (Oscar).
THE WORKS. In 16 Vols. *Each* 6*s.* 6*d. net.*

I. LORD ARTHUR SAVILE'S CRIME AND THE PORTRAIT OF MR. W. H. II. THE DUCHESS OF PADUA. III. POEMS. IV. LADY WINDERMERE'S FAN. V. A WOMAN OF NO IMPORTANCE. VI. AN IDEAL HUSBAND. VII. THE IMPORTANCE OF BEING EARNEST. VIII. A HOUSE OF POMEGRANATES. IX. INTENTIONS. X. DE PROFUNDIS AND PRISON LETTERS. XI. ESSAYS. XII. SALOME, A FLORENTINE TRAGEDY, and LA SAINTE COURTISANE. XIII. A CRITIC IN PALL MALL. XIV. SELECTED PROSE OF OSCAR WILDE. XV. ART AND DECORATION. XVI. FOR LOVE OF THE KING. (5*s. net.*)

William II. (Ex-Emperor of Germany).
MY EARLY LIFE. Illustrated. *Demy* 8*vo.* £1 10*s. net.*

Williamson (G. C.)
THE BOOK OF FAMILLE ROSE. Richly Illustrated. *Demy* 4*to.* £8 8*s. net.* Also a limited edition, £12 12*s. net.*

PART II. A SELECTION OF SERIES

The Antiquary's Books
Each, illustrated, *Demy* 8*vo.* 10*s.* 6*d. net.*
A series of volumes dealing with various branches of English Antiquities, comprehensive and popular, as well as accurate and scholarly.

The Arden Shakespeare
Edited by W. J. CRAIG and R. H. CASE. *Each, wide Demy* 8*vo.* 6*s. net.*
The Ideal Library Edition, in single plays, each edited with a full Introduction, Textual Notes and a Commentary at the foot of the page. Now complete in 39 Vols.

Classics of Art
Edited by J. H. W. LAING. *Each*, profusely illustrated, *wide Royal* 8*vo.* 15*s. net to* £3 3*s. net.*
A Library of Art dealing with Great Artists and with branches of Art.

The "Complete" Series
Demy 8*vo.* Fully illustrated. 5*s. net to* 18*s. net each.*
A series of books on various sports and pastimes, all written by acknowledged authorities.

The Connoisseur's Library
With numerous Illustrations. Wide Royal 8*vo.* £1 11*s.* 6*d. net each vol.*
EUROPEAN ENAMELS. FINE BOOKS. GLASS. GOLDSMITHS' AND SILVERSMITHS' WORK. IVORIES. JEWELLERY. MEZZOTINTS. PORCELAIN. SEALS.

The Do's and Dont's Series
Fcap. 8*vo.* 2*s.* 6*d. net each.*
This series, although only in its infancy, is already famous. In due course it will comprise clear, crisp, informative volumes on all the activities of life.
Write for full list

The Faiths
Edited by L. P. JACKS, M.A., D.D. LL.D. *Crown* 8*vo.* 5*s. net each volume*
The first volumes are:
THE ANGLO-CATHOLIC FAITH (Rev. Canon T. A. LACEY); MODERNISM IN THE ENGLISH CHURCH (Prof. P. GARDNER); THE FAITH AND PRACTICE OF THE QUAKERS (Prof. R. M. JONES); CONGREGATIONALISM (Rev. Princ. W. B. SELBIE).

The Library of Devotion
Handy editions of the great Devotional books, well edited. *Small Pott* 8*vo.* 3*s. net and* 3*s.* 6*d. net.*

Little Books on Art
Well Illustrated. *Demy* 16*mo. Each* 5*s. net.*

Modern Masterpieces
Fcap. 8*vo.* 3*s.* 6*d. each volume.*
Pocketable Editions of Works by A. A. MILNE, JOSEPH CONRAD, ARNOLD BENNETT, G. K. CHESTERTON, E. V. LUCAS, HILAIRE BELLOC, KENNETH GRAHAME, W. H. HUDSON, ROBERT LYND, R. L. STEVENSON, JACK LONDON AND E. V. KNOX.

Sport Series
Mostly Illustrated. *Fcap.* 8*vo.* 2*s. net to* 5*s. net each.*
Handy books on all branches of sport by experts.

Methuen's Half-Crown Library
Crown 8vo and Fcap. 8vo.

Methuen's Two Shilling Library
Fcap. 8vo.

Two series of cheap editions of popular books.

Write for complete lists

The Wayfarer Series of Books for Travellers
Crown 8vo. 7s. 6d. net each. Well illustrated and with maps. The volumes are :—Alsace, Czecho-Slovakia, The Dolomites, Egypt, Hungary, The Loire, Provence, Spain, Sweden, Switzerland, Unfamiliar Japan, Unknown Tuscany.

The Westminster Commentaries
Demy 8vo. 8s. 6d. net to 16s. net.
Edited by W. LOCK, D.D., and D. C. SIMPSON, D.D.
The object of these commentaries is primarily to interpret the author's meaning to the present generation, taking the English text in the Revised Version as their basis.

THE LITTLE GUIDES

Small Pott 8vo. Illustrated and with Maps

4s. net mostly

THE 62 VOLUMES IN THE SERIES ARE :—

BEDFORDSHIRE AND HUNTINGDONSHIRE
BERKSHIRE
BRITTANY
BUCKINGHAMSHIRE
CAMBRIDGE AND COLLEGES
CAMBRIDGESHIRE
CATHEDRAL CITIES OF ENGLAND AND WALES 6*s.* net
CHANNEL ISLANDS 5*s.* net
CHESHIRE 5*s.* net
CORNWALL
CUMBERLAND AND WESTMORLAND 6*s.* net
DERBYSHIRE
DEVON
DORSET 5*s.* 6*d.* net
DURHAM 6*s.* net
ENGLISH LAKES 6*s.* net
ESSEX 5*s.* net
GLOUCESTERSHIRE
GRAY'S INN AND LINCOLN'S INN 6*s.* net
HAMPSHIRE
HEREFORDSHIRE 4*s.* 6*d.* net
HERTFORDSHIRE
ISLE OF MAN 6*s.* net
ISLE OF WIGHT
KENT 5*s.* net
KERRY
LANCASHIRE 6*s.* net
LEICESTERSHIRE AND RUTLAND 5*s.* net
LINCOLNSHIRE 6*s.* net
LONDON 5*s.* *net*
MALVERN COUNTRY
MIDDLESEX
MONMOUTHSHIRE 6*s.* net
NORFOLK 5*s.* net
NORMANDY 5*s.* net
NORTHAMPTONSHIRE
NORTHUMBERLAND 7*s.* 6*d.* net
NORTH WALES 6*s.* net
NOTTINGHAMSHIRE
OXFORD AND COLLEGES
OXFORDSHIRE
ROME 5*s.* net
ST. PAUL'S CATHEDRAL
SHAKESPEARE'S COUNTRY
SHROPSHIRE 5*s.* *net*
SICILY
SNOWDONIA 6*s.* net
SOMERSET
SOUTH WALES
STAFFORDSHIRE 5*s.* net
SUFFOLK
SURREY 5*s* net
SUSSEX
TEMPLE
WARWICKSHIRE 5*s.* net
WESTMINSTER ABBEY 5*s.* *net*
WILTSHIRE 6*s.* net
WORCESTERSHIRE 6*s.* net
YORKSHIRE EAST RIDING 5*s.* net
YORKSHIRE NORTH RIDING
YORKSHIRE WEST RIDING 7*s.* 6*d.* net
YORK 6*s.* net

METHUEN & CO. LTD., 36 ESSEX STREET, LONDON, W.C.2.
1026